The Strange Case of Dr. Mabuse

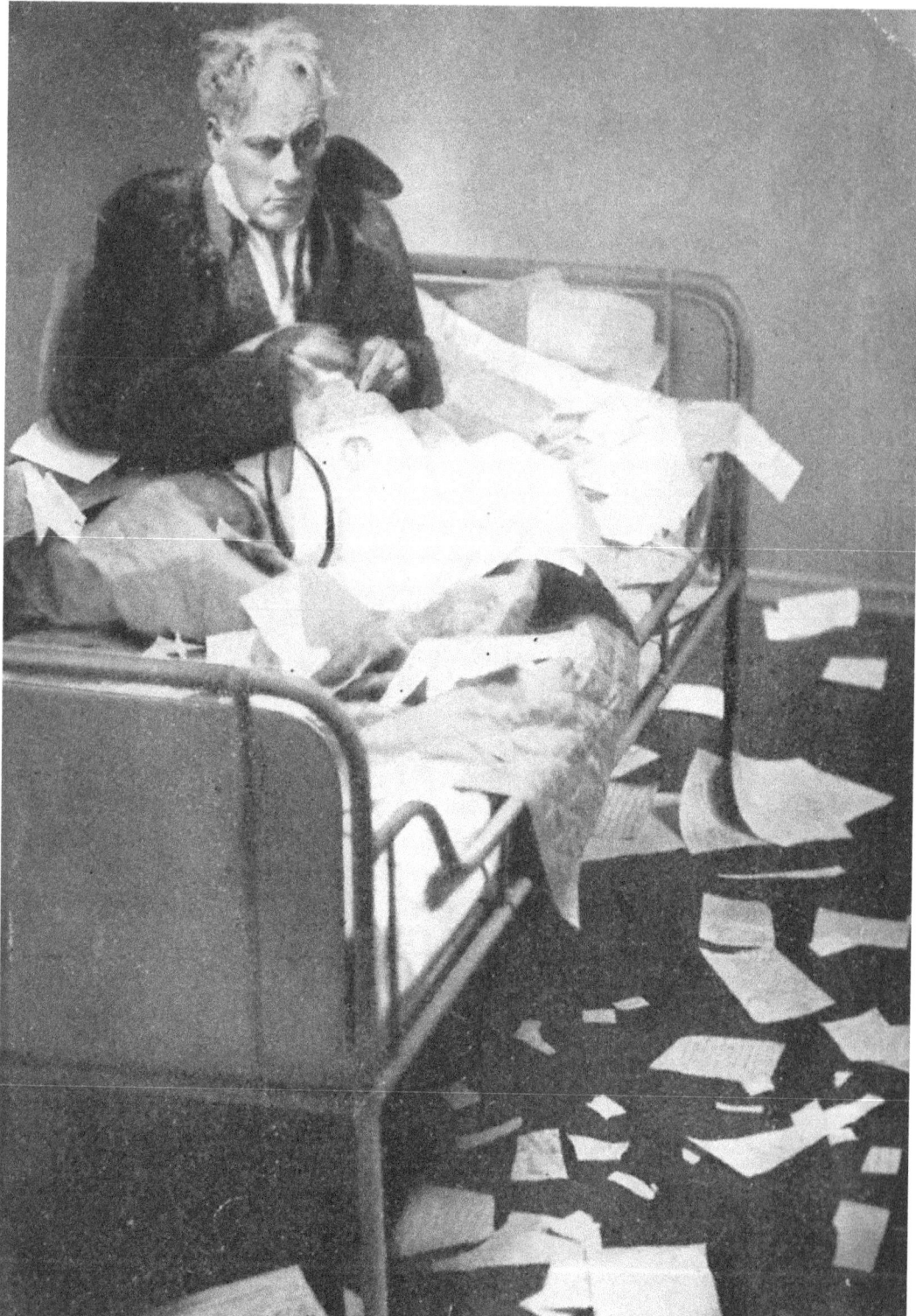

The Strange Case of Dr. Mabuse

A Study of the Twelve Films and Five Novels

DAVID KALAT

McFarland & Company, Inc., Publishers
Jefferson, North Carolina, and London

ALSO BY DAVID KALAT
*A Critical History and Filmography
of Toho's Godzilla Series*
(McFarland, 1997)

*The present work is a reprint of the illustrated case bound
edition of* The Strange Case of Dr. Mabuse: A Study of
the Twelve Films and Five Novels, *first published in 2001
by McFarland.*

Frontispiece: "My name is Dr. Mabuse": Dr. Baum (Oscar Beregi) becomes an inmate in his own asylum.

LIBRARY OF CONGRESS CATALOGUING-IN-PUBLICATION DATA

Kalat, David, 1970–
    The strange case of Dr. Mabuse : a study of the twelve films and five novels / David Kalat.
        p.   cm.
    Includes bibliographical references and index.

    ISBN-13: 978-0-7864-2337-8
    softcover : 50# alkaline paper ∞

    1. Doctor Mabuse films—History and criticism.
PN1995.9.D58K35   2005
791.43′651—dc21   2001030696

British Library cataloguing data are available

©2001 David Kalat. All rights reserved

*No part of this book may be reproduced or transmitted in any form
or by any means, electronic or mechanical, including photocopying
or recording, or by any information storage and retrieval system,
without permission in writing from the publisher.*

Manufactured in the United States of America

Cover art by Bill Chancellor

*McFarland & Company, Inc., Publishers
    Box 611, Jefferson, North Carolina 28640
        www.mcfarlandpub.com*

To Julie Stapel, whose unflagging patience
with this project went far beyond the call
of duty. She is my finest editor
and my greatest inspiration.

Acknowledgments

In 1997, I wrote an essay for *Midnight Marquee* magazine that bore the same title as this book. In that article, I perpetuated a handful of errors and misunderstandings, although I did so in good faith, believing that I was honestly reporting the information I had gathered from reputable sources. As I began to expand that early work into a book, and as I continued to research the subject, I found that while little had been written about Mabuse in English, that already small well was tainted with unreliable information. As I pursued German resources, I found a wealth of material that had evidently never before been presented in English. Part of the motive behind this book is to correct former errors and misunderstandings (including those I have been responsible for), and to collate as much information about this fascinating subject as has ever been gathered in any language.

In this quest, I have occasionally found myself envying Dr. Mabuse. I have fantasized about being locked away from human contact, to concentrate on writing. And indeed I feel a fair bit of this book has issued forth as little more than the fevered ramblings of a demented mind. I am even more astounded that my delirious scribblings have had any tangible effect in the real world, thanks to the intervention not of an army of underworld cronies but by my loyal agents Janet Rosen and Sheree Bykofsky. When I first proposed this project, I fully expected to be laughed out of the room, but instead was greeted with enthusiasm. For their tireless support and assistance I have nothing but the greatest gratitude.

The crafting of this book has, however, made me feel much more like Mabuse's opponents than Mabuse himself. Like the hapless Von Wenk or Lohmann or Joe Como, I have been in pursuit of the Great Unknown. Just when I think I have a handle on my thesis, when I feel I have defined what films and writings I will be addressing and how, a new phantom appears in the periphery, a new clue presents itself, and the whole enterprise is thrown back into doubt and chaos. I began this book as a much simpler, perhaps more focused, endeavor. Along the way, I discovered that Mabuse was working in the shadows in ways I had not recognized. Along the way, more films kept adding themselves to the filmography, more names cried out for biographies, more novels and short stories demanded attention.

In tracking my quarry I have been rescued by much more than a little help from my friends. First I must thank Patrick McGilligan; Cathall Tohill and Pete Tombs; and Günter Scholdt, whose respective writings on Fritz Lang, Jess Franco and Norbert Jacques provided essential points of departure. Ric Menello's expertise on Claude Chabrol, fed to me through enough e-mails to fill a book all on their own, was equally invaluable.

I also wish to thank Richard Gordon, Forrest J Ackerman, Kevin Thomas, Dr. Cornelius Schnauber, Gilbert Mandelik and Bill Warren for sharing their memories of Fritz Lang.

Most of the quotes attributed to Artur Brauner come from an excellent interview by Jorge Dana and Hubert Niogret conducted for their 1998 documentary *Fritz Lang—Circle of Destiny—The German Films*, a transcript of which they very kindly provided me. I also am indebted to Artur Brauner and the staff at CCC Films, including Kristine Klingler, Fabian Nentwig and Fela Brauner-Rozen. Much obscure biographical information came from Matthias Knop at the Deutsche Institut für Filmkunde and his counterpart Manfred Moos at the DIF Archiv.

Without the generous cooperation of Gordon Hessler, Jess Franco, Kevin Collins, Alain Petit, DeDe Fregonese, Gita Reddy and Monika Wagenberg of Women Make Movies, this book would not have been possible. I am also very grateful to the following individuals for their kind words of support and essential acts of assistance: Ed Morrissey, Uwe Sommerlad, Tim Lucas of *Video Watchdog*, Peter Blumenstock of Lucertola Media and Crippled Dick Hot Wax, François Truffart of the French Embassy, Michael Henry Wilson of the Cinémathèque Française, Stuart Galbraith IV, Roger Greenspun, Richard T. Jameson of *Film Comment*, Robert Haller of Anthology Film Archives, David Shepard of Film Preservation Archives and Donald Krim of Kino International. Translation, both professional and amateur, of French and Spanish sources was provided by Lourdes Calatayud, John McCary, James Maysonet and Kristen Gustafson. I am also grateful to Greg Luce of Sinister Cinema, Mike Vraney of Something Weird Video, Jim McCabe of Video Vault and the folks at European Trash Cinema for making most of these obscure gems available on videotape and for helping me access the films themselves.

Ace librarian Sheila Denn provided invaluable sources I could never have tracked down myself. Finally, my deepest thanks to my father Jim Kalat and my wife Julie Stapel for helping shape early drafts.

Contents

Acknowledgments — vii
A Note on the Text — 1
Introduction — 3

CHAPTER 1: The Man Behind the Man Behind the Curtain — 9
CHAPTER 2: The Eyes of Fritz Lang — 20
CHAPTER 3: *Dr. Mabuse, the Great Gambler*: A Picture of the Time — 36
CHAPTER 4: *Dr. Mabuse, Inferno*: A Play About the People of Our Time — 49
CHAPTER 5: Premonition — 61
CHAPTER 6: A Brief History of Nazi Germany — 62
CHAPTER 7: *The Testament of Dr. Mabuse* — 68
CHAPTER 8: The Little Dictator: Fritz Lang in America — 92
CHAPTER 9: *The 1000 Eyes of Dr. Mabuse* — 112
CHAPTER 10: German Trash Cinema: The Story of Artur Brauner — 131
CHAPTER 11: *The Return of Dr. Mabuse* — 143
CHAPTER 12: *The Invisible Dr. Mabuse* — 163
CHAPTER 13: *The Testament of Dr. Mabuse* — 173
CHAPTER 14: *Dr. Mabuse vs. Scotland Yard* — 188
CHAPTER 15: *The Death Ray of Dr. Mabuse* — 203
CHAPTER 16: *Scream and Scream Again* — 213
CHAPTER 17: The Life and Times of Jess Franco — 227
CHAPTER 18: *The Vengeance of Dr. Mabuse* — 239
CHAPTER 19: *The Image of Dorian Gray in the Yellow Press* — 245

CHAPTER 20: The Story of Chabrol   257
CHAPTER 21: *Club Extinction*   267
CHAPTER 22: The Legacy of Dr. Mabuse   281

Bibliography   293
Filmography   297
Index   301

A Note on the Text

This book covers not only the core films of the Dr. Mabuse "canon," but a number of related tangential works as well. The primary films are *Dr. Mabuse the Gambler* (1922), *The Testament of Dr. Mabuse* (1932), *The 1000 Eyes of Dr. Mabuse* (1960), *The Return of Dr. Mabuse* (1961), *The Invisible Dr. Mabuse* (1962), *The Testament of Dr. Mabuse* (1962), *Scotland Yard vs. Dr. Mabuse* (1963), *The Death Ray of Dr. Mabuse* (1964) and *The Vengeance of Dr. Mabuse* (1970). In addition there are three ancillary pictures: *Scream and Scream Again* (1969), *The Image of Dorian Gray in the Yellow Press* (1984) and *Club Extinction* (1989). In all cases, I have used the primary English-language release titles for clarity, as this book is intended for an English-speaking readership. Several of these pictures have multiple English titles, so in these instances I have chosen the title by which the film has come to be best known and or is available on video. In the case of *The Vengeance of Dr. Mabuse*, which has never been released in English, I have used a literal translation of the Spanish title (which is also a fair translation of the principal German title).

For the writings of Norbert Jacques, however, I have elected to use the original German titles. This was done partly to provide an easy distinction between the novel *Dr. Mabuse der Spieler* and its film version *Dr. Mabuse the Gambler*. However, it is also in acknowledgment of the fact that, with the exception of a long out-of-print edition of *Dr. Mabuse der Spieler*, none of these works has ever been translated into English, making English titles rather useless to the interested reader attempting to locate copies.

I must point out that tracking down copies of these books and films will pose a heady challenge even to the most committed fan. While I was able to locate video copies of all 12 films, many of them were either out-of-print or gray market "boots." Part of the purpose of this book is to raise awareness of these motion pictures in the hopes of making them more widely accessible to American viewers. For now, though, too many of these films will be frustratingly hard to find.

I must confess now a personal bias that may affect how you consider my comments. I have a financial stake in a few of the films discussed in this book. In addition to being a writer, I also run All Day Entertainment, a company dedicated to releasing Collector's Editions of "cult movies" on DVD. My passion for the Mabuse series drove me to write this book, and it also drove me to license some of them for DVD release through All Day. DVD editions of *The 1000 Eyes of Dr. Mabuse* and the 1962 version of *The Testament of Dr. Mabuse* are available from All Day; additionally, I contributed to the

DVD release of the silent *Dr. Mabuse the Gambler* on Image's label.

I do not believe that this has compromised my critical integrity in reviewing these films, since both this book and the DVD editions were prompted by my assessment of the films' importance and quality. Still, it is important to acknowledge this possible conflict of interest up front.

Please note that, as I intend this book for English-speaking readers, I have translated all German quotations into English. Any new errors or misunderstandings that may result from my translations are once again my sole responsibility.

Introduction

The time has come to tell the true story of Dr. Mabuse.

It is an expansive story, one that encompasses the tumult of twentieth century German history: the rise and fall of Nazism, the Cold War division of Germany, the tumbling of the Berlin Wall. It encompasses much of the evolution of film: the glories of German silent cinema, the mass exodus of European talent to Hollywood at the dawn of the sound era, the trashy productions of postwar European filmmakers, the revolutions of the German and French New Wave, the universal conflicts between art and commerce.

The story told in this book is true. It may not be stranger than fiction, but it is suspiciously similar to fiction on many counts. The story told in this book is also a fractal one, replete with details that recursively reflect themselves ad infinitum. This is the story of a snake swallowing its own tail: an endless cycle of venomous aggression that leads inevitably into self-destruction.

Specifically, this is a survey of 12 motion pictures produced between 1922 and 1989, whose plot synopses sound eerily parallel to the tales of their making and the biographies of their makers. Both *on* screen and *off*, the story of the strange case of Dr. Mabuse is a story of love triangles and revenge, of murders and suicides and suspicious deaths, of betrayals and paranoia, of fascism and tyranny, of deceptions and conspiracies, of mistaken identities and doppelgängers and pseudonyms, of transformations, of history writ both large and small.

This is the story of a madman's repeated attempts to take over the world, to remake it in his own image. Dr. Mabuse sees himself as a god, and believes himself entitled to decide who shall live and who shall die. The earliest manifestation of Dr. Mabuse, as written by novelist Norbert Jacques in 1922, has the relatively small ambition of establishing his own empire in South America, with him as its lord and master. This incarnation of Mabuse, though, is limited in what power he can exert over one individual at a time. Over the years, he would experiment with various methods of mind control—the better to enforce unquestioning loyalty in his subjects. He would later attempt to make his subjects from scratch, a petty god stitching his Adam and Eve together from bits and pieces of dead bodies.

Dr. Mabuse operates in the shadows, ruling a world that does not even know his name. We encounter him in a basement lair. Only under ground could a creature like this exist. But even here, on his turf, we cannot see him clearly. He is still just a shadow, a figure behind a curtain, the echo of a disembodied voice, barking orders. We need to pull the curtain aside

This detail from a 1922 poster advertising Fritz Lang's first Dr. Mabuse film set an intriguing precedent: few if any of the posters made for the films over the next 67 years made any attempt to actually depict the star player. Instead, as here, Mabuse was shown as a ghastly, ghostly, phantasmagoric presence.

and see his face, to gaze into the eyes of the man who pulls the strings of our world. "Who is behind it all?"

But once we rip away the curtain, we find the greatest horror of all: nothing at all. The shadow belongs to a wooden prop, not a man at all. The voice is the echo of a loudspeaker, not a human throat. We have traced the evil back to its source and still it eludes us. There is no Dr. Mabuse.

In one sense, this is strictly true. To the extent that the name "Mabuse" identifies a single individual, that man goes insane at the conclusion of the first film in 1922 and dies midway into the second film in 1932 (Jacques killed him off at the end of the original novel). The majority of the motion pictures discussed in this book concern his successors, men and women who assume Mabuse's name and cause, and then perversely expend all their energies trying to conceal their newly adopted identity from the world.

"Mabuse" is a secret name, the most taboo of all utterances. It is a name taken by someone for personal use only. In Norbert Jacques' novel, state's attorney von Wenk pursues Mabuse's many aliases, only to find each assumed name leads back to some real person, some poor sap totally unaware that his identity had been appropriated and misused by a villain. But when he researches the name "Mabuse" and finds nothing—there is no Mabuse—he knows he has found the true identity of his quarry.

There is no Mabuse because "Mabuse" is not a name, not in the traditional sense. It is a sign. It is a password. It is an ideology.

In the end, whether the name "Mabuse" is a real one, assigned at birth and officially recorded, is irrelevant. The root of evil is not to be found in any one man—but rather in ideology of tyranny and oppression that, for want of a better word, can be signified by the name "Mabuse." There once was a Dr. Mabuse, but now Mabuse is also people named Born and Baum and Pohland, Jordan and Browning and Farkas, Logana and Haghi, Hitler and Goebbels and Honecker.

Of course, Adolf Hitler is not a fictional character. He existed, and his evil was only too real. But the story of the strange case of Dr. Mabuse is one that has managed to all but lose sight of the distinction between fact and fiction.

In 1993, Dana Stevens wrote a very thoughtful and insightful article on Fritz Lang's *The Testament of Dr. Mabuse* (1932) for the interdisciplinary journal *Qui Parle*, published by the University of California at Berkeley. At the heart of the essay, though, is a factual inaccuracy about Fritz Lang's life—a bogus tale Lang told that became accepted as truth by countless Lang scholars. Read any account of Lang's life, from a one-sentence biography in a paperback video guide to an erudite essay in a scholarly journal like *Qui Parle*, and you will undoubtedly confront this story:

Fritz Lang was called into the office of Dr. Joseph Goebbels in the early days of Hitler's regime to discuss the fate of the film *The Testament of Dr. Mabuse*, one of the first motion pictures to face the Nazi censors. Recognizing the thinly veiled anti–Nazi allegory in the film, Goebbels intends to have the picture banned. But he harbors no ill will towards its maker, and instead offers Lang the job of Führer of Film, to head up Nazi cinematic propaganda. Lang protests: "I am Jewish," he says. Goebbels replies, "No, Mr. Lang, we decide who is Jewish." All the while, his palms sweating, Lang watches the clock outside Goebbels' office window as it ticks away, the banks closing. That night he fled Germany with what cash he had on hand, and started life anew.

It is a fabulous anecdote. From its questions of identity to its desperate escape into the shadows of the night, the story itself sounds so much like a Lang film. As such, the anecdote has been invaluable to Lang scholars looking to interpret his life through his films or vice versa. So the fact that this apocryphal encounter is literally too good to be true has not in any way hindered its continued propagation through academic journals and biographies. This story was thoroughly debunked in 1988, but for most critics, fiction is stronger than the truth.

The Testament of Dr. Mabuse occupies a critical moment in the life of Fritz Lang, regardless of whether he fled Berlin in the middle of the night or months later, so any full understanding of Lang requires an understanding of the Mabuse films, and vice versa. And that in turn requires an understanding of how Lang's spurious encounter with Goebbels has colored the subsequent interpretations of Lang's life and the Mabuse pictures. In this way, fact and fiction get folded together into the same package.

On most occasions, the Mabuse books and films were conceived as deliberate comments on German society, and adapted factual details of the Weimar Republic and the Spartacus Uprising and Hitler's *Mein Kampf* and the Berlin Wall into a fictional context. However, not all of the eerie parallels between real life and the world of Dr. Mabuse can be chalked up to fiction imitating fact, since in no small number of these eerie parallels, the factual events occurred second. Norbert Jacques penned his Dr. Mabuse novels, with tales of a megalomaniac escaping his failed conquest of Germany to the wilds of South America, many years before the Nazis would follow suit. And was Hitler trying to mimic his cinematic counterpart when he, like Dr. Mabuse before him, wrote his last will and testament as a blueprint for his followers to carry on his agenda?

Not all of this story is politics. Certainly much of the strange case of Dr. Mabuse concerns violence and war, insurrection and espionage, the cynical screams of filmmakers who no longer believe in the ability of democracy to defend itself from tyranny. But this is also the story of those filmmakers themselves, who were often less concerned with world politics than the politics of the film industry. This is the story of men and women who have all struggled with the arbitrary separation of art and commerce, struggled to maintain their artistic reputations while engaging in the creation of commercially viable products. The Mabuse series has been looked down upon by posterity as if the fact that it endured for decades and enthralled millions of fans can be taken as proof positive of its worthlessness.

These disparate topics are united in the cinema of Dr. Mabuse. But this cinematic legacy has all but fallen through the cracks. Only sporadically have these films been released in America—some not at all—and what little has been written about them has been marred by fallacy and misunderstanding.

In Germany, Mabuse is a bona fide pop culture phenomenon whose name is recognized as a horror icon on par with Dracula or Frankenstein. By contrast, in the United States a limited coterie of film fans know of *The Testament of Dr. Mabuse*, but may be entirely unaware that any other Dr. Mabuse films exist. In part, this is a consequence of the very different social conditions in America and Germany, such that prosperous American audiences were unconditioned to appreciate the rather specific fears underlying the German pictures. In part also, Americans have been notoriously resistant to foreign pop culture. Compounding these problems, Hollywood has wielded awesome power and influence to maintain global domination of all things cinematic—a hurdle that the makers of Mabuse films had to struggle mightily against.

In 1973, Lang's three Mabuse pictures (*Dr. Mabuse the Gambler*, *The Testament of Dr. Mabuse* and *The 1000 Eyes of Dr. Mabuse*) all happened to be re-released in New York. Each film had met with indifferent reception on its initial U.S. release (in 1926, 1943, and 1966 respectively). Ironically, each was now feted by critics and hailed as a masterpiece. Although the films themselves had not changed, the American social landscape had: In the aftermath of Vietnam, the student protests at Kent State and other schools, the betrayals of Watergate, spiraling inflation and an energy crisis, Americans were finally in a position to "get" what Mabuse represented—the personification of the end of the world.

Those days passed, and subsequent Mabuse pictures like Ulrike Ottinger's 1984 *The Image of Dorian Gray in the Yellow Press* and Claude Chabrol's 1989 *Club Extinction* were ignored stateside.

That is not to say that the shadow of Mabuse has lifted from America. His influence can be felt cinematically to greater and lesser degrees in such recent blockbusters as *The Usual Suspects* (1996) and *Enemy of the State* (1998). American journalists have invoked the name Mabuse to describe such public figures as software tycoon Bill Gates or financial wizard George Soros—it's unclear whether these powerful egos would appreciate the comparison.

As I write this (in the winter of 2000), there is talk of yet another remake of *The Testament of Dr. Mabuse*. In the world of movies, there is always talk of a remake of something or other, so it remains to be seen what if anything comes of it, but the fact remains that filmmakers still see relevance in Dr. Mabuse at the turn of the century, almost eighty years after Norbert Jacques first created the character.

And so this story goes on, into the new millennium. I cannot say what Mabuse films may yet come—I could not even cover films like *The Usual Suspects* that so closely model the Mabuse paradigm without sacrificing coverage of the "core" films. I make no claim that this book is the last word on Dr. Mabuse. Far from it.

I hope it is the first.

Chapter 1

The Man Behind the Man Behind the Curtain

> There are some men who are born to gamble. When he takes just one card in his hand, it's an Ace. He can do whatever he wants. He is stronger than you. He is like a God.
>
> —Cara Carozza in *Dr. Mabuse der Spieler*

The man stands like a giant, towering over the city. He is dressed to the nines in an elegant tuxedo, top hat, white gloves and a black mask. His eyes glow with a vitality that could almost be called atomic—if this were not three decades before the nuclear age was to begin. His name is Fantômas.

Created by Pierre Souvestre and Marcel Allain in 1911, this supervillain, this master of disguise, this diabolical antihero driven not by financial gain but by his own desires for pleasure and self-aggrandizement, has starred in some 32 books and countless motion pictures. These adventures, in which Fantômas wages violent and fiendishly creative war on bourgeois society, appeared primarily before the first World War. Published at a rate of one a month for 32 months (with Souvestre and Allain writing alternate chapters), these pulp novels proved immensely popular.

The Surrealists claimed Fantômas as their hero. Max Ernst, Rene Magritte, Guillaume Appollinaire and others admired how the criminal, the agent of chaos and destruction, adversary of contemporary society, had been made the "hero"— in stark contrast to conventional crime thrillers that followed the exploits of detectives as they reinforced the status quo. Given to anarchy and non-conformity, the Surrealists considered themselves kindred spirits to this defiant lord of crime. Rene Magritte even tried his hand penning brief stories about Fantômas and his nemesis Inspector Juve, and invoked similar imagery in many of his early works—in fact, the period in Magritte's career from 1925–30 is sometimes called "l'époque de Fantômas."

In 1913, legendary French filmmaker Louis Feuillade adapted the property into a series of five feature films. With the outbreak of World War I, Feuillade went off to fight, and returned injured. He never made another Fantômas film. The war claimed the life of Souvestre, leaving Allain to continue the written series alone (and to marry Souvestre's widow). The "Emperor of Crime" continued his exploits in a 20-part American serial, six French sound films and a TV mini-series.

Coincidentally, part of this miniseries

Gino Starace's famous pop-art icon, advertising the 1913 Fantômas film—but see p. 12.

was directed by French New Waver Claude Chabrol, who also directed the 1989 update of Dr. Mabuse, *Club Extinction*. Meanwhile, other New Wave directors showed their respect for Feuillade with a variety of remakes and homages to Fantômas (among them, Georges Franju's *Man Without a Face* [1974], starring Mabuse series regular Gert Fröbe).

Despite this immense creative output, the most enduring aspect of the Fantômas phenomenon is the image described above, the cover of the first book. It was painted by Italian artist Gino Starace, inspired by an engraving by Félicien Rops called "Satan Sowing Tares." Feuillade naturally borrowed the image as the poster art for his film serial. Magritte, fascinated, repainted it in whole and in part on several occasions. *The Backfire* (1943) is essentially Magritte's stroke-for-stroke replica of Starace's *Fantômas* book cover. Only rarely did Magritte borrow so obviously from an inspirational source, but Fantômas obviously had a special place in the painter's heart. Pointedly, in addition to his appreciation of Feuillade's *Fantômas* serials, Magritte also loved the films of Fritz Lang.

When Decla-Bioscop prepared graphics to advertise the opening of Lang's *Dr. Mabuse, the Gambler* in 1922, they appropriated the iconography of this widely recognized poster. In artwork prepared by Theo Matejkos, Dr. Mabuse stands in an evening suit and thick fur coat, gigantic in stature over the city he terrorizes; Mabuse as Godzilla. It would be one of the few concessions anyone made at the time that Dr. Mabuse belonged to any larger literary or cinematic tradition.

Film historian William K. Everson writes in his indispensable *Classics of the Horror Film* that "[a]lthough Dr. Mabuse originated in (and was limited to) only one literary work, Fritz Lang and the movies elevated him to a position equal to those other arch-fiends, Dr. Fu Manchu and Prof. Moriarty." On a strictly factual level, Everson has got it wrong. Mabuse appears in two full-length novels, *Dr. Mabuse der Spieler* and *Das Testament des Dr. Mabuse*. The master criminal also appears in the short story *Dr. Mabuse auf dem Presseball*, the unfinished novel *Mabuses Kolonie* and, in spirit, in two more non-canonical novellas, *Ingenieur Mars* and *Chemiker Null*. However, Everson is absolutely correct that Mabuse is kin to such criminal archetypes as Fu Manchu, Moriarty, Fantômas, Diabolik and all the other such arch-villain antiheroes spawned by the turn-of-the-century literary movement of decadence. Nevertheless, the creators of Dr. Mabuse made a tremendous effort promoting him as a realistic depiction of the unique problems of the time—not a fanciful supercriminal but a true-to-life formulation.

Given this, it should come as no surprise that the father of Mabuse was a journalist. He was also an esteemed author of 55 books as well as hundreds of essays, articles, short stories and sundry unpublished pieces. Thomas Mann considered him a great talent, an opinion shared by many in the early decades of the twentieth century. But by the end of the century, his reputation had dimmed—not out of any aspersion on his creative gifts, but out of an accident of history. He ushered into the world a figure that escaped him.

Norbert Jacques was born in Luxemburg on June 6, 1880. In 1901, Jacques moved to Bonn, ostensibly to study law, but he had a far greater interest in art, music, theater and literature. Around this time he met his first wife, actress Olga Hübner. In 1902, he left the theater to take a steady job as a reporter for the *Oberschlesischen Grenzzeitung*. Jacques quickly distinguished himself as a writer of highly anti-nationalistic pieces.

The budding journalist discovered a

Separated at birth? Artist Theo Matejkos invokes Starace's Fantômas with this poster to the 1922 Dr. Mabuse film.

passion for world travel. His later friend and collaborator Fritz Lang would often claim to be a globetrotter, but Jacques set a standard few could meet. His enthusiasm for foreign cultures influenced his writings—both of the fictional and factual varieties.

In 1907, Jacques took an auspicious trip to Brazil that opened his eyes to new perspectives and inspired new directions for his creative energies. He was hooked. Europe simply could not compete with the exotic South American continent. At that time, utopianism was all the rage—the belief that the hopeful future of man and society would be found by blazing new trails in such untamed wildernesses. Jacques adopted this utopian concept as a literary theme, in such works as *Piraths Insel* and his Mabuse writings. He never did move to Brazil, despite repeated protestations that it was his greatest dream to do so.

In 1912 Jacques remarried (to Margueritte Samuely) and their honeymoon took them on an astounding 16-month world tour, through Ceylon, Sumatra, China, Chile, Rio de Janeiro.... Even when "at home," Jacques flitted between Paris, Berlin, Vienna and Hanover.

The first World War erupted while Jacques was in Switzerland. He tried to enlist, but being foreign-born and an inveterate traveler, he found himself classified an "ausländer." Instead, he found a way to participate and express his patriotism by covering the war for the *Frankfurter Zeitung* as an eyewitness reporter. Of course, this solution also appealed to the world traveler's wanderlust.

As the war drew to a close, so did his journalistic interests in favor of more literary pursuits. He had published his first novel, *Funchal*, back in 1909 to tremendous critical acclaim. In 1917, he scored his biggest non–Mabuse hit with *Piraths Insel* (considered one of the preeminent German utopian novels).

In 1922, Jacques formally became a German citizen. The act was an expression of his increasing patriotism—not in an ugly, Nazi sort of way, but from an honest love of Germany and its people. As an experienced reporter, Jacques was not blinded by his patriotism. He could see the bad as well as the good, and in post-war Germany, the bad was getting pretty bad.

The Weimar Republic was a time of extremes. Poverty, inflation, unemployment, riots, drug abuse and suffering coexisted painfully with newfound wealth and prosperity. The gulf between the haves and have-nots widened. A warweary public yearned for order to replace the chaos, and looked towards the occult, theosophy, psychology—any sort of -ism that promised answers. These were the forces that were leading Germany inexorably towards Nazism, towards a Führer. As yet, the name Hitler meant little outside Munich, but the phantasmagoric presence of evil was slowly manifesting itself.

"There is a devil loose in Germany," Jacques said, "and one day I think I saw this devil myself."

As he later told the story (in the 1950 essay *Dr. Mabuse I Presume*), the peripatetic Mr. Jacques found himself on another of his many journeys back and forth between his home near Lake Constance and ports elsewhere. On this particular three-hour tour, Jacques sat on the deck opposite a singular gentleman who captured the writer's attention. This man never moved, never spoke, but something in his bearing cut to the core of Jacques' being. He felt anxious, afraid. He felt an urge to flee. What was it about this man that exuded such power?

Ever the journalist, Jacques set his mind to observing every detail about this man, to divine the story behind him. Jacques studied his eyes, his forehead, his stature. "Was he a hero, or a villain?"

wondered the author. Fritz Lang, a great believer in phrenology (by which a criminal is said to be identifiable by unique, recognizable physical traits), would have been proud. In this mystery man, who sat motionless and silent all the while, Norbert Jacques read all that was wrong with modern-day Germany.

He was inspired, and returned home to hammer out the novel *Dr. Mabuse der Spieler* in a scant 14 days.

As to the name, Jacques claimed he picked it up on a visit to an art museum. "Mabuse" was the nickname of Flemish painter Jan Gossaerts, and Jacques liked how it sounded. Part-German, part-foreign, "Mabuse" had just the right universal ring to it. It certainly helped that "Mabuse" includes the sound of the German word "Böse," for Evil—a convenient morsel of onomatopoeia.* A Swiss composer named Hans Jelmoli later told Jacques that he had figured the name was a play on French verbs: "je m'abuse, tu t'abuses..."—in other words, the abuse you inflict on yourself.

Dr. Mabuse der Spieler ("Dr. Mabuse the Gambler") depicts a criminal Führer who exploits social decay to his private advantage. Under a variety of disguises and assumed names, he has broken free of the traditional class divisions and invaded the previously insulated enclaves of the decadent upper class.

Mabuse is a doctor of psychiatry, which gives him insight into mankind's weaknesses—but Jacques is less interested in damning the psychiatric profession than he is in making a more generalized point. "Germany knows well from countless experiences the effect titles like Doctor, Professor, or Count can have on trust and respect," Jacques explained in a 1928 essay on Mabuse. "How often have people hung such titles like a curtain in front of certain truths they don't want to have recognized."

Mabuse is a gambler as well as a fake shrink, but for him the gambles are with human lives. The state's attorney Mr. von Wenk suspects a connection behind many country-wide cases of gamblers who have been cheated, defeated and exploited in outrageous ways. Although he believes the cases to be the work of an underground gang, von Wenk's pursuit of the Great Unknown ultimately reveals his opponent is just one man.

Jacques' decision to stage his story in the sundry vice clubs of the era, where gambling, prostitution, drug use and other hedonistic delights abounded, was a propitious one. Gambling may seem like a relatively tame crime by current standards—a threat more from the violence or other crimes that may surround it than from the act of gambling itself—but in the Weimar Republic, gambling was a sin of appalling hubris. The principal players were the newly rich, men of means by inheritance, war profiteering or criminal exploitation, not by the fruits of their own legitimate labor. Worse still, while the average, decent citizens of Germany faced inflation so fierce that their wages devalued in the time between receiving their daily paycheck and making their way to the bread line, these selfish leeches played with money like a toy (the German word for "gamble" is the same as "game").

As Jacques describes it in the book, these gambling dens marked a dangerous transition in the social structure, a development that Mabuse seizes upon and exploits for his own nefarious purposes. "A closed society was a thing of the past," writes Jacques. "Money was the key to all

---

*German speakers pronounce "Mabuse" as "Mah-boo-zah." However, the English dubbing for some of the 60s era films pronounce the name "Ma-bous," which has the onomatopoeic connotations of the word "abuse."

A mysterious Dr. Mabuse gazes out from the cover to the first hardcover edition, 1921.

doors...." Anyone can get in anywhere if you say the password and have the cash to play. In a room full of strangers, foreigners and sundry aliens, the Great Unknown can move about freely.

Jacques may have scribbled his novel in astonishing haste, but he knew what he was doing. In the first year, it sold 100,000 copies. Over time, it sold a half million copies in Germany alone, and became one of the bestsellers of its era. If this number seems small from a modern American perspective, it is worth noting that the book was only published *after* being serialized in the *Berliner Illustrierten* magazine, which exposed millions of readers to the sinister world of Dr. Mabuse.

This serialized edition began in Issue 39 of *Berliner Illustrierten* in September 1921 and ran in five installments over the subsequent issues. The hardback edition came out in February 1922. In April of that year, the film version by Fritz Lang opened. Haste was the watchword all around.

Jacques was proud of the book, but equally proud of the film, on which he collaborated. He feared his book was limited to German-speakers. Although in the end his novel was translated into ten different languages, the universality of silent film brought Mabuse to a global audience.

The tremendous success of *Dr. Mabuse der Spieler* came at a price. On the one hand, Jacques had fashioned a popular, commercial success that won him unprecedented fame and fortune, but on the other hand it stigmatized his literary reputation and stunted his creative growth. Art and commerce do not mix, say the critics. If Jacques' novel is such a hit, it must not be very good. Jacques resented this, since he understood all too well that even artists have to pay the rent.

The book had been published by Ullstein, a publisher looked down upon by snobbish critics as a manufacturer of pulp.

The lurid qualities of the story also placed it in that pulpy tradition, the serialization showed that Jacques was more interested in snaring plebian readers than critical acclaim, and the film version (which followed so close on the heels of the book that the two were virtually inseparable in the public's mind) also carried the mark of a commercial enterprise. Jacques became the first but by no means last in the Mabuse saga to be wounded by this arbitrary and artificial distinction between worthy artistic pursuits and crassly commercial sellouts.

Jacques did not help matters by largely setting his ambitious literary projects aside in a vain attempt to recreate the Mabuse magic. Over the next few years, he penned more and more adventure and crime stories, more than a few of which starred the bad doctor himself.

In Jacques' original novel, Mabuse plunged to his death from an airplane. Thea von Harbou's screenplay kept a sequel option open by simply driving Mabuse insane, but Jacques was in a bind if he wanted to resurrect his character for a literary franchise. In 1923, Jacques wrote a short story called *Dr. Mabuse auf dem Presseball* ("Dr. Mabuse at the Press Ball"). In the opening paragraphs, Mabuse miraculously survives his perilous drop from the plane (which is now a mere 2000 meters up, half the distance he fell at the end of the novel). Making his way back to land, Mabuse decides he needs to rehabilitate his poor public image, and contrives to crash the Press Ball where he can make friends and influence reporters. Mabuse assumes the highly ironic disguise of "Klein-Rogge" (for actor Rudolf Klein-Rogge, who played Mabuse in Lang's film) and is disappointed when von Wenk and the various reporters recognize him immediately. In fact, Mabuse's presence causes such a furor, no one notices when Albert Einstein shows up.

Obviously intended as a satire, *Dr. Mabuse auf dem Presseball* does more than revive the character for future use: It points to how Jacques had even then realized how fully Lang's film version was eclipsing his literary contribution. Klein-Rogge was a poor disguise for Mabuse because for all intents and purposes the movie Mabuse was the real thing.

At first, Jacques did not do much with his reincarnated antihero. Shortly after the *Presseball* short story he wrote a sort of prequel called *Ingenieur Mars* (1923), but the next step in the Mabuse saga occurred several years later. Throughout the 1920s, Jacques had become increasingly involved in the film industry, working on screenplays for a variety of producers. Thanks to his friendship with Lang and von Harbou, Jacques also found himself occasionally consulted on their remarkable pictures.

In September 1930, Lang approached Jacques to review the script for his upcoming film *M*, Lang's first sound film and one of the greatest motion pictures ever lensed. Contrary to stories Lang would later tell, Lang was already scheming a sequel to *Dr. Mabuse*, and wanted Jacques to help work out a new story. The author replied that he had been asked repeatedly by his various producer contacts to script a female version of Dr. Mabuse. Although a Frau Mabuse would not appear until 1984, the notion did set in motion a chain of events that would have profound consequences for Jacques, Lang and the cinema of Dr. Mabuse.

Jacques' efforts at inventing a female Mabuse had led to a new book project, *Mabuses Kolonie* ("Mabuse's Colony"). In the first novel *Der Spieler*, Mabuse's ultimate goal was to take his winnings and establish his own private kingdom in the Brazilian jungle. This Nation of Mabuse, called Eitopomar,* motivated all of his elaborate schemes. *Mabuses Kolonie* features a sinister and mysterious lady known only as Frau Kristina. (Like any good Mabuse figure, Kristina's identity cannot be captured by anything so bourgeois as a name—when asked her full name, Kristina simply says whatever name-like words happen to be printed on nearby signs.) Kristina intends to organize an expedition to find Eitopomar and reclaim for the Fatherland all the money that Mabuse stole in 1922—an eerily prescient analogue to the Nazi program of reclaiming German land from Czechoslovakia, Austria and so forth. The key to Kristina's project lies in Mabuse's last will and testament, which outlined his criminal master plan in detail.

At the time that Lang approached Jacques for input on the Mabuse sequel, the author was shopping his incomplete 86-page manuscript for *Kolonie* to various publishers. Naturally enough, Jacques responded to Lang's query by sending him a copy of the book. Lang tactfully rejected it. His film version of *Dr. Mabuse* had eliminated the Utopian subplot altogether, such that there had been no previous reference to Eitopomar—a handicap to making Eitopomar the central focus of the sequel.

However, Lang did fancy the idea of Mabuse outlining plans for future crimes in his will. Taking this idea as his starting point, Lang worked up an outline for *Das Testament des Dr. Mabuse* ("The Testament of Dr. Mabuse"). Publishers had shown little interest in *Kolonie*, so Jacques abandoned it and shifted gears to writing a novel based on Lang's outline. *Kolonie* was never completed, and only received publication in its fragmented form after Jacques' death.

---

*While "Eitopomar" sounds conspicuously like "Utopia," the authorized translation by Lilian A. Clare renders the island's name as "Citopomar" for English speakers.

On July 28, 1931, Jacques granted Nero-Film the film rights to his novel *Das Testament des Dr. Mabuse* on the condition that Lang direct and Thea von Harbou write the screenplay. In February 1932, Jacques approached the publishing house Goldmann with hopes of getting *Dr. Mabuse der Spieler* reprinted in time for the new film, now that Ullstein's edition had gone out of print. He also told them about his new Mabuse novel, connected to the new film. Jacques had no way of knowing that these two steps, seemingly straightforward means of promoting his work, were on a collision course with each other.

In April 1932, an American promoter asked Thea von Harbou to write a novelization of *M* for the English-speaking market. Accustomed to writing novels and screenplays of the same material at more or less the same time, von Harbou readily agreed. Oh and by the way, the Americans said, we also want a novel of this new Mabuse film. The screenwriter pointed out to them that Norbert Jacques, creator of Dr. Mabuse, had already written such a novel. Not interested, replied the Americans, since nobody over here has ever heard of this Jacques—but you, Miss von Harbou, are a "name."

At least that is how von Harbou told the story when she wrote to her friend Jacques, politely asking him to junk his novel. The Americans only wanted to proceed if there would be no competing book, so to seal the deal she needed him to promise that his version would never be published. Jacques was on financial hard times, though, and had already been begging Lang for money to help pay the bills. To compensate him for his loss, von Harbou offered to pony up a full third of all the revenues from her book. If he agreed, von Harbou argued, they would both make much more money in the long run exploiting the book in the enormous American market.

The problem was that she had not yet written her book and the American deal was not yet a sure thing. Goldmann had meanwhile become interested in publishing *Testament* in a double-edition with the reprint of *Der Spieler*, and had real cash to offer right away.

Jacques floated some counterproposals. Perhaps he could publish *Testament* under a different title, like *Mabuse stirbt* ("Mabuse Dies")? Von Harbou nixed that idea.

Perhaps he could take a novella he was working on, *Der Chemiker des Dr. Mabuse* ("Dr. Mabuse's Chemist"), change it to remove Mabuse entirely, and substitute this for *Testament* in Goldmann's double-edition? Goldmann rejected this plan, maintaining that they were only interested if they could publish the two movie-based novels together. No substitutions. (Ultimately, Jacques did remove Mabuse from the other book and it was published as *Chemiker Null* ["Chemist Zero"] for a 1934 serialization in the *Neuen Zuricher Zeitung*.)

The impasse continued. Hoping to forestall Jacques from caving in to Goldmann simply out of financial necessity, von Harbou paid him out of her own pocket an advance of 1500 Marks. But Goldmann had some 10,000 Marks on the table, and von Harbou's deal in America was looking shakier. Jacques continued to side with his friends, though, and waited.

They had all waited too long. In early 1933, Fritz Lang finished the film and submitted it to the Nazi censors, whereupon Dr. Joseph Goebbels had it banned outright. Lang fled the country, and von Harbou joined the Nazis. The Americans dropped all interest in the von Harbou books.* Neither the original *Dr. Mabuse* nor

---

*In 1968, Simon and Schuster published the M screenplay transcribed from the film by Nicholas Garnham and credited to Fritz Lang, with no reference to Thea von Harbou. Disturbed at how (cont.)

Testament would be screened in either Germany or America for over a decade. In this environment, Goldmann withdrew their offer.

Jacques lost.

The novel *Testament des Dr. Mabuse* would not be published until 1950, retitled *Dr. Mabuses letztes Spiel* ("Dr. Mabuse's Last Gamble"), and it was greeted with indifference. It fell out of print until the late 1980s, when a Mabuse renaissance revived it under its original title. In the intervening years, Jacques' contribution to the second Mabuse film had been obscured by this unfortunate set of circumstances, and most critics blindly assumed that Lang and von Harbou had cooked up *Testament* all on their own.

All in all, the cinematic career of Dr. Mabuse had effectively eclipsed the role of his creator. In September 1953, Jacques granted producer Artur Brauner the exclusive and lasting right to the character and name Dr. Mabuse. Jacques passed away shortly thereafter, on May 15, 1954, from heart failure. Brauner kept Jacques' monster alive, though, rampaging and conniving through a series of seven films from 1960 to 1970. (An additional three variations are discussed in this book despite their somewhat unofficial status.)

In the mid–1980s, a poll of Germans age 17–19 revealed that 95 percent of them were familiar with Dr. Mabuse. Whether they had seen the films or (less likely) read the books, they at least knew that his name stood for diabolical intrigue. However, exactly none of them knew the name of Norbert Jacques.

Jacques had conceived the character as a representative of his time, but Mabuse turned out to be timeless. Like the names Frankenstein or Dracula, Mabuse had become a loaded name, an enduring icon of horror. In that way alone, Jacques had achieved some measure of immortality: He supplied the only lasting literary contribution to that horror tradition to have come from the twentieth century.

With Mabuse, Jacques had struck a Faustian bargain. He had traded a fair measure of his artistic reputation in order to usher into the world this sinister madman. In return, Mabuse overthrew his creator and became something too vast to control. In the early part of the century, Jacques was hailed as one of the most important and talented German authors. By the close of the century, his name was known only to a handful of scholars.

But Jacques was not alone in being overcome by Mabuse's domination. Of the 12 (or so) Mabuse movies, a scant three have been preserved in the minds of film historians. Along with Jacques, Mabuse's other creators and recreators such as Harald Reinl, Werner Klingler, Paul May, Hugo Fregonese, Gordon Hessler, Jess Franco, Claude Chabrol and Ulrike Ottinger have been hidden by the shadow of a strong-willed, dictatorial little man with a monocle. Because for most reviewers, the story of Dr. Mabuse is the story of Fritz Lang.

---

revisionist historians were erasing his wife's contributions from the records of his career, Lang made a point of emphasizing von Harbou's input in subsequent interviews and personal appearances.

CHAPTER 2

The Eyes of Fritz Lang

> It's a pity that there is still a difference between the human eye and the camera; I need a few eyes on the side of my head too.
> —Fritz Lang to Lotte Eisner on the set of *The Testament of Dr. Mabuse*

His image has entered the public consciousness as the definitive icon of the European émigré director: With his monocled eye, barking orders in his German accent, Lang typified Hollywood of the 1930s and '40s. It was an image that swiftly turned into cliché, the sadistic stereotype of the Germanic director.

His name has become celebrated as the creator of one of filmdom's most innovative and influential pictures. The seminal silent *Metropolis* established a visual language for virtually every science fiction film that followed. His self-acknowledged masterwork *M* helped spawn the horror thriller, and is widely regarded as one of the greatest motion pictures of all time. He is also responsible for establishing the genre conventions of the spy thriller (thanks to *Spies*) and was one of the leading pioneers of the *film noir* genre (thanks to such classics as *You Only Live Once*, *Ministry of Fear*, *Scarlet Street* and *The Woman in the Window*).

He was a meticulous perfectionist who painstakingly hand-animated a stop-motion sequence in his silent film *Destiny*, years before Willis O'Brien's landmark work in *The Lost World*. He encouraged and demanded innovation from those around him, too. It was on *Metropolis* that famed cinematographer Eugen Schüfftan first unveiled his Schüfftan Process, a revolutionary method for combining miniatures and live action in the days before optical matting.

He has worked with some of the greatest names in cinema, including Peter Lorre, Marilyn Monroe, Henry Fonda, Spencer Tracy, Edward G. Robinson, Marlene Dietrich, Barbara Stanwyck, Vincent Price, Ida Lupino, Darryl Zanuck, Graham Greene, Bertolt Brecht, Max Steiner, James Wong Howe and Edgar G. Ulmer.

In short, Fritz Lang is a legendary figure in the world of film, which is just how he wanted it. A consummate storyteller, Lang engaged in rampant myth-making on his own behalf throughout his lifetime, editing and embellishing his biography to maximum self-promotional effect.

However, this tendency also impaired the great director. In conceiving his life story as a tale of Man Against Fate, beset on all sides by enemies and sinister conspiracies, Lang may have developed powerful themes and imagery to drive his films but also became a paranoid recluse. He

Despite being a visionary filmmaker, Fritz Lang struggled with vision problems his entire life (courtesy Photofest).

burned bridges both behind and ahead of him, abusing and exploiting all around him. Actors, once through Lang's gauntlet, swore never to work with him again. Meanwhile, Lang hopped from producer to producer, always convinced that they were conniving against him. Lang was the real-life embodiment of his screen characters—alternately the hapless victim of Fate (as he saw himself) or the cruel dictator trying to conquer the world (as others saw him). Lang may have seen much of Hitler in Dr. Mabuse, but his colleagues saw much of Lang himself there too.

He was born on December 5, 1890, in Vienna, Austria, one of the largest and most cosmopolitan cities of the world. His father Anton was a contractor. In Fritz's self-styled myths, though, his father was a more socially advanced and respectable architect. Anton expected the young Fritz to follow in his footsteps; although the future director would later claim to have architectural credentials, it was simply another exaggeration (or lie, depending on one's charitability).

Fritz was hostile and disrespectful towards Anton. The two never reconciled their differences. Instead, Fritz felt himself closest to his mother, Paula Schlesinger Lang, a Jew. Many years later, his mother's Jewishness would raise problems for Fritz, but at the time it was a small matter. The law forbade marriages between Jews and Catholics, and indeed Anton was officially a Catholic, but it was an accepted practice for Jews in such situations to either declare no religion or convert to Catholicism in order to appease the authorities. Oddly, Anton and Paula chose the reverse course, with Anton declaring himself without religion and Paula listing herself as Jewish. Nevertheless, the couple dutifully raised Fritz as a Catholic. When he was ten years old, they underwent a special ceremony to embrace Catholicism for themselves. Fritz Lang would always think of himself as Catholic, and would almost forget his mother's heritage until the Nazi regime later thrust it in his face.

The Lang family lived a life of relative luxury, at a time of incredible turn-of-the-century technological progress. Lang's future visions of fantastic technology in films such as the Mabuse series or *Metropolis* must surely have drawn some influence from this time. He was also soaking up influences from the Viennese theater, which his family frequented several times a month. His personal favorite was the Kratky-Baschik Zaubertheater, which specialized in plays featuring monsters, supernatural occurrences and special effects.

Lang enjoyed the theater, but preferred the cinema. While his parents attended plays about twice a month, young Fritz was seeing movies once or twice each day. Of these, he greatly enjoyed the horror thrillers of director Louis Feuillade, a significant influence on his later filmmaking.

Lang also loved to read, especially trashy pulpy books about super criminals (such as Fantômas), science fiction, crime stories and Westerns. He read books about the occult. He read Jules Verne and Karl May. He read the works of the Marquis de Sade and sundry other banned works of decadence.

He also spent time in the cabarets, both as a spectator and a participant. Lang had been tracked into a technical, vocational school rather than the humanistic, academic track, and was not doing well in his studies. Aspiring to be an artist, not a businessman, Lang spent more and more time working at the cabarets and less and less time in class.

In 1910, Lang left home to travel around Europe, selling sketches and paintings, soaking up the culture. He would later claim to have seen much more of the world than the evidence suggests. His fascination with Oriental art and culture most likely came not from actual visits to Asia as he boasted but from Parisian museums. In 1913, the young man was settled in Paris, eking out a living working in cabarets and selling paintings on street corners.

Unfortunately, just as Lang was adopting Paris as a second home, the world around him was in upheaval. The assassination of Austrian Archduke Ferdinand in Sarajevo on June 28, 1914, resulted in a declaration of war just one month later. Austria's ally was Germany, and Serbia's ally was Russia. Germany's historical enemies were Russia—and France. Suddenly, the Austrian Lang living in Paris found himself in a state soon to be at war with his homeland.

Such a situation would likely have unnerved the average man, but Lang and his fellow Austrian-born artist-wannabes were an apolitical bunch. They remained blithely unconcerned by or unaware of the historical forces at work around them. Days after Austria's declaration of war, though, France was plunged into the conflict. Militant anti–Semites assassinated the socialist Jean Jaurés, the leading anti-war voice in France. By morning, all rail connections between France and either Germany or Austria had been closed. Lang realized he had to get out quickly, and boarded a train to Belgium, intending to reroute towards Germany once out of France. In his haste, Lang had left without the proper visa. Nervously, the future director of many a thriller fingered his Browning revolver in his pocket, worried that he may have to shoot his way out of any incidents. As it happened, the crossing was uneventful, but some permanent scars had been etched into the young man's mind, nurturing a lifelong paranoia.

Like any good patriot, Lang volunteered to serve in the war. Little is known about this period of his life, because in his later years he would reinvent himself as a politically minded opponent of war and tyranny. Voluntary enlistment did not fit this image, so he glossed over it. In fact, though, Lang was a brave fighter. He quickly rose the ranks, earning numerous medals and commendations for valor as he led dangerous reconnaissance missions of the Russian battalions. The first of several war injuries was a relatively mild bullet wound in the shoulder. The second injury, however, temporarily blinded him and may have been the reason he wore that infamous monocle throughout the rest of his life.

While recovering, Lang started a journal of story ideas. Like the stories he loved to read, Lang wrote true crime tales, stories about werewolves and other pulpy, lurid yarns.

A friend from the cabarets suggested they write movie scripts together, and pitched Lang's journal ideas to Joe May. One of the leading lights of the German film industry at that time, May was a producer and a director, running his own production company May-Film GmbH. May had been searching for some new blood to enliven his company, and bought several of Lang's crime stories. This was not yet to be Lang's introduction to the film world, though, for he soon returned to war.

Lang won some more commendations for bravery and was injured a third time. Hospitalized for two more months, Lang decided that he had been shot enough times for one lifetime and asked to be declared unfit for duty. In 1918, Lang's war career ended. He had distinguished himself as a gallant patriot, but he never spoke of it and apparently never adapted his wartime experiences in any of his films. Lang's cinematic world would be peopled with horror of a different variety; the nightmare of World War I was something Lang could not bring himself to face again.

Now a free man, Lang went to see one of Joe May's film versions of his stories. He was appalled. May had taken all the credit, leaving no mention of Lang's contribution. Worse still was the fact that *the movie was badly made.* Lang, who had until now thought of himself as a painter or a writer, now began to think that his place was in films. He knew he could have done it better if he had only had the chance…

Fate gave Lang a helping hand. Erich Pommer was a brilliant producer working for Bufa (Bild und Film Amt), a propaganda unit during the war. After the war, Bufa merged into the larger auspices of Ufa (Universum Film Aktiengesellschaft), then the state-sponsored film agency. Pommer also owned his own production company Decla (Deutsche Éclair). Lang and Pommer met, and immediately impressed one another. Lang moved to Berlin, his new adoptive home, to learn filmmaking at Decla (which would later merge with Bioscop AG, which would in turn later be merged with Ufa).

Lang alternated working for Pommer and Joe May, penning horror and crime scripts while absorbing as much as he could about the manufacture of motion pictures. He became increasingly frustrated with how other directors visualized his scripts. In 1919 he demanded that Pommer give him a chance to direct. The result was *Half-Breed*, which Lang filmed from his own screenplay.

Not long after, Lang moved up in esteem to helm an ambitious project called *Spiders* (1919), a two-part epic about an explorer-hero's adventures battling a secret conspiracy called The Spiders. It was big and lavish. The convention of the day was to make such prestigious blockbuster pictures as gigantic two-part films, with each full-length part filmed and screened separately. Lang enjoyed the spectacle and status of these enormous productions, and would make many of them during his German period.

Part One, "The Golden Lake," was such an instant success that Pommer felt pressure to rush the second installment, "The Diamond Ship," into production. Originally, Lang had been slated to direct *The Cabinet of Dr. Caligari* (1919), but with *Spiders* calling he had to cede *Caligari* to Robert Wiene instead. Lang's brief involvement with this landmark film may or may not have had a lasting impression; as with so much of Lang's biography, the accounts are untrustworthy. But if Lang's contributions are hard to pinpoint with precision, in his version of the story we can see into the man's mind perhaps more deeply than he would wish:

Caligari has been hailed as a masterpiece of Expressionist filmmaking, the film that brought modern art to the masses and proved to elite art lovers that motion pictures deserved serious attention and respect. Consequently, everyone involved in its production has an incentive to claim credit for the decision to stage its eerie narrative with wild, Expressionist imagery. To this end, screenwriter Hans Janowitz has had the most success in claiming authorship of *Caligari*'s daring visual design. Janowitz insisted that he and co-screenwriter Carl Mayer had specified the Expressionist imagery in exacting detail in their original handwritten script, and that they sold this to producer Erich Pommer on the condition that nothing was to be altered in the filming. But in the finished film, the Expressionist imagery is contained within a framing story that establishes the narrative as the mad ravings of a deranged man: The world is bent and distorted because this is the world as seen through an insane mind.

Janowitz railed that this frame story was

> dishonoring our drama ... into a cliché, in which the symbolism was to be lost.

When we came to learn of this plan, we strongly protested. In vain. Then we instructed our attorneys to take the proper steps against this crime. But Wiene succeeded in having his version approved by the production department.

Janowitz first made this claim, many years after the film's international success, to film critic Sigfried Kracauer. Kracauer repeated it as a central element of his thesis for *From Caligari to Hitler*. Since Kracauer's book was as much a landmark work of film criticism as *Caligari* was of filmmaking, Janowitz's self-important posturing was quickly accepted as the truth.

Certainly Janowitz's version of events accorded with the generally held view of film production. Here were two artists, writers with a unique and progressive vision, but the unimaginative "suits" at the studio overruled them and watered down their creation for mass consumption. Soon the received opinion of *Caligari* was that it would have been an even harder-hitting, more revolutionary picture both artistically and politically if Wiene and Pommer had not had cold feet.

Wiene was in no position to argue with this account. He had passed away in 1938, nine years before Kracauer's book. Additionally, Janowitz figured that the script itself had been lost to the ravages of time, not to mention world wars. As it happened, a copy of the original screenplay had survived, in the possession of Werner Krauss, the actor who played Dr. Caligari. When his copy became available in 1978, after the actor's death, scholars finally had a chance to check Janowitz's story.

Janowitz and Mayer made no mention at all of Expressionist imagery in their draft, and furthermore they had already scripted a framing story similar to, but less imaginative than the one in the final film. So if they did not make the decision to stage the action on bizarre sets out of some art director's nightmare, then who did?

Erich Pommer put in his claim, stating that he had assigned the project to his hand-picked design crew. Since he incorrectly identified the designers, though, his position is more than a little dubious. More plausible is the scenario presented by Hermann Warm, one of the designers who (along with Walter Röhrig and Hans Reimann) worked under supervisor Rudolf Meinert. Reimann says that they met with Wiene to discuss the film, and that night Reimann stayed up all night thinking about the script. Reimann returned the next day convinced that only the bold strokes of Expressionism could convey the message of the film. Although skeptical at first, Meinert came around when he realized that, no matter if the film turned out good or bad, the daring experiment would give the film an instant notoriety, and thereby a solid marketing hook. It no longer mattered if the film was a good one; the Expressionism was sure to be box office gold. Meinert turned out to have good instincts, because scholars to this day debate the merits of *Caligari* but its lasting influence and importance as the seminal Expressionist film is undeniable.

And what of Lang, attached to the film for but the briefest of time? He too put in his claim of authorship, but oddly not for its Expressionist elements. No, Lang claimed credit for the *frame story*! In Lang's telling, he reviewed Janowitz and Mayer's script and decided that the audience was just not ready for the weird Expressionist sets, and so such imagery had to be somehow grounded in realism. He then wrote a bookending sequence that presented the tale from the point of view of an inmate in an asylum, explaining away the fantastic visions of the body of the film.

Chronologically, Lang's account is nonsensical. If the Expressionist techniques were cooked up by the design staff only after their initial meeting with Wiene, and Wiene was brought on only after Lang was committed to *Spiders* Part Two, then Lang was too early to introduce any such ideas. For Lang to try to insert himself into this controversy, not to claim authorship of the film's most acclaimed asset but rather for its most notorious defect, says much about Lang's skeptical disdain for Expressionism. His work is often inappropriately identified as Expressionist, but students of *Caligari* know otherwise.

Meanwhile, Lang felt rushed through *Spiders* Part Two, and emerged dissatisfied with the finished product. In what would come to be a recurring scenario, Lang grumbled about how his work was being sabotaged by meddlesome studio executives, and he quit Decla to direct for Joe May instead.

It was around this time that May introduced Lang to the woman who would have the greatest influence on his life and career, at least during this German half of it. Thea von Harbou had a regal bearing from well-bred Prussian stock. Very well educated, she was a prolific writer and poet. Hoping for an acting career, von Harbou started off under the direction of Rudolf Klein-Rogge. During the war years, von Harbou and Klein-Rogge married, and she gave up acting to concentrate on her writing.

In 1917, von Harbou and Klein-Rogge moved to Berlin, where she wrote novels while he acted in films. Within a year, novel-writing had taken a decided back seat to the more exciting world of screenwriting, and von Harbou was penning scenarios for May, F.W. Murnau, Carl Theodore Dreyer and other luminaries of the German cinema.

Lang and von Harbou hit it off instantly, and quickly became a team. Among their mutual interests, the two shared a fascination with the Far East. Von Harbou had written a 1917 novel called

The Indian Tomb that indulged her taste for exoticism, and she began working with Lang on a screenplay adaptation. To suit Lang's grandiose aspirations, it was to be another two-part colossus. Meanwhile, the busy pair also scripted *The Wandering Image* for May.

In a seeming act of largesse, May offered *The Wandering Image* (1920) back to Lang to direct. Always happy to be barking orders to a film crew, Lang accepted. The production would feature at least two names that would resurface in Lang's subsequent Mabuse films. One was production designer Erick Kettlehut, who returned to Lang's employ four decades later to help design *The 1000 Eyes of Dr. Mabuse*. More importantly, Lang cast Rudolf Klein-Rogge in the picture, marking his first collaboration with von Harbou's husband. Klein-Rogge would later star in many of Lang's greatest German films, not least of which as Dr. Mabuse himself.

But while Lang busied himself with *The Wandering Image*, he overlooked how one of his supposed allies was betraying him. May had used *The Wandering Image* gambit to occupy Lang while he took over *The Indian Tomb* for himself. Lang had been cheated. His baby had been taken from him, and (in Lang's estimation) mishandled. Critics hailed *The Indian Tomb* (1921) as one of the best films ever made, which only rubbed salt into the wound. Lang knew that his version would have been ever so much better. Again citing unacceptable sabotage from his producers, Lang resigned from May-Film to return to Pommer and Decla-Bioscop, taking von Harbou with him.

Lang's return to Pommer had given the director his first true hit, a motion picture that marked him as a talent worth watching, a name to remember. *Destiny* (1921) was the first original story that Lang and von Harbou scripted for Lang to direct. The film, which concerns a young woman bargaining with Death to save her husband's life, starred the future opponents of *Dr. Mabuse*, Rudolf Klein-Rogge and Bernard Goetzke.

Thea von Harbou's script about the endurance of love masked the rather tawdry circumstances of her own life. In light of these circumstances, the presence of Klein-Rogge in the cast seems even more surprising. Over time the partnership between Lang and von Harbou had become much more than professional. They found in each other not only perfect creative collaborators, but soulmates and lovers. The affair ruined the von Harbou–Klein-Rogge marriage, but in a sign of sophistication about such things, the three parts of this triangle remained professional partners. Klein-Rogge stuck with Lang, the man who wrecked his home, for starring roles in *The Nibelungen*, *Dr. Mabuse*, *Metropolis* and others.

If Klein-Rogge and von Harbou could sever their matrimonial union amicably, no such thing could be said of Lang himself. It is widely believed that the marriage between Lang and von Harbou in 1922 (shortly after production on *Dr. Mabuse*) was the first wedding for the director. Lang helped cultivate this misimpression himself, and never spoke publicly about his true first wife or her fate. The only person to whom Lang ever confided about this tragedy was Howard Vernon, whom Lang met on *The 1000 Eyes of Dr. Mabuse* and who was also a close friend of *Vengeance of Dr. Mabuse* director Jess Franco.

Since 1919, Lang had been married to Lisa Rosenthal, whom he had met during the war years. Lang's affair with von Harbou was not a very well-kept secret, and it caused understandable friction between the director and Mrs. Lang. They had been arguing, loudly and publicly, but everything came to a head when Lisa walked in on her husband and von Harbou in passionate, naked embrace. And soon, poor Lisa Rosenthal was dead, shot in the chest by Lang's Browning. Lang and von Harbou insisted that it was a suicide, but this was by no means clear. Even some of his close friends believed that Lang had indeed killed his own wife. There was an official inquest, but Lang used his considerable influence to have the matter hushed. Today, no records survive of Rosenthal's death.

Every friend of Lang's interviewed for this book agrees that the Lang they knew was incapable of murder. It is yet easy to see how he would become haunted by the queasy nexus of murder and suicide. Although Lang never spoke of Lisa Rosenthal again, his films became obsessive ruminations on guilt, suicide, innocent parties accused of crimes, and guilty parties trying to conceal their crimes.

Despite having paid such a high price for his relationship with von Harbou, Lang could not bring himself even to be faithful with her. There were many mistresses, many hookers. Yet she understood, and stood patiently by her man; perhaps the memory of her own betrayal of Klein-Rogge kept her from assuming any hypocritical moral high ground. Furthermore, she knew that she and Lang were perfect professional partners, and nothing should be allowed to jeopardize that. Von Harbou later remarked, "We were married 11 years, because for ten years we didn't have time to get divorced."

In those ten years, von Harbou remained a prominent and essential member of the Lang film crew. She was no mere scenarist. In addition to penning the screenplays (which she usually co-wrote with novels, either adapting her novels for the screen or novelizing the film), she was a mediating presence on the set. She knit sweaters for the cast and crew, played the piano, assisted with casting and blunted the director's cruel temper. When the critical situation of the worsening German economy threatened, she took to cooking hot meals on the set at Ufa's expense to feed the cast and crew while her husband enslaved them 'round the clock. In many ways, she was a co-director on Lang's German films, and her absence in Hollywood would leave a void he could never truly fill.

Destiny not only marked a turning point in Lang's career, it marked an auspicious shift in the German film business. Decla-Bioscop merged with Ufa (now a private company) to form the most powerful and important studio outside Hollywood. The new Ufa housed Germany's best and brightest film talents, ran many of Berlin's top theaters, and managed hundreds more theaters across Germany and the rest of Europe. Erich Pommer had taken over as Ufa's chief of production and distribution. This powerhouse considered Lang its greatest asset.

Despite this, Lang remained unjustly obscure in America. *Destiny* went essentially unreleased stateside, as would too many of Lang's great German films. Hollywood dominated world cinema, crowding out other productions both at home and abroad. Then as today, American screens had little room for foreign-language product.

His next film's American reception was not much better. *Dr. Mabuse the Gambler* (1922) began life as a novel serialized in the *Berliner Illustrierten* magazine in 1921, and within mere months made it to cinema screens. The book was written by journalist-author Norbert Jacques as an exposé of the appalling conditions of the Weimar Republic. Lang was developing an affinity that would turn into a character trait: using real-life situations (usually from newspaper clippings) to give authenticity to his films. Lang held a lifelong conviction that cinema was the people's art form, and that if mass audiences were to draw so much of their impressions and attitudes about life from motion pictures, that filmmakers had a responsibility to depict life with honesty and authenticity. His films would always be fiction (and full of fantastic situations at that), but grounded in verisimilitude that he represented with a documentarian's integrity.

Collaborating with a journalist was even better than simply clipping newspaper articles, and to do so on a film intended as a modern-day social critique was a Langian dream come true. Together with Jacques, Lang and von Harbou adapted *Dr. Mabuse* for the screen. Of course, a project this important demanded scope, and Lang made it into another two-part epic running nearly five hours in its gargantuan entirety.

Although *Dr. Mabuse* was a significant critical and commercial success at home, it did not make it to American theaters until six years later, and by then it had been hacked down to a paltry 90 minutes. The "full length" cut did not appear until 1966, and by then some of the original footage had been lost forever.

As if despairing of breaking into the American market, Lang next turned his attention to a fundamentally German project, a retelling of the Ring of the Nibelungen. The original thirteenth century epic poem has long been linked with German nationalist pride. Lang had recently become an official German citizen, and felt a patriotic urge to do something to boost his country's sagging morale.

The conditions of the Weimar Republic, which had been depicted in *Dr. Mabuse* with apocalyptic images of crime run rampant and the ascendancy of a tyrannical overlord, had only worsened. Riots, strikes, protests, mass starvation and poverty had created a crisis situation. The police had given up pursuing thefts or other "minor crimes," their attention diverted by only the most severe transgressions. It was at this time that Thea von Harbou began cooking hot meals on the set for a company that, otherwise, stood a real risk of not getting anything to eat. On the crew of one of the most respected directors working for the most powerful studio outside Hollywood, production designers had to wander the streets scrounging for loose nails with which to construct their sets. For the average citizen living outside the reach of such celebrities, the conditions were even more intolerable.

Lang sincerely hoped to raise the spirits of his new adopted homeland, and put all his creative energies into *The Nibelungen* (1924). He and von Harbou based their adaptation on the epic poem, the famous opera by Richard Wagner, the play by Friedrich Hebbel and their own unique imaginations. They succeeded in their ambitions, and produced a work of powerful artistry and equally powerful nationalist pride. The Nazis loved it. Adolf Hitler and Joseph Goebbels could not see it often enough, deciding that Lang was to be "their" director. "Here is a man who will give us great Nazi films!" said Hitler.

Ironically, *The Nibelungen* was also the first of Lang's pictures to receive serious attention in the United States. Lang and Pommer traveled to New York in 1924 for the premiere, all the while scheming how to wedge their way even further into the American market. The director and his scenarist wife were already developing a screenplay called *Metropolis*, about a dystopian future society ruled by machines and marked by horrific class divisions. A young woman named Maria (Brigitte Helm) tries to soothe the workers' rising anger, but a mad scientist (Klein-Rogge) creates a robot duplicate of Maria to incite the workers into bloody rebellion.

Setting his eyes for the first time on the New York skyline, Lang saw what his future world should look like. Inspired by this imagery, he and Pommer decided to forge ahead with *Metropolis* (1926) as a major undertaking (although it would be a single-part film of somewhat more sensible length).

No expense was to be spared. Ufa planned *Metropolis* as the biggest, most lavish production ever made in all of Europe. They had no real expectation of profit, but instead aspired to create a motion picture event that would break Hollywood's international domination. The expense and scale of the prestigious production gratified Lang, who let his visions soar. It would become arguably his best known and most celebrated film next to *M*. However, the expense nearly ruined Ufa. Lang managed to bust even the already bloated budget, indulging himself to excess. Ufa threatened to shut the production down entirely. Lang dodged that bullet, but only at great personal cost. Ufa's management scapegoated Pommer as the man who let Lang run loose, and removed him from his post as director of production. The new boss did not much care for Lang, and before long the director would be out of a job.

Meanwhile, editors were taking their scissors to Lang's inordinately long director's cut of *Metropolis*. His two-and-a-half-hour-long version would play only in Germany, and would ultimately be lost forever. For foreign markets, Ufa trimmed the picture to blunt its rather Communist message about the evils of heartless capitalism.

The film that Ufa hoped would conquer Hollywood did indeed ignite audiences and critics and leave a lasting influence on the entire science fiction genre, but would leave Hollywood none the worse for wear. Ufa signed a deal with Paramount to allow extensive distribution of Paramount and MGM's titles in Germany in exchange for some desperately needed cash. Ufa needed the money to offset *Metropolis*' costs, but got little else from the deal. Certainly, the Hollywood studios would not make any effort to get Ufa films screened in America.

In fact, when *Metropolis* arrived in the States, even the lean international cut Ufa had prepared was deemed too foreign. A promoter named Channing Pollock recut the picture drastically, to not only reduce its running time but change the story as well. Now missing some 45 minutes from its original length, the Pollock cut riled Lang bitterly. Lang refused to ever see this bastardized version, and added the incident to his mental list of injustices committed against him—a growing catalogue of evil producers tampering with his creative visions.

Lang had more immediate concerns. Ousted from Ufa, he was adrift. Erich Pommer had moved on to Hollywood, and extended an offer to Lang to join him. For now, Lang declined.

Instead, he established Fritz Lang Film GmbH to produce his own pictures, which would then be exclusively distributed by Ufa. It was a compromise agreement that relieved Ufa of the day-to-day worries of Lang's financial excesses, yet allowed them to take advantage of his inestimable reputation as a filmmaker of the highest rank. Even still, Ufa hoped to rein in Lang's extravagance as much as possible from afar.

Under this new order, Lang attempted his first independent iteration of the Mabuse scenario *Spies* (1928). With this film, Lang and von Harbou demonstrated that they did not need Norbert Jacques to conceive of a world of disguise and deception, trap doors and secret conspiracies.

Where *Metropolis* established the iconography of the science fiction genre, *Spies* set the standard for espionage films. Pointedly, the spy film boom of the 1960s owes more to the genre conventions laid out in this silent-era classic than even the

Lang and von Harbou (in hat, far right) on the set of *Metropolis* (courtesy Photofest).

numerous espionage thrillers with which Lang and Alfred Hitchcock peppered the screen during the 1940s.

The proto–James Bond hero is Agent 326, Donald Tremaine (a curiously Anglo-Saxon name for a German hero), who faces "the most dangerous man in Europe," the Great Haghi. As played by Rudolf Klein-Rogge, Haghi is a dehumanized supervillain, a cold and calculating monster more akin to the Mabuse figures to come in the 1960s than the lusty sadist depicted in the 1922 *Dr. Mabuse the Gambler*.

Haghi is the man behind the scenes, the puppet master yanking the strings, but his principal puppet is the lovely and seductive agent Sonia. The seamy world of international intelligence-gathering first captured public attention during the First World War through such vampish figures as Mata Hari and Maude Allan. To the average citizen, espionage was a game of sexual exploitation whereby enemy agents pried information from their targets by manipulating human desires and weaknesses. What high-ranking VIP could avoid letting state secrets slip in the passionate embrace of an illicit lover? But in a move that would anticipate many a James Bond film to come, Tremaine's sexual magnetism compels Sonia to switch her allegiance.

Sonia initially weasels her way into Tremaine's confidence by preying on his chivalry, and manipulating him into covering up a (fake) murder—a strategy later repeated in *The 1000 Eyes of Dr. Mabuse*. Tremaine believes himself to be acting on his own free will, but is only entangling himself in Haghi's evil web. Sonia has Tremaine right where Haghi wants him, but then she falls for Agent 326 and allies herself with him against Haghi.

For all of Tremaine's efforts, though, the Mabuse-like Haghi ultimately brings himself down. The police and the secret service are representatives of a failed social order—their motivations may be pure and their investigations may uncover the criminal conspiracy, but they are unable to defeat it. Sonia is a far greater threat—a femme fatale from Haghi's inner circle who defects. She inflicts more damage on Haghi's organization than Tremaine ever could. In the final scene, though, neither she nor Tremaine gets the pleasure of defeating the most dangerous man in Europe: He commits suicide. The Mabuse Principle demands that Mabuse destroy himself. It was a familiar pattern that would be recycled with minor variations time and again in the films that followed.

Other, smaller plot devices would also get a dry run here before reuse in later Mabuse pictures: a bad guy disguised as a clown (*The Invisible Dr. Mabuse*), the rescue of a murderer from death row in order to recruit him as an agent (*Dr. Mabuse vs. Scotland Yard*) and a climactic encounter aboard a train that reworked ideas from *Dr. Mabuse the Gambler* and would later inspire *Ministry of Fear* and *The Return of Dr. Mabuse*.

To get one sequence just the way he wanted, Lang fired real bullets at his cast to achieve truly realistic onscreen gunshots and bullet holes. It was not the first nor by any means the last time the director would put his underlings in harm's way. In *Metropolis*, when the robot Maria is put to the stake, poor Brigitte Helm was surrounded by real fire; the flames ignited her dress, but Lang interceded with a fire extinguisher before she was (physically) harmed. Actors under Lang, from stars like Peter Lorre and Henry Fonda to nameless extras in the crowd, suffered all manners of injury and indignity. He would pinch them, shoot at them, hoist them by wires or nearly drown them in freezing water. All onscreen explosions were real—set off by the director himself. These were the actors who wondered aloud once if Lang would go so far as to actually kill one of them, just to get an authentic death scene. These were the people who had no trouble believing that Lang had killed his first wife.

Spies introduced lovely young actress Gerda Maurus, whom Lang prized as his "find." By day he filmed her, by night he slept with her, and throughout it all he abused her. She had to suffer the same mental torture as any other Lang cast member, but as his mistress she also bore the brunt of his sadistic temper. Her bruises revealed the torrid depth (and cruelty) of their relationship, but von Harbou continued to look away discreetly.

Von Harbou had work to do. Fast on the heels of *Spies* was yet another science fiction spectacle, *By Rocket to the Moon* (1929). In her novel written concurrently, von Harbou created one more Mabusian arch-criminal and master of disguise. As if tiring of that kind of character, Lang downplayed that aspect in the finished film. *By Rocket to the Moon* was yet another deluxe production with all the usual cost overruns. During production, sound recording techniques revolutionized the industry, and silent films were rapidly losing audiences. Ufa asked Lang to add some sound effects to his new film as a minor concession to the changing marketplace. At least, they pleaded, add some blast-off sounds when the rocket is launched.

Lang refused. In fact, he railed so adamantly against the executives who asked him to "butcher" his artistic creation that the Ufa bosses began to grow very weary of this temperamental and inflexible renegade. When the film opened to disappointing business, Ufa felt vindicated. Lang was not infallible, they realized, and what makes sense artistically has nothing to do with what is needed commercially. In the face of lackluster box office returns, Ufa finally had an excuse to give up on the man they once considered their prize director. Without Ufa as a distributor, Fritz Lang Film GmbH was no more.

Enter Seymour Nebenzahl, a producer with some very impressive credits on his résumé despite his young age. He had already ushered in G.W. Pabst's *Pandora's Box* and Robert Siodmak's *People on Sunday*, and was now courting Lang and von Harbou to join him in Nero-Film. It would be a step down in budget and prestige to go with such a small company, but Lang no longer had the luxury of being picky. Moreover, the advent of sound had changed the film production landscape, and Nero was willing to let Lang enter the sound age in his own idiosyncratic way. Film buffs the world over should celebrate that fact, for it made possible the unusual, challenging, sublime motion picture called *M* (1931).

It was technically Lang's first "talkie," but *M* uses little dialogue, favoring more inventive and effective uses of sound. Far from the stagy productions being made in Hollywood that resembled little more than filmed plays, *M* is a visual feast that has hardly dated. Almost 70 years after its date of manufacture, *M* is still vital and entertaining as if it had been made yesterday. In fact, its artistry and execution are more ambitious and more successful than many modern films.

At first, Lang and von Harbou developed a crime story about the author of anonymous "poison pen" letters, before deciding that the most horrific crime imaginable was the murder of children. The real-life case of mass murderer Peter Kürten (the Monster of Düsseldorf) was in the news at the time, and provided the essential touch of authenticity that Lang held so dear. Kürten killed adults as well as children, but in their screenplay the killer's only target is little girls.

Lang cast Peter Lorre in the lead role, and boasted that he had discovered this prodigious talent. In fact, Lorre had long been a feature of the stage and had already appeared in a few films, but the role of child killer Hans Beckert made him an international star (and typecast him forever in creepy roles). Beckert is a sick man, driven against his own conscience to commit acts of depravity that horrify even him. Police Inspector Lohmann (Otto Wernicke) valiantly pursues the case, but lacks clues. The police force clamps down hard on all crime, hoping to catch the killer, but instead corrals only gamblers, prostitutes, and bank robbers. The criminal underworld realizes that their livelihood is threatened, and organizes a coalition of criminals and beggars to catch the child killer themselves. A tense showdown climaxes the film as the underworld captures Beckert and puts him on trial for his life.

The most memorable aspect of *M*, besides Lorre's masterful performance, is Lang's skillful cross-cutting between Beckert's crimes, the police procedures, and the organization of criminals trying to outdo the cops. Lang and von Harbou borrowed from reality the idea of petty criminals banding together to track a worse criminal, with Lang producing the requisite newspaper clippings as corroboration. In turn, Inspector Lohmann was closely modeled on Commissioner Genath, Berlin's star detective, who had worked the Kürten case. Of course, Lang made sure Lohmann's screen image stayed true to published accounts of Gernath's behavior.

Both Otto Wernicke and Peter Lorre were veterans of the influential Volksbühne theater. Wernicke reprised his role for Lang the following year in *The Testament of Dr. Mabuse*, which was both a sequel to *Dr. Mabuse* and to *M*. While

Wernicke returned to Lang's employ, though, Lorre severed all ties to the man who made him a star. Career-making roles are one thing, but Lorre had had his fill of abuse. Once both men had emigrated to Hollywood, Lorre stayed aloof towards Lang.

M was a much smaller production than Lang had been accustomed to, but not merely because of the smaller resources available to Nero-Films. The director himself was growing weary of the bloated blockbuster epics that he had made his stock-in-trade. As he moved away from fantasy and towards gritty realism, he also moved towards smaller, more personal pictures. Ironically, *M*, the tale of a child murderer, would be one of the filmmaker's most human movies. Thanks in large part to Lorre's incredible performance, the film has an emotional realism that Lang's work, for all its vaunted factual realism, rarely matched.

Originally, Lang and von Harbou called their project *Mörder unter uns* ("Murderer Among Us"). In preparation for filming, Lang scouted a location in a massive zeppelin hangar he felt would be perfect. Lang knew the hangar's manager, and asked permission to work there. Solemnly, the man refused, recommending that Lang abandon the project altogether.

A portrait of the artist as a young man: Fritz Lang circa 1938 (courtesy The Everett Collection).

"You will hurt the feelings of many who will become very important," the man said, "It will be very bad for you." Baffled, Lang wondered how his movie would hurt anyone's feelings. Granted, the script lacked a romantic subplot, which might hurt it commercially...

As Lang wondered these thoughts aloud, the manager began to doubt himself and asked just what Lang's movie was about. "A child murderer!" replied the director. Oh, then go right ahead and shoot your film here after all, relented the manager. He had mistakenly assumed the title referred to Hitler, and that *Murderer Among Us* would be an anti–Nazi film. To avoid unnecessary misunderstandings, Lang changed the title to *M*, in reference to the chalk mark the beggars place on Lorre's shoulder to brand him as the wanted murderer. Years later, East German filmmaker Wolfgang Staudte borrowed Lang's unused title for the first overtly anti–Nazi film to be made in Germany, 1946's *Die Mörder sind unter uns* ("Murderers Among Us").

With no indelicate confusion over the title, Dr. Joseph Goebbels, already a Lang fan from *The Nibelungen*, fell in love with *M*. To his decidedly myopic interpretation of the film's moral and political complexity, Goebbels saw it as a pro–death penalty rant (Lang intended quite the opposite). Goebbels' own star was on the rise; he had slowly built the Berlin branch of the Nazi party from a mere fledgling into the heart of the movement. Lang remained rather naive about politics. He posed for pictures with Goebbels and tried to curry favor with the new regime, but still had little idea what Nazism was all about.

Meanwhile, the Nazis were compiling lists of Jews in the film industry (much as the United States House Un-American Activities Committee would later catalogue the Communists working in Hollywood). It amounted to a virtual who's who of the picture business. On the list, to no one's surprise but his own, was Herr Lang. Thanks to his mother's heritage, the self-styled Catholic Lang was considered a Jew. What this might mean to his personal or professional future was still not known.

Lang realized the time was nigh to learn what all the fuss was about. He attended one of Hitler's rallies and was dumbstruck. The crowd around him raised their arms in salute ("Heil Hitler!") as the filmmaker stood in terrified silence.

In the same year that *M* was released, the Nazis had amassed power. Nineteen thirty-two, the year of Lang's *Testament of Dr. Mabuse*, would be the last year of the Weimar Republic. The social crisis had reached its breaking point. With unemployment at six million, the desperate masses were ready for a leader to impose order. That such a leader would be a hateful and exploitative tyrant had already been predicted by Lang and Jacques. History was catching up with art: Dr. Mabuse had arrived.

The urgent social problems that had compelled Lang and Jacques to tell the first Dr. Mabuse tale had only grown more dramatic. Throughout production on *M*, Lang, Jacques and von Harbou had already been planning a Mabuse sequel, to be called *The Testament of Dr. Mabuse*. Just as his trip to New York had provided the essential spark of inspiration to fuel the visualization of *Metropolis*, Lang's experience at the Nazi rally gave him new insight into the new project.

In the years that followed, Lang would mythologize *Testament of Dr. Mabuse* as a daring anti–Nazi polemic. With each telling of the tale, the legend grew, and the supposed political subtext of the film grew with it. Indeed, *Testament*'s content supports such an interpretation, which is only the more unusual given that it had been written for the screen by Thea von Harbou, who would months later officially join the National Sozialistische deutsche Arbeiter Partei herself.

Von Harbou's brand of Nazism was never so ruthless, though. She had spent a lifetime vigorously supporting women's rights issues. Yet she was a fierce nationalist, and cast her lot with the Mabuses of the world.

The last time that Lang saw his wife was at a grand summit meeting of the leading lights of the German film industry, held by Joseph Goebbels. Surrounded by storm troopers, the largely Jewish crowd listened in apprehension as Goebbels singled out films like *The Nibelungen* as examples of what would be permitted under the new rule of Nazi censorship. After Goebbels' speech, Lang spoke with the propaganda minister about the fate of *Testament of Dr. Mabuse*, which had suffered the misfortune of being the first film reviewed by the new regime. *Testament* was banned, and soon Lang fled the country in what would come to be his greatest (if also the most embellished) legend of his life. Von Harbou stayed, to continue writing films for Goebbels' new order. She passed away in 1954.

Lang, however, had a second life ahead of him.

CHAPTER 3

Dr. Mabuse, The Great Gambler: A Picture of the Time

[P]olitically, *Dr. Mabuse the Gambler* negates bourgeois codes in order to reveal their inadequacy and vulnerability to subversion from dangerous, tyrannical forces.... [I]n not offering the spectator anything positive with which to identify and to posit against the decadent old world, the new order appears as simply an underground, more powerful version of the order that is being overthrown. We are caught between two equally undesirable ways of being, two worlds neither of which offers us the comfort, security, peace and community symbolized by the old, stable social structures.

—E. Ann Kaplan,
Fritz Lang and German Expressionism

The first part of the monumental film version of *Dr. Mabuse the Gambler* covers roughly the first half of Norbert Jacques' novel—chapters 1 through 11 out of 21. By and large, director Lang and screenwriter von Harbou remained faithful to Jacques' writings. In the epic-length two-part film, there was footage aplenty to accommodate Jacques' story; screen time was not rationed miserly. For each subplot or nuance that von Harbou and Lang deleted, they substituted something new. The differences between the book and the film may be few and subtle, but they are telling; the alterations have less to do with the act of translating a written work to the screen than with the different takes these various artists took with the subject matter.

Certainly the almost continuous inner monologues of the characters that constitute the bulk of Jacques' book would not translate easily to the stylized visual language of silent cinema. Without dialogue, actors like Bernhard Goetzke and Rudolph Klein-Rogge had to rely on suggestive gestures and exaggerated poses to convey their character's thoughts and feelings. Four hours of intertitles would have strained the patience of even the most indulgent filmgoer, so instead Lang offers less insight into Mabuse's psychology. This choice has the distinct advantage of taking the character one step closer to becoming a phantasmagoric apparition, and less a specific individual man with all-too-human foibles.

3. Dr. Mabuse, the Great Gambler

The most obvious hero of Jacques' book is State Attorney von Wenk,* a war hero who has worked his way up the police department ranks by virtue of his hard work and dedication to duty. He is the ultimate civil servant. However, von Wenk does not appear in Lang's film until a third of the picture has unspooled. Von Wenk would rise in prominence in the second installment, but in Part One the central figure is the charismatic anti-hero Dr. Mabuse. Lang opens the film with an extended sequence, a bravura piece of filmmaking, that embellishes the myth of Dr. Mabuse. The sequence is perhaps too well-made for its own good; the rest of the gargantuan picture cannot quite live up to the promise set by the first 20 minutes.

The movie begins with Mabuse shuffling a hand of cards, and selecting one at random. The cards are not ordinary playing cards—they are the faces of his many disguises. The card he picks determines which of his faces he will wear next. His servant, Spoerri, is in no condition to help the mastermind with his costume, having just taken cocaine. Mabuse scolds Spoerri about his drug habit; the lackey responds by threatening suicide.

Mabuse writes a coded message on a piece of currency (a visual pun: a literal bank note) and leaves his house disguised as an elderly businessman. He is accosted by a beggar on the doorstep, and drops a bill into the man's hat; the beggar is one of his henchmen, and he has just delivered the coded message. Mabuse gets into a car and is driven away, but his journey ends abruptly in a traffic accident. The other driver offers Mabuse a lift and they drive off together, leaving Mabuse's demolished vehicle. Again, appearances are deceiving; the accident was planned, the

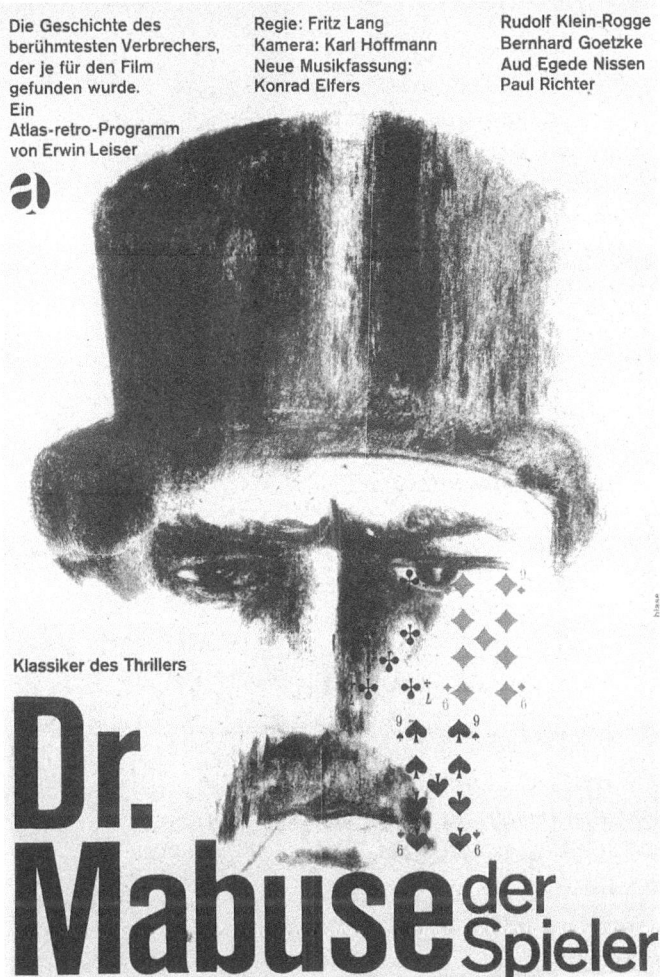

This poster for the German re-issue of Fritz Lang's *Dr. Mabuse der Spieler* boasts a clever playing card motif (but no genuine representation of star Rudolf Klein-Rogge).

---

*Norbert Jacques did not give either of his main characters first names. They are simply Mabuse and von Wenk. For the film, Lang gives von Wenk his creator's given name, Norbert.

other driver is also in Mabuse's employ. Everything that happens in this world, no matter how accidental or natural it may seem, is orchestrated by this man according to his master plan. These complications do not serve any evident purpose, other than to provide a smoke screen around everything that Dr. Mabuse does—a smoke screen so thick that any policeman bothering to watch would find it next to impossible to divine what was happening. To the audience, the effect is the enhancement of Mabuse's godlike dominion over all things.

Meanwhile, Mabuse's personal assassin Georg has attacked a Dutch businessman on a train and stolen some vital corporate contracts. This, too, is all part of the plan. (Georg is a character type that would recur in future films, played by actors like Howard Vernon and Andrew McCarthy. Here he is played by Adalbert Schlettow.)

Rudolph Klein-Rogge as "the old professor," one of his more memorable disguises from *Dr. Mabuse der Spieler.*

Mabuse arrives at the stock market, knowing that word of the theft will soon produce a panic. He helps get the panic started, and soon stock prices are plummeting. As the crash hits its nadir, Mabuse begins buying the worthless stocks. On cue, exactly as he has timed it, Mabuse's agents arrange the "discovery" of the contracts and their safe return. This news breaks, and the stock prices begin soaring back up. Now Mabuse can sell his winnings, having made a fortune without breaking a sweat.*

Film critic Noel Burch, one of *Dr. Mabuse*'s most ardent admirers, regards this sequence as nothing more than an elaborate introduction of the character of Mabuse. He notes that the sequence began with Mabuse's face cards and ends with the threatening, supernatural superimpo-

---

Jacques apparently liked Lang's embellishments, since the author included the stock market sequence in his follow-up novel Das Testament des Dr. Mabuse. *No such scene appears in the film of the same name.*

sition of Mabuse's leering visage over the ruins of the stock exchange:

> Bracketed by these "face-parades," everything seen thus far has been a prologue: only one character has been introduced and he has demonstrated his apparently absolute powers; conflict has yet to manifest itself, let alone plot. Lang and Harbou delay the "beginning" of the plot for more than twenty minutes (although it is true that the film lasts for over four hours and that they have time ahead of them).

What Burch does not realize is that the onset of the "plot" marks the moment at which the book's story begins—when Mabuse cheats Edgar Hull at the 17 + 4 Club—and all of this extravagant prologue is original to the film and therefore clearly identifiable as von Harbou and Lang's contribution. Tracing the authorship of elements within this film is a tricky matter, since Jacques, von Harbou and Lang shared so many common interests and worked together professionally and as friends. The novel already reads like a novelization of a Lang film, and Lang would show a propensity for reworking the same images and ideas in his other non–Mabuse films. Yet the beginning of Part One and the finale of Part Two are unique to the film version and therefore express Lang's approach to the material independent of Jacques' contributions.

What makes this question of authorship even more interesting is that this opening sequence is a virtual remake of the opening sequence from Louis Feuillade's second *Fantômas* serial. Feuillade began the four-episode-long *Juve contra Fantômas* (1913) with a series of dissolves through the various disguises that the master criminal (played by René Navarre) would wear in the serial. This was followed by a scene aboard a train, in which the disguised Fantômas robs a courier transporting a bundle of bank notes.

Feuillade himself reworked the same scene in the fourth episode of his famed *Les Vampires* serial (1915–16), concerning the exploits of a criminal mastermind and master of disguise known as the Great Vampire. In *Les Vampires: The Spectre*, the Vampire Gang attack a financial VIP aboard a train, the first step in a larger plot to destabilize the stock market. In concept, visualization and motive, this sequence and Lang's introduction to *Dr. Mabuse* are almost identical. Lang's debt to Feuillade has been examined in detail by other critics, but the connection here is palpable.

Germany of 1922, though, would perceive an attack on the stock market differently than French audiences in Feuillade's day. The scenes may look the same, but Lang intends his for a different and more deeply relevant meaning. As Lang scholar Paul Jensen observes,

> He uses Mabuse as a symbol to unite all the negative factors in Germany at the time. The sporadic and spontaneous outbreaks of violence are shown to be planned and controlled by a single figure, and in this way a form is imposed on otherwise haphazard acts.... Mabuse's counterfeit money is intended to destroy the European banking system in the same way that wholesale printing of almost worthless paper money confused and lowered the value of the mark.... Mabuse's manipulations of the stock exchange also gives him credit for its erratic fluctuations.

Lang's Mabuse is more than just the embodiment of social ills; his will reaches also into the personal sphere. Whether one falls in love and with whom, whether one wins or loses at cards, whether one takes one's own life—such choices may seem to be random or natural or the result of free will, but in fact they are nothing but steps in Mabuse's master plan.

It would be typical of the paranoid Lang to visualize the world in this way.

The "true" face of Dr. Mabuse, such as it is: Klein-Rogge sans make-up from the 1922 film.

by Thea von Harbou from Norbert Jacques' novel of the same name, director Fritz Lang has set his sights on making not a blockbuster, not a detective story, nor a mere film about society, but rather following the suggestion of the novel to forge a picture of the time, in which the year of its creation is every bit as important a performer as the actors, the set designers, the photography. Every epoch has had its epic dramatic works in which the spirit of the age is made more or less vital and evident. This film stands as a new dispatch, powered by characteristic directness, intended as a picture of the times, a document for future generations. The world of this film is the world in which we all live.... This gambler Dr. Mabuse was not possible in 1910, and perhaps—you might say hopefully—will not be possible by 1930. But for the time around 1920, he is a larger than life likeness—almost a symbol, at least a symptom.

Horrible things are happening, so he sees the chaos not as the consequences of random social forces but as the planned and meticulously executed plots of a vast conspiracy. Bad things happen because devils make them. Dr. Mabuse may look like a character out of a Feuillade film or a comic strip, like a Fantômas or a Fu Manchu, but it is in the specific kinds of havoc he wreaks that Jacques and Lang are building their allegory. This film was billed as "A Picture of the Time" for a reason.

The program to the 1922 film begins:

> In the two-part Uco-Film from Decla-Bioscop, *Dr. Mabuse the Gambler*, adapted

Interviewed in 1964, Fritz Lang had similar things to say:

> The period after World War I was for Germany a time of deep despair, hysteria, cynicism, unrestrained vices. Horrible poverty was juxtaposed with new wealth, and Berlin coined a new word: "Raffke" (Snatchers), from the greedy accumulation of money. "Raffke" is what we called these newly wealthy. Dr. Mabuse is a prototype of this time.

When introducing a screening of his 1928 *Spies*, a sort of remake of the Mabuse scenario, to the University of California in 1967, Lang described the Weimar era (quoted by Lotte Eisner):

> After the defeat in World War I, and after the obligatory but senseless—because emotional—social upheaval, followed by the equally obligatory but much more successful counter-revolution by the reactionary forces (because the counter-revolution was cold-bloodedly conceived and executed), Germany entered a period of unrest and confusion, a period of hysteria, despair and unbridled vice, full of the excesses of an inflation-ridden country…. Money lost its value very rapidly. The workers received their money not weekly but daily, and even so when they arrived home after working hours, shops were closed and the following morning their wives could hardly buy a couple of rolls or half a pound of potatoes for a day's work.
>
> At the same time the nightclubs were in full swing, supported by the easily earned money of uncaring war—and inflation; the profiteers, who thought or knew they could buy anything and everything, including the starved and impoverished women of the former upper and middle classes. In cellars and private flats, obscure little night spots popped up nightly only to disappear two or three days later—as soon as they became too well known to the general public and the police.
>
> In these places, the up-and-coming classes of the new rich could gamble and the sky was the limit. Their rich and jaded wives visited them too, morbidly looking for unequivocal invitations, vulgar and sordid as they came—every sex deviation found fulfillment.
>
> Crime prospered. From time to time some loner tried to stop this witches' Sabbath. One morning there appeared wall posters throughout Berlin showing a half-naked voluptuous woman in the arms of a skeleton with the caption: "Berlin—you are dancing with Death." But who cared? After four years of war, Death had lost its terrors.

In their efforts to make *Mabuse* a timely social commentary, though, Lang and von Harbou also enhanced some of the subtexts of the novel. The book makes no reference to counterfeiting, which is a central aspect of the film's iconography and a recurring motif in the future Mabuse films as well. Counterfeiting is a natural analogue for Mabuse's skill with disguise: in this world, people, money, even buildings can all be disguised. Nothing is what it seems.

Not all of Lang and von Harbou's tinkering added to the material. In the book, Mabuse is motivated by a desire to establish his own country in the Brazilian jungle. The film dropped all references to such an ambition, and instead presents Mabuse as a man motivated by pure ego. As the character himself explains at one point, the only thing he believes in is the will to accumulate power. That the utopian subplot does not survive in the film unfortunately robs the Mabuse series of what would have made a very eerie coincidence. Subsequent events and subsequent films would forge a link between the cinematic Dr. Mabuse and Adolf Hitler; that many Nazis would flee to South America after World War II could not have been foreseen by the makers of *Dr. Mabuse*. Without a recognizable motive, though, Lang and von Harbou have begun the process of dehumanizing the character—an important first step in creating this franchise.

In this first film, as in the book, though, Dr. Mabuse (Rudolf Klein-Rogge) is still a distinctly human creature. He can love and be loved (although these two relationships involve two different women). He gets drunk. He feels fear. Most of all, he must tolerate dissent from his underlings. The Mabuse of the book calls his agents "slaves," but the fact is that his conspiracy is comprised of gangsters who have chosen to join Mabuse's employ, since he offers them wealth and security in the midst of a crumbling chaotic society. A normal criminal might break the law in

Capitalism gone mad: Mabuse presides over a counterfeiting plant run by blind workers.

order to line his own pockets, but Mabuse commits acts of terrorism for terrorism's sake. This upsets some of his men, especially underling Pesch, who wants to quit Mabuse's gang but knows the boss would have him liquidated. For now, the mastermind has to put up with this kind of disloyalty from his troops because he commands them only so far as they are paid. Like Fritz Lang himself, Mabuse treats his employees with cruelty and sadism, berating them for the slightest mistakes. Only the future Mabuses of the continuing movie series would really command an army of slaves, once the Doctor had learned that the best way to ensure loyalty is to rely on various chemical or technological methods of mind control.

Opposing Mabuse is state prosecutor von Wenk (Bernhard Goetzke): the only person to ever put up an effective mental resistance to Mabuse's psychic powers, the only opponent Mabuse ever faces who recognizes the value of a good disguise, the only gambler in Berlin with a shred of social conscience. Yet von Wenk arrives late on the scene in Part One, and will be deprived of his victory in Part Two.

Between von Wenk and Mabuse is the Countess Dusy Told (Gertrude Welcker). Skulking for clues in the secret gambling clubs of Berlin, von Wenk is distracted by the sight of this elegant and beautiful woman, so bored by life she can barely keep her eyes open. Her identity is unknown to the club regulars—they call her "Lady Passive." She does not play. Instead she watches, a voyeur on the heightened emotions of others as they win and lose fabulous sums of money. Only by watching the destruction of other people's lives can she combat her own intense boredom. In her thrill-seeking and her ambiguous identity she is a little like Mabuse, but von Wenk inspires her to join his cause in search of the Great Unknown. While she and von Wenk are the heroes of the book, and central figures in the film, neither is introduced in the film for some time. At first, the playing field is Mabuse's alone.

The second main character to be introduced after Mabuse is the dancer Cara Carozza (Aud Egede Nissen), who performs a sexy stage act at the Folies Bergère. But the crowd is scarcely titillated by her raunchy show—there just aren't enough thrills in the world for these degenerate people. They turn to drugs, gambling, prostitution, but can never fill the emptiness in their souls. Only Mabuse has found true thrills, in gambling with the lives of human beings. His latest victim is Edgar Hull (Paul Richter), the only son of an industrialist. Mabuse projects his psychic will into Hull's mind and contrives to be invited to the 17 + 4 Club* where he will defraud the young man of 170,000 marks (it is a sign of rapid inflation that in the months between the writing of the book and its translation to the screen, Lang and von Harbou had to substantially increase the amount Mabuse wins from the 30,000 described in the novel).

American viewers often make the mistake of expecting Hull to be a romantic hero. He is young, good-looking, rich—all the things that Hollywood teaches audiences to admire. His is a rather brutal fate in the film, though, and anyone expecting him to save the day and win the girl are in for a sad awakening. Noel Burch writes, "We must not for a moment be allowed to mistake Hull for a central character, or to empathize with him…. Hull is a puppet and will soon cease to have any autonomous role to play at all. La Carozza having got him under her thumb, and the state attorney having placed him under police protection, Hull becomes a mere pawn between two masters."

In his essay on the film, William K. Everson chastised Lang for callously having Hull, "ostensibly the hero in part one," killed off in a long shot so ambiguous that his fate is unclear until a subsequent title card. Actually, Lang lets Hull off easier than Jacques did; at least Lang bothers to depict Hull's murder at all. In the book, the reader only learns of Hull's demise when von Wenk is informed after the fact. Neither Jacques nor Lang intended audiences to identify Hull as a romantic hero. Hull is a symptom of what is wrong with Germany, a worthless playboy with nothing better to do with his time and money than waste both in gambling parlors.

The film version brightens Hull's image somewhat by deleting a subplot in which Hull's father approaches von Wenk. The elderly Hull, who worked for his wealth and supported his only son with a monthly allowance, is now very sad and alone. He regrets how his son wasted his life, and asks von Wenk for advice on how to spend the money he had been sending to Edgar. Together they find socially beneficial uses for that money, in a pointed contrast to Edgar's selfish profligacy.

Mabuse has contrived for Hull to fall in love with Cara Carozza, and while Hull believes himself to be following the lead of his own heart, he is slowly sinking into the trap. She will set Hull up for Mabuse's assassins the instant he presents a risk of exposure. Mabuse's cunning victimization of

---

*In some English prints, the name of the club is translated as "The Incognito Club," which is actually more evocative.

Patsy Edgar Hull (Paul Richter, left) faces the ultimate gambler (Klein-Rogge, right).

Hull at the 17 + 4 Club has attracted the state attorney's attention. Von Wenk believes the rash of gambling-related cheats and cons around Berlin are connected, but he has yet to suspect that what he ascribes to a gang of criminals is actually the work of just one man in many different suits. Mabuse does not want the police to talk to Hull any more, so Hull must "disappear."

Hull actually receives advance notice of his doom. He discovers one of Mabuse's messages to Cara and relays it to von Wenk. Von Wenk, too, then has advance warning of the threat. Nevertheless, the murder is committed exactly as Mabuse planned and Hull is killed while under police protection! It is Mabuse's greatest strength that he can continue to run his operation in plain sight.

Unfortunately for the great criminal, Cara is arrested for her part in setting Hull up to be killed. She refuses to talk, so von Wenk sends the Countess into the same cell with a cover story of having been arrested in a raid. Dusy Told tries to pry some information out of her cellmate, but to no avail. Cara loves Mabuse, and will not divulge anything. Dusy Told mistakes Cara's distraught manner for grief over the death of "boyfriend" Hull and tries to comfort her. Cara in turn mistakes the Countess' remarks as meaning that *Mabuse* has died, and she flies into a panic. Once the Countess realizes that Cara is not crying for Hull, and Cara realizes that the Great Unknown is still safe and alive, the dancer spits out, "Who should be able to kill him? Only he can destroy himself!"

Cara's outburst gives voice to a prevailing theme throughout the Mabuse series, one that could be called The Mabuse Principle. If Mabuse is such a powerful god-like force, then naturally the police pose no significant threat to his plans. Yet drama means conflict, and if Mabuse is to be the central character of these films, then something must present a danger to him. If not an outside enemy, then Mabuse must face the threat from within himself. The notion of Mabuse as a self-destructive force makes for more psychologically interesting drama than the cops 'n' robbers paradigm of straightforward crime pictures. The world of these films is full of suicidal and self-destructive impulses—in other words, the world in which Fritz Lang himself resided.

Certainly Cara Carozza is her own worst enemy. She refuses to cooperate with the authorities, but her intense love for Mabuse is by no means reciprocal. She receives flowers from admirers at the Folies Bergère, but the only thing Mabuse sends are orders. In Part Two he will have her assassinated to keep her quiet, without ever comprehending how her emotions were doing just that for him.

The Countess Told too acts as her own destroyer when she freely invites Dr. Mabuse to her home for a social evening (one is tempted to recall the legend that vampires can only prey on those who invite the monster into their dwellings). She first met Mabuse at a psychic's seance and discovered their common outlook on life. Mabuse senses a link between himself and Dusy, and quickly becomes obsessed with winning the Countess as his ultimate prize. No sooner does the predator arrive at the Told estate than he orchestrates the disgrace of the Count and the kidnapping of the Countess. The final image of the film is Mabuse in triumph over Dusy's unconscious body, as he shouts "MINE!!!"

As the second part unfolds, her husband the Count will be emotionally tortured and driven to suicide. Like Hull, Count Told is a weakling who should not be mistaken for a sympathetic central character. The Count is a wasted, withered relic of an age gone by, and can no longer offer his wife the life she needs. Instead she must seek thrills in vice dens, leeching off the pain she watches. The Count is too feeble even to recognize his own wife's disaffection. In both the book and the film, the Count is damned for being a collector of modern art—a sure sign of moral decline. Mabuse, when asked his opinion of modern art, replies that it's a way to pass the time, like everything else in life—something to fill the void until death. As it happens, the film is not quite as hostile towards Expressionist art as the book; Lang was an art collector himself, and was known to dabble in Expressionistic techniques in his films from time to time (including the odd occasion in *Dr. Mabuse*, often cited incorrectly as an Expressionist film).

The Count is not long for this world. He is an obstacle in the love triangle brewing between the Countess, von Wenk and Dr. Mabuse. Von Wenk is a gentleman, and his amorous intentions towards Dusy Told are very discreet and subtle in the film (the book is much more romantic). By contrast, Mabuse is not one to let anything stand in his way, and will hasten the Count's death.

Lang and von Harbou understood love triangles and their possible tragic outcomes. While Norbert Jacques was busy first writing the tale of Mabuse, von Wenk and Dusy Told, the film director and the screenwriter were entangled in the tawdry stuff of their affair. Lang intruded on von Harbou's marriage to Rudolf Klein-Rogge, but that breakup was amicable enough for the actor to continue to appear in Lang's films, starring here as Dr. Mabuse himself. Lang's own marriage did

Love at second sight: Dr. Mabuse meets Lady Told at a seance (Rudolph Klein-Rogge and Gertrude Welecker, second and third from left, respectively).

not end so peacefully. When Mrs. Lisa Rosenthal Lang discovered her husband in von Harbou's arms, she wound up dead, shot in the chest with Lang's revolver in what would be officially decreed a suicide. Following production on *Dr. Mabuse*, Lang and von Harbou would marry each other and launch a professional and personal partnership that would last until the film's sequel ten years later, *The Testament of Dr. Mabuse*.

Despite the obvious fit between Jacques' topical and sensational story and that of the Lang–von Harbou team, at first the studio chiefs at Decla announced Hanns Kobe as the director of *Dr. Mabuse*. Lang and von Harbou were instead slated to administer their attentions to a three-part epic to be called *The Pirates*. As it happened, *Pirates* would never see the light of day and Fate would unite Lang, von Harbou and Jacques.

Work began on the project in late 1921 while the book was still being serialized in the *Berliner Illustrierten*. Veteran Lang stars Rudolf Klein-Rogge and Bernhard Goetzke took the lead roles of Mabuse and von Wenk. Paul Richter, who had become a star in Joe May's *The Indian Tomb* (1921), played Edgar Hull while his erstwhile wife Aud Egede Nissen played Cara Carozza. Alfred Abel played the Count Told, and would return a few years later for Lang's *Metropolis* (1926).

Lang packed *Dr. Mabuse* with innovative special effects that taxed the limited resources of the day. Superimpositions, animations and ghostly images abound. In one memorable shot, the camera picks out the face of Mabuse in a crowded nightclub; the rest of the room darkens, leaving just Mabuse's evil countenance; and then that face comes leaping out of the screen as if it could escape the screen altogether and attack the audience.

Ever the perfectionist, Lang was not averse to endangering his cast and crew to make these visuals look true-to-life. When on-screen gunshots were called for, Lang took a loaded pistol in hand and fired live ammunition at his cast. Glass and wood shattered and splintered on cue, lifelike, and Lang never missed his target. His terrified employees, naturally, delivered authentically frightened reactions for the camera.

To modern viewers, the original impact of one sequence is all but lost. As von Wenk speeds down the streets of Berlin in breathless pursuit of Dr. Mabuse, audiences of the day were given to spontaneous applause and howls of appreciation. Never before had nighttime photography of automobiles been attempted with such success. The sparkling headlights against the deep, inky night sky was an image of real life now rendered in the cinema for the first time.

The newspaper *B.Z. am Mittag* wrote:

> In this film the techniques of the film camera are brought to perfection. The problem of how to film lit-up streets at night has been solved for the first time. It is unbelievably impressive to see the glaring lights of speeding cars flash through the night or the rapid passing of an elevated train or the initially blurred, then gradually focused glimpse through a pair of opera glasses on to the variety stage, the nuances of light and shade—these things alone prove the value of film documentary.

It was with showstopping images like these that Lang started busting the budget. Producer Erich Pommer had already given the picture substantial funds for its epic scope, but the director always found expensive ways to indulge his perfectionism. They fought repeatedly over money, but the producer often gave in to appease his temperamental genius.

For all of Lang's abuse of Pommer, the producer was just as committed to making an excellent work of cinematic art as Lang. Pommer also recognized the social relevancy of the subject, and had his own ideas of what Mabuse symbolized: "*Dr. Mabuse* portrays the battle between the Spartacists and the liberal conservatives," Erich Pommer later explained. "Mabuse himself was conceived as a Spartacist."

The Spartacus League was a renegade band of hard-line Socialists who objected to the slow, feeble pace of reforms by the Weimar Republic's Social Democrats. Believing that the best way to effect change was with cold, brutal violence, they adopted the name Spartacus, after the Roman gladiator whose army of slaves terrorized Italy from 73 to 71 B.C. (a man Mabuse would certainly have admired).

Between December 1918 and June 1919, Berlin and other parts of Germany endured strikes, riots and acts of terrorism that amounted to an effective civil war. Street fights erupted. Some of the worst violence came in February, as the Spartacists tried to disrupt the newly elected National Assembly, resulting in five days of total anarchy. In just nine days (from April 30 and May 8), some 557 people—civilians, hostages, prisoners—were killed in the violence. The Social Democrats put down the Spartacus uprising by using the same violent tactics they had deplored in the old order; an uneasy, unstable Republic emerged to wobble its way through the decade until the Nazis tore it asunder.

Lang later claimed that the film originally opened with a prologue featuring actual footage of the Spartacus rebellion and other violent recent events. This montage of documentary scenes concluded with a title card asking "Who is behind all this?" and a second title card answering the question, "I." The following image was Mabuse selecting a disguise by playing cards with himself. Whether this sequence ever really existed, and (if so) when it was removed, is a question film scholars have never been able to answer. Even Lang's friend and biographer Lotte Eisner, who was inclined to accept the director's most outrageous fabrications and exaggerations as gospel, seemed skeptical about the existence of this prologue.

By the time *Dr. Mabuse* made it across the Atlantic to the United States, much more than just the prologue would be excised.

CHAPTER 4

Dr. Mabuse, Inferno: A Play About the People of Our Time

> Commenting upon this film, Lang once remarked that he was guided by the idea of rendering the whole of society, with Mabuse everywhere present but nowhere recognizable. The film succeeds in making of Mabuse an omnipresent threat which cannot be localized, and thus reflects society under a tyrannical regime—that kind of society in which one fears everybody because anybody may be the tyrant's ear or arm.
>
> —Siegfried Kracauer, *From Caligari to Hitler*

Motion picture sequels are an unloved lot. Critics and professional film writers often regard sequels and movie series with disdain. This prejudice is a consequence of a pervasive belief that cinema consists of two kinds of productions: commercial, and artistic. In this mindset, serious and worthy films represent the unfettered expression of an artist's personal vision, as compared to the many movies that are churned out by a manufacturing process, guided only by the desire to exploit some market demand.

Sequels, by design, are examples of this latter group. Nobody believes that a starving artist lives hand to mouth, hoping for a chance to make a *Lethal Weapon 5*. Movies whose titles include roman numerals, or the words "Son of," "Return of" and "Strikes Back," are produced because they are a relatively light risk. The success of a forerunner has demonstrated a market for a particular kind of film, and as long as the makers of its sequel do not deviate too greatly from the qualities that made its predecessor popular, the success of the sequel is almost assured.

This dim view of sequels, though, rests on the assumption that a meaningful distinction can be made between art films and commercial movies. Although this is a cherished nugget of cinematic wisdom among critics, it has little connection to the real world of film production.

Of all forms of creative expression, motion pictures are by far the most expensive. A single artist can create a novel, an opera, a painting or a play while working alone with few resources. The manufacture of a film, though, demands a team of numerous skilled technicians, expensive specialized equipment, rigorous scheduling and budgeting procedures, and the investment of huge sums of cash.

The film business is risky enough even for the most experienced players, so

49

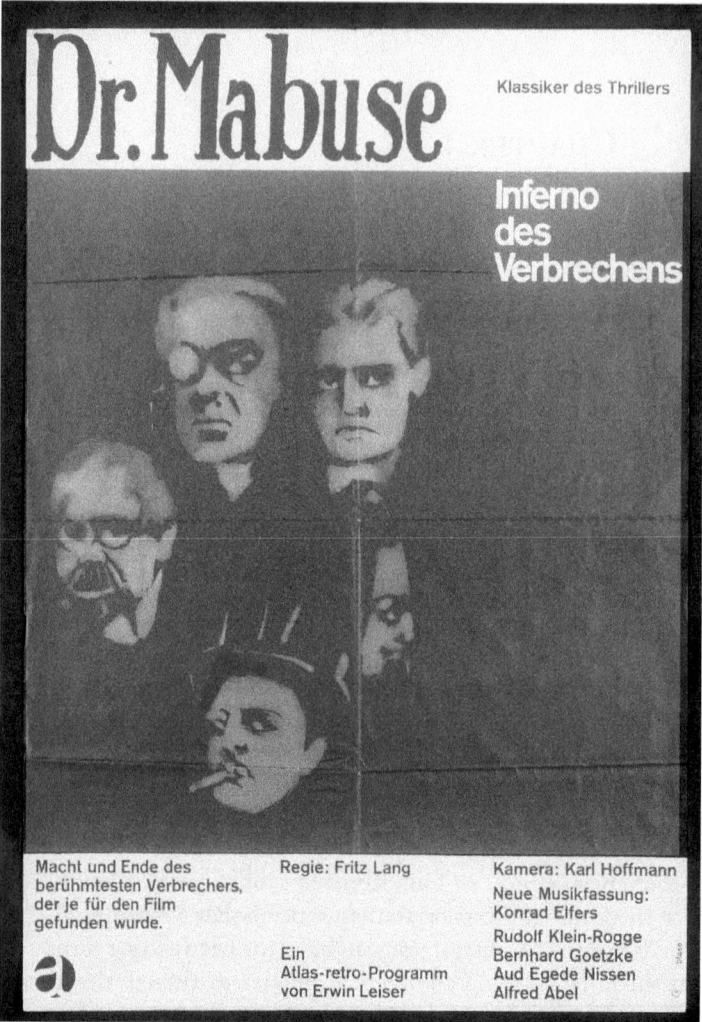

A rarity in the world of Mabuse: this re-release poster for *Inferno* (1922) actually depicts the many faces of star Rudolph Klein-Rogge.

absence of a commercial motive, but in the size of the market segment being targeted. "Art films" appeal to a specialized audience, and are marketed to that audience. If a film is conceived that expresses a valuable, personal artistic vision but which is too arcane to be marketed for profit, it is unlikely to be funded in the first place, and unlikely to be screened even if it manages to be made. To work in an expensive medium like film, artists must make certain concessions to the marketplace.

Beyond the purportedly crass economic reasons behind their manufacture, sequels are also dismissed for being derivative. While literally true, such a complaint is factually meaningless. All films are derivative to a degree. Many are adaptations of literary works (be it novels or comic books), television programs, songs or fairy tales, or are sequels or remakes of previous films. At the very least, most films can be categorized in certain genres, whose conventions and standards have been established by previous films. Not only are the stories, settings and stylistic touches of films recycled, but actors too carry with them the baggage of their previous roles. While in the worst cases, this can limit the actor's career by typecasting, in many cases it can allow filmmakers to take advantage of these audience associations. Casting choices can

no sensible investor will commit funds to a film without at least some prior anticipation of the intended market. The avenues for film distribution are limited. Unless a motion picture is sufficiently commercially competitive to gain access to one of the restricted number of available screens, it will never be seen by audiences or critics regardless of its artistic merits.

All films have some mercantile motive. So-called "art films" and big summer blockbusters differ not in the presence or

Dr. Mabuse romances Countess Told on one of Otto Hunte's eye-popping sets.

imbue characters with narrative, thematic or sympathetic connotations above and beyond the specific character development contained within the film itself.

This process of adaptation, cannibalization and cross-reference is not a deficit of filmmaking or an aspect deserving of critical rebuke; it is a fundamental aspect of the cinematic language.

Sequels take advantage of the derivative aspects of cinema to a specific and unique effect. A solitary, stand-alone film must contain its entire narrative, character, and thematic development within the boundaries of its opening fade-in and climactic fade-out. This roughly two-hour temporal restriction is partly due to film industry conventions and partly due to the limits of audience patience. By contrast, a sequel begins at frame one with the tacit assumption that the audience has at least a passing familiarity with the characters and events of the preceding film or films. Sequels and ongoing movie series are consequently opened up to encompass more ambitious narrative and character arcs.

That is not to say, though, that sequel makers take full advantage of this freedom. A writer begins an epic novel with an advance knowledge of how many pages are available for the story to unfold. Television producers sign contracts with networks stipulating how many episodes will be broadcast during a season. This advance knowledge allows the creators to develop and pace their narratives accordingly.

By contrast, movie series evolve haphazardly. A single picture is successful, so a sequel is commissioned. Its success spawns another sequel. Gradually, a franchise emerges. Along the way, filmmakers and cast members come and go. The series continues, not until its story is completed, but rather as long as it remains profitable. Narrative and character development may be freed to fill up more screen time than is the case in single films, but it must also endure illogical disruptions and derailments. Off-screen events can dictate on-screen developments not wholly justified by the films' content. Stories may continue past the point of their logical conclusion, or they may stop abruptly; it is a question of how long the audience keeps coming back for more.

This peculiar characteristic of movie series can be seen as a defect, but it is also a unique attribute deserving of critical attention. Movie series exhibit a form of narrative progression not to be found in any other media. While it may produce some oddball stories, full of continuity errors and mystifying character changes, even these worst-case scenarios represent something special and interesting.

The Dr. Mabuse series is an exemplary movie series, containing all the best and worst characteristics of an long-running franchise. In the nearly seven decades that elapsed between 1922 and 1989, a total of 12 motion pictures have been produced concerning the ongoing exploits of Dr. Mabuse.

Then again, perhaps there have been 13.

In 1922, just one year after the publication of Norbert Jacques' novel *Dr. Mabuse*, Fritz Lang directed an epic-length filmic adaptation. The movie version ran a staggering 20 reels, unspooling on the silver screen for over four hours. However, there are limits to human endurance, and *Dr. Mabuse* was actually screened in two parts.

It was a convention of the day to make epic-length films in two parts. These projects were manufactured and presented separately. So, *Dr. Mabuse, the Great Gambler* (Part One) and *Dr. Mabuse, Inferno* (Part Two) were filmed individually and projected on consecutive nights. The two parts are distinguishable from one another stylistically. The events of *Inferno* take place within their own set of opening and closing titles. Audiences today only have access to *Dr. Mabuse* on home video, and its two pieces are distributed separately, sold individually. It can be plausibly argued that *Dr. Mabuse, Inferno* is a sequel to *Dr. Mabuse,* the *Great Gambler*. As such, the total count of Mabuse features to date would then be 13.

However, *Dr. Mabuse, Inferno* is not truly a self-contained film. Its narrative is incomplete on its own, and depends on audience familiarity with the events of the *Great Gambler* to make sense. Only when the two halves are viewed together does an intact story unfold, with the final sequence of *Inferno* making a visual and thematic complement to the first scene of the *Great Gambler*. The two parts were conceived together and produced in tandem by the same cast and crew. Although screened on different evenings, the makers always intended the two parts to be a pair, and expected the audience from Part One to return the following month for the conclusion. When shown abroad, the two-part extravaganza was condensed into a single, normal-length feature. By this reasoning, *Dr. Mabuse,* the *Great Gambler* and *Inferno* comprise a single entity, and the inclusive count of Mabuse's cinematic career is therefore 12.

The ambiguity of *Inferno*'s identity as a motion picture in its own right or as an element of an indivisible whole is eerily appropriate; the movie series it spawned has been singularly obsessed with questions of identity, masquerade and counterfeiting.

In a wonderful example of the Mabuse Principle at work, von Wenk (Bernhard Goetzke, left) advises Count Told (Alfred Abel, right) to seek psychiatric help from a certain Dr. Mabuse.

By the time *Dr. Mabuse* arrived in the United States, though, its two halves had been joined together, compressed and condensed, that lacked much of what made the project successful in Germany.

Social commentary, like comedy, tends not to translate well from culture to culture. Audiences naturally look to connect a film to their own personal experiences. Thus, audiences in Germany and America engaged *Dr. Mabuse* from different social contexts. The 1920s were for Germany a time of severe unrest, while in the United States the decade would be marked by a distinctly more positive and progressive brand of decadence. Germany's screens were filled with images of monsters: Dr. Mabuse, Dr. Caligari, Nosferatu the Vampire, the Golem. American cinemas were the place of comedians: Charlie Chaplin, Buster Keaton, Harold Lloyd, Laurel and Hardy. When *Dr. Mabuse the Gambler* finally made it across the sea to the United States in the summer of 1927, a good five years after its manufacture, it met with a decidedly chilly reception.

The *New York Times* review said the five-year-old film looked to be at least ten years old, marred by the hyperbolic overacting that was common to German silents. The film had been already cut down from Lang's two-part edition, and even still the reviewer felt it was overlong. Notably, this American premiere saw Lang's apocalyptic vision paired with a Charlie Chaplin short subject.

It took 46 years for America to "get" *Dr. Mabuse*. In the interim years, Lang had proven his worth as a filmmaker of justifiable repute, Hitler had reared his diabolical head, and sundry other Mabuses had popped up across the globe. Lang's creation could no longer be seen as out-of-date. In 1973, Lang's full-length version finally surfaced as part of the New York Film Festival. This time, the same *New York Times* that panned the original release embraced the film as "something very good." Nora Sayre's review reported that "some have called *Dr. Mabuse* the hit of the festival and, without belittling the best selections, it's pleasing to think that a rare classic got its due." Even still, the aging Lang deeply regretted that *Dr. Mabuse* was not better known in America, and desperately showed the *New York Times* clipping to any and everyone near in an effort to revive his forgotten classic.

Contributing to America's rather jaundiced reception of *Dr. Mabuse* in the 1920s, the edition that appeared in the U.S. lacked more than half of the original's footage. The almost five-hour epic had been trimmed, trimmed and trimmed again until it ran a mere 90 minutes, released under the title *The Fatal Passions of Dr. Mabuse*.

Lang's epic vision had already suffered some cuts back in its native Germany: Censors decided that scenes such as Mabuse's drunken celebration and the climactic final shootout with the police included images threatening to public safety and morality, and snipped off about a minute in all. The sanitized German edition made it to France and England more or less intact, where the local importers translated the title cards into their own languages. The American distributors chose not to expend any time, money or effort on reworking *Dr. Mabuse* into its new matinee-friendly length, and simply took the British release and hacked off huge chunks of it. Since the distributors did not re-design the title cards to fill in for the scenes that had been deleted, the resultant picture was an incoherent mess.

In his survey *The Cinema of Fritz Lang*, Paul Jensen described the confusing cuts:

> [O]ne of the card games is entirely inexplicable because the scenes that reveal Mabuse's opponent to be Wenk in disguise are missing. Later, when Wenk attends a theatre to see Sandor Weltmann's show, he does so without any apparent reason. In fact, the character [one of Mabuse's alter egos, a professional hypnotist] is not even mentioned beforehand. At the film's conclusion, Mabuse flees to his counterfeiting room, but since neither the setting nor the criminal activity involved has been introduced into the plot, viewers have no way of knowing where the character is or what money he is throwing around.

The full-length cut was believed lost for many years, victim of the Nazis who had banned it. Luckily, the complete print resurfaced in 1966. Although by now the lessons of *Dr. Mabuse* had been put into their historical context by the rise and fall of Nazi Germany, American viewers were still conditioned to see the picture through their own cultural lenses; not having experienced the destitution of the '20s or the violent social discord and revolutions that resulted, Americans focused their attention on the fantastical elements of *Mabuse*—the Expressionistic techniques, the supernatural powers of its Fu Manchu-like star—rather than the social conditions that gave the film its ultimate meaning.

"Sometimes one forgets entirely that this is a modern story, and it is quite a shock to see an automobile emerging from the Caligari shadows," wrote William K. Everson. "It must have seemed even less contemporary in 1922, when the real thing surrounded it on all sides."

Quite to the contrary, the critics in 1922 Germany responded exactly as Jacques and Lang wanted.

Das Tagebuch: "A mirror of the age."
Vorwärts: "An archive of its time."
Die Welt am Montag: "A document of our time."
B.Z. am Mittag: "The portrait of an age set in motion."
Roland von Berlin: "At last, a film that has something to say to us that represents the present, daringly shot, contemporary history relentlessly photographed."

Arguably the preeminent scholar of *Dr. Mabuse* and Norbert Jacques, Günter Scholdt, believes that Mabuse's modernity is central to his importance: Of the great German movie phantoms such as Caligari, Nosferatu and the Golem, only Mabuse inhabits the same world as the spectator; of literary monsters who have become lasting cinematic icons, figures like Dracula, Frankenstein's monster and Jekyll and Hyde, only Mabuse hails from a twentieth century novel, *about* the twentieth century. In fact, *Dr. Mabuse* was the first major German film of any genre to be staged in the modern day; previously, German cinema was populated by historical dramas and fantasies.

Decla's program book for the premiere of Part Two began:

> Where the first part of *Dr. Mabuse the Gambler* attempted to depict the breathless, chaotic bustle of our time, how the fates of individual people are thrown about in a crooked whirlwind, drawn helplessly into the vortex of a strong, evil will—the second part, *Inferno*, is concerned with showing the inescapable consequences of these destinies—not least of which is the fate of this powerful criminal himself, whose final ghostly gamble loses, even though he holds the trump cards.... A higher justice has taken this situation into hand and laid the criminal, who had gambled with lives and social order, across His knee.

The fate of Dr. Mabuse at the end of Part Two is another striking manifestation of the Mabuse Principle of self-destruction. There may be a "higher power" at work in Mabuse's defeat, but it surely is not the work of the police. State's Attorney von Wenk does not get his man, at least not until after his man has gotten himself. Lang claimed that "we abandoned much of the book and only adapted the basic elements," but this is not entirely true. The vast majority of *Dr. Mabuse* faithfully follows the events of the book, with the principal exception of the beginning of Part One and the ending of Part Two. In these bookends, Lang and von Harbou allowed their inspiration to take hold.

Inferno begins where *Gambler* ended. Dusy Told is the prisoner of Mabuse while her husband wallows in shame and disgrace after having been forced to cheat by Mabuse's hypnotic will. Von Wenk still has Cara Carozza in jail, but no useful leads on the increasingly confusing case. Count Told consults von Wenk about his recent experience, which the State's Attorney instantly recognizes as the work of the Great Unknown. Unfortunately for them both, von Wenk has yet to suspect who his Great Unknown may be, as he advises the distraught Count to seek therapy from—psychiatrist Dr. Mabuse!

In consulting Dr. Mabuse for help, the Count effectively signs his own death warrant. Mabuse will quickly isolate the poor man from all human contact, convince the outside world that the Count is away on vacation, and play to the doomed fool's rawest nerves and deepest insecurities. Soon, the Count will take his own life, another so-called suicide in the wake of Mabuse.

Before the film ends, there are several

Class warfare personified: Mabuse crushes the effete Count Told like a bug.

more suicides, pseudo-suicides and homicides, as the doctor moves to eliminate his risks of exposure. Cara's imprisonment is problem number one, but he soon faces an even greater problem. Mabuse sends underling Pesch to bomb von Wenk's office. The lawyer survives this assassination attempt and arrests Pesch, who had vocalized his desire to quit the organization early in the previous film. In a devilishly clever scheme, Mabuse (in disguise) stirs up an angry mob to force the police to free "Johannes Gutter." Who is Johannes Gutter? It makes no difference, because the whole scenario is simply a ruse to get the police to reveal their prisoner. It's Pesch, of course, not Gutter—and assassin Georg gets a clear shot at him.

Von Wenk is understandably furious at Mabuse's brazenness. This Great Unknown can kill with impunity, and right under the police's collective nose. First Edgar Hull, stabbed while under police protection in a situation where both the victim and the cops had prior warning, and now Pesch, shot by a sniper while in a paddy wagon under double guard! Mabuse tops it all when he liquidates Cara while she's alone in her cell in the women's prison.

Cara had no intention of revealing anything to the police; her love for the madman had made her blind. Yet Mabuse's agents, disguised as prison guards, misunderstand something they overhear while spying on Carozza, and Mabuse orders her execution. Georg delivers a vial of poison to the lovesick girl, who dutifully kills herself because that is what her man asked her to do.

The final suicide is the image that concludes the film. Georg, Mabuse's strongest and most loyal supplicant, has been arrested. (In the book, the police mistake him for Mabuse, allowing the mastermind to escape. This confusion of identities was unfortunately removed from the screenplay.) Georg will not turn states' evidence on the great man whose cause he so ruthlessly defended: Let Spoerri, Mabuse's coke-addled butler, play the coward. Georg hangs himself from the iron bars of his cell window, but not before scrawling a final screed at his jailers. In the book, he writes "Merde" in reference to Waterloo—the famed last words of Napoleon's Gen. Comte Cambronne at the hands of the English, which has also been translated (more politely) as "Death before surrender." In the film, Lang changes the reference to the more Germanic "Götz von Berlichingen," from a Goethe play about a sixteenth century knight who sides with a peasant revolt. In either rendition, Georg's last words amount to a profane and politically charged curse.

"I am no longer the man I was," Mabuse laments after the assassination of Pesch. "I am making mistakes." Although he can efficiently dispose of all risks of exposure, to have to worry about such risks is new to him, and these risks oblige him to eradicate his own people. Von Wenk's investigation into the Count's suicide reveals a clue that puts all of Mabuse's empire at risk—a risk not so easily mitigated. For the first time, von Wenk connects his Great Unknown with the name Dr. Mabuse—and the hunt is on.

Up until this point, *Inferno* has followed the book reasonably well. Once von Wenk suspects that Dr. Mabuse is his master criminal, though, the story takes some new directions. Mabuse confronts von Wenk directly in his office (to the amazement of all, who cannot quite figure out how he entered the office). Mabuse hopes to forestall suspicion by appearing forthright, so he proffers the theory that poor Count Told was a victim of an evil influence that hypnotized him first to cheat and later to compel suicide. In other words, von Wenk's own theory of the case. This is a tactic that Mabuse's successors would use again in future films, especially in *The 1000 Eyes of Dr. Mabuse* where Mabuse feeds genuine if unhelpful clues to his opponents in order to deflect suspicion away from his own activities. Like an expert magician, Mabuse knows how to divert the audience's attention: There's nothing up my sleeves, says the conjurer, knowing that his empty sleeve has nothing to do with the legerdemain at work.

Dr. Mabuse takes von Wenk into his confidence and suggests that the attorney attend a performance of magician and hypnotist Sandor Weltmann, whose act consists of compelling people to do whatever he commands.

Sandor Weltmann does appear in the book, and in both cases von Wenk comes to the realization that Weltmann and Mabuse are one and the same, only then to succumb to Mabuse's hypnotic will. However, in the book the confrontation results in von Wenk's becoming a helpless prisoner of Mabuse's as the criminal takes flight. Dusy Told then kicks Mabuse from his own airplane, killing him and saving von Wenk's life. The film deletes the entire episode with the airplane, and instead concludes the Sandor Weltmann scene with a moment transplanted from an earlier position in the book: Under Mabuse's influence, von Wenk almost drives himself off a cliff.

Rescued from the car just seconds before it plunges over the rocky slopes, von Wenk regains his own will and leads the police in a raid on Mabuse's headquarters. This sequence too hails from the book, but it originally preceded the Sandor Weltmann encounter. Lang directs the siege with gusto, and manufactures a visual feast that seems far more original, and more Langian, than its literary source might suggest. In addition to Jacques' treatment of the shootout, though, Lang turned to real-life incidents as well. Lang said that a fan had sent him a book about Chicago gangster Al Capone, and that the legend of Capone had inspired this sequence. Lang returned to the Capone-style imagery repeatedly over the years, and was always eager to season his visualizations with authentic details. Along with the Capone references, Lang also took inspiration from recent headlines of the Parisian robber Chavrol, who was cornered in his house by a police siege. Alfred Hitchcock (who freely borrowed from Lang, much to his ire) took inspiration from this sequence for a very similar climax in his 1934 picture *The Man Who Knew Too Much*. Director Carol Reed also borrowed from *Dr. Mabuse*, recycling the notion of the villain's retreat into the sewers for his 1949 film *The Third Man*.

As in the text, Mabuse makes use of hidden passageways to escape the police siege of his hideout, and at this point all correspondence to the novel ends. Von Wenk rescues Countess Told from Mabuse's lair, and she is practically a vegetable after all the emotional torture she has endured.

The Countess is undoubtedly the true hero of Jacques' book, but her role in the film is lessened significantly. That Lang made this change is atypical; otherwise his filmography is rife with dominant females and ineffectual males. Even Lang's later Mabuse and pseudo–Mabuse pictures like *Spies* (1928), *The Big Heat* (1953) and *The 1000 Eyes of Dr. Mabuse* (1960) would turn on the actions of their respective female stars.

The curious reduction in Dusy Told's role in this film may have something to do with issues of class. She is a symbol of the decadent aristocracy, and her heroic triumph in the book represents the victory of the old order over the revolutionary spirit of Mabuse. Much is made in Jacques' book of Mabuse's crossing class lines: social structures that used to keep lower class threats like him out have broken down, and now this creature is invading the once sanctified halls of the upper crust.

Lang, of a decidedly more plebeian bent than Jacques, was unlikely to buy into this attitude. Lang was the working class kid who pretended to be rich. If anything, he would be likely to have identified with Dr. Mabuse. Instead of seeing Mabuse as a threat to the class system, Lang depicts his Mabuse as a threat to democracy.

Je m'abuse: Dr. Mabuse is defeated by his own evil designs at the climax of *Inferno*.

Consequently, the Countess Told and the old world she represents does not defeat Mabuse. She emerges as a victim stricken with post-traumatic stress disorder, in no position to combat her tormentor.

That is not to say that the film elevates von Wenk to that heroic position in her stead. True to form, Lang maintains a jaundiced, cynical outlook on the effectiveness of the authorities. Von Wenk may be a valiant, good-hearted chap, but members of the Establishment lack the tools to fight the kind of pervasive evil that Lang sees in the world. Mabuse will end his own reign of terror, and without Dusy Told as the agent for that self-destruction he will be seen to defeat himself more directly.

In the opening to Part One, Lang's embellishments featured a secret counterfeiting plant operated by blind slaves. Concluding the epic feature with a parallel structure, *Inferno* reaches its climax back in this clandestine lair with its sightless inhabitants. Mabuse has eluded the police, but he cannot outrun his own conscience. Trapped in his vault of fake money, the ghosts of Mabuse's victims—mostly his own underlings—haunt the criminal. Visions of Cara and Pesch surround Mabuse. By the time von Wenk and the police batter down the door, their prey has gone out of his mind. The visualization of a guilty conscience became a favorite device of Lang's, reused in such pictures as *Fury* (1936) and *Scarlet Street* (1945). As Mabuse loses his grip on reality, he imagines the vault's door metamorphosing into a monstrous face—an image Lang reworked in *Metropolis* (1926) to international acclaim.

Although they were not yet anticipating a sequel, von Harbou and Lang left open such a possibility by allowing Mabuse to survive the events of the film, albeit insane. A decade later, Nazi censors would object to the subversive attitude of the picture: Lang never depicts the triumph of order over chaos, but simply the self-destruction of chaos. To a paranoid misanthrope like Lang, though, it was a coherent worldview of a society careening towards disaster.

In Russia, genuine revolutionaries had pulled off a successful overthrow of the old order, and thus found less offensive about *Dr. Mabuse* than the Nazis did. If anything, it only confirmed their suspicions about the despicable character of Germans. According to Lang biographer Lotte Eisner (possibly repeating an account by Lang himself), the famed Russian filmmaker Sergei Eisenstein, an admirer of Lang's, undertook a Russian re-edit of *Dr. Mabuse*. Rather than unthinkingly mincing the picture as the Americans did, Eisenstein approached his re-edit thoughtfully. Eisenstein's cut differed insignificantly from Lang's; the master of montage could not improve on Lang's choices.

In fact, this is another fallacy masquerading as truth, a fiction that persists in cluttering up Lang's heritage. When the Russians imported *Dr. Mabuse*, Eisenstein was just an apprentice editor with Esther Shub, learning the craft of film montage by recutting foreign films for the Soviet market. Specifically, the Soviet authorities charged Shub and her team with "correcting" the politics of pre-revolutionary and foreign pictures. They made significant cuts to *Dr. Mabuse* in order to alter its ideological outlook, reducing the two-part feature into a single film under the title *Golden Putrefaction*.

In any case, Eisenstein could hope to learn much from studying Lang's *Mabuse*. Critic Noel Burch credits much of the film's importance to its use of "alternating montage":

> Lang always establishes clear relationships between the end of one scene and the initiation of another (or between the suspension of one scene and its resumption). This connection sometimes assumes the rather crude form of a question and answer ... sometimes a rather more subtly cerebral counterpoint, when the thoughts or acts of one of the participants in this emotional quadrille worthy of Corneille (La Carozza loves Mabuse, who loves Countess Told, who loves no one, not even her discreet admirer von Wenk) lead quite naturally to the appearance of one of his partners. In a more general way, and no matter what its particular function, each sequence change takes over the relay, makes the necessary transmission of *narrative movement* ... hence the dialectical tension produced by each change of the scene in the film, which on this level prefigures Eisenstein's dialectic.

Lang did not yet fully appreciate how rapidly his world was indeed careening towards disaster; it would be during work on the sequel that he would finally open his eyes politically. After concluding his work on *Dr. Mabuse the Gambler*, Fritz Lang took two important steps in his personal life. Firstly, that summer he married Thea von Harbou. Secondly, he formally became a German citizen. The full meaning and consequences of that second act, though, would not manifest themselves for some time...

Chapter 5

Premonition

"Fully half of the secret weapons and munitions supplies had been stolen. The struggle between the classes had grown into a war that daily claimed more lives, more victims. Rumors of the assassinations of high-ranking public officials circulated without restraint.

"In Magdeburg, Milan and other states, thieves executed covert robberies of poisons, leaving behind the money.

"There were frequent thefts of vast quantities of explosives. These were never solved.

"On June 16, 1931, at the Austrian customs office in Riefersburg—some 25 kilometers from Begrenz—two men appeared in a car loaded with weapons. At gunpoint they told the customs officials that revolution had broken out in Bavaria, and that they were taking the revolution to Austria. Afraid for their lives, the officers had no choice but to let the men through. Afterwards, they made their report to Begrenz, and the garrison was alerted. The guards stood at ready for two days, full of anticipation and courage as they awaited the next dangerous event.

"Word came from England of airplanes on maneuvers, outfitted with some new kind of poison gas guns.

"The poison gas catastrophe in Maastel that began on December 5, 1930, claimed over a hundred lives and resulted in 300 casualties. It is still unsolved. The Belgian government was powerless against the coming of the gas, and had no alternative but to distribute 20,000 gas masks to the affected areas.

"Within a few months it actually became fashionable in Holland to be seen in a gas mask.

"...From this summary of recent events, what meaning can we deduce? Can we recognize the coming apocalypse? What horrible future do these signs portend?"

—Norbert Jacques, *Mabuses Kolonie* 1930

Chapter 6

A Brief History of Nazi Germany

> Hitler understood the significance of film.... The artistic organization of these mass ceremonies, recorded on celluloid, and even the organization of the final collapse, were part of the overall program of this movement. Hitler saw the war and its newsreel footage as his heroic epic.
>
> —Dr. Joseph Goebbels

Kaiser Wilhelm led his people straight into the maw of the beast. The Great War that Fritz Lang fought and Norbert Jacques reported left Germany defeated, devastated and demoralized. Something had to be done.

The so-called "German Revolution" of 1918 may have indeed dismantled the monarchy and established a democratic republic in its place, but the consequent Weimar Republic was an unstable creation. It was as if the ruling class had done little more than don a mask and assume a new name: the same social problems persisted, the same industrial interests were prioritized over average citizens, the same corruption and decadence remained. Germany had changed in only superficial respects, and the same elite ruled over the same underclass—only now the gulf between the haves and the have-nots began to widen greatly. The transfer of power from the emperor to an elected body of representatives had been achieved with astonishingly little violence. But perhaps the almost bloodless nature of the German Revolution was its downfall: Unlike in France or Russia or America, there had been no great violent sacrifice to win freedom, no sense that the Republic had been bought with blood and was therefore something precious to be ardently defended. Instead, the German people remained somewhat passive recipients of the revolutionary change, and lacked the sense of personal investment in democracy.

The new Republic was a tentative coalition of fractious political parties, with little consensus and much internecine squabbling. From 1918 to 1932, the Weimar Republic would be shaken, disrupted and put back together time and again. With each reassembly, the parts fit together less well. The Republic became gradually more and more fragile, until at last it just fell apart completely.

Conditions were ripe for revolution in 1918: The privations of war had left the public desperate, impoverished and bitter. In many ways, the German folk hated Wilhelm II far more than they hated the notion of the monarchy, and if he had stepped down earlier there was a chance the monarchist system would have survived.

Various socialist factions had been the most vocal advocates of a revolutionary change; on October 5, 1918, the Independent Socialists called for a worldwide socialist uprising. Although they lacked the organizational resources to make good on their sloganeering, events around them were taking shape. On October 30, a group of sailors, influenced by the Independent Socialists' propaganda, defied their commanding officers. The men feared rumors that they were being readied for an attack on the English fleet, which at this stage of armistice negotiations would have surely scuttled hopes of peace and plunged Germany back into the full throes of war. They had endured enough war, and refused to follow any further orders from their corrupt commanders. In response, the officers arrested some of the sailors, provoking a mass demonstration by the others. The officers opened fire on the demonstration, killing eight and wounding almost 30 more. Word of the incident rippled across the nation.

As other isolated revolutionary episodes followed, the government realized the urgency of the situation. Some feeble reforms were promised, but without the abdication of the Kaiser nothing would quell the public's concerns. Already, a handful of the Majority Socialists (a more moderate movement than the Independents) had joined the cabinet to work behind the scenes on an orderly transfer of power. On November 6, they presented a list of demands, which included the abdication of Wilhelm. Hoping to avoid a widescale violent uprising, the government agreed to all demands—except the abdication. The socialists agreed to wait until the ninth.

The eve (November 8) arrived with no move towards Wilhelm's departure, so the socialists resigned from the cabinet and readied themselves for massive strikes and demonstrations. When the government troops sided with the socialists, Prince Max decided he had to act to preserve peace. He announced the abdication of the Kaiser and appointed Friedrich Ebert the new "Reich Chancellor."

The Bavarian province, however, had been moving towards a socialist republic much faster than the country at large. Separatist Kurt Eisner staged a successful coup over the early days of November, and issued a proclamation on November 8 declaring Bavaria a unique and independent democratic state. This forced Berlin's hand. Desperate to keep Bavaria within Germany, Majority Socialist Phillip Scheidemann issued a proclamation of his own on November 9, declaring all of Germany a constitutional republic. Ebert was furious. To his mind, Scheidemann had no business declaring Germany to be *anything* until after the Constituent Assembly had met. Now, the outcome of that Assembly had been predetermined—and all that remained was trying to put together the coalition needed to make that democracy work.

This was the hard part. The events of November 9 had created a democracy in name, but had done nothing to build cooperation between competing factions or faith in democratic institutions. The Weimar Republic would last from 1918 until 1932, but during that time it would be largely ineffective in realizing any of its promised reforms. Instead, no-confidence vote would follow no-confidence vote as radical minority parties would drive wedges into the republican process. Government would follow government, each more short-lived and brittle than the one that preceded it.

The Spartacus Uprising was a portent of things to come. The Socialists were united only in their opposition to Kaiser Wilhelm, but unable to find common ground beyond that. The Revolution came and went with only 15 people killed on November 9—one of the most bloodless of all revolutions—yet the victors then engaged in fierce fighting that left a body count worthy of a revolutionary war. The Spartacists were a hardline faction of socialists who took their name from an infamous Roman warrior. They believed the Majority Socialists were weaklings incapable of achieving meaningful reforms, and initiated a civil war. The new republic put down the Spartacists by relying on the same anti-democratic principles of rule by force that they had deplored in the hands of the Kaiser. Although they lost, the Spartacists had proven a point: the new order did not look so different from the old.

By February 1919, the constituent assembly convened and drew up an emergency constitution. A coalition of three parties led the government, designed as a federal union of individual states. However, the Bavarian separatist movement remained a powerful voice of dissent and a point of no small vulnerability for the fledgling republic. Norbert Jacques carefully set *Dr. Mabuse* in Munich, the heart of Bavaria, for just this reason: Where better for a tyrant to launch his campaign than from this most sensitive pressure point? A real-life Dr. Mabuse named Adolf Hitler would later make the same choice, and find Munich the ideal entry point onto the national political stage. For now, the constituent assembly addressed their fears of Bavarian secession by passing Article 48, granting the president the right to govern by decree in emergencies.

From the public's perspective, inflation was a far greater threat than arcane issues of federalism. The imperial government had used inflationary measures to finance the war, leaving the postwar Mark worth only 20 percent of its former value. While the spiraling inflation hit the middle and working classes hard, the industrialists profited from inflation by taking out short-term loans, and then repaying the loans with devalued currency. Since the voices of the "inflation profiteers" spoke louder in the legislative halls than the voices of average citizens, the government made no serious efforts to stabilize the currency for many years.

Furthermore, the Treaty of Versailles imposed on Germany a punitive measure demanding reparations be paid to the Allied victors. The war had left Germany already in a state of severe economic distress; Germany could not possibly pay the reparations. Paying the reparation debt with devalued currency allowed the German government to adhere to the letter of the treaty if not the spirit.

German workers could scarcely buy bread, and lived under conditions of extreme deprivation, while the upper classes actually benefited. The class divisions could not have been more acute or contentious, yet it was not the people of this so-called democratic republic who managed to convince their elected representatives to take their suffering seriously; it took the French army to step in and demand a stabilization of the Mark. The French had long been angry at the Germans for skirting their reparation obligations, and invaded the Ruhr district in early 1923 to force the issue.

Meanwhile, the subjects of the Weimar Republic became increasingly cynical about their democratic institutions. Moderate leaders like Walter Rathenau and Matthias Erzberger were assassinated by right wing nationalists. The National People's Party (DVNP) formed specifically to advocate the overthrow of democracy—and managed to paradoxically use that platform to win democratic elections, becoming the second largest party in the Reichstag by 1924.

The ability of the DVNP to undermine the Republic from within paled next to the threat posed by the German Worker's Party (DAP), which ultimately evolved into the National Socialist German Worker's Party—better known as the Nazis. The embryonic DAP first appeared in 1919 as just one of many local parties in Munich calling for Bavarian independence. Formed by Anton Drexler and Karl Harrer, the DAP flailed about with a handful of noisy rallies that attracted the attention of the Bavarian Reichswehr authorities, who assigned a young advisor by the name of Adolf Hitler to report on the party's activities.

Hitler reported back that the DAP was an organizational fiasco, but he had to admit he liked their brand of anti–Semitism. In most other respects, the DAP represented a dime-a-dozen right-wing agenda, but its vicious anti–Semitism made it distinctive, and to Hitler attractive. He joined up in September 1919 and quickly rose through the ranks on the strength of his skills as a public speaker. Within months he was chief of propaganda and an executive committee member.

Hitler was far from content with his swift promotions. He thought it especially problematic that the DAP espoused anti-democratic views, yet operated under complex democratic rules of its own. He thought that the DAP would be able to effect large-scale change if and only if it transformed itself into a model dictatorship, with the party ruled by a single authoritarian figure.

The essential conflict between Hitler and the leaders of the DAP turned on this point. Hitler actually *wanted* to overthrow the Weimar Republic while the DAP was otherwise content to merely *advocate* such a thing. The old guard resisted Hitler's attempts to reform the party's structure, and (in an attitude that would be tragically repeated over the years to come) deluded themselves into believing they could contain his ambitions by throwing him a bone now and then.

By 1920, the party had renamed itself the National Socialist German Worker's Party.* A massive influx of new members joined up thanks to Hitler's effective propaganda rallies; while the swelling ranks gave the NSDAP a greater prominence in public affairs, it also gave Hitler a wedge against the old guard. The new members owed their loyalty first and foremost to the charismatic demagogue who recruited them, rather than to the party as a discreet entity.

In July 1921, Hitler played this trump card. He resigned from the party, threatening to take with him the bulk of the membership. Two days later, he stipulated the conditions under which he would return. Top of the list: Hitler demanded to be appointed party chairman with full dictatorial powers, capable of expelling any member who disagreed with him. The following day, the executive committee gave in to his demands. The NSDAP would no longer be a political party in the traditional sense, but a cult of loyal disciples slavishly obeying their leader's will.

With the NSDAP conquered, Hitler's next goal was to take over Bavaria, and from there the rest of the republic. Germany's future seemed uncertain and tenuous by the fall of 1923. Seizing the moment, former Bavarian Prime Minister Kahr took over as near-dictator of Bavaria and began moving towards secession. The Berlin leadership invoked Article 48 to declare a state of emergency. As Munich moved towards independence and Berlin considered how to respond, Hitler took action.

Kahr was slated to give a speech on November 9, the fifth anniversary of the German Revolution, to a large patriotic assembly. Hitler charged the stage, gun in

---

*"Nazi" comes from the first two syllables of the first word (in German), Nazional.

hand and backed by his storm troopers, and announced that a revolution had overthrown the governments of both Munich and Berlin. He was to lead the new Bavarian Republic, with Kahr as his Regent and Pöhner as Prime Minister. At gunpoint, the stunned Kahr agreed. The morning editions carried the sensational news of what would come to be known as the "Beer Hall Putsch."

The midday editions of the same papers printed a retraction of the earlier scoop. Kahr and his colleagues had changed their minds (once out of Hitler's gunsights), and it became clear that Hitler did not have the support his revolution would need. He held a disastrous demonstration in which 19 people were killed. Hitler himself was injured in the violence, and arrested shortly afterwards.

On trial for high treason, Hitler defended himself with stirring and defiant rhetoric. The sympathetic court he faced sentenced him to five years in prison, of which he only served a mere nine months. During his imprisonment, Hitler wrote his manifesto, outlining his angry philosophy and his plans for the future, *Mein Kampf*. He was released in December 1925, ready to see those plans into action.

The economic crisis worsened as 1929 drew to a close. As millions of people suffered unemployment, their ranks swelling daily, the government ran out of funds to pay the dole. The leading political parties differed on how to confront the crisis, and failed to reach a compromise. The Chancellor resigned on March 27, 1930. His successor, Bruning, formed a minority government but was unable to get any of his economic reforms passed by the bickering factions of the Reichstag.

Bruning asked the President, the ailing old man Hindenburg, to declare an emergency under Article 48 and impose the reforms by decree without the Reichstag's involvement. Recognizing the antidemocratic nature of this move, the Social Democrats spoke out in bitter dissent. Unwilling to debate the issue, Bruning simply had Hindenburg dissolve the Reichstag.

New elections took place in mid-September against a background of staggering unemployment. Radical minority parties like the Nazis and the Communists used the civil unrest to win surprising gains, and the new Reichstag was more splintered and factious than ever before. Bruning no longer even tried to get the elected representatives of the people to agree, and instead circumvented them by persuading Hindenburg to impose reforms by decree under Article 48.

When Hindenburg's term expired in the spring of 1932, Bruning risked losing his power. He had never functioned in the parliamentary system at all, relying entirely on the near-senile Hindenburg to be his puppet. Bruning convinced Hindenburg to run again. Hindenburg won the election, but Hitler received an impressive and ominous percentage of the vote. Against his better judgment, Hindenburg agreed to Bruning's demands to ban the SA, the Nazi's violent paramilitary force.

By June, Hindenburg decided he was tired of playing puppet to Bruning and replaced him with the reactionary and shortsighted von Papen. One of von Papen's first misguided moves was to agree to dissolve the Reichstag and lift the ban on the SA storm troopers in exchange for Hitler's assurances that the Nazis would support his new government. The Nazis won enough new seats in the July 31 elections, though, that Hitler's party could block any measures by von Papen that they wished. With Hitler's promise broken, von Papen reverted to Bruning's method of ruling through presidential decree under Article 48. Presidential decree was also imposed a few weeks earlier to deal with Communist-vs.-storm trooper street fighting in

Prussia—the upshot of which was to place the majority of the Republic's police force under the direct control of the Chancellor.

The new Reichstag convened in mid-September, with the Communists planning to vote no-confidence in the government. Von Papen tried to prevent this by, once again, dissolving the Reichstag, but he was too late. New elections were held (the third in just over a year), again producing a fractious government of antagonistic and radical interest groups. Von Papen resigned.

In December, Schleicher took over from von Papen. His term of office lasted only a few weeks, because behind the scenes the bitter von Papen engineered a terrible compromise. He approached Hitler and worked out an agreement for Hitler to assume the Chancellorship and von Papen to take over as Minister of the Interior for Prussia. Von Papen arranged for Hindenburg to agree to this deal and appoint Hitler Chancellor of Germany.

On January 30, 1933, Hitler stood triumphant on the chancellery balcony as hundreds of thousands of his supporters marched in his honor. His supporters were rabidly faithful followers, but the Nazis had never laid claim to a broad support from the German people. Hitler's rise to power had been the result of secret deals and handshakes behind the scenes. Von Papen held the delusion that he had somehow captured Hitler, that somehow he—a vice-chancellor in Hitler's cabinet—was still in charge. Like Edgar Hull inviting Dr. Mabuse to the private 17+4 club, von Papen would quickly discover that he had made a grave error in working so hard to bring this predator to the Chancellery.

The Nazi storm troopers suppressed all political opposition (with murder, as needed) in the March elections, ensuring a NSDAP majority in the Reichstag. On March 23, the Reichstag voted to grant Hitler full dictatorial powers.

Under Hitler's tyranny, the nation would be once again led into the maw of the beast. By the time World War II drew to a close, Europe would have lost twice as many lives to the conflict as the total number of dead from World War I, with tens of millions more wounded and uprooted.

Chapter 7

The Testament of Dr. Mabuse

> We are psychiatrists; we are Germans; we have read Nietzsche; we know that to gaze too long at monsters is to risk becoming one.
> —Richard Huelsenbeck, *En avant dada*

The key image of *The Testament of Dr. Mabuse* (1933) is the name "Mabuse," half etched—backwards—in a pane of glass. It is a fragmentary, elusive clue, and ultimately a rather unhelpful one. Although this scrawled inscription may be the most important clue that Inspector Lohmann ever receives in his illustrious career in the Berlin Homicide Division, by itself and out of context it is misleading and incomplete. Knowing that a "Mabuse" is the sinister force behind the elaborate and far-reaching crime spree terrorizing the nation is of little comfort since Dr. Mabuse has just died, after spending the last ten years in an insane asylum where he has lived, mute and deprived of all human contact. It is hard to see how the master criminal could possibly be up to his old tricks again. That is not say he is *not* up to his old tricks, merely that it is *hard to see*.

The film itself is like that scratched piece of glass: incomplete, misleading, yet of critical importance. *The Testament of Dr. Mabuse* is one of Fritz Lang's finest works, joining the ranks of *Metropolis*, *Spies*, *M* and *The Big Heat* as his immortal contributions to the history of film. Yet only recently has this flawed masterpiece come to light. When it was made, *Testament* was banned in Germany by the Nazis and ignored in Hollywood. The two places that Lang called home had no room for one of his most significant creations.

Along the way, critics and film commentators wrote much that was misleading or mistaken about the picture, drawing unsubstantiated conclusions from the fragmentary evidence at hand. Part of this mistaken analysis centered on the film's importance in Lang's life. *Testament* is at the heart of Lang's emigration from Germany to America, and as such became embroiled in the director's rampant rewriting of his own biography. Few films have become the subject of legend as much as *Testament*, and Lang himself styled most of this legend. According to the director, here is how it happened:

Fritz Lang walked down the stone corridors of the Third Reich's newly inaugurated Ministry of Propaganda. He had been summoned by the Minister himself, Dr. Joseph Goebbels, to discuss the fate of *The Testament of Dr. Mabuse*. Lang heard his footsteps clang through the cold halls, a vivid echo of his own nervous heartbeat. Armed soldiers stood guard at regular intervals, reminding him how much was at stake.

The film director entered Goebbels' massive office, struck at once by the sheer enormity of the man's desk. Whatever tension Lang felt, though, Goebbels himself seemed to ignore. In person, the Minister of Propaganda was all unction and charm. *The Testament of Dr. Mabuse* is a closed question, Lang was summarily informed. Although there were some changes Goebbels could suggest to eliminate its political problems and clear it for distribution, in all honesty he did not expect the filmmaker to accede to these requests. Instead, Lang would have to resign himself to the fact that *Testament* would be a casualty in the larger war—a war that Goebbels expected Lang to fight. A war for the Aryan soul of the German nation.

Yes, Mr. Lang, Goebbels said, we want you to be the head of all film production in the Third Reich. You shall be Filmmaker Number One in the New World Order.

Lang listened, or pretended to listen. Was it a problem that Lang had manufactured such a controversial picture? No, Goebbels explained, he just needed to be nudged back onto appropriate subject matter—like *The Nibelungen*, Hitler loved that film. Was it a problem that his mother was Jewish? No, said Goebbels, because *we decide who is Jewish and who is not*.

Not just the poster is in French: Fritz Lang actually made two versions of this horror masterpiece, one in German and one in French.

Throughout, the filmmaker stared out the window behind Goebbels' head at the clock tower across the street, as the hands slowly clicked away the minutes, the hours. Lang knew the fix was in. He had to leave or risk whatever awful fate the Nazis had in store for him. Lead the Third Reich Film Ministry indeed. But his heart sank as he watched the time pass: banks were closing. If he was going to leave, he had little time to make it to the train station, and would be unable to withdraw any funds from his accounts before fleeing.

The interview concluded, and Lang requested 24 hours to consider the Minister's generous proposal. They shook hands, Lang praying his sweaty palms would not give him away. Fearful of being followed, Lang hurried home to gather what possessions he could carry. That very night, he left Germany, his belongings secreted away in his train compartment—taped behind the bathroom mirror, shoved under the mattress, crammed into nooks in the floorboards. He had escaped the Nazis, and would not return to Germany for almost 30 years. Although *Testament of Dr. Mabuse* had been banned, it had not been destroyed—an alternate French-language version had been spirited across the border into France where it would prove Lang's genius. Artists can be threatened, but art can never be silenced.

That these events never happened has not been in any way an impediment to the proliferation of the legend. The story of his confrontation with Goebbels has become a key point in Fritz Lang's largely dubious personal history, the proof of his stalwart anti–Nazism. In turn, generations of film critics have hailed *Testament* as the first motion picture to address the evils of Hitler, a pioneering work of political bravery that guarantees its place in the annals of film history.

Any important film must suffer the inevitable distortions and mythologizing that come from so much attention over so much time. Select any classic at random—*Casablanca*, *Citizen Kane*, *The Wizard of Oz*—and one is sure to find any number of legends, exaggerations and outright lies. A great film is like an old building, rendered quaint by the growth of ivy across its walls. *Testament of Dr. Mabuse*, though, has long ago passed such a stage, and is now almost completely obscured by innuendo and error. This building has been eaten alive by kudzu.

It is true that *Testament of Dr. Mabuse* occupies a place of significance in film history, German history and Lang's own personal history. Lang's rendition of the story is far simpler, more cinematic and direct than the messy and complex truth. To understand the real significance of *Testament*, one needs to set aside the legend and dig into those messy complex facts.

There is no doubt that Hitler and Goebbels both greatly admired Lang. Each was quoted on several occasions praising the director and saying how, as long as he was dealing with the right kind of subjects, he could be The Great Nazi Filmmaker. However, Goebbels' diary makes no mention at all of this auspicious meeting with Lang; his memoirs are otherwise maddeningly comprehensive. For his part, Lang never referred to the event until some ten years after it purportedly took place.

The Nazis came to power in January 1933, as production on *Testament of Dr. Mabuse* was nearing its end. Lang had shot two versions simultaneously with German and French speaking casts. The French-language footage had been sent to editor Lothar Wolff in Paris while Lang completed work on the German version—far from sneaking the film reels out in luggage filled with dirty linen, as some accounts of the legend had it. Lang may not have met Wolff, but Wolff was following Land's explicit instructions in the preparation of *Le Testament du Dr. Mabuse*, which would be a fully authorized cut of the picture assembled before Lang had any inkling of problems with the Nazi censors. (It is worth noting that this French cut runs almost 30 minutes shorter than Lang's German language "director's cut.")

The German cut was announced for a March 24 premiere at the Ufa-Palast am Zoo, the same theater that had hosted the premiere of *Dr. Mabuse the Gambler* 11 years earlier. On March 14, ten days before

The Nazi-era parable of *Das Testament des Dr. Mabuse* comes through in this striking poster to Fritz Lang's 1932 classic.

"Mabuse" is as elusive as a name etched in glass.

the scheduled opening, Hitler established the Ministry of Public Enlightenment and Propaganda, to be headed by Dr. Goebbels. Only at this time did it become apparent that anything about film censorship would change under Nazi rule. *Testament* was not yet finished, though, and would not be available for Goebbels to screen until March 23. Consequently, the premiere would have to be delayed to allow for the censors to review it first.

On March 24, following the initial examination by Goebbels' office, the opening of *Testament of Dr. Mabuse* was again postponed, for "technical reasons." The official announcement that *Testament* was banned came on March 30, when the German Board of Film Censors decreed that the film posed a threat to law and order and public safety.

Two days earlier, Goebbels hosted a party at the Hotel Kaiserhof for the leading lights of the film industry. Ostensibly, the event was to raise morale for the film community and inspire the reinvigoration of a new Nazi cinema. Between the lines, though, the mostly Jewish attendees looked around at the storm troopers lining the walls and listened to Goebbels' pronouncements of what constituted pure and permissible filmmaking, and understood that everything had changed. The German film community would soon experience a mass exodus as filmmakers great and small emigrated to France and America to escape the coming disaster. Reportedly, Lang and Goebbels spoke briefly with one another about the future of *Testament of Dr. Mabuse*.

According to the legend, it was a few

days later in April of 1933 that Goebbels summoned Lang to his office to renew the discussion, and make his momentous proposal. Although it is not unlikely that Goebbels made some such offer, the rest of the account—especially Lang's urgent overnight departure—can be easily refuted. Lang's own passport shows that he did not leave Berlin until no earlier than June 23, 1933. During June and July, Lang made several trips back and forth to Belgium, and withdrew some 1366 Reichsmarks from his bank. His final departure from Berlin took place four months after the alleged meeting with Goebbels, on July 31.

Lang had been considering leaving Germany for some time before that meeting, whether or not it occurred. He had been speaking openly with his friends and colleagues about the possibility of relocating to Paris or to Hollywood, and had been entertaining these thoughts before Goebbels became propaganda minister. His wanderlust was fueled in no small part by his recent discovery of wife Thea von Harbou's infidelity. Of course, Lang had felt no compulsion to remain faithful to von Harbou, and had slept around extensively and openly. The fact that his loyal, long-suffering wife had taken up a lover (Indian leftist journalist Ayi Tendulkar) had shaken the filmmaker as he began production on the Mabuse sequel. In addition to the disintegration of his family life, his diminished stature in the German cinema gave Lang pause, and he wondered if his career might be better served abroad.

By the time Lang arrived in Hollywood, the amount of cash and personal property he had salvaged from his former home belied any claim he might make about a rushed overnight scramble from Berlin. And, many years later when he waged a minor skirmish with Seymour Nebenzahl, producer of *Testament of Dr. Mabuse*, over the legal rights to *M*, Nebenzahl remarked acidly that Lang had plenty of opportunity to sort out such matters during his protracted decision whether or not to leave Germany.

So much for the hasty exit.

The Goebbels story first surfaced in 1943, after Lang had been living and working in Hollywood for some time. An outsider from the rest of the German emigre community, Lang felt a certain need to establish his political credentials. He had been politically naive in Germany, ignoring the threat of Hitler until it was too late, cozying up to the Nazis for personal advantage. After his flight, though, Lang had matured in his outlook and had become a hardened anti-fascist. His hatred of the Nazis ran deep—deep enough for him to voice a desire that the entire nation of Germany be decimated with an atomic bomb to wipe out all traces of the Nazi character. In Hollywood, Lang had carved a little niche for himself as the director not just of socially minded films like *Fury* (1936) and *You Only Live Once* (1937), but anti–Nazi films like *Man Hunt* (1941) and *Hangmen Also Die!* (1943).

Lang based the narrative of *Hangmen Also Die!* on the real-life assassination of Reichsprotektor Reinhard Heydrich, the so-called Hangman who led the occupying Nazi forces in Czechoslovakia. Lang had once said that it was "out of the Mabuses came the Heydrichs, the Himmlers and the Hitlers." Nineteen forty-three was not only the year that *Hangmen Also Die!* was released, but also the year that *Testament of Dr. Mabuse* finally appeared in the United States. Lang saw *Testament* and *Hangmen* as a sort of pair of anti–Nazi bookends, socially minded filmmaking that confronted the evils of tyranny.

In publicity for *Hangmen Also Die!*, Lang described the Mabuse film as "an allegory of Hitler's processes of terrorism," that it was pointedly "an anti–Hitler picture" in which he had been "putting all the

The dead Mabuse bequeaths his hateful ideology to his successor.

Nazi slogans into the mouth of criminals."

For the New York premiere of *Testament*, Lang announced, "This film meant to show Hitler's terror methods as in a parable. The slogans and beliefs of the Third Reich were placed in the mouths of criminals. By those means I hoped to expose those doctrines behind which there lurked the intention to destroy everything a people holds dear."

"I remember one [slogan] in the film," Lang later told Peter Bogdanovich. "'The belief of the normal citizen in the powers he has elected must be destroyed. And when everything is destroyed—on this we will build the realm of crime.' Which is exactly what the Nazis said."

In the context of such remarks about his deliberate anti–Nazi polemic, Lang for the first time told of his encounter with Dr. Goebbels and his urgent overnight escape. The story was gripping, cinematic, easily summarized. It soon found its way into every reference to *Testament of Dr. Mabuse*. Here were the words from Lang's own mouth, why should anyone doubt him?

The version of *Testament* that appeared in America in 1943 was the French-language version prepared by Lothar Wolff, now retitled *The Last Will of Dr. Mabuse*.* The subtitles had been written in part from Thea von Harbou's script, but were not translated directly. Instead, the distributor also took into account what

---

Unfortunately, this title has fallen into disuse, replaced by the more direct translation The Testament of Dr. Mabuse. The Last Will, *however, contains all the same meaning as* The Testament *as well as an English-language pun on the word "will" that excellently suits the picture's themes.*

Lang *said* was in the picture, and thus produced subtitled dialogue that was even more pronounced in its political sentiments than had been true of the original work. Little by little, the legend was coming true.

When an English-dubbed version was created in 1952 under the title *The Crimes of Dr. Mabuse*, translator Leo Katcher would similarly base his screenplay on what he expected to find in the film, creating a more explicitly political film than Lang had in fact originally fashioned; *Crimes* restages the action from 1932 to 1939, placing the events squarely within the Nazi regime. Only in 1973, 40 years later, did an unretouched rendition of the German-language cut surface in American theaters, by which time the belief that *Testament of Dr. Mabuse* was a deliberate anti–Nazi allegory had become so entrenched that no one thought otherwise.*

That the content of *Testament of Dr. Mabuse* seems so elusive is perhaps to be expected: Even those who have seen and studied the film at length find themselves at a loss to summarize its plot. Herewith, an attempt:

A disgraced policeman, expelled from the force for accepting bribes, has undertaken an unofficial undercover infiltration of a counterfeiting gang in hopes of redeeming his sullied reputation. He has discovered a vast conspiracy responsible for a wide array of elaborate crimes. At its head is one "Dr. Mabuse." Before the ex-cop Hofmeister can relay this information to Inspector Lohmann, his former superior, he is caught by Mabuse's gang and, somehow, driven insane. Hofmeister does manage to leave a clue to Lohmann, however, etching Mabuse's name backwards into a pane of glass just before losing his mind.

Lohmann looks up the old case file and learns that Dr. Mabuse, while having been responsible for a similar spate of crimes ten years ago, has been an inmate of a mental institution ever since. Mabuse can barely move; he has been locked away in a solitary cell for a decade, deprived of all human contact; he has not spoken a word in all that time.

That is not to say that Mabuse is uncommunicative. A few years back, the asylum's director Dr. Baum discovered that Mabuse was desperate to write. Since that time, Mabuse has spent every waking minute scribbling dense, almost incoherent notes detailing future crimes. Baum has kept these scribblings, bound under the title "The Testament of Dr. Mabuse," in hopes of divining some insight into the man's dementia.

A colleague of Baum's visits one day and makes a startling discovery. Mabuse's Testament describes in exacting precision a set of crimes that have just recently occurred. How can this be? The colleague tries to report his suspicions to the police, but is assassinated en route.

Mabuse's gang is not without its weak links. One agent, Thomas Kent, wants out. He is an ex-con who has faced staggering unemployment in Germany's deteriorated economy—in such hard times, even young men *without* criminal records cannot find work. Mabuse has exploited this fact, offering Kent good money to participate in his program of terrorism, but Kent and his girlfriend Lily decide it is better to risk death at Mabuse's hands or imprisonment rather than continue to help the monster. Kent surrenders himself to the police.

Kent's story, that he has been an agent of Dr. Mabuse, upsets Lohmann. On the one hand, Lohmann has struggled

---

Bosley Crowther's 1943 New York Times *review of the premiere of the French version* The Last Will of Dr. Mabuse *inaccurately claimed that the German version had previously played in the States.*

to connect the name on the glass to the crimes in question, but on the other hand Mabuse has recently died in Baum's care and thus cannot be the mastermind of any underworld empire. Kent, though, identifies Mabuse by the one characteristic he knew the man by—his voice, amplified over a loudspeaker. The voice Kent recognizes, the voice he knows as Dr. Mabuse, is none other than Dr. Baum. In his intense scrutiny of Mabuse's mind and writings, something terrible occurred. In a supreme example of doctor-patient transference, Baum has become Mabuse—without even realizing it himself—and has continued the criminal's plans in his proxy.

Once exposed, Baum/Mabuse's psyche becomes completely unhinged and he checks himself into his own asylum. With hollow eyes, the broken man introduces himself. "My name is Dr. Mabuse."

The Testament of Dr. Mabuse can well be read as a political film, with Mabuse as an allegory of Hitler. Lang's notion of Mabuse's Testament inevitably invites comparison with Adolf Hitler's *Mein Kampf*. In 1924, two years after Dr. Mabuse had been committed to an asylum and one year after Hitler was sentenced to prison for his failed coup in Bavaria, the future Führer wrote his autobiography and ideological plans for the New Germany. *Mein Kampf* was already a top seller by 1930, when its two volumes were compiled into a single package, and would therefore be an obvious source of inspiration for Mabuse's very similar literary activity in the 1933 film.

Weirdly, Hitler later did pen his genuine last will and testament, shortly before killing himself in 1945. Certainly Norbert Jacques and Fritz Lang had no way to see into the future, but they predicted it nonetheless. Hitler's testament, like Mabuse's, is the final word of a dying man, outlining in precise detail his plans for the future, a blueprint for his followers, the way to perpetuate his program after his death. It is almost as if Hitler had watched *The Testament of Dr. Mabuse*, cribbing notes on how to be a power-mad tyrant.

But how many Nazi-era parallels were intentional, how many were eerie prescience à la the first Mabuse film, and how many were a case of the real world unintentionally patterning itself on art?

Certainly Goebbels recognized a political threat from the film. "I wouldn't tolerate this film," said Goebbels, "because it showed that an extremely dedicated group of people are perfectly capable of overthrowing any state with violence."

In Lang's account of his meeting with the Minister of Propaganda, Goebbels supposedly told him that his principal concern with the film was its conclusion. He was dissatisfied that the evil criminal mastermind simply implodes, rather than being defeated by the people. The film needs a Führer, Goebbels said, to step in and save the day.

However, Lang had claimed that there is a Führer figure in the film—Dr. Mabuse. And the message was not to inspire criminal rebellion against an orderly (Nazi) state, but to equate the criminal underworld with the Nazi state. If Goebbels' remarks are taken at face value, then, he saw menace in the picture but arrived at a wholly different interpretation than Lang intended.

In 1938, Goebbels addressed the Reichsfilmkammer and, of all things, raised the subject of the long-since banned Mabuse picture. "I have recently seen a film that was filmed at the end of 1932 and completed at the beginning of 1933. This

Opposite: Das Testament des Dr. Mabuse first arrived in the U.S. in 1943, as a subtitled release of the French version.

THE SCREEN'S SUPREME THRILL DRAMA

S. S. KRELLBERG
Presents

The Last Will of Dr. Mabuse

A TRIUMPH BY THE MASTER DIRECTOR
FRITZ LANG

DISTRIBUTED BY GOODWILL PICTURES CORP. 630 NINTH AVE, NEW YORK CITY

film was banned for political reasons, but that is not the aspect that interests us in this context. More interesting is another fact. This film was lauded by experts in its day as a technical and visual sensation. It broke new ground. But now when we come back to it just five years later, we are struck by the dullness of its portrayal, the coarseness of its construction, and the inadequacy of its acting."

Publicly, Dr. Goebbels could deride the film with such harsh words, but his private actions told another story. He had only had the occasion to review the film so long after its original dispute because it was a treasured part of his personal collection. Lang may have left Germany, but he had not left Goebbels' heart. Whatever else he was, the Minister of Propaganda was an ardent film buff. From time to time, he would project Lang's uncut, uncensored version of *Testament of Dr. Mabuse* in his own private screening room for close personal friends.

To view *Testament* as the expression of Lang's solo artistic and political voice ignores the contribution of many important figures, whose political leanings might have been in conflict with such an agenda. Norbert Jacques, creator of Dr. Mabuse, was not a Nazi by any measure, but he chose to stay in Germany throughout the Nazi regime despite numerous opportunities to follow his Jewish wife and children when they fled. Screenwriter Thea von Harbou, however, was a Nazi, as was her former husband Rudolf Klein-Rogge, who plays Mabuse himself. How could Lang insert such overt political sentiment into the film without the knowledge or interference of his screenwriter or star?

And then there is the problem of chronology. It is here that our story gets most messy, where the truth has been the most obscured, because while the fate of *Testament of Dr. Mabuse*—its censorship by the Nazis and Lang's flight to America—has been recounted before,* the origin of *Testament of Dr. Mabuse* has never before been clarified in print. Lang's obfuscations and misrepresentations have gone too long unchallenged.

In 1965, the Nouvelle Vague critics at *Cahiers du Cinema* spoke with their idol Fritz Lang about his career, and the elder director remarked that he had been strong-armed into directing a sequel to *Dr. Mabuse* by producer Seymour Nebenzahl. The producer, eager for a follow-up to the blockbuster hit *M,* had noticed the commercial prospects of *Mabuse* and encouraged the sequel. Lang said he resisted at first, concerned that having left Mabuse in an insane asylum at the end of the previous film made a sequel difficult, but that he relented when he realized he could use the film as a platform for his anti–Hitler views.

"*Testament of Dr. Mabuse* had nothing to do with [Jacques'] book," Lang told *Film* in 1956. "It was an invention by Thea von Harbou and myself."

Although less pervasive than the Goebbels myth, this myth too has taken hold in the annals of film criticism: Lang was pressured into making a sequel, but he made a concession to the marketplace in exchange for using the film for socially relevant subtexts. On closer inspection, there are a few suspicious questions; for example, why would Nebenzahl be so fixated on the box office prospects of a sequel to a film 11 years old? Furthermore, early in the film Lang treats the viewer to an extended recapitulation of the events of the first film to fill in those viewers joining the saga already in progress—something Lang would hardly have deemed necessary if *Testament* were simply, as he

---

*Lang's bogus Goebbels story was debunked by Gösta Werner in 1988.

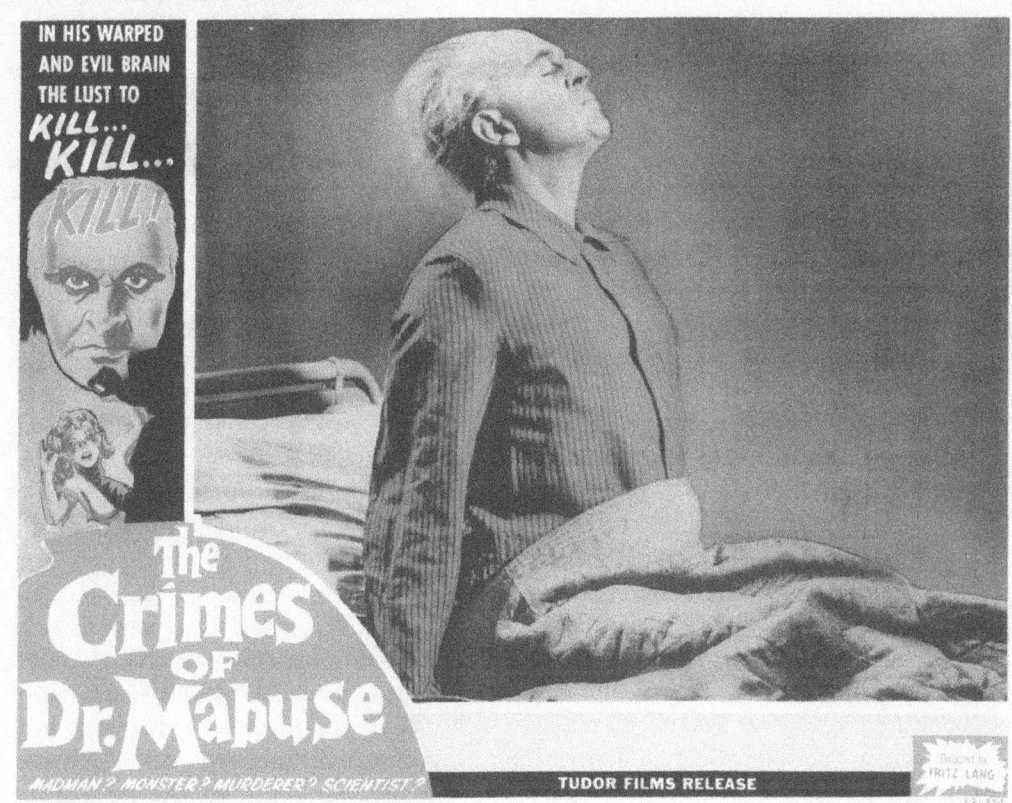

The American version of Lang's film firmly rooted the events of the story in wartime Germany.

suggested, a concession to overwhelming public demand for a *Mabuse* follow-up.

For his part, Norbert Jacques had discovered that the market for Dr. Mabuse had begun to dry up. His original novel had gone out of print. Hoping to recapture the kind of mass market popularity that *Mabuse* had tapped, Jacques all but abandoned his more high-brow literary pursuits to focus on reviving his arch-criminal anti-hero.

In addition to writing books, Jacques had also been working with the film industry on screenplays. Some of his producer contacts had suggested that he conceive of a female Dr. Mabuse so that one of Germany's great leading ladies could get that kind of scene-stealing role. In response, Jacques began work on a novel called *Mabuses Kolonie* ("Mabuse's Colony"), in which a mysterious Frau Kristine takes over Mabuse's legacy, using the doctor's last will and testament as a master plan.

Meanwhile, Jacques had maintained his friendship with Lang and von Harbou, who were not above asking him for advice on their screenplays. In September 1930, Lang wrote to Jacques asking his input on the script for *M*, which at that point was still called *Murderer Among Us*. In the same letter, Lang mentions his desire to film a sequel to *Mabuse*, and wonders if Jacques has any story suggestions. Far from being coerced by his producers to stage a follow-up to *M* in the wake of its success, Lang was planning *Dr. Mabuse II* before *M* was made, before he had worked for any meaningful amount of time with

Nebenzahl, and—most significantly—before the Nazis solidified power. Hitler did not come into power until 1932, by which time the bulk of *Testament of Dr. Mabuse* had already been written.

Jacques replied to Lang that he had this work-in-progress called *Mabuses Kolonie* that could serve as the basis for the new film. Sensing that Jacques' story lacked the essential cinematic spark, Lang rejected it and proposed an idea of his own (which borrowed Jacques' idea of Mabuse's last will and testament being a meticulous documentation of a future world of crime). Lang outlined his plans for *Testament of Dr. Mabuse* in 1930.

Von Harbou developed the screenplay from Lang's outline, and at the same time Jacques wrote a novel from the same story. Then in July 1931 Jacques signed over the Nero Films the right to make a movie with the same title and plot as his book *Testament of Dr. Mabuse*, on the condition that the film would be written for the screen by von Harbou and directed by Lang. It was a legal formality that preserved Jacques' ownership of the Mabuse character and name. Since the film was not technically an adaptation of his book, though, no reference to Jacques' work would be credited on the film prints. While Lang proceeded with the development and production of the feature, Jacques attempted to find a publisher for the new book (see Chapter 1 for full details). He was unsuccessful, and his novel would not be published at all until 1950, and even then only under the title *Dr. Mabuses letztes Spiel* ("Dr. Mabuse's Last Gamble"). For all but the most dedicated of researchers, all evidence that Jacques had been involved in the creation of the second film had been suppressed or obscured, and Lang would be free to make whatever spurious claims he wanted about the origins and ownership of the film's ideas.

In some respects, the roots of *Testament* actually reach back even farther than *Mabuses Kolonie*, all the way back to the climax of Jacques's original novel *Dr. Mabuse der Spieler*: Von Wenk has ended up in Hungary in the parlor of psychic Sandor Weltmann. Gradually, horrifically, von Wenk realizes that Weltmann is Mabuse, and that he has had the misfortune to submit himself directly into the hands of his enemy. The trigger for this devastating realization is the genesis for *Testament*'s plot: Von Wenk had been taking notes on the various crimes and fraudulent gambles that he believed were connected. Mabuse orchestrated the theft of this notebook in order to deprive his nemesis of this critical information. Now von Wenk recognizes that the games unfolding in Weltmann's den match those he described in his notes, as if Weltmann is playing from von Wenk's playbook. It cannot be coincidence that the written word is coming to life before him, so Weltmann and Mabuse must be the same man. Learned Hand once said that every idea is an incitement; Mabuse does him one better. In the world of Mabuse, the distinction between words and actions is erased.

Although Lang substantially altered the Weltmann sequence in the first Mabuse film, he recreates its spirit in *Testament*. Once again, the real world crimes match those on the printed page, and this link provides the essential clue to connect the crimes with Mabuse. In one impressive sequence, a psychiatrist named Dr. Kram accidentally knocks a sheaf of papers off Baum's desk during a visit to the asylum. As he reads the pages in an effort to reassemble them in order, Kram is flabbergasted by the striking similarities between Mabuse's insane documentation of anticipated crimes and recent events described in the newspaper. One case in particular, a jewel robbery where the thieves placed a sort of "closed for lunch" notice on the door and gassed the employees, matches almost word for word between the newspaper account and Mabuse's fanatical scribblings.

But does *Testament of Dr. Mabuse* reach back yet farther even than that? In creating the story of *The Testament of Dr. Mabuse*, did Lang look to *The Cabinet of Dr. Caligari* for inspiration?

Both films tell the story of a mysterious crime spree centered around an insane asylum, where a psychiatrist has collapsed the distinction between his identity and that of a subject, allowing the thrall of obsession to metamorphose him into a mad criminal. In both films, the identity of the killer is almost a given—suspicion turns early on both Caligari's Cesare and Baum's Mabuse, but the real question is less whodunit than howzitdone. If Cesare and Mabuse are each safely locked away and under constant observation, then how is it they can also be out and about committing mayhem?

Lang had originally been slated to direct *The Cabinet of Dr. Caligari*, and so the narrative of this most famous of all German silent classics may well have stayed on his mind. Lang's only purported contribution to *Caligari* was to provide a frame story that presents the fantastical events as the delusions of a madman, to perhaps reassure skittish audiences that everything's okay, it was just a dream. By sharp contrast, he fashioned *The Testament of Dr. Mabuse* with a zeal for realistic detail. This time it's really happening.

The student of *Dr. Mabuse the Gambler* faces the difficult challenge of distinguishing between the various overlapping contributions of Jacques, von Harbou and Lang; *The Testament of Dr. Mabuse* presents an easier method for tracing authorship. Through this unique set of circumstances, parallel literary and cinematic approaches to the same material appeared almost simultaneously. Neither is the book a novelization of the film nor is the film an adaptation of the book; instead, each represents the end product of an artist working from the same starting point in their different chosen media. Any similarities between the two can be assumed to be common elements from Lang's original outline; differences can be assumed to be individual choices of the different creators.

A quick perusal of Jacques' rendition reveals that even as early as 1930—before cameras even started rolling on *M*—Lang had already planned to use the character of Inspector Lohmann in both films. Lang made a well-considered decision here. The presence of actor Otto Wernicke playing the same character in both pictures helps ground *Testament* in a realistic style despite the inclusion of certain supernatural touches.* Wernicke brings with him much of *M*'s reputation for hard-edged realism, establishing a set of audience expectations that *Testament* can play against. In this context, *Testament*'s fantastical elements—such as Mabuse's ghostly apparitions, his exposed brain throbbing in his dissected skull—chafes against that realistic style, rendering those fantastical elements that much more alien, foreign, and threatening. Nevertheless, Lang later said that he regretted the inclusion of these paranormal scenes in *Testament* and that if he had it to do over again he would not have violated the realism of the approach; indeed, when he returned to Mabuse in 1960's *The 1000 Eyes of Dr. Mabuse*, Lang pointedly excised all paranormal or fantastical elements that otherwise occur in greater or lesser degrees in all of the other films in the series.

In writing the novel, Norbert Jacques

---

*Wernicke does not play Lohmann in the French edition. Instead, actor Jim Gérald appears in the role, with only Klein-Rogge appearing in both the French and German versions.

An evocative collage of crucial images from the film adorns this page from the German programme.

necessarily lacked an understanding of how Inspector Lohmann's character would be developed in the yet-to-be-made film *M*. Between them, Thea von Harbou, Fritz Lang, and Otto Wernicke fashioned Lohmann as a cynical, sarcastic piece of work. He sleeps in his office, chomps on cigars, jokes with cruel gallows humor and inspires fear in the criminal underworld. Yet in Jacques' book, Lohmann seems bland and uncharismatic, a mere shell of his screen self.

Although in broad strokes, the book and film tell the same story, they do so in sometimes strikingly different ways. Lang tells his story in a strange, elliptical way that frustrates some viewers, accustomed to more straightforward drama. Jacques focuses his narrative by eschewing the eerier aspects of the mystery and concentrating instead on character development. Early on he reveals that which Lang reserves for the climax: that Mabuse is dead and well and living in the soul of his psychiatrist. Mabuse is dead, long live Mabuse.

For the last ten years, the master criminal has been a virtual invalid, eking out the barest whisper of an existence in a mental institution run by Dr. Born (Dr. Baum in the film). Mabuse is wheelchair-bound and mute, but desperate to communicate. At first, he cuts open his fingers to scrawl on the walls in his own blood. Born thoughtfully provides pen and ink, and the result is the Testament: an immense work-in-progress outlining his plans for a future world of crime. Born collects the papers and studies them, hoping for some insight into Mabuse's madness— or his genius. Somewhere along the way, Born's fascination with the case turns into hero worship, and then that hero worship turns into insanity. As Nietzsche said, "When you look into the abyss, the abyss also looks into you." Born has become Mabuse.

Lang's treatment of the story doles out in measured doses the clues that Baum has assumed Mabuse's identity. In the film, Baum has long since lost his soul; it is as if Mabuse has taken over the man's body. Jacques prefers to examine in greater detail Born's descent into madness. He presents Born as a man susceptible to fascism, whose respect for a Great Man overtakes his will. Nazi Germany would soon enough be overrun by Borns, enthralled by Hitler's cult of personality.

Jacques also includes a number of ideas unique to his version of the tale. Before Born takes the name Mabuse as his own (or at least before Born realizes that he has named himself Mabuse), he has already split off an alter ego in the form of a chemist named Rauschmann. In this role, Born almost succeeds in deluding himself that he has circumvented the middle man in acquiring psychoactive drugs for use in his legitimate practice, but the reader understands that his true motive is to manufacture poison gas for use in acts of Mabusian terrorism.

The film includes none of the book's emphasis on gas. At the climax of the novel, Lohmann realizes just how close to the brink of apocalypse they had come, that Mabuse-Born was going to unleash gas warfare on Germany immediately. It is a detail that separates Mabuse from the man often cited as his real-world counterpart, Adolf Hitler. During WWII, Hitler had maintained an enormous stockpile of gas weapons, but he dared not use them. As historian Stephen Ambrose explains in *Citizen Soldiers*:

> The Germans had inaugurated gas warfare in the trenches of World War I, a criminally stupid mistake because the prevailing winds in Europe blow west to east. Consequently German generals in World War II wanted no part of gas. But of course they could not make a final decision, only Hitler could. But even in early

April 1945, when he was at his most desperate and most crazed, he never ordered gas warfare. Apparently this was because he had been gassed in World War I. So it was not true that Hitler would stop at nothing; he drew the line at gas warfare.

Jacques also includes a character named Lara, who is a sort of composite of Dusy Told from the original book (not her enfeebled filmic incarnation) and Frau Kristine (the villainess from the unfinished *Mabuses Kolonie*). She is Born/Mabuse's love interest, but unlike Dusy Told this strong-willed woman is a willing enabler of Mabuse-Born's dastardly schemes. She is drawn to his power, and her admiration for his darkest qualities keeps Born from retreating from the edge of destruction when he might otherwise have been able to do so. Lara contributes little else to the proceedings, and the only substantive consequence of her absence from the film is to deprive Mabuse-Baum of any recognizable human relationship.

The book's Born not only has a girlfriend but a daughter as well, in the form of the virginal Helli Born. A sheltered girl, she has no experience with which to evaluate her emotions, and without realizing it she has become attracted to the wrong kind of guy. That wrong kind of guy is ex-con Thomas Kent, currently employed as a criminal odd-jobsman for Mabuse's underworld gang. Kent's role is essentially the same in the book as in the film: In both, he is beholden to Mabuse only as a consequence of the crippling unemployment in Germany that denies him any other option. In both versions, his conscience ultimately gets the better of him and he exposes all to Lohmann.

However, while Jacques may evidence a greater and more nuanced understanding of Born's character than Lang, the film director shows that he appreciates Helli's (Lily in the film) importance more than the novelist. Lang changes her name and deletes any suggestion that she is related to Dr. Baum—as with the exclusion of Lara, Lang is shunting all normal human relationships away from Mabuse-Baum. (Not until Claude Chabrol's 1989 entry would Mabuse have any such human ties again.)

Lily may not be biologically related to Mabuse, but Lang has placed her at the very heart of the drama in a way that highlights a more subtle relationship to Mabuse. Kent is just a pawn; without Lily to inspire his better nature, he has no motivation to defect from Mabuse's gang. But in providing Kent with motivation and purpose, in giving his life meaning, she also demands sacrifice. Taking on Mabuse is an almost suicidal act, and Kent will only barely escape with his life. Lily inspires Kent to put his life at risk, and in this way she has some Mabusian characteristics of her own. Her manipulation of Kent is motivated by the best and most honorable of intentions, but she is manipulating a man's psyche to stake his life in a cosmic game of chess between the Forces of Good and Evil in just the same way that Mabuse inspires his minions to commit suicide at his whim. This is Lang's insight into Lily, and his reason for excluding Lara—one character can serve both functions at once. Lang's Lily is the fusion of Jacques' Helli and Lara (even suggested by the fusion of their names), a woman attracted like a moth to the flame of crime, and in her urge for self-destruction yet manages to lure the man she loves to his doom as well.

Helli Born is a wide-eyed innocent blissfully ignoring all warning signs about Kent's past or present employment; Lily by contrast is a masochist who knows full well what Kent is and sticks with him anyway. In a fabulous scene that is tragically cut from the English-dubbed edition *Crimes of Dr. Mabuse*, she stares with frightening glossy eyes at Kent as he confesses

Dr. Baum's transformation from psychiatrist to criminal echoes the classic German silent film *The Cabinet of Dr. Caligari*.

his sins to her, responding to each new bombshell with an intractable "I love you."

Kent, tortured by his conscience in that time-honored Langian manner, hopes to scare his sweetie off so she will not be implicated in his crimes. He tells her he was once in prison, for killing two people. She continues to smile at him starry-eyed like some love-struck stalker. He tells her he is now a part of a criminal conspiracy involved in counterfeiting, armed robbery and murder. Still, she stares at him with unwavering devotion. No matter how unpleasant the revelations Kent can dig up about his darker side, Lily remains undeterred. Her self-destructive approach to love will soon land her in a sealed underground chamber with a bomb.

Lily is a manifestation of a recurring character type in Lang's filmic universe. The director, who collected women like trophies and treated all of them with dictatorial cruelty, had a sexual fixation on women who found appeal in the wrong man. Cara Carozza (whose masochistic tendencies had originally been crafted by Norbert Jacques) was an early example of the type, and her attraction to Dr. Mabuse got her killed. Lily follows in her footsteps. Lang would rework the character again and again in his Hollywood pictures, with characters like Joan Bennett's Kitty March in *Scarlet Street* (1945) or Barbara Stanwyck's Mae Doyle in *Clash By Night* (1952) perhaps the most extreme examples of women aroused by a man's sadism.

Lily refuses to hear what Kent has to say, instead reacting to his startling confessions as if he were whispering sweet nothings in her ear. It is a small example of a larger phenomenon in Lang's *Testament of Dr. Mabuse*, which is a cinematic rumination on what one does, and does not, hear. This was Lang's second sound film, and he continued his experiments in sound begun in the previous *M*. *M*'s experiments were formal—offscreen whistling used to designate an unseen murderer, for example—but *Testament*'s sonic experiments are thematic. One of the most important characters in *The Testament of Dr. Mabuse* is not Mabuse, Lohmann, Baum or Lily, but sound itself. And like these other characters, sound is deceptive.

The film opens with a celebrated sequence in which undercover ex-cop Hofmeister infiltrates Mabuse's counterfeiting plant, is discovered and flees for his life. The sequence utilizes Lang's finely honed skills with silent filmmaking, because the only sound heard is a grinding drone—the sound of the printing machines is deafening, and drowns out everything else.

A similar technique appears in what is undoubtedly the film's most famous sequence (a sequence that Lang would remake, with pointed alterations, in 1960's *The 1000 Eyes of Dr. Mabuse*). Baum's colleague Kram has made an inconvenient discovery linking Mabuse writings to the recent crime wave, and is underway to report his suspicions to the police. Mabuse sends an assassin in a car to intercept Kram. The assassin's car pulls up alongside Kram's at a stoplight, and begins honking the car's horn. This incites the other drivers to honk as well. Even Kram gets in on it, witlessly honking his horn, oblivious to the fact that the racket is providing the killer with sufficient cover to murder him undetected. The criminals drive away, taking the crime scene with them, and only after all the witnesses have also driven away does the traffic cop on duty discover Kram's lifeless body in his car and a bullet hole in the windshield.

But if noise can conceal information, others sounds can simply be absent altogether. Hofmeister places his call to Lohmann, but is driven insane before he can speak the one word he so desperately needed to say. Only by etching the name "Mabuse" into the window pane can Hofmeister communicate that which spoken words cannot. Mabuse himself has traded spoken speech for etchings. Silent film star Rudolf Klein-Rogge reprised his role as Mabuse; like the silent film refugee Klein-Rogge is, Mabuse cannot speak for himself, but must rely on written words to convey his thoughts.*

Mabuse has a voice in the film, but it belongs to Dr. Baum. Here, too, sound lacks its crucial communicative aspect. Thomas Kent knows Mabuse only by his voice (or by the written messages he sends), since he has never met the man behind the curtain. When Kent meets Dr. Baum for the first time, though, he fails to recognize "Mabuse." It is only later, when he hears Baum's voice reproduced over a phonograph's loudspeaker, that he recognizes his master's voice. In the book Jacques makes no such distinction between a recorded voice and a living one—Kent recognizes Dr. Born as Mabuse the instant he hears him speak on their very first encounter. Sound is not a character in Jacques' literary treatment of the story.†

The events leading up to the moment

---

*Klein-Rogge does speak in the film, but only after Mabuse has died, his voice the ghostly whisperings of a phantom.

†In the 1962 remake, with "talkies" no longer self-conscious, the filmmakers avoid such an emphasis on sound: The counterfeiting plant does not make a deafening noise, there is no car-assassination scene, Mabuse can speak in his own voice, and there is no scene where a character suddenly recognizes the asylum's director as the new incarnation of Mabuse.

when Kent recognizes Baum as Mabuse, putting all the pieces of this jigsaw puzzle finally into place, represent some of Lang's finest directorial showmanship. Lang's editing pattern marks a culmination of the question-and-answer–style cutting of the first Mabuse picture. Each transition carries the story forward from the previous scene, each cut a link in the chain that suggests the hidden connections that Lohmann is tracing. The world of Mabuse is a giant web, and the cinema of Mabuse reveals these camouflaged joints.

Lang crosscuts between parallel lines of action to great and thrilling effect in what ought to have been the film's climax. One part of this action-packed sequence finds a number of Mabuse's gang under siege from the police, in an echo of the finale to *Dr. Mabuse the Gambler*. The cunning jewelry heist that aroused Dr. Kram's suspicions, and got him killed, has finally yielded a clue to the weary cops trying to solve the case. Although the police have yet to recognize the link between Kram's murder and the jewelry caper, they have seen a known gangster's moll trolling the streets with some of the stolen gems around her neck. Two detectives go undercover (naturally!) to the girl's apartment, and find no less than five of the conspirators holed up there. Although the better part of this crowd is willing, albeit reluctantly, to surrender, there is one nasty holdout who has decided that he will not be taken by the cops alive. A shootout ensues.

While Mabuse's underlings scramble to find escape from the apartment, poor Thomas Kent and Lily are in even more dire straits. They too were prepared to be arrested, and were on their way to Inspector

Lang's conception of Lily's character differed meaningfully from Jacques'.

Wera Liessen as the syrupy femme fatale, Lily.

Lohmann's to turn themselves in and reveal all they knew about the conspiracy. Scarcely a few feet from Kent's home, though, some of Mabuse's agents capture them and deliver the pair to the doctor's secret underground lair. The man behind the curtain explains that the consequence of Kent's insubordination will be death. They are imprisoned in a locked room, surrounded by bricks and steel, with a ticking time bomb. The minutes pass, the hours pass, and every effort to find a way out is met with greater disappointment and desperation.

These parallel scenes form the core of *Testament*'s bleak message: There is no escape. Not for Mabuse's robbers, not for Kent or Lily, not even for Herr Director Lang himself when he faced the Nazi regime. The coming catastrophe cannot be averted. The very best that anyone can hope for is that when the disaster comes, that they may survive it.

"I think that is the main characteristic, the main theme that runs through all my pictures," Lang told Peter Bogdanovich, "this fight against destiny, against fate. I once wrote in an introduction to a book that the fight is important—not the result of it, but the revolution itself. Sometimes, maybe, with a strong will, you can change fate, but there is no guarantee that you can. If you just sit still, however, and say, 'Well, I cannot do anything—' bang! At least, you have to fight against it."

Survival does come, at a cost, to those who choose to fight. Lang managed to leave Germany and start a new career in Hollywood. Kent and Lily come up with an ingenious plan to flood the room, so that the bomb's blast is absorbed by the water. The resultant explosion, followed by the flushing out of a roomful of water through the hole in the floor as the two lovers struggle against the tide, is a marvelous action set piece that would not be out of place in any modern summer blockbuster. As for Mabuse's gang trapped in the apartment, they too survive the siege to be arrested by Lohmann. That is, all but that one stubborn little man survive; he takes his own life rather than face jail. This would not be a Mabuse picture without at least one suicide, after all. His suicide is the counterpoint to survival: Those who do not accept the coming of Fate destroy themselves. This is the Mabuse Principle—*je m'abuse*.

It is the aftermath of these two

sequences, how they affect Dr. Mabuse, that fully expresses Lang's fatalism. Thematically, the consequences of these two events is the Mabuse Principle at its most haunting—cinematically, though, Lang has extended his picture a little too long. Kurt Weill once remarked that Lang's films were "zu Lang": too long, too Lang. There is still a quarter of the film's running time left, even though its emotional climax has just now ended.

Lang described his films as a chronicle of the struggle against destiny.

Mabuse-Baum has set his own demise in motion by trying to kill Kent. At the very least, he made a fatal mistake in electing not to simply shoot Kent but to stage an overly complicated trap that he then does not oversee. Such cliffhangers would be stock-in-trade for James Bond and Batman, but do not constitute sound megalomaniacal policy. Having escaped Mabuse-Baum's bomb, Kent and Lily make a beeline to Inspector Lohmann's, just as they had planned. Meanwhile, Lohmann has recently arrested the jewelry store thieves, and discovered that the gun used for the gangster's suicide was the weapon used to kill Kram. Furthermore, Lohmann learns that Kram spent his last hours at Baum's sanitarium. Critical clues are coming into place that connect the various crimes with each other, and with Baum.

Lohmann arranges for Baum to make an appearance at the police station, hoping that some of the gang will be able to identify him as their mastermind. This fails, since Mabuse-Baum has never revealed his face to his lackeys. Yet Mabuse-Baum knows that Lohmann is on to him, and that it is only a matter of time before he is caught. Lang presents a high angle long shot as Mabuse-Baum walks dejectedly through the station house hallways—a doomed man who knows his days are numbered. This was the Ubermensch that had the world at his feet, that was going to usher in a New Order of Crime and Terror. Now, he seems a very small man after all.

However, Lohmann has yet to snag a single scrap of evidence that conclusively fingers Baum as being involved at all. Proving that he is his own worst enemy, Mabuse-Baum provides that clue to Lohmann himself. Although none of Mabuse's agents recognize Baum, *Baum recognizes Kent*. Although he quickly tries to deny it, Baum is clearly surprised, and angry, to learn that Kent is alive. Since Baum has no reason to know Kent, and Kent does not know Baum, Lohmann has a conundrum. In this moment, Lohmann realizes the key to his puzzle: Mabuse is not Mabuse at all. It does not matter that the "real" Mabuse is dead; Baum can be Mabuse. Anyone can be Mabuse.

The rest of the film is a chase scene as Lohmann and Kent pursue Mabuse-

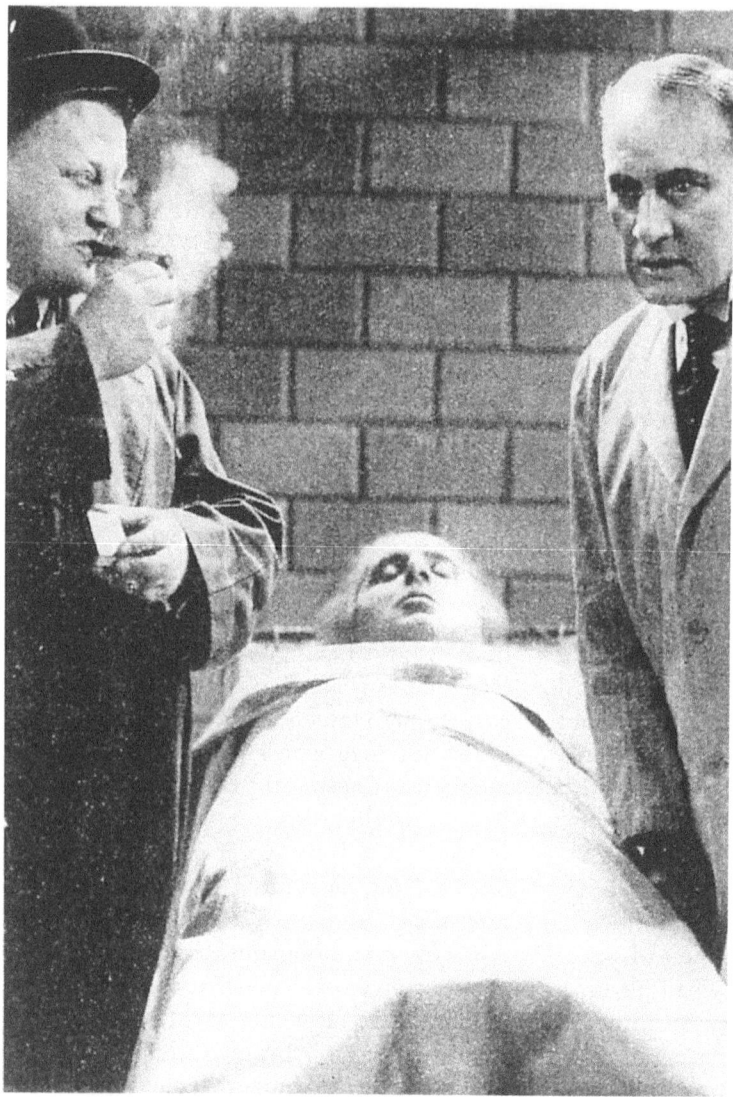

Dr. Mabuse is dead, long live Dr. Mabuse (from left to right: Otto Wernicke as Lohmann, Rudolph Klein-Rogge as the deceased Mabuse, and Oscar Beregi as his disciple Dr. Baum).

catch up with his prey after this has happened, when there is nothing left to say or do. Perhaps the demons of Baum's mind include his own guilty conscience. Perhaps he is also damning himself as punishment for having failed. Either way, the punishment is one he imposes on himself.

This proved to be the sticking point for the Nazi censors, who would have preferred to see the unequivocal triumph of law and order over such unruly elements. Although Goebbels told Lang that he would ban the film, in fact he did allow its distribution in Nazi Germany after Lang's departure, albeit with changes. A new framing sequence was filmed with Otto Wernicke as Lohmann explaining that the events in the film took place back in the bad old days when the Jews ran the country. Curiously, the American edition *Crimes of Dr. Mabuse* added an opening sequence stating that the events took place during the height of the Nazi era when Hitler's goons ran things. It would be some time before either of Lang's homes, Germany or the United States, would see the unexpurgated version of the film, with all its ambiguities unembellished.

Like *Dr. Mabuse the Gambler* before it, *Testament* suffered the indignities of

Baum across Berlin. Their efforts are futile: Mabuse's fate was sealed the moment that Kent survived the bomb blast and the cops arrested the jewel robbers. Baum is running now not from Lohmann, but from the phantom of Mabuse that haunts his mind. Driven by this ghost, Baum will end up at his own asylum. He will head for a cell, announce himself as Dr. Mabuse and retreat into madness. Lohmann will only

being a film before its time; that is, until its time came, the film was maligned and ignored. Lang may have arrived in the United States in 1935, but *Testament* did not follow for many years. Finally, in 1943, in the thick of World War II, the French version appeared (the German cut being understandably out of reach). Reviewing the picture for *The New York Times*, Bosley Crowther grumbled that it was a "battered antique," and disputed Lang's claims that Mabuse was a cinematic allegory of Adolf Hitler.

Like the first film, *Testament* enjoyed a reissue in 1973 featuring his original edition, and like its predecessor this fact was heralded by a glowing review in *The New York Times* by Nora Sayre. The "immensely refreshing" *Testament of Dr. Mabuse* "yields a torrent of images that almost make the nineteen-seventies seem tame." By the 1970s, of course, the world of Dr. Mabuse had expanded considerably.

CHAPTER 8

The Little Dictator: Fritz Lang in America

> Lang makes you want to puke. Nobody in the whole world is as important as he imagines himself to be. I completely understand why he is so hated everywhere.
>
> —Kurt Weill

Dr. Mabuse lay in hiding. The world thought him dead, or locked away in an insane asylum, or both. In the 1931 film *Dracula*, Van Helsing says that the vampire's strength is the fact that people will not believe in him; the same can be said of Mabuse. He is never more dangerous than when he goes unnoticed.

In the years between Lang's departure from and return to Germany, though, there was little by which to recognize the hand of Mabuse. Following the debacle with his book version of *Das Testament des Dr. Mabuse*, Norbert Jacques gave up on reviving the character as a literary property. Following his equally dispiriting experiences with the film version, Fritz Lang had also abandoned Mabuse.

But Dr. Mabuse had not abandoned Fritz Lang, and in many ways it was as if the mad conspirator had traded identities with the film director. During his years away from Germany, Lang kept in shape to ultimately revive Mabuse—by living a life ripe with deceit and intrigue, abuse of power, and sadism.

Lang fled Nazi Germany in the summer of 1933, and like so many of his peers his initial destination was Paris, the city that had been home to him as a teenaged starving artist so many years before. His producers Erich Pommer and Seymour Nebenzahl were already there, and Pommer arranged for Lang to direct a peculiar romance called *Liliom* (1934) from the play by Ferenc Molnár. Like so many of his German classics, *Liliom* was never formally released in the United States, but it was one of the director's personal favorites and he often screened it for his Hollywood friends.

During Lang's stay in Paris, his mistress Lily Latte made repeated journeys back and forth between Berlin to export as many of Lang's assets as possible. It was a treacherous pastime, as Latte was Jewish, but she had a low enough profile not to attract Nazi attention. In her devotion to the great director, Latte never balked at such duties. Other friends, though, were another matter. As work on *Liliom* progressed up, Lang sent word to his friend and editor Conrad von Molo that he was needed on the new Erich Pommer project, and, oh, please bring my mail.

Von Molo was eager to escape the horrors of Nazi Germany, and thrilled at the prospect of working again with Lang, having previously served as assistant editor on *M* and *Testament of Dr. Mabuse*. Only upon arrival in Paris did the poor man discover just what was in the "mail"—some hundred thousand Marks that he had smuggled out unwittingly on Lang's behalf. Like a character in a Mabuse film, von Molo had done just what the puppet master wanted, without even realizing it. Had von Molo been caught, he could have paid with his life. In repayment for this act of friendship, Lang did *not* hire von Molo on *Liliom*, and blithely expected the editor to return to Hitler's Fatherland. Von Molo stayed in Paris, but his relationship with Lang was over.

Meanwhile, Lily Latte's husband and daughter left Germany to join her in Paris, but she chose to divorce her family to stay by Lang, who was already cheating on her with the Parisian girls. When Lang left for America, she would follow along behind, carting his belongings like a faithful slave.

Hollywood came courting Lang in 1934, just as *Liliom* opened in French theaters. While on a European head-hunting jaunt, MGM's mogul David O. Selznick signed Lang. By June, Lang was en route to New York where much celebration and publicity awaited his arrival. The American film industry would be a new beast, though, and Lang would soon find himself alone and adrift.

In Germany, the film community looked upon the creator of *Metropolis* and *M* with almost unqualified respect, and he commanded the cast and crew like a despot. Every aspect of his films would pass through his hands, from the screenwriting to the casting to the production design to the editing. When the critics of *Cahiers du Cinema* would develop their auteur theory in the 1950s and '60s and single Lang out as a prime example of the auteur director, they chose well; at least in his German productions, he could claim creative authorship of virtually every detail.

In Hollywood, the director was a contract employee within a massive factory. Power resided in the studio system itself; it assigned directors and actors to scripts already developed. It would be the rare director who could command enough authority on his own to alter or affect studio decisions, and these men would earn this power only through box office success, not artistic triumphs. Lang arrived in a land that scarcely knew of *Metropolis* or *M* or *Dr. Mabuse*. He arrived with entrenched habits of riding roughshod over cast and crew in pursuit of his singular visions—arrived in a land where stars were the top bananas, crews were unionized, and production style was dictated by studio brass. And most of all, he arrived in a land with a strange culture and language that he would need to learn quickly if he hoped to connect with local audiences.

Lang had never developed any teamwork skills, and this deficiency would hinder his career at every turn. Time and again he antagonized and alienated major Hollywood stars, powerful studio executives and entire unions of technicians and craftspeople. Lang never saw himself at fault. In his view of the world, he was always the injured party: a visionary artist hampered at all sides by philistines, his creations always marred by the unwanted intrusions of others. To Hollywood, however, Fritz Lang was a temperamental misfit who was his own worst enemy.

For the first year, Lang failed to get any films past a rudimentary planning stage. Instead he concentrated his energies on learning English and the intricate politics of the studio system. He vowed to stop speaking German, began traveling

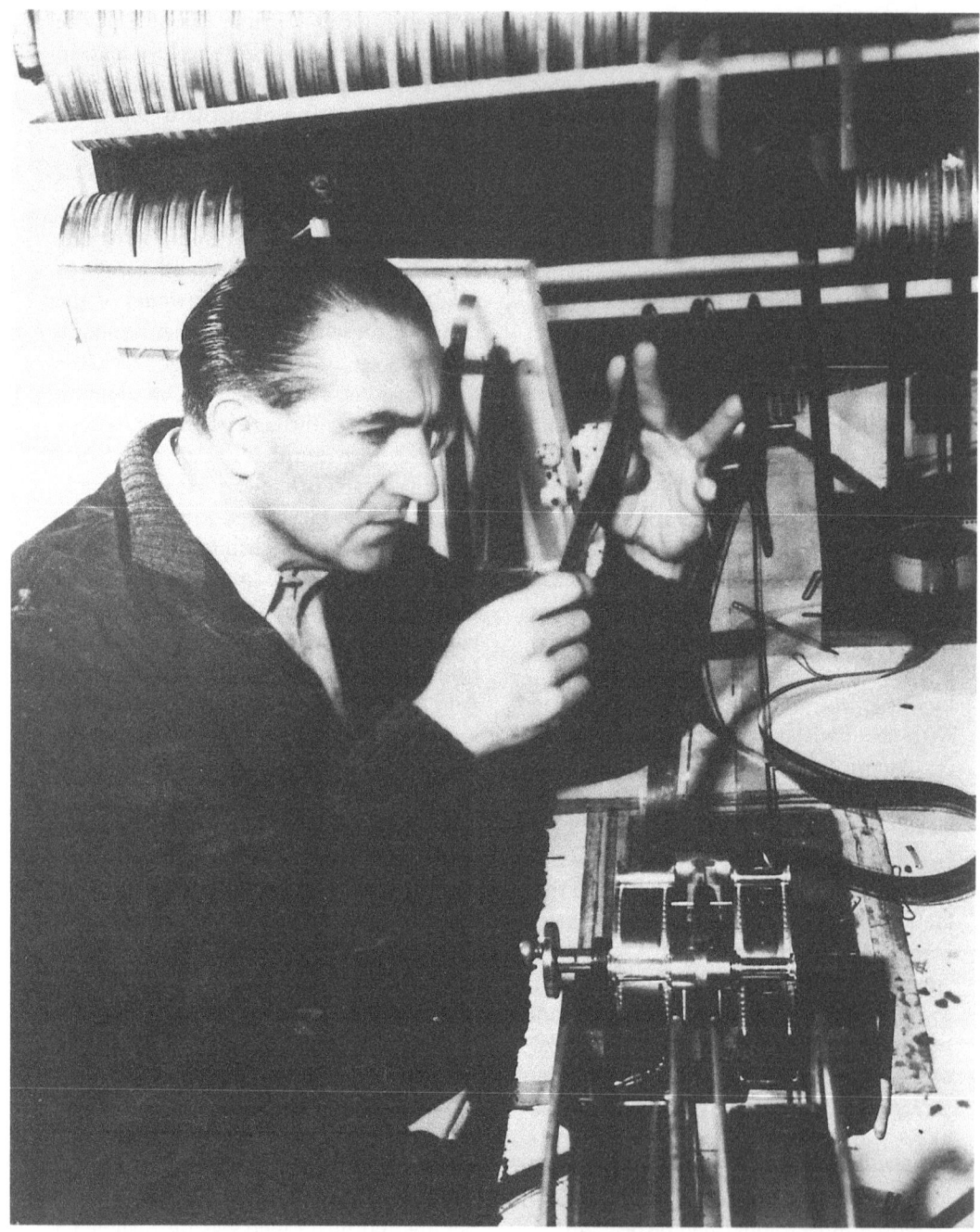

Fritz Lang was a perfectionist, which was not always a good thing to be (courtesy Photofest).

across the continent and read as many comic books as he could.

Finally, in 1935, he made a film. If *Fury* would rank among his best works, though, the dark tale—of a man almost lynched by an angry mob, who then orchestrates a sham trial of his tormentors in a vengeful plot to see them executed—was too bitter for American tastes. A critical triumph, *Fury* was also a popular bust, and in Hollywood the only thing that counts is ticket sales.

Right from this very first film, Lang established a pattern of misdirected hostility. He fought with everyone, from cameraman Joseph Ruttenberg to star Spencer Tracy. Lang so enraged actor Bruce Cabot that physical violence nearly erupted. He worked the crew through lunch without breaks (he did not go hungry; he had his customary lunch of a nutritional pill and a sandwich prepared by Lily Latte). This was a violation of union rules and an act of cruel disrespect to his staff, and Tracy responded by leading a walkout of the entire production team. Only then did Lang relent on the issue of lunch breaks, but compensated by working the crew for 20 hour days six days a week.

One day, producer Joseph L. Mankiewicz had to race to the set to save his director's life: The crew had rigged a light to fall on Lang. It was not the first time that Mankiewicz had saved Lang; throughout the entire project the producer had given Lang a wide berth, defending him to the studio bosses, indulging his most idiosyncratic whims. Against his better judgment, Mankiewicz allowed Lang to shoot a scene depicting Spencer Tracy's guilty conscience confronted by ghostly apparitions of his victims—a conceit familiar to fans of *Dr. Mabuse the Gambler*. Mankiewicz thought it silly and unnecessary, but gave the director the benefit of the doubt and allowed him to test it on preview audiences. When, to no one's surprise, the sequence was met with laughter and derision, undermining the tension of the rest of the picture, Mankiewicz had it cut. Lang railed furiously against the producer, who had been his only true ally, accusing Mankiewicz of ruining the film. When word spread of Lang's harsh treatment of the well-liked Mankiewicz, the director was well on his way towards becoming a pariah.

However, there was one person on *Fury* who emerged from the experience without a hatred of Lang. In fact, actress Sylvia Sidney recognized him as an artistic genius. Without her intercession, it might have been the end of Lang's Hollywood career then and there. The studio had little interest in pursuing a relationship with the director of a flop; everyone else thought him a sadistic bastard. Thanks to her, producer Walter Wanger hired Lang to direct Sidney and Henry Fonda in the Bonnie and Clyde–style crime drama *You Only Live Once* (1937). Lang seemed a wise choice, in part due to his experience with crime thrillers and in part due to his growing reputation as a filmmaker of socially relevant pictures.

Lang took eagerly to the assignment, touring prisons to conduct research. When it came to production, though, Lang's worst side reemerged, and he abused Fonda verbally and emotionally. Fonda grumbled, "He is the master puppeteer, and he is happiest only when he can manipulate the blank puppets."

When *You Only Live Once* performed poorly at the box office, an unsurprising fate for a downbeat drama with a tragic ending, Lang took to the press to excoriate Wanger. Lang, who actually had a contractual right of final cut, accused Wanger of excluding Lang's desired prologue to the film, which was to have shown the social conditions that led Fonda's character to a life of crime. (Like the prologue to *Dr. Mabuse the Gambler*, this appears to have existed only in Lang's mind.)

His hostility towards Wanger backfired. Already on shaky ground following his temperamental behavior on *Fury*, Lang had now alienated the only producer who had been willing to give him a second chance. For the next six months, Lang tried unsuccessfully to launch his own independent production company. In this vein, he developed a number of abortive projects that he shopped around Hollywood in search of financing: How about a film about Al Capone? Or notorious bank robber John Dillinger? What about an epic of American history? Or another espionage thriller like *Spies*, about a doomsday weapon?

Giving up hope on establishing his own independent company, Lang took the spy picture idea to Paramount, a studio known as a haven for German émigrés. Paramount responded by signing the onetime pariah to a two-year, three-film contract. Once again, Lang had Sylvia Sidney to thank. Paramount had an eye on wooing the young star to their studio, and she was willing only if she could again have Herr Lang as her director.

The result was a socially minded musical called *You and Me* (1938). Hoping to imitate the style of a Bertolt Brecht Lehrstuck, Lang hired Kurt Weill to compose the songs. Almost immediately, Lang and Weill began an embittered war of words. Lang ordered the crew to work overtime; he insulted and maltreated the cast. In his perfectionist zeal, he allowed the production to fall behind schedule, angering the studio bean counters. Weill felt that his songs had been ruined, and blamed Lang for destroying his artistic vision. When *You and Me* opened to dismal reviews and audience apathy, Lang sheepishly admitted that "it was—I think deservedly—my first real flop."

Plucky as ever, though, the director continued with his plans for the spy film, now titled *Man Without a Country*. Over the course of numerous script rewrites, the villain was gradually evolving into another Dr. Mabuse. True to the Mabuse paradigm, the villain ultimately is blinded by his own death ray, goes mad and is tortured by his own guilty conscience. This Mabuse knock-off never saw the light of day. The project fell apart, and the studio negotiated an end to Lang's contract.

There were not to be two more films for Paramount, and the most hated man in Hollywood burned yet another bridge behind him.

Things began to look up in 1939, when Lang met agent Sam Jaffe. The two men hit it off immediately, and Jaffe became an instrumental figure in rebuilding Lang's deteriorated career. Nineteen thirty-nine was also the year that Lang had officially become an American citizen, and he was soon selected to helm that most American of genres, the Western. Lang had long been a fan of Westerns, and so was especially pleased when Jaffe convinced 20th Century–Fox to give this displaced European, this director of socially relevant *noir* thrillers, the job of directing *The Return of Frank James* (1940).

Keenly aware of the potential consequences of his misbehavior, Lang indeed tried to play nice. Fortunately, *The Return of Frank James* turned out to be a modest commercial hit, and Lang was given the chance to direct another "oater," *Western Union* (1941). Throughout it all, Lang played the pliant, submissive employee the studio system expected him to be. Although the director had to sacrifice his trademark control freak persona, in turn he had won such benefits as a chance to explore filming in color, making Westerns and proving his box office worth to the studio chiefs.

His third picture for Fox, 1941's *Man Hunt*, returned Lang to more familiar thematic ground and provided his first collaborations with screenwriter Dudley Nichols (the closest thing to Thea von Harbou he would find in the States) and actress Joan Bennett (with whom he would later launch a covert love affair and an overt business venture). Additionally, the project's assistant editor, Gene Fowler, Jr., would become fast friends with Lang and a recurring creative partner. The wartime espionage drama concerned an

Fritz Lang with Marlene Dietrich, a onetime flame and fellow German émigré (courtesy Photofest).

Englishman behind enemy lines, attempting to assassinate Hitler. For the director who claimed to have helmed the very first (if veiled) anti–Nazi film, *Man Hunt* was to be an appropriate and prestigious undertaking.

Studio head Darryl F. Zanuck became worried that Lang had too much free rein on *Man Hunt*, and assigned as producer a meddlesome fellow who would keep tabs on the renegade director and report all suspicious behavior back to Zanuck. Before long, Lang was banned from the editing room, on the grounds that he was spending too much time perfecting his cut. Fowler and Lang conspired to sneak in after hours to work off the clock on their ideal cut, without the studio knowing. The result was a worthy comeback and a solid commercial success.

Unfortunately, success went easily to Lang's head and his worst character traits were soon on full display. Zanuck assigned him to helm *Confirm or Deny* (1941), another wartime spy film and another Joan Bennett starring vehicle. Lang scarcely arrived on the set before he threw a temper tantrum and walked off the production entirely, to be replaced by Archie Mayo. Relations between Lang and Zanuck were worsening, but the movie mogul hoped Lang might redeem himself with *Moontide* (1942). Once again, Lang found fault with the script, his co-workers, Zanuck's suggestions and anything else that came to mind. Once again, Lang walked off to be replaced by Archie Mayo. This time there would not be a second chance: In 1942, Zanuck and Jaffe worked out an end to Lang's contract.

The United States had recently joined the war, following the December 1941 bombing of Pearl Harbor. Many of Hollywood's best and brightest patriotically enlisted, but Lang rightfully felt that he had served his time in World War I, so he stayed behind. With so many great directors off to war, Lang would now have a better chance at prestigious assignments, and fewer peers to be compared against. The war years would allow Lang to prove himself creatively and commercially.

Nevertheless, there was a certain stigma to staying behind, as if he was something of a coward, or a fascist supporter. This could not have been farther from the truth. Lang may have blossomed late in terms of political consciousness, but he had become a vocal and active anti-fascist. He hated the Nazis with a passion, so much so he avoided contact with other displaced Germans in Hollywood. He happily lent his name to any leftist cause and surrounded himself with fellow travelers. As he later explained to Peter Bogdanovich:

> When I came to this country, the Big Powers—England, France too—tried to appease Hitler, and what actually happened? No one really gave a damn about what was going on in Germany. Some of us saw it coming, but the only ones who were really opposed—we *thought* they were the only ones—were the Communists. That was one of the reasons why so many people in Hollywood turned to the Communists—because they *believed* that the Communist Party was the only group really fighting the Nazis.

Perhaps to deflect any criticism for not enlisting in the war effort, it was in 1943 that Lang first spoke publicly about the legendary meeting between himself and Dr. Goebbels to discuss the banning of *The Testament of Dr. Mabuse* (see Chapter 7). The Mabuse film had just opened in America, some ten years late, and Lang was eager for it to be received as the anti-fascist parable he had crafted it to be. Simultaneously, Lang had just released his most recent creation, the more overtly anti–Nazi *Hangmen Also Die!*

Back in the summer of 1942, the hated Reichsprotektor Reinhard Heydrich (derisively called "The Hangman" by the Czech citizens he terrorized) had been assassinated in the town of Ludice. The Nazis responded by cracking down on Ludice with a wave of brutality and retaliation intended to force the townspeople to surrender the assassin. Remarkably, they did not.

A Czechoslovakian refugee by the name of Arnold Pressburger just happened to be a Hollywood producer, and wanted to dramatize the story on the silver screen. Pressburger discovered that Fritz Lang also saw the cinematic possibilities. With Pressburger's blessing, Lang invited the famed playwright Bertolt Brecht to work with him on a screenplay.

For years, Lang had wanted to work with Brecht, or at least help the great writer find a foothold in Hollywood. Lang and Lily Latte had been instrumental in raising money for Brecht to flee Nazi Germany. Lang's respect for Brecht could only go so far, though, and soon Lang would realize that he had invited into his inner circle a dark-minded egotist just like himself. For every rant Lang had made at his producers for hindering his artistic freedom, Brecht would soon echo right back at Lang himself.

Brecht hated Hollywood. He saw only decadence and opulence, a city of worthless human waste—Lang included. He accepted the assignment to write *Hangmen Also Die!*, but soon found his approach clashing with Lang's. Brecht wanted the film to be a grand paean to the power of the people. The misanthrope Lang distrusted "the people," and had spent his career showing how easily "the people" can be turned into a vicious mob. Brecht wanted to cast some of his closest friends, including his wife Helene Weigel, for whom he specially wrote a part. Lang would have none of it, insisting that the Czech roles be played by ordinary, accent-free American stars so that American audiences could be made to feel the effects of an enemy occupation—something the U.S. did not experience in either World War.

Lang wanted the film to be a commercial success, and knew from his extensive experience how to fashion a crowd-pleasing suspense thriller. Brecht objected to Lang's "hackneyed situations, intrigues, false notes." He said that the entire experience made him sick to his stomach.

> [Lang] sits with all the airs of a dictator and old movie hand behind his boss-desk, full of drugs, and resentment at any good suggestions, collecting "surprises," little bits of suspense, tawdry sentimental touches and falsehoods, and takes "licenses" for the box office. i [sic] feel the disappointment and terror of the intellectual worker who sees the product of his labors snatched away and mutilated.

In turn, Lang griped that Pressburger was violating *his* creative integrity.

For all the backstabbing, *Hangmen Also Die!* was a deserved success both critically and popularly. It was one of the rare instances after his departure from Germany that Lang could claim significant authorship in a film, and was about the closest he would ever come in Hollywood to the creative autonomy he enjoyed in the days of *Dr. Mabuse*, *Metropolis* and *M*.

After directing *Ministry of Fear* (1944) from the Graham Greene novel, Lang finally began to move towards the goal he had been striving for ever since Fritz Lang Film GmbH dissolved after *By Rocket to the Moon*: the formation of his own production company. The impetus for this development came on the set of *The Woman in the Window* (1944). Lang had lucked into a producer he could tolerate, Nunnally Johnson. Johnson was a screenwriter as well as a producer, and his script for *Woman in the Window* was a fine piece of work. In addition to giving Lang a good script with which to work, Johnson put together a solid team that included Edward G. Robinson and Lang veterans Joan Bennett and Dan Duryea, and then gave the director considerable freedom. True to form, Lang abused his cast and crew—so much so that Johnson advised him not to attend the wrap party lest someone try to murder him—but delivered another box office hit.

Giddy from his career upswing, Lang embarked on some negotiations with David O. Selznick. Projects were mooted, contracts were signed, but Lang and Selznick parted ways without a single frame of film being exposed. The Selznick deal fell apart, but in the meantime a more attractive option had developed.

Walter Wanger (producer of *You Only Live Once*) was willing to work with Lang again, because his wife Joan Bennett had convinced him. Wanger did not know that Bennett and Lang had been carrying on an illicit affair, which may have biased her attitude towards the endeavor. At any rate, the somewhat incestuous threesome united under the banner Diana Productions in the spring of 1945. Like Fritz Lang Film GmbH before it, though, Diana would be a rather short-lived venture. Lang was on a hot streak, and hoped to dominate Diana while exploiting Wanger's name and connections. For his part, Wanger hoped to control Lang's rebelliousness by ceding stock seniority to the director.

If Wanger believed that Lang would

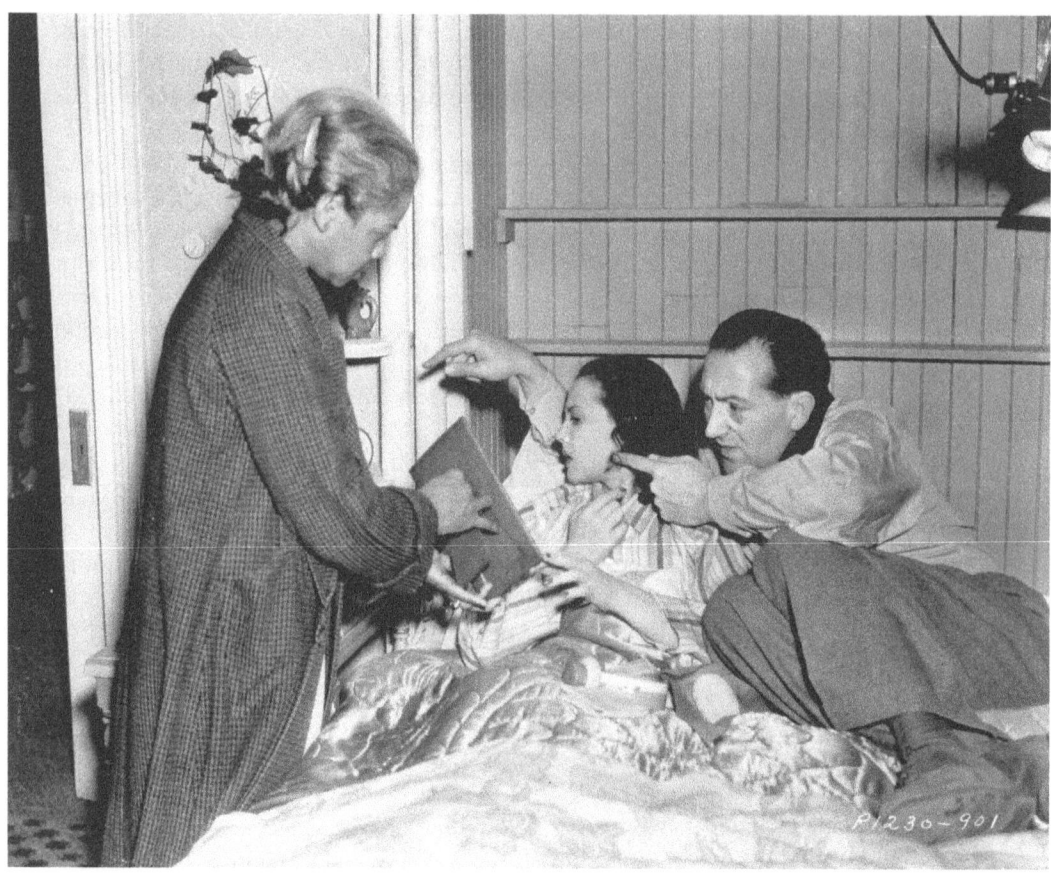

It has been said that Lang went to bed with many of his actresses—but this picture actually just shows him directing Sylvia Sidney on the set of *You and Me*, 1938 (courtesy The Everett Collection).

show more restraint now that he had some of his own money at stake, he was sorely mistaken. Typically, Lang went over-schedule and overbudget on *Scarlet Street*, a remake of Jean Renoir's *La Chienne* (1931). *Man Hunt* screenwriter Dudley Nichols (a partner in Diana Productions) wrote the screenplay, and Lang reunited his *Woman in the Window* stars Edgar G. Robinson, Joan Bennett and Dan Duryea for this tale of sexual betrayal, murder and guilt. When Lang delivered a typically epic-length film, Wanger felt forced to recut the picture to a more manageable running time. Lang denounced Wanger as a butcher and casually defected to direct *Cloak and Dagger* (1946) for producer Milton Sperling. Soon, Lang and Wanger found themselves forced to ally in defense of *Scarlet Street* to prevent a third party from cutting even more.

Scarlet Street's bleak world full of prostitutes, sexual masochists, faked suicides and unpunished killers was destined for trouble with the censors. The Legion of Decency was the first to denounce the picture, and soon after the New York State Board of Censors banned it outright. Atlanta and Milwaukee followed suit. Lang had been down this path before; the apocryphal story of his confrontation with Nazi censors had become the greatest anecdote of his biography. Walter Wanger took up the fight, arguing that Lang's film was all the more moral because rather than depict Edward G. Robinson's character being arrested and punished for his murder of Joan Bennett (and subsequent framing of Dan Duryea for the crime), he must live forever with his own guilty conscience. He must endure a living hell—a fate he shared with many a Langian protagonist, including Dr. Mabuse. Screenwriter Dudley Nichols made his own impassioned and eloquent arguments against censorship of any kind. The censors relented, and compromised on a few minor cuts. The censorship battle proved good publicity, and Diana Productions was off to a healthy start.

During the months that Wanger and Nichols were fighting on behalf of *Scarlet Street*, Lang had relocated to the Warner Brothers lot to helm *Cloak and Dagger*. The war had ended, but that did not stop Hollywood from making war movies. Producer Milton Sperling had wanted to make a film about the Office of Strategic Services (OSS), and was not about to let a mere armistice get in the way of moviemaking. He figured nobody could do the wartime spy thriller better than Fritz Lang, but the two fought throughout the project, with Lang convinced that Sperling was incompetent. Lang made a point of banning Sperling from the set, and then turned his attentions to attacking his star, Lilli Palmer. Under constant verbal abuse from her director, Palmer almost suffered a nervous breakdown. She retreated to her trailer, and the entire crew staged a walkout in sympathy. The walkout lasted a full three days, and only ended when studio brass intervened to promise an on-site manager who would ensure that Lang would not maltreat her any more.

Deprived of the ability to abuse his star, Lang returned to bickering with Sperling. At issue was the ending to the film. Lang's preferred climax was to have had Gary Cooper heading back into Germany to destroy an atomic bomb factory, only to discover the Nazis have hidden it, leaving open the possibility of future catastrophe. Sperling felt that the audience knew the Nazis had no nuclear capacity, and the ending would be laughable. He allowed Lang to film it, at no small expense, and include it in the first cut. When the Warner executives balked, Sperling cut the ending, and Lang let loose with the acrimony.

The director returned to Diana, apparently more interested in arguing with Walter Wanger than with strangers. Wanger tried to be conciliatory in the face of Lang's accusations and complaints, but Dudley Nichols sensed disaster in the air and sold off his stock in the company. With Nichols gone, the new film was to be penned by Lang's latest lady love, Sylvia Richards. And so began the beginning of the end.

Lang had always been an inveterate womanizer. Lily Latte had left her family behind to follow Lang into the New World, only to find him sleeping with every starlet and hooker in his path. Feeling guilty, Lang tried to encourage Latte's affairs, while he kept her on as a domestic manager. Over the years, Lang had enjoyed liaisons with such luminaries as Marlene Dietrich, Miriam Hopkins and Joan Bennett. Although he was now a business partner of Bennett's (and her husband's), Lang had moved on to a new young thing. The tension created between him and Bennett affected their ability to work together both on the set and in the boardroom, and by itself posed a severe threat to the new project.

Worse still was Sylvia Richards' utter lack of experience as a screenwriter. She was not qualified to take Dudley Nichols' place in such an important artistic enterprise, and Lang was too blinded by love and lust to see that fact. Richards put together a weak script for *Secret Beyond the*

Door (1948), and from that Lang made a very weak film.

He went over-time and over-budget. He fought with Bennett and her co-star Michael Redgrave. He fought with the crew. He fought with Universal's marketing team. When preview audiences reacted negatively towards the film, Universal executive William Goetz took over and recut the film—and Lang fought with *him*. *Secret Beyond the Door* turned out to be Universal's worst flop of the year. Wanger was kicked out of Universal for his role in the debacle. Diana Productions folded. Wanger and Bennett divorced.* And Fritz Lang found himself under investigation by the U.S. government.

It was a powerful sense of deja vu. Not so long ago, Lang had been targeted in Nazi Germany by listmakers drawing up inventories of all Jews working in the film industry. He had fled such totalitarianism to America, where he took up the fight against fascism with its most strident opponents—the political left. Now, thanks to those associations, Lang was once again on a list. It had started back in 1940, when a Los Angeles grand jury had been convened to investigate Communist sympathizers in the film industry. They had a list of subversive elements, and Lang was on the list. As soon as Congress began looking into the allegations, though, Hollywood had fought back. The Dies Committee (named for Martin Dies) faded away, but not before laying the groundwork for the House Un-American Activities Committee (HUAC).

Ironically, while the Right was investigating Lang's Communist ties, the Left was criticizing the filmmaker for being too conservative. His association with German Expressionism was seen as a fascist tendency, and his misanthropic depictions of human events were Politically Incorrect: A true leftist would depict the triumph of the masses over tyranny. Communist critics denounced films like *Dr. Mabuse the Gambler* as evidence of Lang's fascist leanings.

"I hate Hitler—I hate Stalin—I hate all dictators and dictatorships!" Lang said in his defense. But HUAC was not listening. They saw the paper trail, all those Communist organizations Lang had lent his name to, all those Communist petitions Lang had signed, all those Communists he had hired to work for him over the years. In May 1947, and continuing over the next ten years, HUAC subpoenaed filmmakers they accused of Communist subversion, and imprisoned anyone who refused to cooperate. Hollywood responded this time by blacklisting anyone who might end up on a HUAC list, and thereby ruining the careers of countless artists.

Lang was never called. Although he believed himself blacklisted, it is doubtful that he ever was; his horrible reputation in Hollywood provided excuse enough for producers to avoid his company. However, Lang's circle of friends and associates were called in for questioning, blacklisted or sent to jail; among those victimized by HUAC was Sylvia Richards. The FBI had been keeping a file on Lang since as early as 1939. Lang biographer Patrick McGilligan, who conducted a Freedom of Information Act (FOIA) search of the FBI files, describes Lang's file:

It is necessary now to add a strange footnote to this story, yet another little nugget of confused names, betrayed love, and violence: Wanger discovered that Joan Bennett had been cuckolding him with a Mr. Lang, but the Lang this time was a Jennings Lang—*an executive at Universal. Wanger confronted this other Lang in the Universal Studios parking lot, pulled out a gun and shot him ... in the crotch. Wanger, not surprisingly, served time in prison for this act. Immediately upon his release, Wanger and director Don Siegel made the film* Riot in Cell Block 11 *(1954).*

In Lang's case there is also the customary degree of misinformation. An interview with a fortune-teller, prognosticating about the director, is included. Lang is sometimes confused with another man; the report refers to him as 'alias Fred Lang,' married and the father of one child. Typically, the FOIA papers offer more blacked-out sections, representing either covert sources or even wilder misinformation, than legible text.

Following the breakup of Diana Productions, Lang cast about in a vain search for other independent company prospects. He did manage to link up with Howard Welsch, the prosperous head of Fidelity Pictures, to direct a few films. Among these projects was a very personal project for Lang, a Western that would star his ex-lover Marlene Dietrich in a story of "hate, revenge, and murder." *Rancho Notorious* (1952) took several years to develop, and along the way Lang directed a few minor films, and fought typical battles with casts, crews and producers.

Originally titled *The Legend of Chuck-a-Luck*, *Rancho Notorious* was a bitter *film noir* of a Western, and joined *Hangmen Also Die!* as that rare moment in Lang's Hollywood career when he managed to see a project through to the screen from his own story idea. It was Dietrich's first Western since her landmark 1939 *Destry Rides Again*, and Lang had written the role especially for her. While Lang and Dietrich fought like the ex-lovers they were, the resultant picture was an artistic triumph for Lang following his recent difficulties. Lang had found a way to marry his distinctly European sensibilities with the distinctly American genre of the Western—something that had eluded him in *Frank James* and *Western Union*.

Perhaps the difference was that Lang had seen a link between the Western and his German work: "The Western is not only the history of this country," Lang told Peter Bogdanovich, "it is what the saga of the Nibelungen is for the European." For the man who had made *The Nibelungen*, this was a critical insight. Many critics, especially those in France, had come to see Lang's Hollywood career as a means of remaking his German classics. If his Westerns were an American equivalent of *The Nibelungen*, if his spy pictures were revamps of *Spies*, if *Fury* and *While the City Sleeps* (1956) were American versions of *M*, then *The Big Heat* (1953) was undoubtedly his American *Dr. Mabuse*.

Thirty years had passed from *Dr. Mabuse the Gambler*, 20 years from *The Testament of Dr. Mabuse*. William McGivern's novel *The Big Heat* had been serialized in *The Saturday Evening Post* in 1952–53 much as Norbert Jacques' novel had been serialized in the *Berliner Illustrierten* in 1921–22. McGivern's books had inspired many a classic crime film (and he had penned scripts for several film and television *noirs*), and screenwriter Sydney Boehm had been a crime reporter for some 14 years before moving to Hollywood to oversee over four dozen films noir. Boehm's script for *The Big Heat* would be awarded the Edgar Allan Poe Award by the Mystery Writers of America. Between them, somehow, McGivern and Boehm had copied to the letter the Mabuse genre's conventions.

The film follows Police Sgt. Dave Bannion (Glenn Ford), an American working-class Lohmann, who is learning that his world is controlled by a sinister underworld conspiracy run by an untouchable crime lord named Mike Logana. Logana's agents are everywhere, even in the upper echelons of the police force, and Bannion is a marked man for daring to investigate this syndicate. Logana's assassins make a mistake, however, and a car bomb intended for Bannion kills his wife instead. When Bannion vows revenge on the gang that destroyed his family and took

A film noir of the highest order and one of Lang's finest creations, *The Big Heat* translated the Mabuse paradigm for American audiences (courtesy The Everett Collection).

away the mother of his little girl, the police brass suspend him. He hands over his badge, but keeps the gun. "That doesn't belong to the department—it's mine. Bought and paid for."

McGivern told Lang biographer McGilligan that Lang had felt a personal attraction to *The Big Heat*, "That one heroic man, the character played by Glenn Ford, stood up and fought back. He appealed powerfully to Lang's own sense of frustration and humiliation at being forced to leave Germany. In a sense, Lang said, he himself had stood up to Goebbels and Hitler, but did so by running away."

Lang also once said that deep in everyone is "the desire that good shall conquer evil. Could it be that people see in [Bannion] a symbol of hope in these days of taxes, insecurity, and the H-bomb?"

Bannion's fight against Logana, though, is not necessarily any more successful than Lang's was against the Nazis. Like von Wenk and Lohmann before him, and characters from Kras to Hartmann who follow him, Bannion cannot ultimately defeat the Forces of Evil. He learns that a corrupt cop on Logana's payroll killed himself after writing an incriminating letter. The dead man's widow, Bertha Duncan, has been using that letter to extort payments from Logana. She can rest assured that Logana will continue to pay her hush money and not attempt to assassinate her, because she's arranged that should she die the letter will be made public. If Bannion kills Duncan, though, he can bring down "the big heat" on Logana and exact his revenge.

In true Mabuse Principle fashion, *The Big Heat* kicks off with a suicide (courtesy The Everett Collection).

But even though he is no longer officially a cop, Bannion cannot bring himself to kill the widow. He has come up to the edge of the abyss, but turned back with his soul intact, and with a continued faith in the rule of law.

The crux of McGivern's novel is Bannion's inner struggle with his anger. Driven by hate, he becomes no different than the gangsters he despises. His redemption is when he turns back from his vengeance, accepts the kindness of his friends and learns the see the goodness in the world, too. Many Lang scholars seized on *The Big Heat* as evidence of a new maturity in Lang's worldview, until now dominated by misanthropy and paranoia. "[Bannion] understands that it is not for him in the final resort to exercise justice," writes Lotte Eisner, voicing the opinions of many Lang enthusiasts. "The way leads from *M* to *Fury*, to *Rancho Notorious* and *The Big Heat*, as Lang heroes move towards a maturity and wisdom which no longer contains bitterness or contempt for their fellow men."

This interpretation, though, ignores an important and inconvenient fact: While Bannion does not kill the widow, she is nonetheless killed. The big heat is brought down on Logana; it *has* to be for Bannion's return to the police force to be a happy ending of any kind. Bannion can see the downfall of the Mabuse figure without dirtying his own hands because someone else pulls the trigger for him.

That someone else is Debby (Gloria Grahame), moll to Logana's enforcer Vince. Vince is a brute of a man, wielding violence and force to effect Logana's will.

Never underestimate the power of a dame: Gloria Grahame is the true soul of *The Big Heat* (courtesy The Everett Collection).

At one point he callously throws scalding coffee in Debby's face, scarring her forever. She has endured abuse for a long time, but as her skin boils away she decides the time has come to put an end to all of this. She has seen in Bannion a genuine decency, a noble spirit she thinks she can rekindle in her own soul.

Debby kills the widow, throws coffee in Vince's face as scarifying repayment, and unleashes a torrent of violence and chaos that brings Logana's operation to its knees. She dies for her troubles, but Debby always knew that hers was a suicide mission. She has redeemed herself and slain her own dragon.

Debby is key to understanding Lang's worldview, key to understanding the Mabuse genre. Although the film was rushed through production by an impatient Columbia, Lang nevertheless took pains to fine-tune and revise Boehm's screenplay. By charting the alterations to Debby's character from McGivern's book through to the screen, we can see how Lang deliberately altered Debby's role in such a way as to undermine the somewhat naive moralizing of McGivern's novel. Debby is Lang's avenging angel, the agent of destruction who does what Bannion cannot or dare not do. She is the whore with a heart of gold, a recurring Langian archetype familiar from *Rancho Notorious*, *Scarlet Street*, *Woman in the Window*, *Clash by Night* and any *other* Lang picture, for that matter.

McGivern only introduces her after half the story has unfolded; Lang introduces his Debby in the opening sequence of the film. In the book, Bannion is surprised and shocked when Debby, using her own weapon, takes it upon herself to assassinate Mrs. Duncan—he had informed Debby of Bertha's significance, but only by way of venting his own frustrations. The book's Bannion is only dimly aware that Debby is even listening. In Lang's version, Bannion all but assigns the task to Debby. First he carefully explains why he wishes he could summon the guts to murder Bertha in cold blood. Shortly later, he gives Debby a gun for self-defense. He arms her first with information and then with bullets.

"Bannion's remarks here are tantamount to asking Debby to kill Bertha Duncan," writes Colin McArthur for the British Film Institute. "There is a strong suggestion in the way the film is put together that Bannion, consciously or unconsciously, cedes his impulse to kill Bertha Duncan to Debby. There is no such implication in the novel."

Already a lost cause for her sleazy lifestyle and selfish decisions, she can take on Bannion's mission of vengeance without compromising her soul, without compromising his. With her bandaged scars, she is literally two-faced. One side is all sweetness and light, but beneath her bandages, under her burning flesh, lies a motivation no less vengeful than Bannion's. She does not retreat from the abyss; she drives everyone else over it with her. Thanks to Debby's presence, *The Big Heat* is every bit as harsh and pessimistic as *Dr. Mabuse* before it.

Lang certainly had every right to his pessimism. The horrible conditions of the Weimar era were the direct result of a war undertaken by the nobility with no regard for the citizens for whom they were responsible. The Republic that was established in the wake of the Great War was ostensibly a democratically elected government representing the people, but it too indulged in economic policies designed to benefit the rich at the expense of the average German. For all its platitudes, for all its promises of reform, the government of the Weimar era proved daily that the authorities were no help against the Forces of Evil.

In the case of Hitler and the Nazis, it was easy to see that the authorities could be the Force of Evil itself. At least when the First World War ended, there had been a public reaction against the corruption of the old order and a revolutionary effort to bring about something better. By stark contrast, there was no domestic opposition to Hitler's regime. Up until the very end when the Allies won, there were no revolutionary uprisings in Germany, no attempts to overthrow him from within. Czechoslovakia and Poland had experienced valiant local rebellions throughout the Nazi occupation. Mussolini had been toppled by Italians. Not so in Germany, and Lang knew this.

When the war ended in May 1945, Lang spoke out in all seriousness that the only way to truly stop fascism was to "kill five million Germans." His secretary Hilda Rolfe confirmed Lang's attitude: "He used to say to me the only way you ever change the German character is to drop a bomb on the whole country and decimate it."

This was the pessimism behind the Mabuse films, the pessimism behind *The Big Heat*. The great people's revolution that Bertolt Brecht was so certain would come, that he was so angry at Lang for not depicting in *Hangmen Also Die!*, never materialized. The Communists criticized Lang for his lack of faith in the ability of the masses to overthrow their tyrants, but history proved Lang right (at least in regard to Germany). The forces of "law and order" could not stop the Hitlers and Mabuses of the world; if they were not already part of the machinery of evil, they were powerless to see their good intentions through to action. The people, victims of the forces of evil, were also unwilling or unable to save themselves. So where could someone like Lang look for hope? Only within the machinery of evil, within the inner retinue of Hitler's regime or Mabuse's gang, could come a meaningful threat to tyranny. Despite their best efforts at maintaining total subservience and loyalty from their subjects, the Mabuses of the world cannot completely extinguish the spirit of individuality from everyone. Inside a few, a rare few, there would remain an irreducible, stubborn spark of defiance, just enough to divert the course of the tyrant's master plans.

In *Dr. Mabuse*, the mastermind is endangered not by von Wenk's investigations but by the various real or imagined threats of exposure from such gang members as Pesch, Spoerri or Cara Carozza. In *Testament of Dr. Mabuse*, only the defection of Kent threatens Baum's plans to terrorize Germany. In *Spies*, the Great Haghi's downfall comes about through the defiance of his principal agent Sonja. In *The Big Heat*, Logana's top enforcer's girlfriend tears his empire down. It was a pattern that would be repeated in Mabuse films to come, from *The 1000 Eyes of Dr. Mabuse* (1960) all the way to *Club Extinction* (1989).

The Big Heat was a low-rent rush job as far as Columbia was concerned, Fritz Lang no longer meriting the kind of fawning treatment he once enjoyed. The studio bought McGivern's novel in January 1953, and completed the film within four months. The shoot itself lasted a scant 28 days. Preview audiences gave the picture top-notch marks, but it opened to lukewarm business in the states and hostile, dismissive reviews by critics. *The Big Heat* became known as the most violent thriller of its day, remembered if at all for the cruel scalding of Gloria Grahame's Debby.

Abroad, in France, it was hailed as a major artistic achievement. There, a group of film analysts writing for *Cahiers du Cinema* were developing a theory that ascribed to certain directors the distinction of being auteurs: directors with such a unique and recognizable style that their films bore their maker's personality like a brand. These analysts, who would soon become the directors of the Nouvelle Vague (see Chapter 20), lined up to sing Lang's praises.

Although *The Big Heat* lacked the bigger budgets or marquee name stars of his earlier Hollywood works, and although it had been raced through production at breakneck speed, it stands as one of Lang's greatest accomplishments and an enduring *noir* classic. If only the films that followed on its heels could have better followed in its footsteps, perhaps Lang's career might have taken a different path.

Human Desire (1954) marked the second time that Lang remade a Jean Renoir film, in this case adapting *Le Bête Humaine* ("The Human Beast," 1938). Hoping to woo Peter Lorre to star as a psychopathic train driver, Lang dragged out the development of the script. Unwilling to believe that the man he made a star refused to work with him again, Lang held out hope for Lorre until producer Jerry Wald decided enough time had been wasted, and cast *Big Heat* stars Glenn Ford and Gloria Grahame as the leads. Lang quickly lost faith in Wald and reverted to his worst habits, riding roughshod over cast and crew and driving the production over schedule. When it bombed on release, Columbia kicked Lang out of his contract.

MGM invited Lang back to head a widescreen Technicolor swashbuckler called *Moonfleet* (1955). It was just another example of Lang battling his producers over the final cut, yet another domestic failure that found champions in the French critics.

Recognizing that his talents were better appreciated abroad than in Hollywood,

Glenn Ford and Gloria Grahame in a publicity pose for *The Big Heat* **(courtesy The Everett Collection).**

Lang's thoughts began to drift overseas, and to the postwar conditions in Germany. At the conclusion of the war, Lang had become concerned about the copyright ownership of his German pictures. He was especially interested in *By Rocket to the Moon*, which he entertained dreams of remaking with hi-tech special effects.

He was right to worry about the issue of ownership. While Lang had been in the development stages on *Rancho Notorious* in late 1949, Seymour Nebenzahl had asked the director to assist in a remake of *M*. Lang rejected the idea outright; he knew *M* was his masterwork, and spent his entire life looking to it as the prime example of what he could do when left alone by impertinent producers and studio big shots. To Lang's horror, Nebenzahl went ahead with the remake without him, hiring Joseph Losey to update and Americanize Lang's most treasured creation. Lang attended the film's premiere in order to initiate a vicious shouting match with the producer, calling him a thief. Nebenzahl countered that he was well within his rights, as he had legally licensed the screenplay from Thea von Harbou and therefore had no responsibility to secure Lang's consent.

The incident stuck in Lang's craw. Sure, he had been a hired hand at Nero Films, and Nebenzahl had a legitimate claim to ownership as a result, but he had hoped for better loyalty from von Harbou. The director had always taken care to defend her reputation in the States, and to credit her properly for her immense creative contributions to his German films. She may have betrayed him, she may have become a Nazi, but he still loved and honored her.

After the war, she had been interred in a British prison camp in Staumühle for a fairly lengthy period. She defended her membership in the Nazi party as being nothing more than an expression of her nationalism and support for Indian independence. She said that she rejected the racial politics of the Nazis but joined the party to help the Indian cause. Her work for the NSDAP had been as a filmmaker or a volunteer emergency medic, hardly inflammatory stuff. Yet she had been a well-paid associate of Dr. Goebbels, and never renounced her Nazi participation.

She ended up as a "Trümmerfrau" (rubble woman), scouring the wreckage of the German streets for salvageable materials with which to rebuild her country. Later, she got a job dubbing Hollywood films for German audiences. In mid-summer of 1954, von Harbou attended a special screening of *Destiny* held in her honor. She answered questions from the audience, and felt her heart surge with pride at being recognized for her talents once again. It seemed so far away that she had Fritz Lang had been the toast of the town. She fell and injured herself on her way home from the event, and never fully recovered. Thea von Harbou had been ill for some time, and passed away a few days later at the age of 65. As it happened, Norbert Jacques died the same year, less than two months earlier.

Some nine months before that, Jacques had signed over the rights to *Dr. Mabuse* to producer Artur Brauner, who had a grand plan to revive the Germany film industry and woo back those great silent-era directors who had fled from the Nazis. Beginning in 1954, Brauner began his overtures to Lang, hoping to entice him back to German soil. Brauner had difficulty winning Lang over with his intention to remake the successful films of Germany's past. Not particularly interested in remakes of his classic works, Lang played hard to get.

He still smarted from the Joseph Losey remake of *M*, though, and found himself amenable when producer Bert E. Friedlob suggested a sort of low-rent Hollywood version of *M*. Although based on a book by journalist Charles Einstein, *While the City Sleeps* (1956) turned out to be a crude pastiche of Langian elements.

Since *While the City Sleeps* performed well at the box office, Friedlob followed it with another lash-up full of Langian clichés, *Beyond a Reasonable Doubt* (also 1956). Over the preceding 20 years, Lang had fought almost everyone in Hollywood, from the most revered of moguls to the most anonymous of technicians. He had battled over matters of serious artistic consequence and petty triviality. Now he was just old and tired, and very weary of the same old conflicts time and again. What good had the fighting ever done him? Who cared?

Then, Friedlob crossed the line. The producer wanted to conclude the film with the on-screen execution of the criminal. A lifelong opponent of the death penalty, Lang refused, and stood his ground. A bitter, drawn-out standoff ensued. Lang was not about to lose this fight, and shot the finale his way. One of Friedlob's spies on the set reported Lang's disobedience, and the producer stormed down to confront his renegade director.

"You son of a bitch," Lang told his producer. "I don't want to have anything to do with you any more or the American motion picture industry."

And with those words, Fritz Lang's Hollywood career came to an end.

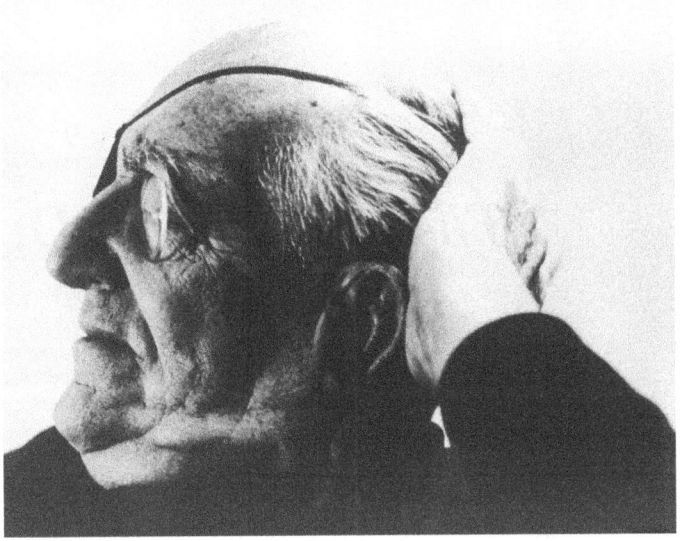

Gretchen Berg's famous photo of Lang captures the tragedy of his blindness (courtesy Photofest).

CHAPTER 9

The 1000 Eyes of Dr. Mabuse

> *The 1000 Eyes* is a superb film, dense, complex, exuberant, mysterious, … and deserving much more than the ignorant indifference that met its arrival.
> —Roger Greenspun, *Film Comment*

"I already killed that son of a bitch!" said Fritz Lang when he was approached to direct a third Dr. Mabuse picture.

However, just as the characters in Lang's films were hopelessly trapped by Fate, the director himself was being guided by Fate to return to Germany, to return to the character he had immortalized. The die had already been cast…

The story of Dr. Mabuse's triumphant return from the grave properly begins in 1921. While Norbert Jacques was writing the novel *Dr. Mabuse*, Fritz Lang and Thea von Harbou were hard at work writing the screenplays for *The Tiger of Eschnapur* and *The Indian Tomb*, involving a fantastic journey through a fictional India that represented all the fascinations Oriental art and culture held for Lang. But no matter how much the project meant to Lang personally, he would be denied the opportunity to helm the epic spectacle himself.

Instead, director Joe May maneuvered to direct the Indian films, stealing Lang's "baby" from him. May was then one of the heavyweights of German film. As a producer-director with his own studio, May-Film, he had helped nurture Lang's directorial career, and had even introduced Lang to von Harbou. For Lang, it was as if he had been stabbed in the back by his own father. May won accolades for his rendition of *The Indian Tomb*, which was proclaimed "the world's greatest film" by *Der Film*. Lang knew that he could have made it even better, and deeply resented the attention May was getting in his stead.

The incident stuck in Lang's craw. Being a paranoid man given to harboring grudges, Lang continued to rankle about this injustice for decades thereafter.

Flash forward in time about 35 years, to 1958. Lang has now had a long and successful career in Hollywood. His films have earned critical and popular admiration around the world, and many will be celebrated as classics for all time. Lang himself is unsatisfied, though, and harshly critical of his own cinematic legacy. Far from recognizing the excellence of his work, Lang has fixated on the notion that alone in his canon, *M* stands as the only masterpiece. Lang has further concluded that *M*'s superiority is due entirely to the fact that he had total creative autonomy on the project, and that ever since then he has been suffering the foolish interference of producers and studio bosses.

Enter Artur Brauner. Brauner has

Left: The German poster for Fritz Lang's final film, *Die 1000 Augen des Dr. Mabuse. Right:* The Belgian poster to *Die 1000 Augen des Dr. Mabuse.*

survived World War II, but with nothing to his name save his gentlemanly charm. With a sense of mission, Brauner sets himself to rebuilding the German film industry.

Before the Nazis, Germany's motion picture production had been the toast of the world. As Hitler rose to power and began his reign of terror, though, those brilliant German filmmakers left their homeland, emigrating to the United States. Thanks to the infusion of expatriate European talent, Hollywood quickly established itself as the preeminent force in world cinema. Following the ravages of war, European theaters were far more likely to be screening imported American product (to an audience of American occupying forces) than anything from the now devastated domestic industries. Germany had lost the most, falling far from the dizzying pinnacle of its Golden Age.

Brauner established the first postwar studio in Berlin, when he retooled a Nazi-era poison gas factory in 1946 to house CCC (Central Cinema Company) Films. He then set about acquiring the rights to pre-war German classics and hiring back many of those German filmmakers who had fled the Nazis. Little by little, Brauner was resurrecting the glories of German film.

It had long been Brauner's dream to lure Fritz Lang back to Germany. Brauner had been a fan of Lang's since his childhood, when he had a picture of the monocled director on his bedroom wall (along with a poster of Buffalo Bill, one of Lang's idols). Brauner had already made a few overtures to Lang, hoping to entice him into the CCC fold. Having had no success so far, the producer offered Lang terms he could not refuse: total creative control, and

Gert Fröbe, soon to be famous as Mr. Goldfinger, plays Inspector Kras in *Die 1000 Augen*.

the all-important screen credit "A Fritz Lang Film." In all his years in Hollywood, Lang had never won these concessions from the studios.

The deal clincher, though, was Brauner's choice of subject matter: a remake of *The Tiger of Eschnapur* and *The Indian Tomb*. Denied the opportunity to make these films originally, Lang relished the idea of a second chance. Ironically, Brauner did not recognize what it meant to Lang: Brauner was unaware that Lang had been involved with the original and was ignorant of the entire story of Lang's history with Joe May. As far as Brauner was concerned, he was simply pairing a remake of a golden oldie with one of the leading lights of the old school.

Opposite: **When Ajay Pictures reissued** *Die 1000 Augen* **in the U.S. as** *Eye of Evil*, **they simply affixed stickers with the new title on top of the existing posters struck for** *"The 1000 Eyes of Dr. Mabuse"* **a few years earlier.**

In 1958, Lang and Brauner signed a deal, and the press enthusiastically trumpeted the director's return "home." Lang was dispirited to discover, though, that Berlin was nothing like he remembered. Twenty-five years and a World War had transformed his Berlin into a pale memory. Lang, already pushing 70, began to call himself "The Last Dinosaur."

If burying his thoughts in the production of the two Indian films eased Lang's nostalgia, it did not quite offer the "total creative freedom" Lang had expected. Lang had accepted a smaller salary from Brauner than he was used to back in Hollywood, since the two films were already budgeted far above the postwar film industry average. As Lang exercised his creative autonomy, though, the CCC bean counters watched him push the already expensive project dangerously over budget and behind schedule. This provoked bitter disputes between Lang and his production manager Eberhard Meichsner. Meichsner tried to encourage Lang to be more frugal in his approach: shoot fewer takes, shoot only what he knew he would use in the film, and so on. Meichsner tried to explain tactfully to the director how things are generally done in the cash-strapped German film industry. Lang resented these intrusions.

Brauner had to intercede. Lang was an old hand at battling studio bosses, and the mild-mannered Brauner hated to argue, so Lang usually won the disputes, with Brauner backing down simply to keep the peace. So Lang kept shooting, kept spending money, having the time of his life.

His indulgent, personal epic was panned by the German critics. Most of the criticism was personal, directed at Lang rather spitefully: This uppity ex-patriot had abandoned Germany and now returned with the gall to show them "how it should be done." Despite the hostility of the German intellectual elite, the two Indian films were tremendous commercial successes. The films did not make it intact to America, Lang's adoptive home, though. American International Pictures (AIP) compiled, condensed and dubbed them into *Journey to the Lost City*. Once he quit Hollywood, Lang had all but vanished from American popular culture.

Stung by the hurtful comments by German critics, and realizing that his much-vaunted second chance at the Indian films did not even warrant serious attention back in America, Lang vowed never to return again to Germany. His homecoming had turned sour.

"I can no longer work in this country," he told Brauner. "I'm sorry."

Brauner had other ideas. Of all the once-great filmmakers he had hooked, Lang was the prize catch, and the Indian films had been hits. Forget the critics, Brauner implored, let's do another one! So he tried to tempt Lang back for another remake of an old German classic (remakes being a much more sensible investment than a risky new project). How about *Metropolis*? *The Cabinet of Dr. Caligari*? *Destiny*? How about *The Nibelungen*?

Lang soundly rejected remaking *The Nibelungen*. He felt that its archaic dialogue could seem grandiose and impressive when read from silent movie title cards, but that there would be no way to put such words in the mouths of actors and have it sound anything but stilted and silly. The director had long ago abandoned expressionistic techniques in favor of naturalism, and *The Nibelungen* could not be called a realistic story.

It may also have played a part in Lang's decision that of all his early German films, *The Nibelungen* had been wholly embraced by the Nazis as a true Aryan masterpiece. Returning to the rubble of war-torn Germany, Lang was eager to avoid such connotations, both for the benefit of his German audience and his own public image. (As it happened, Brauner was not easily dissuaded, and he later produced a remake of *The Nibelungen* in two parts, directed by Harald Reinl—the same director who took over the Mabuse series when Lang quit.)

Brauner then proposed a remake of *The Testament of Dr. Mabuse*. Lang had no desire to repeat himself (the Indian films were a special case), but he felt his resistance waning. Brauner, who had seen Lang's *Dr. Mabuse* some two dozen times as a child and become a staunch Mabuse fan, had acquired the rights to Jacques' novel. Jan Fethke had already worked up a story outline, and Heinz Oskar Wuttig was writing a screenplay. Meanwhile, Lang still smarted from the 1951 American remake of *M* which had been mounted without him, and worried that if he refused, Brauner would go ahead with the project anyway.

So, Lang consented to make a new Mabuse picture—not a remake—and flew back to Berlin to confer with Wuttig. Although some of the story had already been developed prior to Lang's commitment, the director had never met a script that did not need his improvements.

Lang's most significant contribution provided the movie's setting and its title, *The 1000 Eyes of Dr. Mabuse*. As always, Lang saw the Mabuse project as an opportunity for socially relevant commentary. Whereas the last Mabuse had been "a little Hitler," Lang avoided making an overt connection to Hitler this time around. He was undoubtedly aware of how important it was to remain discreet—the German press already had a grudge against his return, and the German people were understandably touchy about Nazism.

Lang let the old Mabuse, with all his Hitlerian connotations, stay dead. Instead, this film and its sequels depict another brilliant super criminal who has chosen to follow Mabuse's example, and has assumed the name of his hero both to celebrate his legacy and to confound the cops. The true name and identity of this self-appointed "Mabuse" remains forever obscure.

The director had found a different way of linking Mabuse with the Nazis, though. He had read about Nazi plans to outfit Berlin's Hotel Adlon with a variety of covert detection devices, in order to spy on visiting foreign dignitaries after the War. In the film, this becomes the Hotel Luxor, a fabulous luxury hotel that has, indeed, been outfitted by the Nazis for postwar espionage with a myriad of video cameras and other spy devices—Mabuse's thousand eyes.

The new Dr. Mabuse (Wolfgang Preiss) has acquired the hotel, and turned it to his own nefarious purpose. He lurks in a secret basement (a literal criminal underworld), where he watches the private lives of his guests unfold on an array of video screens. Not only does this covert information give him essential insight into how to stage his meticulously planned crimes (which have resulted in 15 unsolved murders of VIP guests), but also serves another purpose, intricately linked with his inconstant identity. Not only is Mabuse's true character never revealed, he scarcely even appears as "Mabuse" in the film.

Instead, his presence in the film is divided between two roles. One half of his split identity is psychiatrist Dr. Jordan, and the other half is psychic Cornelius. Jordan may be the more threatening figure, carefully manipulating people's destinies, but Cornelius is the more pervasive and interesting. With the aid of his "thousand eyes," Cornelius can affect a gift for clairvoyance, even while he pretends to be blind. In truth, Cornelius can see in the traditional sense but cannot in the supernatural sense, but the ruse is key to his larger plans.

In an interview with Peter Bogdanovich, Lang explained that his intention with the Mabuse update was to "again say certain things about our time: the danger that our civilization can be blown up and that on its rubble some new realm of crime could be built up."

In addressing the Cold War nuclear fear, Lang managed to render the theme somehow timeless. Most of the films contemporary with *1000 Eyes* that dealt with such fears depicted the enemy as a foreign nation, an opponent in an ongoing ideological battle. Dr. Mabuse as a lone madman with his finger on the nuclear trigger is a villain more appropriate for today, the post–Cold War era in which the threat comes from terrorists and individuals rather than countries.

Actually, the new Dr. Mabuse does not yet have his finger on the button. Instead, the film uncovers his exceptionally elaborate scheme to get his hands on nukes. The key to his plot is American businessman Henry Travers (Peter Van Eyck playing a wealthy playboy in the mold of *Dr. Mabuse*'s Edgar Hall), owner of a nuclear plant Mabuse hopes to acquire. Travers has the misfortune to be staying at the Luxor, unaware that everything he does is observed by Mabuse.

Being a voyeur himself, Mabuse's tactic is to awaken voyeuristic tendencies in his victims. In his Dr. Jordan persona, he places in Travers' path a lovely young woman named Marion Menil (Dawn Addams). Believing himself to have saved her from a suicide attempt on the rooftops of the Luxor, Travers becomes ensnared. Before long, Travers will be a mini–Mabuse himself, watching Marion through one of the Luxor's ubiquitous eavesdropping devices.

The 1000 Eyes of Dr. Mabuse is unlike the previous two Mabuse features (and those that follow) in its claustrophobia. Lang's earlier outings were spread across a large geographic canvas, as Mabuse's sinister web spread across the country. In this film, almost all of the action takes place in the Luxor, with occasional forays to the police station or the extravagantly furnished parlor of clairvoyant Cornelius. This minimalism is in part a consequence of Lang's feeling out of place in postwar Berlin: unable to recognize the landscape, he had no ability to translate it cinematically. However, the restricted terrain also serves to focus the film's energies. This Mabuse picture is also unique among the series in the demands it makes on the audience's attention: Everything may be taking place in the Luxor, but what the hell is going on is not at all easy to figure out.

Lang, along with Alfred Hitchcock, was one of the pioneers of the suspense thriller, and like Hitchcock he had specific ideas about how best to construct a thriller. Lang disliked the murder mystery approach, in which the audience is kept in the dark while the mystery unfolds and then, in a surprise ending, all is revealed. He felt such a style lacked depth. Lang preferred to approach his thrillers as a game of chess, in which the good guys and the bad guys are pitted against one another in a protracted and interconnected struggle. As one side makes their move, it forces the opposing side to respond, with each action changing the playing field and prompting the next move.

The 1000 Eyes of Dr. Mabuse is atypical for Lang in that it does follow something of the murder mystery paradigm. The question is not whodunit, but who is Dr. Mabuse? The police have recognized the criminal's methodology (in part due to a recreation of the famed assassination sequence from *The Testament of Dr. Mabuse*—both Mabuses are reading from the same playbook), but Mabuse is supposedly dead and buried these last 30 years.

The film is still structured as a chess game, but the identity of the players is in question. With very few exceptions, none

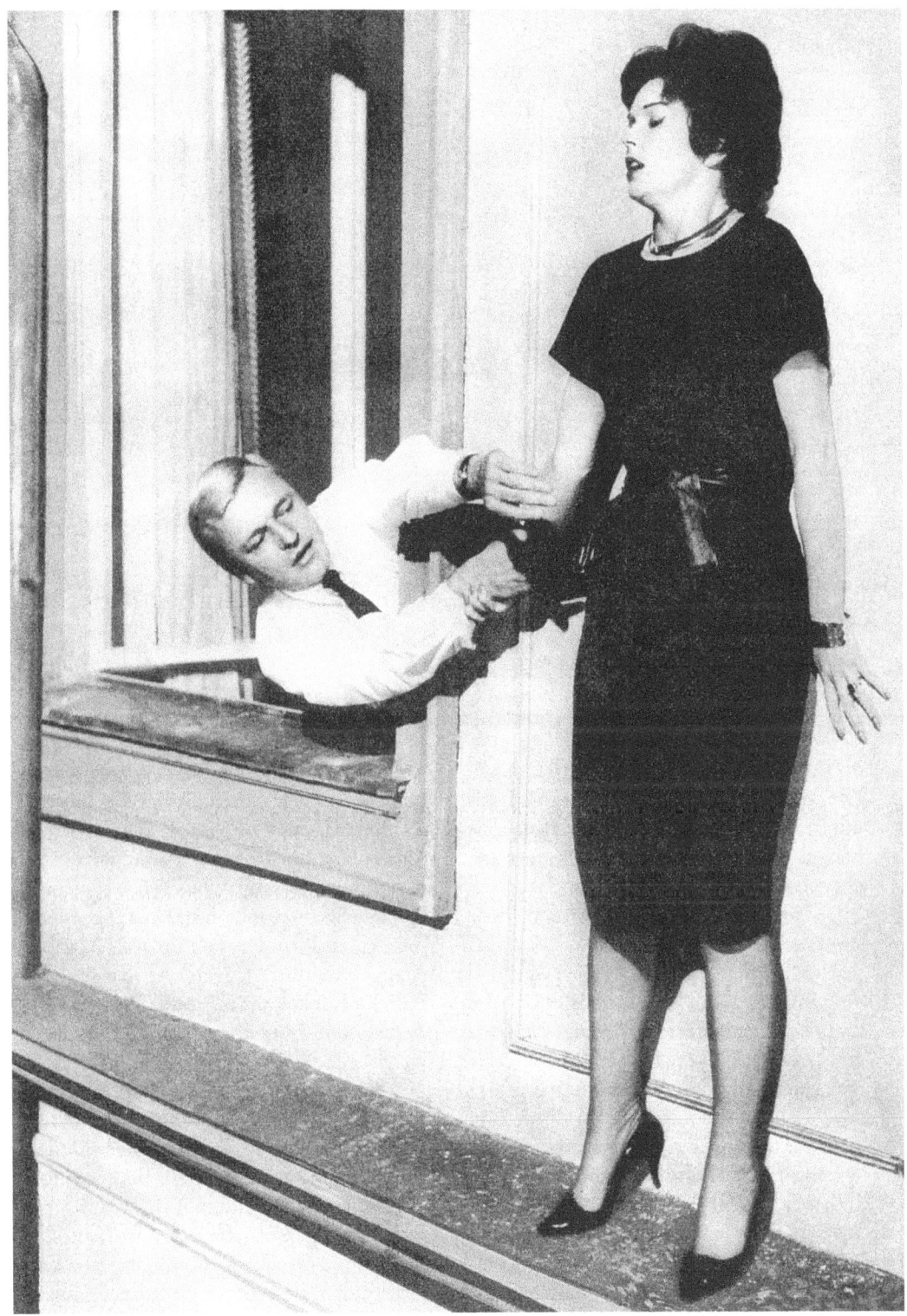

Peter Van Eyck "rescues" Dawn Addams from a pseudo-suicide attempt at the Hotel Luxor.

Fritz Lang directs Dawn Addams on the set of *Die 1000 Augen*.

of the characters are what they seem. Everyone is wearing at least one mask, if not several, and more than one scene is played out in which the characters exchange nothing but lies with one another.

The multiple disguises and false fronts assumed by the characters virtually guarantee that the average viewer will draw unwarranted conclusions about the nature of the menace: suspecting the good guys, overlooking the bad, and missing the real agents of Mabuse for the many decoys. Lang withholds critical information vital for a proper understanding of the story until its climax, by which time the audience is trying desperately to reevaluate what they have seen in light of these new revelations.

Once Henry Travers has rescued Marion Menil from her suicide attempt, he takes her under his reassuring wing. He wants to find out what dark secret she is hiding, and is tempted by an offer to rent a room adjacent to hers in the Luxor, a room which includes a one-way mirror to spy on her. His guilty conscience squirms, but as the unctuous hotel manager lets him watch through the mirror as Marion changes clothes, Travers' resolve cracks. Although reluctant to invade her privacy, Travers does rent the room, and he does watch.

What he witnesses through the mirror is her abusive, clubfooted husband threatening her life. Acting on instinctual chivalry, he crashes through the looking-glass to shoot the clubfoot dead and conspire with Marion (and Dr. Jordan) to conceal the crime.

In fact, despite the personal anguish and self-reflection that Travers expends on his decisions and actions, everything he

Voyeurism is a dominant theme in the film, as this collage from the German programme suggests.

does has been prescribed by Mabuse. Sure, Marion has a dark secret to hide, but it's not what Travers thinks and there's no chance he will discover it by spying through the mirror. She has been under Mabuse's hypnotic power all along. Her suicide attempt was a fake, she is not married to the clubfoot, and their struggle was staged purely for the benefit of Travers, who was rented the one-way mirror by another of Mabuse's agents. When Travers conspires with Marion and Jordan to remove the body from the hotel, he does not know he fired mere blanks from a prop gun at the man (another of Mabuse's agents, only pretending to be dead).

No sooner has the clubfoot's body been spirited out of the Luxor, though, than he is killed for real, by Mabuse's assassin Number 12 (Howard Vernon), who fires a thin steel needle into the man's brain with an experimental rifle stolen from the American military. The rifle and its unique ammunition was another of Lang's contributions to the screenplay. Like the Luxor setting, it was based on an article Lang had read, concerning an American top secret weapon that fired poison pellets.

Lang's filmography is a harrowing chronicle of the power of destiny, his recurrent theme the hapless man trapped by the hand of Fate. However this theme usually manifested itself in the circumstances of the plot, how the machinations of Fate gradually backed the hero into a corner from which all avenues of action are blocked save the one that he has struggled to avoid. A prime example of this typical Langian worldview would be *You Only Live Once* (1937), in which ex-con Henry Fonda tries vainly to reform himself, only to discover he has been branded by his past in a way he can never escape. In *1000 Eyes*, though, the hand of Fate is moving in a far more sinister and subtle fashion.

Henry Travers believes, and the audience believes with him, that his actions are the product of his own free will. Travers' plight is most unsettling because he (and the audience) remain unaware of it. Only in the climax of the film does he recognize how he has been manipulated without his knowledge. His guilty conscience over renting the one-way mirror is all a waste. He never really had a choice. He has been Mabuse's pawn in this cinematic chess match.

Travers, with his dashing good looks and charming manner, and Police Inspector Kras (Gert Fröbe), the representative of law and order, would appear to be the film's ostensible heroes. Yet Travers is a dupe, and Kras is ineffectual. Kras concocts a number of clever schemes to entrap Mabuse and reveal the criminal's plot, but none are successful. Along the way, he is nearly killed twice, has his files on the original Dr. Mabuse destroyed, wastes his resources sending in an undercover cop to investigate another undercover cop, and receives his only meaningful clues directly from Mabuse himself (in the guise of Cornelius, perversely feeding the cops information about the activities of his other personality). Kras triumphs in the end not through any facility of his own, but the combination of good luck and the intervention of someone far better suited to battling someone like Mabuse.

Travers and Kras are decoy heroes, characters who look the part but are not the real thing. While the audience is fooled into accepting them as the heroes of the film, they fail to see the real heroes working quietly in the shadows—characters who, like Mabuse, have managed to sublimate their own identities and move about in his shifting, untrustworthy universe in ways the guileless characters cannot. (Kras at least understands the importance of guile: He lies freely and hires others to do undercover work, but since he never puts on a disguise himself, he lacks the necessary conviction to combat Mabuse on his own turf.)

The only policeman capable of playing by Mabuse's rules on Mabuse's chessboard is Heironymous B. Mistelzweig (if that is indeed his real name, played by Werner Peters). His cover story is fairly obviously a front: As a pushy insurance salesman with a fascination for astrology, Mistelzweig invites a healthy dose of skepticism. While Kras, and the audience, suspect that he is part of Mabuse's operation, he is in fact an Interpol agent working undercover to unearth the secret of the Luxor Hotel.

If Mistelzweig is Kras' camouflaged counterpart, Travers' parallel persona is Marion Menil. She appears to be a damsel in distress, but is really a tool of Mabuse. Her character is a representative vision of Lang's attitude towards women. Lang had been raised Catholic, and came to see women in dichotomous terms as whores and Madonnas. Being a lusty man, though, Lang decided that whores were better than Madonnas, or at least more worthy of his attention. He populated his films with examples of the fallen woman who, like Mary Magdalene, can be redeemed through the events of the film. Marion Menil is a corrupted woman, controlled by the force of indomitable evil. Yet she is never merely a victim nor a villain. Her will has been temporarily dominated by Mabuse's, but her spirit manages to reassert itself and throw off the evil influence. She confesses all to Travers, saving his life and ruining the criminal's plot.

Mabuse foolishly and arrogantly believes that he can not only move people about like chess pawns, but that he can dictate their emotions as well. The linchpin of his master plan is that Travers will fall in love with Marion and marry her. If he succeeds in manipulating Travers' heart, though, Mabuse has overlooked the risk that Marion might genuinely fall for her target and switch allegiance altogether. We have already seen how a woman's love can be the most substantial threat to a Mabusian operation (*Spies'* Sonia; *Big Heat*'s Debby).

In some respects, though, Lang took the opportunity with *1000 Eyes* to explore some new thematic territory. In fact, the supernatural element in this film is perhaps the least of any of the Mabuse features, and certainly stands as a rational contrast to the spooky qualities with which Lang peppered his earlier Mabuse films. Lang had been an avid follower of the occult, especially in his youth. In the years since *The Testament of Dr. Mabuse*, though, Lang had become more interested in realism, and wanted to make this Mabuse film a social critique, in which Cold War nuclear fears are conflated with the cops 'n' robbers characteristics of *noir* thrillers.

Consequently, Lang downplayed the stylizations that had marked the previous Mabuse entries. Although Cornelius the psychic is a central character, his clairvoyance is a trick. The original Mabuse had the ability to hypnotize, mind-read and project his will into others. This one relies on purely technological means to create an illusion of mental powers. This, for Lang, is the real fear behind Mabuse: that modern scientific advances make a pulpy, cartoonish super-villain like Dr. Mabuse possible. The original Mabuse was a genius with a highly developed, unique mental faculty. The new Mabuse has gadgets. Interestingly, as the Mabuse series evolved without Lang, the supernatural element was added back in (to co-exist with technological trickery).

Producer Brauner, a trifle disappointed that he was getting an all-new Mabuse instead of a new-and-improved remake, wanted to bill the picture as the adventures of Dr. Mabuse's son, to establish a direct link between the old and new generations of the character. Lang rightfully saw this idea as silly and blocked it. His Mabuse was a new villain, inspired by the original legend to recreate his criminal legacy. Although no familial link appears in this or the subsequent films, Brauner went ahead and made the claim in CCC's promotional materials for *1000 Eyes*. Thanks to this, some commentary on the film—including Jean Douchet's *Cahiers du Cinema* review—incorrectly repeats the assertion that Jordan/Cornelius is the Son of Dr. Mabuse.

Mabuse's heir, be it biological or metaphorical, was played by Wolfgang Preiss, a veteran of Continental B-movies. Preiss was billed under his own name for the role of Dr. Jordan but assumed the pseudonym Lupo Prezzo for the character of Cornelius, the better to keep the audience fooled about Mabuse's split identity. The ruse worked all too well: For his article in *Film Comment*, reviewer Roger Greenspun even based some of his analysis on the mistaken belief that two different actors played Mabuse's two alter egos.

The dual role would allow Preiss the most screen time he ever enjoyed in his many years in the Mabuse series. Despite playing the title character in all of the '60s-era films, Preiss usually appeared in little more than a glorified cameo, while other actors played his various secret identities. Ironically, Preiss had generic features that could easily be concealed by makeup—Preiss could certainly be disguised much more easily and more effectively than Rudolf Klein-Rogge had been—but the filmmakers concluded that the best way to keep Mabuse's hidden personalities secret would be to engage other actors to play them. So Preiss would be shoved into the background, trotted out only in the final minutes to rip away a rubber mask.

As Inspector Kras, Gert Fröbe lent his considerable talents to the production. Although his portly frame denied him the leading man roles, Fröbe's undeniable skill and screen presence made him one of Europe's busiest character actors. He was born Karl-Gerhard Fröebe in Saxony on Christmas Day, 1912—or was it February 25, 1913? (In the world of Mabuse, it is so hard to pin such things down with any precision.) The actor later dropped the spare "e" to render his name more accessible to foreign audiences. Over the course of his extensive and prolific career, Frobe worked with top visionaries, from Fritz Lang to Orson Welles to Luchino Visconti to Georges Franju to Ingmar Bergman. Although he starred in such English-language productions as *The Longest Day* (1962) and *Those Magnificent Men in Their Flying Machines* (1965), by far and away his best-known role was the titular villain in the James Bond classic *Goldfinger* (1964).

During production on *Goldfinger*, Fröbe had objected to a scene where he gasses his enemies, worrying that such imagery would offend victims of the Holocaust. His fears were justified, because while that scene in particular raised few hackles, the ghosts of Nazi Germany would soon rise to haunt him and the film together. *Goldfinger* had opened to strong box office success in Israel when word began to spread that star, Fröbe was a former Nazi. Soon the state censors stepped in to ban the film. Producer Harry Saltzman began to panic. Israel was not only a significant territory to have to forego, but before the controversy hit, the picture had been a hit with Israeli audiences. Fröbe tried to defend his reputation. Yes, he admitted, I was a Nazi, but my mom paid my Nazi membership dues.

Such feeble entreaties got him nowhere. Who cares who paid your membership fee?, the Israeli censors replied. The point is what you believed.

All right, said Fröbe, I did support the Nazi social program, but I never actually read *Mein Kampf*.

So what?, responded the Israeli government.

So Fröbe played his trump card. I didn't want to bring this up before, but you've left me no choice, he explained. During the war I was in Vienna, where I saved a Jewish woman and her son.

And sure enough, the little boy came forward to identify Fröbe as his benefactor. Problem solved, and *Goldfinger* had its reprieve.

Now, perhaps what Fröbe said was true. Perhaps the only meaningful controversy in his life was the two-month gap between his variously stated birthdates. But it must be remembered that during the postwar reconstruction of Germany, there were any number of prominent business and political and cultural leaders who had been Nazis during the War, but had not been hardcore war criminals. Something had to be done to acknowledge the horrors of Nazism and rehabilitate the country, but to banish or prosecute all Nazis would have deprived the New Germany of almost its entire population. Somehow, some method had to be established to turn a blind eye, as it were, to overlook or forgive the Nazi past of much of Germany simply in order to move on. So it was not at all uncommon for Jews to be paid (or occasionally otherwise coerced) to name certain individuals as their saviors, so that those people could thereby be forgiven their Nazi party connections and be accepted back into civilized society. In some respects it was a reverse image of the witch hunts of HUAC: Instead of phony allegations of Communist sympathies being used to ruin people's careers, phony declarations of altruism were concocted to save people's careers. There is no reason to impugn Fröbe's reputation unnecessarily, but there is also no reason to take his claims at face value. The legacy of Nazi Germany tainted the word of many a decent man or woman, and left truth in rubble and ruins like so many bombed-out buildings.

Fröbe's co-star Peter Van Eyck had been born in Germany but naturalized as an American citizen. Although he would come to be one of postwar Germany's favorite stars, and a regular headliner for Artur Brauner's nascent studio, Van Eyck first encountered Brauner as a representative of the American film industry, an agent for Hollywood's imperial interests (see Chapter 11). He is best known to film buffs for his roles as a doomed truck driver in Henri George Clouzot's superb *Wages of Fear* (1953) and the complex East German spymaster in *The Spy Who Came In from the Cold* (1965). Despite his distinctly Teutonic features, Van Eyck would be cast as an American or an Englishman in each of his three appearances in the Mabuse series.

Like Van Eyck, Werner Peters reappeared in several future installments in different roles. While Van Eyck would recur always in heroic roles, though, Peters switched sides freely, playing good guys and bad guys with equal ease. Here, he exercises his duplicitous capabilities in the role of Heironymous Mistelzweig. As Van Eyck's love interest-cum–Mabusian secret agent Marion Menil was actress Dawn Addams. With one of the more eclectic résumés of the cast, Addams had been Charlie Chaplin's leading lady in 1957's *A King in New York*, and one of the stars of the seminal widescreen epic *The Robe* (1953), before moving on to Hammer horror in *The Two Faces of Dr. Jekyll* (1960) and *The Vampire Lovers* (1970).

As filming approached, a multi-lingual and multi-talented actor named Howard Vernon approached Lang for a role. Vernon would appear in *Alphaville* (1965), Woody Allen's *Love and Death*

Howard Vernon, here seen as Number 12, became Lang's best friend.

(1975), and would shortly star in the title role of Jess Franco's most famous concoction *The Awful Dr. Orlof* (1962). Vernon's friendship with both Franco and Lang would be one of several strange coincidences between the lives and career of the two directors. Franco once said that his close friend Vernon could have been a major star if he had tried, but that he had chosen obscurity in order to enjoy the freedom to select only the roles that appealed to him.

Had Vernon met Lang earlier, he might have won a meatier part in the film. Lang and Vernon discovered they shared much in common, and quickly became friends. (For Lang, a distrustful man given to burning bridges behind him, this friendship was an unexpected but welcome development.) With the film essentially already cast, though, the best Lang could offer Vernon was a minor role as Mabuse's assassin Number 12. Given little screen time and even fewer lines, Vernon's powerful charisma and distinctive appearance meant that this bit part became one of *1000 Eyes*' most memorable features.

To help compensate for the abbreviated role in *1000 Eyes*, Lang lobbied to win his friend a more prestigious slot in the cast of *The Secret Ways* (1961), a job Vernon desperately wanted. Vernon became one of Lang's closest confidants, and the only person he ever spoke to about the unfortunate fate of his first wife (see Chapter 2). Lang was a longtime homophobe, but when he learned that his best friend Vernon was in fact openly gay, he softened his views on the subject, asked thoughtful questions about the homosexual lifestyle, and began to regret how he had equated homosexuality with criminality in some of his past films (*The Big Heat* among them). It was a testament not only to Lang's flexibility in his old age, but to the tenderness and sincerity of his relationship with Vernon.

Recalling Lang's success with the

simultaneous filming of French- and German-language editions of *The Testament of Dr. Mabuse* back in 1932 (see Chapter 7), Artur Brauner asked his American representative Emile Lustig to seek a co-production partnership. Lang was keen on the idea of a genuine English-speaking edition, one that would have a greater chance at success in the American market, but Brauner could not afford to finance the dual shoot on his own.

Lustig found no interest in Hollywood, and turned his attention to England. A British producer would be able to provide the requisite English speaking cast at a fraction of Hollywood's prices. Since Lustig and independent producer Richard Gordon happened to be office neighbors in New York at the time, Gordon was the natural choice.

London-born Richard Gordon had immigrated to the U.S. during the 1940s with his brother Alex to work in the American film industry. While Alex went on to Hollywood to eventually help found American International Pictures, Richard settled in New York to start his own firm, Gordon Films, initially to distribute imported British pictures in the States. As he gradually began to broker international co-production deals, Richard found himself increasingly interested in producing his own features. Having achieved moderate success with such admirable low-budget endeavors as *Fiend Without a Face* (1957) and *First Man Into Space* (1959), Gordon was excited by the prospect of raising his prestige by working with such an acclaimed screen legend as Fritz Lang.

Gordon described his first encounter with Lang to *Midnight Marquee*:

> On the occasion of his first visit to my office in 1960, he appeared, on a cold and rainy day, wearing a trenchcoat with the collar turned up, a soft hat pulled down almost to his eyes, one of which was covered by the famous black patch, and when my receptionist, who did not know we expected him, asked his name, he replied, "Dr. Mabuse, of course."

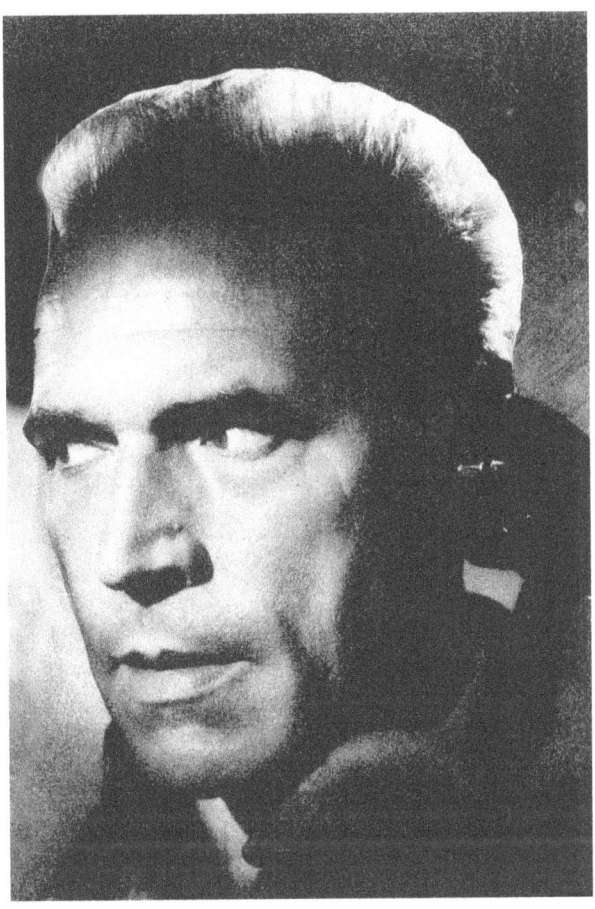

Wolfgang Preiss (a.k.a. "Lupo Prezzo") stars as the new Dr. Mabuse.

Gordon managed to interest London's Rank Studios in backing the English-language *1000 Eyes*. Actors Richard Todd and Belinda Lee were discussed as stars. Then, suddenly, the plans were scotched when Rank's executives got wind of Lang's advanced age and ailing health. Their insurance carrier refused to cover the production unless Lang agreed to have an English director on hand as a standby.

With bizarre, irrational promotion like the campaigns seen here, Lang's final film received poor distribution in the United States.

When Lang rejected that notion, Rank withdrew entirely. Gordon faded from the scene, and Lang was left to content himself with the German version alone.

Over the years that followed, Lang and Gordon remained friends and launched several unsuccessful attempts to make a film together. Although Lang never directed again after *1000 Eyes*, Gordon continued to produce or distribute low-budget shockers, among them the 1964 *Cave of the Living Dead* with Wolfgang Preiss.

Lang feared (and rightfully so) that the German-speaking *1000 Eyes* would face the same difficulties in finding an American distributor that his Indian films had. Foreign-language features faced a double-edged sword in the U.S.: American audiences derided the cartoonish quality of dubbed soundtracks, yet also resisted subtitling. To the extent a market existed (or still exists) for subtitled pictures, it was an audience disinclined towards the kind of pulpy thriller that Lang was making. The mere absence of native English speakers in the cast essentially doomed *The 1000 Eyes of Dr. Mabuse* to obscurity in America, the largest film market in the world.

Right from the beginning back in 1922, Dr. Mabuse represented Lang's penchant for personifying the problems of the world. Is your country spiraling towards fascism? Don't blame anonymous social forces, it's the doing of an evil genius. Is your latest motion picture facing distribution problems in America? Don't blame your age, your own intransigence, or the myopic tastes of American filmgoers, blame your German cast.

So with the exception of Howard Vernon, Lang voiced deep disappointment with his cast. Lotte Eisner, echoing Lang's own feelings, called them "the scum of the German film industry." That industry had changed, though, and the kind of actors Lang had been able to cast in both in his German period and in Hollywood were not the kind of actors now working in Germany. Brauner and his competitors could find success trading on the past glories of Germany's Golden Age, but these were just past glories: has-been filmmakers remaking classics. Lang was certainly no has-been, but in the eyes of his stars he was. Lang, conditioned to find slights in every interaction, grumbled that Fröbe and Preiss were disrespectful and inattentive.

If Lang felt his cast was a comedown, he hoped to compensate with the crew. On the two Indian films, Lang had planned to reunite with cinematographer Fritz Arno Wagner, his friend and collaborator on films like *M*. In the end, that had proved an elusive dream, but with *1000 Eyes* Lang managed to hire Wagner's former assistant Karl Loeb. On the art direction team Lang and Brauner brought in Erich Kettelhut, one of the greats from the days of Ufa (the same art director who had worked with Lang on the 1922 *Dr. Mabuse*, no less), and Kettelhut's current colleague Johannes Ott.

Together, this motley team of great and lesser filmmakers, friends and enemies, artists and hacks, managed to put together a film as schizophrenic as its heritage would suggest. Lang was both on unfamiliar terrain and yet still working on the same old themes. His film resurrects

Goldfinger vs. Dr. Mabuse is at least as sensible a title as *The Shadow vs. The 1000 Eyes of Dr. Mabuse*, but that isn't saying much.

Mabuse, but as a technological threat rather than a supernatural one. *The 1000 Eyes of Dr. Mabuse* is at once a B-movie thriller and a complex tapestry from a visionary artist. It appeared in theaters in 1960, to a critical reception of equal ambivalence.

The German critics still harbored an anti–Lang prejudice, and blasted *1000 Eyes* as they had the Indian films. As with the Indian films and Lang's earlier Mabuse films, the American market never really got a chance to evaluate the picture properly. Six years passed before a dubbed edition appeared in the United States, more for television broadcasts than a serious theatrical issue. Its "premiere" in New York occurred in 1973, a full 13 years after its creation and just in time to greet the first appearance of Lang's *Testament of Dr. Mabuse*, 41 years after its date of manufacture.

However, *1000 Eyes* turned out to be a popular hit in Germany, and a critical success in France. French critics were already in the process of lionizing Lang, and found *1000 Eyes* to be a perfect coda to Lang's stellar career.

That it would be Lang's swan song was not immediately evident. Brauner knew that the box office receipts from *1000 Eyes* demanded a sequel, and asked the 70-year-old director to take on the franchise. Lang's relationship with Brauner was rapidly souring, though (a recurring cycle in Lang's dealings with his producers). The more Brauner reined in Lang, to avoid the kind of excess that marked the Indian films, the more resentful Lang grew. Lang saw Brauner as a no-talent huckster exploiting his name and reputation. Every interaction with Brauner, no matter how innocent, became a source of strife. Before long, the once-partnership between filmmakers had devolved into an acrimonious dispute over royalties. They never worked together again, and Lang never directed another film.

The director had become obsessed with the fear that *M* was his one and only great work, and that the only way to redeem his legacy was to acquire unfettered creative autonomy. The promise of such freedom had brought Lang and Brauner together, but the misfit between their definitions of creative control drove them apart again. Lang later claimed that his only purpose in directing *1000 Eyes* was to persuade some producer to once again grant him total control.

The world had changed, though. Motion pictures had grown more costly, the markets increasingly dominated by Hollywood. Brauner's offer was not unreasonable, and Lang had much to be proud of in *1000 Eyes*. Lang's inflexible notions of the working conditions he required, and how he would evaluate his success, prevented him from appreciating the full scope of his achievement.

Instead, the aging director traveled the world, writing scripts for movies that would never get made and speaking at film festivals to a new generation of fans.

While Lang kept looking futilely for a chance to make another *M*, Brauner kept on making more *Mabuse*s.

CHAPTER 10

German Trash Cinema: The Story of Artur Brauner

> When I was five or six years old, I saw some of Fritz Lang's films: *Dr. Mabuse, Metropolis, The Nibelungen*, and I was fascinated, especially with *Mabuse*. I decided when I was, as best as I remember, fifteen or sixteen years old that I would somehow, how should I put it, engage Mabuse, in entirety.
> —Artur Brauner

In 1960, the year of *The 1000 Eyes of Dr. Mabuse*, the German film industry was in a state of crisis. What had already been a small circle of underfunded studios cranking out a limited number of low-budget films, was now in danger of total collapse. Many studios were forced out of business altogether, many others merged to pool their sparse resources. The bankruptcy of so many companies put the screws on the banks: Those producers who remained in business would find it nearly impossible now to borrow money. The result was fewer films, lower budgets and a concerted effort to minimize risks all around.

A few years into the crisis, producer Artur Brauner made a dramatic proposal. Brauner offered to single-handedly "save" the German film industry by establishing a new branch of his successful CCC Studio dedicated to making art films. As Brauner saw it, the reasons filmmakers were not pushing the artistic envelope were largely economic. With producers and financiers in a crunch, the opportunities for innovative risk-taking were all but non-existent. Using the same logic that Hollywood would employ several decades later with the founding of such divisions as Sony Pictures Classics and Fox Searchlight, Brauner's CCC-Kunstfilm was to produce a small number of modestly budgeted art films financed with the profits from the main CCC-Film studio, which would continue to pursue mainstream commercial success. Brauner boasted that if his initiative failed to revive the German cinema "in the coming days," he would resign and close his studio's doors.

His pronouncement was greeted with almost uniform skepticism. Some critics derided Brauner for confusing "artistic quality" with "cheap"; others insisted German cinema had no need of anything new; and others questioned Brauner's choice of seeking out and promoting unproven new talent. And then there were those who said that Brauner himself was the cause of the industry's woes and that he had no right seeking to "save" the film business that he had driven into the gutter in the first place. Who does this Artur Brauner think he is?

In his essay *Herrschaft des Verbrechens*

("Empire of Crime"), film scholar Hans Schmid wrote:

> In John Ford's *The Searchers* (1956), John Wayne tells the story of a White man who rides his horse until it's on the brink of death, and then proceeds on foot. A Comanche comes along and finds the horse, and manages to get it on its feet again. He rides it another twenty miles, and then eats it. The film journalist Joe Hembus wrote of Artur Brauner's role in the 1960s that he was the Comanche of German cinema.

Hembus' cruel comparison referred to Brauner's tactic of hiring has-beens of the once great German film industry—directors like Fritz Lang, Robert Siodmak and William Dieterle who had emigrated to Hollywood and already fulfilled the promise of their careers. Hoping to revive the German cinema, Brauner wooed these men back across the ocean to helm low-budget programmers, milking the promotional value of their well-known names for all they were worth.

Brauner had built his CCC-Film GmbH into a powerhouse in European filmmaking with the regular manufacture and exploitation of situation comedies, musicals, pulpy crime thrillers, sequels and remakes. He had played a vital and extensive role in the rebuilding of Germany's film industry; he was the first to make a film in postwar Germany, and rose to become the most commercially successful producer in all of postwar Europe. But the industry he built bore little resemblance to the one that existed in the Golden Years of the 1920s and '30s. No matter how many oldtimers Brauner dug up, no matter how many classics of the bygone era he remade, the world of CCC-Film GmbH was a world of play-it-safe commercialism. The world of Fritz Lang, G.W. Pabst and F.W. Murnau seemed farther away with each passing day.

This would be the legacy of Artur Brauner. As would happen time and again throughout the history of film, commercial success was bought at a price to one's artistic reputation. For everything that Brauner did to revive and reinvigorate German cinema, he would be forever regarded as a glorified P.T. Barnum. But this is not the real Artur Brauner, it is just a public image—a shadow man concealing the real deal behind the curtain, behind the loudspeaker. The true story of Artur Brauner is messier and more complex. It is the story of a man who struggled mightily with the same conflict between art and commerce that frustrated all of the players in this book. If Brauner's choices differed from those of Fritz Lang or Jess Franco or Claude Chabrol, it may have had something to do with the peculiar set of social, political and economic situations in which Brauner found himself.

Next to Fritz Lang and Norbert Jacques, Brauner is one of Mabuse's three "fathers." He placed his stamp on no fewer than seven of the 12 pictures discussed in this book, and worked with eight of the nine directors in question. He brought the Mabuse legacy out of the Nazi era and into the Cold War. He has been variously known as Artur Brauner, or Atze Brauner, or Art Bern, or Art Bernd. But who was he?

The most powerful film producer in postwar Europe was born in Lodz, Poland, on August 1, 1918, just a few short months before the German Revolution that created the Weimar Republic. The oldest of five children, he showed an aptitude for music at a very young age. But it was the cinema that attracted him the most; he hung photos of Tarzan and the cowboy heroes of American Westerns over his bed. As a small boy, one film in particular got under his skin. It was Fritz Lang's *Dr. Mabuse.*

"It was the first true gangster film,

From left to right: **Fritz Lang, Debra Paget, and Artur Brauner.**

garnished with every delicacy that would then become typical of this genre: the clattering of the machine guns, the use of cars as tools as murder, trains racing through the night, witnesses who die under mysterious circumstances, and so on. Today a matter of course, but back then a monstrous, completely illicit sensation," Brauner recalled later. "And who among the family fathers in Lodz thought something of himself, would take care to lock up his sons during the run of these films to save them from the influence of this super-gangster, this arch-criminal Mabuse with the thousand faces. But you see, I had my rope ladder."

When he was a teenager, Artur saw Lang's *Testament of Dr. Mabuse* and experienced an epiphany. This film spoke deeply to him. He knew then that somehow, Dr. Mabuse was his destiny. He was inspired to become a filmmaker.

When he was 19, Artur Brauner traveled to the Mideast with a group of young Jews. He was increasingly aware of European anti–Semitism, and thinking about where in the world people of his faith could feel safe. While this would lead him later to become a vocal supporter of Israel, for the time being such havens would remain fantasies. When he was 21, Germany invaded Poland.

The Nazi Occupation interred his family in a ghetto. He was forced to wear the identifying star, the first of many humiliations and horrors yet to come. During the course of the war, some 50 of his relatives were murdered. He and his brother Wolf survived to reunite with the rest of his immediate family when the Red Army defeated the Germans.

There were those in his family who decided simply to get away, to the United

States perhaps. Certainly Artur felt the pull of Hollywood. But along with his brother Wolf and a young lady named Maria Therese Albert (whose family had been killed in the concentration camps), he decided to settle in Berlin instead. Partly, he hoped to play a part in rebuilding and de-Nazifying Germany, to help clean away the institutional evils and prejudices that had victimized his family in the first place. Partly, he recognized a rare opportunity in the rubble of postwar Berlin to establish himself as a major player, something that would have been impossible in the competitive environment of Hollywood. Like Dr. Mabuse, he found profit in chaos. And finally, there was the old saying that to live well is the best revenge: If he could become rich and powerful in Berlin, the very heart of the place that had tried to exterminate him and his family and his people, then he would have triumphed indeed.

To establish himself as a movie mogul, though, Brauner would first have to contend with the Orwellian bureaucracy of occupied Berlin. During the Nazi years, Goebbels and his cronies operated the film industry as a direct adjunct of Hitler's government. Cinema was explicitly propaganda to promote Nazism. Consequently, the four Allies assumed control of the German film industry as part of the overall de-Nazification program. Nevertheless, each of the various occupying forces took a slightly different stance. France and England had a relatively laissez-faire approach. The Soviets decided to aggressively pursue a revival of the film industry precisely to continue its propaganda function, only now with socialist values as the message. By sharp contrast, the United States wanted to suppress the local industry as much as possible in order to keep Germany a wide-open market for the import of Hollywood's films.

In order to produce films in Berlin, a prospective company had to obtain a license from the military force occupying that sector. Brauner's desired location happened to fall in the American zone, but the U.S. military wished to keep the domestic cinema weak and therefore made it exceptionally difficult for any producers to obtain film permits.

Brauner was a young man, just 28 years old. He had neither a license to film nor any experience with filmmaking. What he did have was desire, and money. So in September 1946 he founded the Central Cinema Company (CCC Films) in the American sector of Berlin. He got around the license dilemma by collaborating with a licensed studio in another sector, Studio 45 in the English zone, using their aegis to legitimize his involvement. Brauner sold his mother-in-law's fur coat on the black market and funneled the money into the very first film made in postwar Germany: *Sag die Wahrheit* ("Tell the Truth").

Despite the provocative title, the film was entirely unpolitical, a comedy about a man who can only speak the truth and thus ends up in an asylum (not far off from the 1997 Jim Carrey film *Liar Liar*). Critics blasted it as pointless froth, and asked whether in such historic times the first film of this new era should have some real substance. Brauner learned an important lesson on this inaugural project, because despite such grousing *Sag die Wahrheit* turned out to be successful. Critics are one thing, Brauner learned, and audiences are quite another.

Nevertheless, Brauner agreed with what the critics said. He knew he was pandering to the lowest common denominator, but he had a larger purpose in mind. He wanted to depict the horrors of the Holocaust and the Nazi reign of terror on the screen, to truly "tell the truth" about what he had lived through, but to do so properly he needed more money than he

Artur Brauner consults with Fritz Lang, his star director.

could get hocking fur coats. He intended to work up to his Holocaust film, *Morituri* ("Mortuary"), in stages by producing commercially successful if less ambitious features first. So, on the heels of *Sag die Wahrheit*, CCC produced *Herzkoenig* ("King of Hearts"), a lightweight musical comedy. This time he circumvented the license problem by paying 5 percent of his receipts to Ernst Liepelt, a producer in the French sector, for the rights to use Liepelt's name as the "official" producer of a film Liepelt otherwise had nothing to do with.

In 1947, Brauner felt himself ready to undertake *Morituri*. This was to be his most personal film, a dramatization of his own wartime experiences and attitudes. And if Brauner was only the film's producer, not its director, he considered himself its ultimate auteur. Throughout his career, Brauner placed his stamp on the films he produced so definitively that whether he wrote the screenplay or not (which he sometimes did under pseudonyms), he knew that they would always be first and foremost *his* films.

One major roadblock still stood in the way of *Morituri*, however: the Allied powers. It enraged Brauner that these hypocritical occupying forces would not support his anti–Nazi picture, that they would actively stymie his efforts and then make grandiose proclamations that the war had been to benefit people like him. Hah, he thought. With or without the permission of the authorities, Brauner was going to tell the truth about Hitler.

However, this time Liepelt was not interested in lending his name, so Brauner's lack of a permit became a critical issue. The producer met with the representative of the U.S. Military, Peter Van Eyck, to see if they could find some common ground.

Yes, this was the same Peter Van Eyck who would later quit the U.S. Film Office to join Brauner's company as a movie star. The same Peter Van Eyck who would square off against Dr. Mabuse in *The 1000 Eyes of Dr. Mabuse* (1960), *Scotland Yard vs. Dr. Mabuse* (1963) and *The Death Ray of Dr. Mabuse* (1964). The same Peter Van Eyck who back in 1945, speaking on behalf of the U.S. occupying forces, had warned filmmaker Wolfgang Staudte that the Germans had better not think about making any films for the next 20 years if they knew what was good for them.

In fact, Wolfgang Staudte had traveled Artur Brauner's path before him. Staudte had a script for an anti–Nazi film that he had shopped around Berlin at the end of the war. There was little interest, in part because local producers sensed that German audiences had no desire to see the ugliness of the recent past exposed on the screen; lighthearted pabulum of the *Sag die Wahrheit* variety was far preferable to actually telling the truth. But the Americans' imperialistic protection of Hollywood's interests angered Staudte, and he approached the Soviets. From their perspective, Staudte's proposal was an ideal vehicle with which to begin their campaign to wash away the Nazi influences in their sector. So the very first anti–Nazi film made in Europe, *Die Mörder sind unter uns* ("Murders Among Us") was produced in the Russian zone in the old Ufa studios. Ironically, the title was almost identical to the title Fritz Lang had originally selected for *M*, but which had been rejected for its apparent anti–Nazi connotation.

Brauner also turned to the Soviets for the support that the Americans would not give. As with Staudte's film, Brauner found the Soviet authorities very receptive to his anti-fascist ideas and easily won their approval. Brauner's team spent much of the year rebuilding decimated concentration camps in the Russian zone for use as locations. To play up the A-list prestige of the project, and not incidentally to obtain the best possible quality for this most personal of his undertakings, Brauner set to assembling a team of former luminaries from the pre–Nazi film era. This would be the genesis of his trademark approach, hiring back the "names" of Germany's Golden Age of cinema to boost marquee value and to revive that classic look and style.

The epic *Morituri*, though, turned out to be a noble failure. His production team, packed as it was with ex–silent film greats, leaned too heavily of creaky old silent film techniques. The script itself was overwrought and obvious. But the greatest liability of all was not in the film itself but in the culture, for even if *Morituri* had been the unassailable classic Brauner had hoped it to be, there was nothing he could do to force it down a reluctant public's throat. The Soviets could approve as many anti–Nazi films as they wanted, but the German people simply did not want to watch them.

In a 1962 interview, Brauner explained, "We don't like self-criticism—not political, not social, and not personal. The people here don't want to see reality, or it must be depicted as rosy. Problems can only be shown when they're untruthful, or minimized."

The critics, who just a few short years earlier had chided Brauner for producing films without substance, now announced that the time had *already* passed for such films, and that in 1948 it was too late to be rehashing the sins of the past. Audiences demanded their money back. Some jeered so loudly at screenings that theater managers often canceled shows.

Brauner had no regrets about his choice—he had made *Morituri* out of a sense of personal moral obligation—but he also knew he would not attempt anything like it again. Between *Sag die Wahrheit* and *Morituri*, Brauner had seen what his future held: Forget the critics, give the public what it wants.

The tension between the American and Soviet sectors was much grander, much more dangerous, than a trifling disagreement over the local film industry. In the context of the events of June 24, 1948, the complaints over Peter Van Eyck's official position would pale. Suddenly, the Cold War hit full on, and the Soviets blockaded Berlin, resulting in U.S. airlifts of supplies into Western Berlin.

Many producers decided that the Cold War was bad for business — who knew when the Russians would seal them in forever? — and vacated to reestablish their studios in other cities. Brauner cautiously opened branches of CCC in Hamburg and Geiselgasteig, just in case, but stubbornly stayed behind in Berlin. This had been his chosen home, after all, and it would take a lot more than a paltry blockade to scare him off. He figured that if Stalin were to ever to try to take Berlin, he would risk total war, and that was unlikely, even for a madman like Stalin. The USSR had already lost 20,000,000 in the war with Germany, and Stalin would be reluctant to deliberately sacrifice more. Brauner knew that eventually the blockade would end, and Germans would once again turn to rebuilding Berlin, and there he'd be, already established and right in the heart of it all.

Brauner kept moving forward with his efforts to obtain official permission from the Americans to be in the film business. He turned to Erich Pommer, the brilliant producer behind so many of Fritz Lang's classics, for help. Brauner had to temporarily relocate CCC to the English sector, but Pommer was able to improve relations with the U.S. military over the next two years. Ultimately, thanks to Pommer's diplomacy, Brauner returned CCC to its original home, with the necessary papers signed and approved by the American officials.

For its part, though, the United States had effectively crippled the local film industry. Most pictures shown in Germany were foreign, and most of those came from Hollywood. Of the films produced in Germany, most were produced by foreign producers. Almost all of the money flowing through the German film industry was therefore ending up in foreign hands. It became a political issue, especially for the Christian Democratic Party, to rebuild German cinema to its glory days of the 1920s and '30s.

Of course, that was impossible. The U.S. had forbidden the kind of vertical monopolies that had made Ufa great. German-made films were at a competitive disadvantage even in Germany, with such theatrical domination by Hollywood imports. Producers simply could not afford to take risks. Making fluffy popular films became a necessity simply in order to nurture the economic infrastructure of studios and develop a local audience that could, perhaps later down the line, support more adventuresome or controversial filmmaking.

With his experience on *Morituri*, Brauner understood well the conflict. "Back then, the German film industry had financial security, which meant it could afford to experiment," Brauner told the magazine *Bunte* in 1958. "If a film did poorly with audiences, the producers had the opportunity to make back their losses through two or three more conventional films. That is no longer true."

Consequently, CCC led the pack in making low-risk films: comedies, lurid crime thrillers known as "krimis," musicals, romances, war films and, whenever possible, remakes and sequels galore. To maintain an air of artistic endeavor,

Brauner wooed back such former lights as director Robert Siodmak, cinematographer Fritz Arno Wagner, star Lil Dagover. He also promoted the new stars of German film: Peter Van Eyck (now an actor after leaving his job with the U.S. Film Office in 1950), Dieter Borsche, O.E. Hasse and Gert Fröbe—all of whom would star in the Mabuse series to come. By following this proven formula, Brauner quickly turned CCC into the most successful studio in continental Europe.

His new stars were local heroes only, though, with little international appeal. Even the former Ufa greats he so studiously sought out often had minimal name recognition outside Germany. To reach audiences abroad, Brauner decided it best to remake classics that had previously enjoyed international success.

Through all of this, Brauner's holy grail was to lure back Fritz Lang, the greatest name in German cinema, bar none. Lang's creepy visions of horror and suspense had originally inspired Brauner to work in films, and he wanted nothing more than to somehow find a way to work with the Great Herr Lang. In 1954 Brauner was beginning work on an ambitious film about the real-life 1944 assassination attempt on Hitler's life. Anxious not to let another *Morituri* happen on his watch, Brauner was keen to assemble top-flight talent for this major project. He commissioned a screenplay from a man with the right anti-fascist credentials, Jochen Huth, who had fled Hitler to work at a factory in America. Now the question was to choose a director with marquee value who would understand the subject matter. Brauner asked New York–based agent Paul Kohner for advice, and Kohner agent recommended Edgar G. Ulmer for the job. Instead, Brauner saw his opportunity, and telegrammed Fritz Lang.

Lang showed interest in the project and asked to see the script. Brauner miscalculated, though, and had approached Lang too late in the cycle of pre-production; there simply was not enough time for the elaborate courtship ritual Lang would demand from Brauner. Instead, Falk Harnack would helm *Der 20 Juli*. Nevertheless, Brauner had planted a seed, and he would now be able to water and fertilize that seed over the next few years. At the time, Lang was still a major Hollywood director, and there was nothing Brauner could offer to compete with that kind of prestige or money. But a year later, when Lang walked off the set of *Beyond a Reasonable Doubt* in disgust (see Chapter 8), the director was suddenly adrift, and therefore more receptive to Brauner's entreaties.

The key to Lang's soul was his vanity, and to win him over Brauner knew he would need to stroke the man's ego. "You are a great artist," Brauner told Lang. "You know that you are an extraordinarily talented director, that the public loves your films and the critics do as well, that you have made the most important films in Germany, before Hitler, and for that I respect you, but even more so because you left Hitler's Germany and would not cooperate with the Nazis."

The great Fritz Lang could not be seen to *need* the CCC job, he would have to be won over with just the right script in order to preserve his self-image. It just so happened that the hand of Fate intervened serendipitously, and without even realizing it Brauner offered Lang exactly the right film.

Vaguely, Brauner knew that Lang's ex-wife Thea von Harbou had written the script to the two-part Indian epic *The Indian Tomb/The Tiger of Eschnapur*, but he was otherwise ignorant of the importance this had in Lang's past (see Chapters 2 and 10). Brauner proposed to Lang that he come over to Berlin to direct a remake, simply thinking it made sense to pair Germany's greatest filmmaker with such a classic project. To Lang, though, it was a once-in-a-lifetime second chance, to reclaim the film that Joe May had stolen from him so many years ago.

Although Brauner was thrilled to be working with his idol Lang, the producer entered the game with his eyes wide open. "The film community naturally warned me about Fritz Lang," Brauner recalled in an interview for French TV. "They explained everything: there was no question that Fritz Lang had driven Ufa into bankruptcy, and that no one had ever been able to work with him, that he is a dictator, that he can work absolutely heartlessly, and that he doesn't care if he ruins the studio along the way or not. That was Fritz Lang."

Although Brauner had been sufficiently warned, and had hired Lang knowing full well his reputation as a perfectionist spendthrift, there were still the inevitable battles between Lang and his producers over budgets and shooting schedules; the kind of bickering that had now become de rigueur for a Lang film. Through it all, the producer who had built his empire on low-budget filmmaking steeled himself stoically. He had fought so hard to bring Fritz Lang into CCC's stable precisely because of the man's unique vision. Brauner had to trust that Lang knew how to spend the money wisely, that the exorbitant production costs would result in a motion picture he could feel proud of.

So the immensely hostile reactions by German critics to the two Indian films hit Brauner and Lang especially hard. Brauner was used to being on the wrong side of the critical establishment, but he had hoped that the name "Fritz Lang" would insulate him on this particular project. Lang became so disillusioned and despondent as a result of the critical trashing he received that he told Brauner he would leave Germany and never work there again.

Brauner would hear none of it. He realized that the critical response had almost nothing to do with the content of the films themselves but constituted instead a venting of personal invective against Lang himself. Even during his heyday, Lang had been a figure more respected than liked. His sadistic personality had generated far more enemies than allies over the years. And there was another thing.

From the perspective of Brauner or Lang's colleagues in Hollywood, the director's celebrated defection from Nazi Germany in 1933 had been a principled act—some in the U.S. had even taken Lang to task for not leaving Germany sooner, for staying too cozy with the Nazi officials before his departure. However, from the point of view of the German critics, Lang's exit took on an entirely different cast. For whatever their own positions had been on the Nazi agenda—be it in part, in whole, or not at all—they had nevertheless chosen to stay behind. In his words and deeds, Lang had proclaimed himself better than them. Why, he had even announced that the lot of them deserved to be blown away by A-bombs! Here was a chance for them to take Herr Lang down a notch.

Brauner pleaded with Lang. Sure we fought over the budget, he said, but that comes with the territory. All in all we worked efficiently and professionally together, why throw that away? The German critics may have panned the Indian films—but the German public is eating them up—these are highly commercially successful films. You still have your fans after all. And listen to what those Nouvelle Vague guys over in France are saying. They're calling the Indian films some of the best works of cinema ever—isn't that exactly the praise you felt had been stolen from you by Joe May all those years ago?

In the end, Brauner persuaded Lang

CENTRAL-CINEMA-COMP.
FILM GmbH
STUDIOS UND PRODUKTION

Herrn

Norbert Jaques
Schlachters bei Lindau /B

BERLIN-SPANDAU
VERLÄNGERTE DAUMSTRASSE 16
TELEFON SAMMEL-NR. **37 41 21**
BANKKONTO BERLINER BANK AG
KURFÜRSTENDAMM 62, KTO. 82 087
POSTSCHECK BERLIN-WEST 119 39
TEL.-ADR. CE CE CE FILM BERLIN

Ihre Zeichen	Ihre Nachricht vom	Unsere Zeichen	Tag
trifft Dr. Mabuse		ab/1a	29.9.53

Sehr geehrter Herr Jaques!

In Beantwortung Ihres Schreibens vom 23.9. teilen wir Ihnen mit - damit eine absolute Klarheit in Bezug auf unsere Anfrage besteht - dass uns nicht am Roman "Dr. Mabuse, der Spieler" oder "Das Testament des Dr. Mabuse" liegt, sondern an der Figur des Dr. Mabuse selbst, die zweifellos, abgesehen von dem bestehenden Roman und vergebenen Filmrechten, Ihnen gehört. Wir wären Ihnen deshalb dankbar, wenn Sie uns mitteilen würden, was Sie für die Figur des Dr. Mabuse fordern; mit anderen Worten: Die CCC-Film erwirbt von Herrn Norbert Jaques gegen eine Summe von DM ..... das uneingeschränkte Recht zur Benutzung der Figur des Dr. Mabuse, die seine eigene Erfindung darstellt.

In Erwartung Ihrer umgehende Antwort begrüssen wir Sie

mit vorzüglicher Hochachtung
Central - Cinema - Comp
Film G. m. b. H.

The contract transferring ownership of the Dr. Mabuse character from creator Norbert Jacques to Artur Brauner.

to direct at least one more movie. If the two Indian films had been Brauner's way of indulging Lang, this time the producer wanted to be indulged. It was time, he decided, to pay his respect to the man who got him into cinema in the first place. It was time to revive Dr. Mabuse.

Back in 1953, Brauner had taken the steps of licensing from Norbert Jacques all relevant rights to the name, character and extant stories of Mabuse. Brauner had done nothing with those rights for years, perhaps because he was in the process of luring Lang across the sea and he knew that if he could manage it, nothing would be more apt than to pair Mabuse with the filmmaker who gave him life. Lang was not interested in remaking *The Testament of Dr. Mabuse*, though, and was only on board if a new, modern update could be developed.

Like the Indian films before it, 1960's *The 1000 Eyes of Dr. Mabuse* faced universal critical antagonism in Germany. That it, again, received overwhelming popular support and kudos from the French critics did not soften Lang's disappointment. He had tried to come home but did not find the open welcoming arms he wanted. Lang and Brauner went their separate ways, and Lang never directed another film. Brauner continued to hold Lang in very high regard, knowing that the opinions of the critics meant nothing. As the 20th century drew to a close, Brauner could look back on a prolific and successful career; he had produced or helped to produce nearly 300 motion pictures. Of them all, he considered the three by Fritz Lang to be the greatest—artistic triumphs, box office hits and enduring classics that continued to garner new fans and admirers decades later.

The success of *The 1000 Eyes of Dr. Mabuse* had been so great, Brauner quickly launched a series of sequels that kept the franchise going for many years. In 1960, he could ill afford to let such a cash cow go by without milking it dry. Nineteen sixty was the year of the Crisis.

In 1960, the already tentative German film industry was imploding rapidly. Theaters were closing, studios going out of business, German films bombing at the box office at home and abroad. As in the rest of the world, television posed a serious competitive threat, but in Germany the film industry had so little with which to fight back. In the summer of 1961, the Berlin Wall went up, exacerbating the crisis even further by posing the serious threat that someday soon Berlin's borders might close forever.

The economic crisis thus provoked, or aggravated, an artistic one. Films became more predictable, more conventional, cheaper looking and less original. It was in this environment that Artur Brauner stepped up to make his controversial proposal. He had been inspired by the French Nouvelle Vague, which had reinvigorated a tired French film industry with an influx of young directors who could make internationally successful art films on limited budgets. Hoping to spark the same kind of development in Germany, Brauner started with the name. He called his movement the Riskante Welle, or "Risky Wave." As Brauner saw it, the problem with German films was the inability to take risks. If he could set aside money from his more conventional productions to finance films that did not need to worry about the bottom line, he hoped to encourage the kind of artistic experimentation that had flourished in the Golden Age of the 1920s and '30s, and that now flourished in France. In 1962, Brauner launched CCC-Kunstfilm, with the mission of producing three films on a year on a set budget which, by being low, he could afford to lose. CCC-Kunstfilm was supposed to discover and promote new, young talents both in front of and behind the cameras. To get the thing started, Brauner hand-selected the first three screenplays.

As with so many of Brauner's most personal ventures, CCC-Kunstfilm was greeted with skepticism and hostility by the German film establishment. The first three films Brauner chose were made, released to an indifferent public, flopped and were forgotten as quickly as if Brauner had simply dropped coins into the Rhine. All that came of Brauner's noble mission to save German cinema was that CCC-Kunstfilm switched over to sex films.

Brauner's success in the crisis years of the '60s was not to do with "risk," but with the tried and true. While so many of his peers went under, Brauner found prosperity with Dr. Mabuse, Sherlock Holmes, a third remake of *Donovan's Brain*, teen flicks with German pop stars, Edgar Wallace thrillers, remakes and sequels.

In the 1970s, long after Brauner's proposal had been forgotten and CCC had settled into a comfortable rut of exploitation films, a real German New Wave did in fact emerge. Directors like Werner Herzog, Rainer Werner Fassbinder, Volker Schlöndorff, Wim Wenders and Ulrike Ottinger (see also Chapter 19) set out to make artistically challenging and unique films that fought against what they perceived as the trashy character of contemporary German cinema. Ironically, the only reason the industry had survived and prospered enough to nurture their experimental digressions was because it had stayed so conventional, so trashy.

They owed it all to Brauner. He had revived the decimated industry after the War and kept it alive during its darkest days. He managed to do so while simultaneously struggling against the oppositions of the American military, the conflicting tastes of the German audiences and critics, and the economic and political crises of the '60s. Perhaps he had not made the most memorable or most artistically satisfying of films, but he had made the right films for the time and paved the way for the future.

In his own way, Artur Brauner did save German cinema.

CHAPTER 11

The Return of Dr. Mabuse

> The name Mabuse is just a personification of criminality. It seeks for power and is motivated by megalomania.
> —the Reverend Briefenstein

The anxious little man sits alone in his train compartment, his briefcase handcuffed to his wrist. The door to the compartment opens, and a traveler tries to enter. Nervously bringing his briefcase closer to his chest, the first man gruffly announces that his compartment is closed; the intruder had best seek another place to sit. Wearily, the intruder points to his wooden leg and asks for compassion. Feeling pangs of guilt struggling against his natural suspicion, the little man apologizes to the cripple and offers him a seat.

The following morning, the anxious little man's body will be found in a ditch, his briefcase—and its contents, documents incriminating the Chicago Mafia—removed.

The Return of Dr. Mabuse opens with a sequence familiar to fans of Fritz Lang, yet another reworking of the great train robbery that Lang had himself borrowed from Louis Feuillade and adapted over and over again in *Dr. Mabuse the Gambler, Spies* and *Ministry of Fear*. But despite appearances, this was not A Fritz Lang Film; he had retired from directing after *The 1000 Eyes of Dr. Mabuse*. Lang may not have wanted the Mabuse films to continue, but the choice was not his to make. Whatever other characteristics Mabuse and Lang may have shared, Lang could not control the wills of others. Dr. Mabuse would return, *The Nibelungen* would be remade and the corpse of Germany's Golden Age would be dug back up and displayed in all its rotting glory whether Herr Lang liked it or not. He could opt himself out of Artur Brauner's plans, but his place in the grand scheme of things was fungible. If Lang would not cooperate, his low-rent doppelgänger Dr. Harald Reinl would.

The name Harald Reinl is essentially unknown outside of Germany, but that obscurity conceals his true importance to film history. Where Artur Brauner was the most commercially successful producer in postwar Germany, Reinl was the most commercially successful director. He could crank out by-the-numbers genre pictures in any by-the-numbers genre you care to mention. For all the worst, most exploitative, least imaginative aspects of Germany's postwar film industry, he was its finest practitioner. It may not have been a legacy most filmmakers would aspire to, but it must also be said that Reinl possessed a genuine talent and visual flair. If

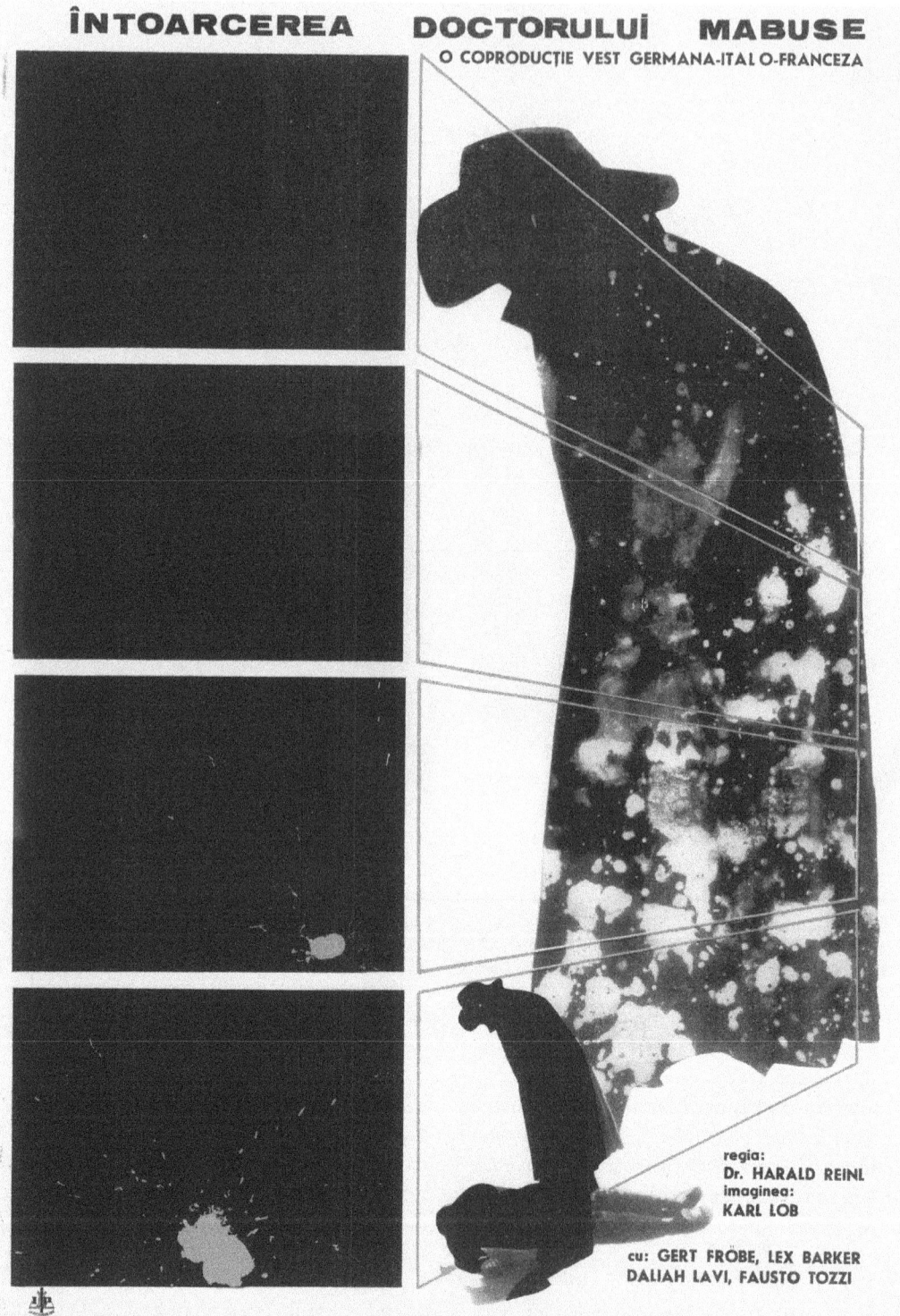

This lovely Romanian poster is as much a work of art in itself as it is a piece of commercial advertising.

his films were derivative and routine, they were also superbly crafted, thrilling entertainment.

Reinl retooled the Mabuse genre he inherited from Lang. Discarding any pretensions to art, he rebuilt it as a franchise, with an easy-to-follow formula. And his contributions were significant: Lang directed three Mabuse films, Reinl two. In addition to codifying a set of genre conventions and iconography for Brauner's Mabuse programs, Reinl also, whether by design or accident, altered its political subtext. By degrees, the Nazi metaphors which had dominated Lang's approach would be shoved into the background in favor of more contemporary Cold War concerns: nuclear holocaust, technology run amok, mind control.

Which is not to say that the specter of Hitler had completely passed. In fact, the climax of *Return of Dr. Mabuse* invokes some of the most direct and obvious Nazi imagery of all the Mabuse films: a ruthless megalomaniac inspires a fascist uprising in Germany from his prison cell. In the closing minutes of the film, Führer Mabuse leads an army of mindless soldiers, each slavishly devoted to Mabuse's deranged ideology. However, while Norbert Jacques, Fritz Lang and Artur Brauner had found in Mabuse a venue to voice their respective oppositions to Hitler's evil, Mabuse's new "father" could claim no such anti-fascist credentials. Harald Reinl was a man with a past.

He was born in 1908 to Hans and Ida Reinl, and studied law at Innsbruck. His twin brother Kurt became a lawyer, but Harald hemmed and hawed, unconvinced that government work was his destiny. As he was a world champion skier, Reinl bided his time and paid the bills as a ski instructor, waiting for inspiration to strike.

Enter Arnold Fanck, a pioneering spirit in German cinema in the 1930s. In pointed contrast to the eerie forebodings that directors like Fritz Lang were envisioning, Fanck was a leading light of an entirely different breed of film: the Heimatfilm. The word translates as "film about home." There is no equivalent to this curiously German genre in Hollywood's lexicon; its best known example on these shores would be the kitschy, maudlin *Heidi* (1937). To Americans, the very idea of a film whose sole purpose is to romanticize the rustic countryside must seem painfully quaint, naive. But in a nation with countryside as awesome as Germany's truly is, and in the early days of the Third Reich when overweening pride in the Fatherland was an end in itself, Fanck and his followers were very popular indeed. Fanck asked ace skier Reinl if he would be willing to ski around for Fanck's cameras for some of his upcoming mountaineering pictures. Sure, said Reinl, and a partnership was born. During the 1930s, Reinl skied up and down a variety of mountains for several of Fanck's films, and gradually came to provide some technical assistance to the crew as well. By the end of the decade, he was working on documentaries with a group of ex-colleagues of Fanck's.

None of this could really be called a career, though, and Reinl found himself under pressure from his family to start putting his law degree to some practical use. And then in 1940 came a chance encounter with Leni Riefenstahl, fascist filmmaker extraordinaire. She too had ties to Fanck, having learned the craft of cinema under his tutelage. Indeed, she had starred with Reinl in Fanck's *Stürme Über dem Mont Blank* (1930), so the two had crossed paths before. Reinl admitted to her that he really wanted to work in films instead, but felt he had no choice. Riefenstahl asked him if he would quit law altogether if she would hire him on the spot as her assistant director. Reinl pointed out that he had no practical experience. From what she had seen of his skills, said she, Reinl had innate talent. That's what counts most, she told him; technical skills you can learn but talent is in the blood.

And if there was anyone in German film thinking about issues of blood and lineage, it was Leni Riefenstahl. She had made a name for herself with two classic documentaries, *Triumph of the Will* (1934), about Hitler's Nazi rally in Nuremberg, and *Olympia* (1938), covering the 1936 Berlin Olympics. In later years, some would charge that she had been Hitler's mistress. Her standard reply: I only made movies for him.

Her latest project, *Tiefland*, was to be her most personal picture, in that it had been her idea from the start, as opposed to being commissioned by Goebbels for a specific propaganda purpose. Reinl happily joined her team as assistant director. It was a fruitful partnership for both. Riefenstahl greatly appreciated having Reinl's company both as a creative collaborator and as a friend; Reinl learned filmmaking from a master.

Riefenstahl was undeniably a master, an innovator, an artist of the highest order. She was also a Nazi. It was a taint she could never escape. Fritz Lang had fled Nazism all the way to America, renouncing his homeland in bitter acrimony. Artur Brauner found himself and his family persecuted, hunted and murdered by the Nazis. Thea von Harbou and Gert Fröbe sheepishly admitted their membership in the Nazi Party but desperately backpedaled on any association with what that Party stood for. Yet Leni Riefenstahl had no wiggle room. She had been a willing acolyte of Goebbels, explicitly using the power of cinema to promote the Nazi agenda. When the war came to an end, and that Nazi agenda wound up on the losing side, she found that she had a lot of explaining to do.

So it came to pass that Riefenstahl was arrested by the American military and imprisoned with the likes of Hermann Göring—filmmaker as war criminal. She escaped and was rearrested three times before the U.S. authorities decided that she had been "de-Nazified," and released her. The French military, though, could not have cared less what the U.S. authorities thought, and promptly arrested her themselves—they had grievances, too.

While she sat in a French-run insane asylum for three months, the greatest fascist filmmaker of all time consoled herself with what fragments of silver linings she could make out on the storm clouds hanging over her. She had gotten word that Reinl and some of her other former colleagues had taken her camera equipment and formed their own production company, churning out documentary shorts and Heimatfilms for the new postwar German audiences. That brought a smile to her lips; she was glad that good people like Reinl were building new lives for themselves. Perhaps through him a little piece of her would survive.

Between 1947 and 1949, the French undertook repeated legal proceedings against her. One of the charges accused Riefenstahl of involvement with a concentration camp where countless Gypsies had been gassed to death. One Gypsy woman came forward to name Riefenstahl specifically, and she had a compelling story to tell. During production on *Tiefland* (which was still unfinished, thanks to Riefenstahl's legal plight), Riefenstahl had allegedly procured a number of Gypsies from the concentration camp, used the poor folk on camera and then returned them to the camp to be executed. If true, Riefenstahl was not directly responsible for any deaths, but the cruelty and callousness of her attitude would be damning enough. Riefenstahl insisted the charge was false, and summoned Harald Reinl to her defense.

Reinl took the stand to give his testimony. It was a powerful testament to his loyalty and courage for him to do so; all of Riefenstahl's other friends and co-workers had abandoned her. Even Arnold Fanck denied knowing her. But Reinl had been intimately involved in the making of *Tiefland*; in fact he had been the one who found the gypsies for Riefenstahl. If anyone could explain the true circumstances of the filming, it was he.

Reinl gave the following testimony, as quoted in Riefenstahl's memoirs:

> The claim that the Gypsies were brought from concentration camps is a deliberate lie, since any child in Salzburg can tell you that no concentration camp ever existed in Maxglan; it was merely a reception camp for wandering Gypsies. I make this statement under oath.

Oh sure, the place to turn when you want to know about war crimes conducted in secret is to little children, by far the finest source of trustworthy information. Now perhaps what Reinl said was true, but his words sound discomfortingly similar to those that have been offered up time and again in the subsequent decades by revisionist historians claiming that the Holocaust never happened. There were no concentration camps, just glorified trailer parks that the Nazi government operated on behalf of wandering Gypsies. Sure.

The French authorities decided to ignore Reinl's dubious testimony in its entirety, much to Riefenstahl's fury. Ironically, in the end, the best evidence to acquit her came not from any witness but from her accuser. The Gypsy woman had attempted to substantiate her charges against Riefenstahl by identifying specifically some of those people she said she had seen gassed to death. The names she named, though, belonged to a family of Gypsies who were quite alive, and friendly with Riefenstahl's family.

In 1949, the French released Riefenstahl declaring her at last de–Nazified. She tried to put her life together again, but the specter of Nazism haunts her reputation to this day. In 1954, the year that Brauner bought the rights to *Dr. Mabuse* and began wooing Lang back to Germany, Riefenstahl released *Tiefland* to an indifferent, even hostile audience.

If Riefenstahl's career was circling the bowl, Reinl's star was on the rise. His association with Riefenstahl all but vanished into the ether. The accusations that dogged her never applied to him, and he quickly became one of the most prolific directors in the resurgent German industry.

He collaborated with Riefenstahl on a script in 1953 but found much greater success on his own. After a string of Heimatfilms, in 1955 he helmed a Spanish Civil War drama called *As Long as You Live*, the success of which inspired him to direct two more war pictures in 1958. That in turn led to a number of action-adventure films. With his 1959 production *Fellowship of the Frog*, he launched what became arguably the most successful and important subgenre in the postwar German market, the Edgar Wallace series (see also Chapter 14). He directed four more Wallace pictures soon after: *Hand of the Gallows* (1960), *The Forger of London* (1961), *Room 13* (1964) and *The Terror* (1965), as well as Bryan Edgar Wallace's *The Strangler of Blackmoor Castle* (1963). In addition to his two Mabuse films, Reinl directed the first of CCC's Karl May Westerns, *The Treasure of Silver Lake* (1962), and all three of the exceptionally popular and influential Winnetou films, also from May's books. Reinl oversaw the 1965 European take on James Fenimore Cooper's *Last of the Mohicans*, the 1967 Edgar Allan Poe flick *The Pit and the Pendulum* and the two-part remake of *The Nibelungen* that Fritz Lang had refused. Reinl made krimi thrillers, Jerry Cotton

Note how this U.S. poster rhymes "Mabuse" with "excuse."

He was married three times, initially to Corrina Frank, from 1946 to 1950. In 1954 he married actress Karin Dor, who became a recurring feature, naturally enough, in his films. Dor stars in Reinl's second Mabuse entry, *The Invisible Dr. Mabuse*, along with two other Reinl regulars, Lex Barker and Joachim Fuchsberger. Dor and Reinl divorced in 1968, however, and shortly thereafter the filmmaker made the mistake of marrying actress Daniela Maria Delis. During Leni Riefenstahl's darkest hours, Reinl proved to be the only person she knew who valued loyalty and friendship over personal convenience; he risked his own reputation to stand up for her when everyone else bailed out. And on October 9, 1986, this deeply loyal man met with a most inapt fate—literally stabbed in the back by his wife Daniela. He died in Tenerife, Spain.

films, Kommissar X films, documentaries, comedies, Heimatfilms and plenty of sentimental schmaltz for good measure.

Few of his films found much of an audience stateside (many of his creations belong to genres or subgenres Americans have never even heard of), but in Germany Dr. Harald Reinl was box office gold. His prominence in the world of the postwar German film industry is so great that he has been the subject of two made-for-TV biographies.

Called away from his vacation to head the investigation, Inspector Lohmann (Gert Fröbe) stands over the body of the murdered courier. The briefcase is missing, and with it the evidence against the Chicago mob. Surely someone connected to the Mafia is responsible? Feeling the quagmire of the case congeal about his feet, Lohmann heads to the prison where Alberto Sandro (Ady Berber), a hired thug with ties to the Chicago syndicate, is serving his life sentence. Lohmann consults with Warden Wolff (Fausto Tozzi), hoping to interview Sandro and maybe obtain a clue. Wolff is doubtful the killer will have anything to say to the cops, but happily grants Lohmann the chance to find out.

As Wolff's associate Böhmler (Werner Peters) brings Sandro from his cell, Lohmann looks around Wolff's office. The walls are decorated with life casts of the faces of the greatest criminals of the century. Certainly a morbid choice of decor for a prison warden? The images inspire Lohmann to ponder the whole notion of masks, the false fronts everyone puts up to conceal their secrets inside. The whole case is about masks and false fronts, phony leads, vanishing evidence, lies and deception, tantalizing suppositions, but never anything tangible. The criminals are always one step ahead of the cops, always, meticulously covering their tracks. If only he can get a solid clue to catch up with them, to leap ahead perhaps, then he might have a chance at catching the spider instead of flailing about helplessly in the web.

Böhmler brings Sandro into the office. The massive brute is silent, as if he were drugged, and Lohmann has to concede yet another tiny defeat.

When Fritz Lang brought back Otto Wernicke as Inspector Lohmann in 1932's *The Testament of Dr. Mabuse*, it was an inspired crossover, linking the preternatural horrors of Mabuse with the documentary-style realism of *M*. With his gruff humor and keen mind, Lohmann became archetypal. Decades later, even in Hollywood, the spirit of Lohmann lived on, in such characters as Peter Falk's Columbo, who even parroted Lohmann's dress sense. Naturally enough, Gert Fröbe's role in *The 1000 Eyes of Dr. Mabuse* was a Lohmann-figure, even if he was named Kras. So when Fröbe reprises his role in this sequel to *The 1000 Eyes*, with the same mannerisms, the same clothes, the same haircut, the same memories, the same job, but with the name "Lohmann" substituted for "Kras," the audience should not be too greatly concerned. This is the same man, and by any name this Lohmann still smells as sweet.

By contrast, Werner Peters makes a return appearance in a decidedly different role. While he was last seen as an intrepid undercover Interpol agent, he is now a ruthless proxy for Dr. Mabuse. Peters would appear twice more in the series, in two more distinct roles: once again as a right hand man for the mad doctor, and once again as a cop. In a cinematic world where identity is so mutable and appearances always deceiving, the fact that some actors reprise the same roles while other actors return as the same characters with new names and yet other actors appear as all new characters, the disorienting effect is just part of the game.

Concealed by the night's darkness, Mrs. Pisaro makes her way to the Bimbo Bar for her rendezvous. She is one of two emissaries of the Chicago syndicate, sent to Berlin to contact a mysterious figure, a man who has already struck terror in her heart and she has yet to meet him. Fears both real and imagined haunt her. Where is her partner? Has he been caught by the cops, or has some worse fate befallen him?

Poor Mrs. Pisaro has good reason to worry. Whatever threat her Great Unknown may pose, she is also being watched—by the cops, by a blind beggar, and by a sinister figure posing as a souvenir salesman, carefully gliding his cart along the street to stay in sight of his target. One signal from the souvenir vendor, and a laundry truck careens around the corner to block Mrs. Pisaro's path. A panel opens on the van's side, and a jet of flames spew forth, incinerating the frightened woman. The police race from their squad car, but they are already too late. The poor wretch has burned alive.

Luckily, the blind beggar is a witness. Of course he saw nothing, but he heard the distinctive rapping sound of a wooden leg against the pavement. As he hears the souvenir vendor glide past, the beggar realizes that his words now decide his fate: He clams up, and claims to know nothing.

Infuriated, Inspector Lohmann has the blind man arrested. Perhaps they can entice him to speak back at the station house. Suddenly there is a flash of light—a photojournalist (Daliah Lavi) has forced her way to the front of the crowd and snapped Lohmann's picture. She wants a quote for her paper, but like his reluctant witness Lohmann keeps his lips shut.

The reporter decides to follow Lohmann. What he won't tell her perhaps she can see for herself. A strange, charming young man (Lex Barker) tags along with her, for reasons he too refuses to voice. There is something decidedly odd about him, some secret he is hiding. He says his name is Joe Como, and makes a macabre joke about being a murderer. She introduces herself as Maria Sabrehm—why does he find that name familiar?

Meanwhile, their target is on the move. Inspector Lohmann has discovered a book in Mrs. Pisaro's purse, a weird little tome called *The Devil's Anatomy—The Criminal Instinct of Men*. Written by a Reverend Briefenstein, the book is divided into four chapters, covering "Crime and Sin," "The Vampire Myth," "The Wolfman Myth" and "The Dr. Mabuse Myth." No sooner has he read this last line than the veteran detective anxiously finds a pay phone and makes a call. Across the street, Joe Como reads Lohmann's lips. Doing so, he feels a chill run down his spine.

"He's on the wrong track. He's got it all wrong," Como says, but the tone of his voice is unconvincing. "He's talking about a man who died long ago. Inspector Lohmann's overworked—he's seeing ghosts."

One of the biggest stars to grace CCC's Mabuse cycle, Lex Barker's fame and fortune befell him almost exclusively in Europe. Alexander Chrichlow Barker, Jr., was born in 1919 into wealthy New York Society, a direct descendant of Roger Williams, the man who founded Rhode Island. After the usual program of athletic and academic excellence in all the best schools, Lex abandoned his studies at Princeton to pursue a career as an actor. That decision infuriated his tony family, which disowned him.

Barker's acting career got off to a shaky start, and was soon put on hiatus by World War II. Barker enlisted as an infantry private, and left as a major. When he returned to Hollywood, he skipped around from studio to studio as casting directors deemed him too tall and upstagingly handsome for supporting parts, but not enough of a "name" for starring roles either.

Finally, in 1949, he snagged his first starring role, as the Lord of the Jungle in *Tarzan's Magic Fountain*, scripted by German emigré Curt Siodmak. Barker, who took over the role from Johnny Weissmuller, headlined a total of five Tarzan pictures between 1949 and 1953 before moving on to Westerns. At about the same time, he married screen legend Lana Turner (Barker's third wife, out of what would ultimately number five). Barker grew tired, though, of living in the shadow of his wife's superstardom. When they divorced four years later, Barker decided that being a big fish in a little pond was preferable to the reverse, and he moved to Europe to seek the celebrity Hollywood would never give him.

Being a consummate overachiever, Barker was fluent in French, Spanish, Italian and German, which made him all the more valuable a commodity to the struggling postwar film producers of the Continent. Traveling from France to Germany to Spain to Brazil to Italy to Yugoslavia to Lebanon, Barker would star in some 50 motion pictures during this highly successful phase of his career. Although he appeared in esteemed foreign production like Fellini's *La Dolce Vita* (1960), his performance as Karl May's *Old Shatterhand* in CCC's 1963 film of the same name, directed by *Death Ray of Dr. Mabuse*'s Hugo Fregonese, was one of the most popular. Lex "Shatterhand" Barker soon became a regular feature of the low-budget spaghetti Westerns being cranked out in Yugoslavia. He would also reprise his role as Joe Como in Harald Reinl's *The Invisible Dr. Mabuse* (1962). Through his allegiance with Reinl and his immense marquee value, Barker became one of CCC's regular players. Barker passed away in 1973, felled by a heart attack.

Shadowed by Maria Sabrehem and Joe Como, Inspector Lohmann heads for the St. Thomas Church to interview Pastor Briefenstein about his book, *The Devil's Anatomy*. The reverend explains his belief that the Devil is a spirit that can take many different bodily forms in its various incarnations. Lohmann is most interested in just one of these manifestations, a master criminal long believed dead, a phantom known as Dr. Mabuse. A sudden sound interrupts their conversation, and the pastor is obliged to rush off to investigate the unauthorized misuse of his church's bells. Left alone in the reverend's office, Lohmann realizes he has been locked in—with a bomb tossed into the room by a man with a wooden leg. Thinking quickly, he barely manages to survive the blast.

"You must have very powerful enemies if they pursue you into the house of God!" exclaims Briefenstein as Lohmann's singed body is pulled from the wreckage. "I'll get a doctor."

"I'd prefer a drink!" protests the cop.

Joe Como approaches and introduces himself as an FBI agent. He has been sent to follow Mrs. Pisaro to try to find out just who or what in Berlin is trying to strike a deal with the Chicago Mob. She may have been killed simply to throw detectives like him off.

Their conference is interrupted by a voice over the church loudspeaker. It is no sermon, but a warning—from whom? As Lohmann races to find the source of the mysterious voice, Como talks with it. To the Voice, Como tells a radically different story. Now he introduces himself as Nick Scapio, Mrs. Pisaro's partner from Chicago, who is using the cover of "Joe Como" to avoid police interference. Before he can agree to any of Mabuse's terms, his associates in America want to see a demonstration of Mabuse's alleged fantastic power. The Voice assures him that the demonstration will exceed his wildest imaginations.

Briefenstein's church is an awesome gothic spectacle, its artistry all the more impressive because Reinl stages just this one sequence there; few low-budget thrillers would put such effort into small details. *The Return of Dr. Mabuse* is marked throughout with some of the finest art direction the Mabuse genre would ever boast, thanks to the involvement of veteran production designers Otto Erdmann and Hans Jürgen Kiebach. Erdmann was one of the greats of classic 1920s–1930s German cinema, reactivated by Brauner to lend CCC postwar productions a touch of old-school class. His eye for detail had previously enriched such enduring masterpieces as G.W. Pabst's *The Joyless Street* (1925) and *Desire* (1928), as well as the highly influential science fiction drama *Alraune* (1930) with stars Brigitte (*Metropolis*)

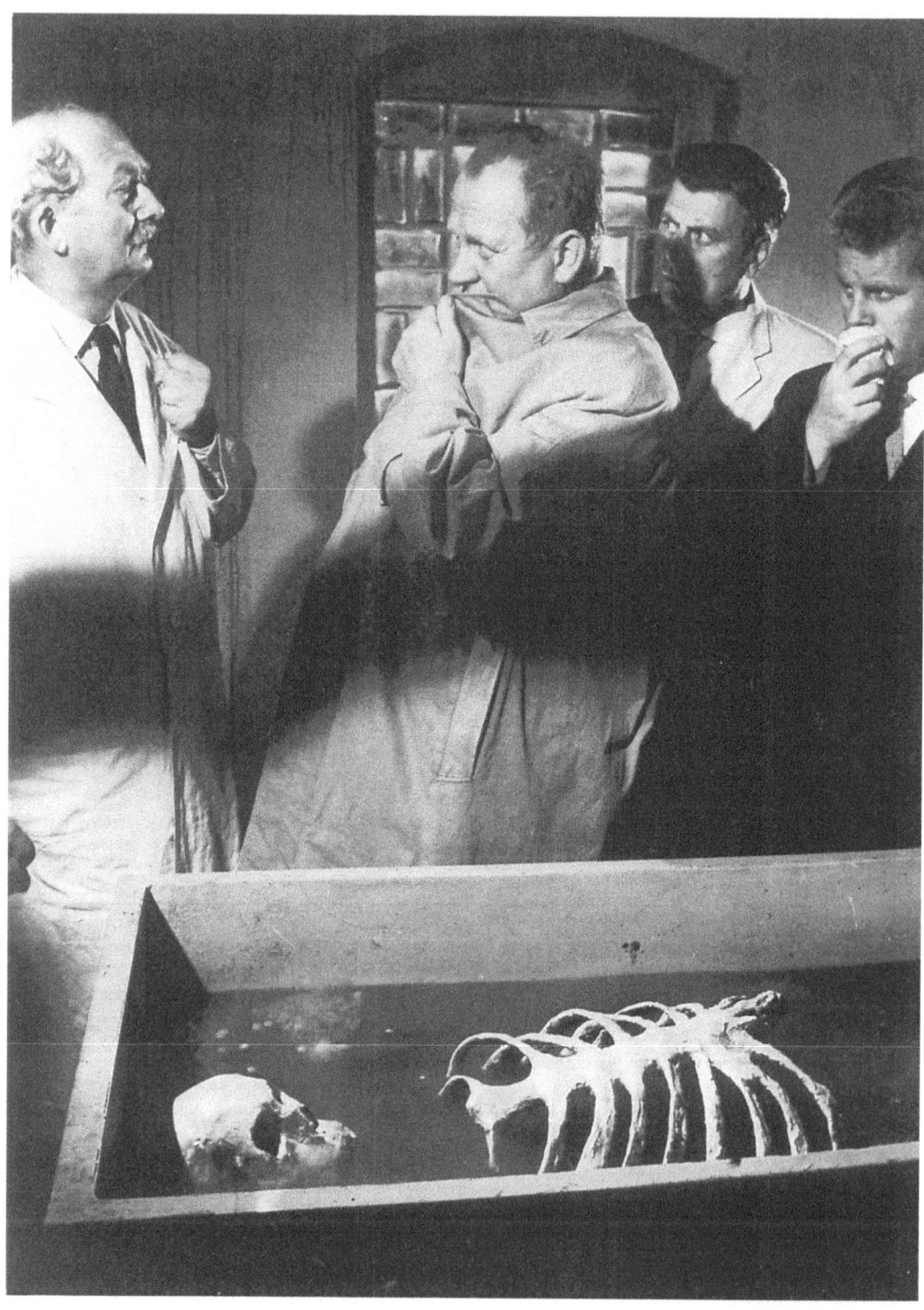

Im Stahlnetz des Dr. Mabuse significantly upped the level of graphic violence in the series.

Helm and Bernhard (*Dr. Mabuse the Gambler*) Goetzke. Partner Kiebach would, in contrast, do his best work in the brave new world of German filmmaking. Kiebach's designs can be seen in such Edgar Wallace entries as *The Phantom of Soho* and *The Monster of London City* (both 1964), the 1969 AIP production *De Sade* (see also Chapter 16) and the acclaimed 1972 picture *Cabaret*.

Photographing their exquisite sets was ace cinematographer Karl Löb. Having already lensed *Der 20 Juli* (1955) and *The 1000 Eyes of Dr. Mabuse* (1960), Löb would go on to specialize in Edgar Wallace thrillers and Westerns, making him quite a valued team member indeed for CCC Films.

If *The Return of Dr. Mabuse* was a bastard child of Lang's lofty artistic ambitions, if it was a routine B-movie thriller intended to launch a continuing movie franchise, if its purpose was first and foremost commercial, it was nevertheless an impressive collection of on-screen and off-screen talent, all working at the peak of their skills. Rarely has a B-movie been graced with such a surfeit of artistry; rarely has a B-movie reached such heights of craftsmanship.

With Rev. Briefenstein's book a tantalizing but ambiguous lead, the only substantial clue Lohmann has yet uncovered in this baffling and frustrating case is the blind beggar, whose reference to a peg-legged man might just lead to a suspect—if only they can get him to talk on the record. So Lohmann is angry and frustrated to learn that his assistant Voss (Joachim Mock) has released the recalcitrant witness.

Lohmann rushes to St. Thomas' Church, where the beggar is expected to join other poor Berliners in seeking weekly handouts from Pastor Briefenstein's congregation. They arrive in time to see the blind man crushed by the same laundry truck that incinerated Mrs. Pisaro. Lohmann and Joe Como, who just happened to be nearby, chase the van, oblivious to the souvenir vendor quietly going about his business on the street corner.

The two detectives chase the van down an alley, only to watch the driver crash the vehicle, desperately choosing certain death over capture. Barely managing to pull his still breathing body from the flaming wreck, they are shocked to see the face of Alberto Sandro, the mob hitman who is supposed to be serving a life sentence.

Lohmann confronts Warden Wolff with a very sensible question: Just how is it that one of his inmates is not in his cell, but instead wandering loose in Berlin committing violent crimes? Wolff answers that Sandro cannot be the man Lohmann arrested, since Sandro is most definitely in his cell. He has Böhmler take Lohmann to Sandro's cell to prove it, but the body in Sandro's cell is the strangled corpse of a man with a wooden leg.

This is all very familiar to Lohmann. This has all happened before. Criminals locked away, purportedly removed from decent society altogether, who nevertheless manage to continue their crimes undaunted by prisons, or asylums, or death—it is the hallmark of Dr. Mabuse.

Wolff cannot believe his ears. Is Lohmann seriously suggesting that a ghost is behind all this?

"The dead sometimes return," is his reply.

Although Reinl deserves much of the credit for recreating the spirit of Fritz Lang's Mabuse, the success of *Return of Dr. Mabuse* is also due to the sharp-witted and intricately structured screenplay by veteran scribe Ladislas Fodor (1898–1978). Unfortunately for the cause of film history, not much is known about Fodor, but a glance at his prolific output reveals that he was a vital element in European pop cinema, and an influential figure whose true importance may never be properly assessed. Beginning in the mid-1950s he forged an alliance with Artur Brauner that proved highly profitable to both. Over the ensuing three decades, he would pen some 24 screenplays for Brauner, not counting the various scripts adapted from his previous writings. In other words, approximately half of Fodor's screenwriting resulted in approximately one tenth of CCC's films.

Fodor was one name that Brauner did not pull from Germany's Golden Age, but rather from Hollywood. The writer had begun as a playwright, and Hollywood found his plays excellent source material for films. One play became the James Whale melodrama *The Kiss Before the Mirror* (1933), which Whale also later remade under the title *Wives Under Suspicion* (1938). Another play provided the basis for the Charlie Chan mystery *City in Darkness* (1939). After a dozen or so of Fodor's plays were adapted to the silver screen, he took up screenwriting more directly, working with some of the biggest names in cinema. Fodor wrote films for John Wayne, Marlene Dietrich, Errol Flynn, Rita Hayworth, Ginger Rogers, Henry Fonda, Edward G. Robinson, Barbara Stanwyck, David Niven, Ethel Barrymore, Gregory Peck, and on and on. He wrote two screenplays for director Robert Siodmak, and penned *tom thumb* (1958) for fantasy film auteur George Pal. Immediately before drafting *The Return of Dr. Mabuse*, Fodor wrote *North to Alaska* (1960) for John Wayne. However, that was to be his last Hollywood work, as he now relocated full time to Germany to work primarily for Brauner's CCC. There he wrote five of the six 1960s Mabuse pictures; the wildly successful Karl May Western *Old Shatterhand*; a number of the Edgar Wallace entries like *The Strangler of Blackmoor Castle* (1963) and *The Phantom of Soho* (1967); the two-part *Nibelungen* remake (1966); 1967's *The Corrupt Ones* starring Robert Stack, Elke Sommer and Werner Peters; and the epic failure *The Fight for Rome* (1968, Part II in 1969) that Robert Siodmak helmed for Brauner with an all-star cast including Orson Welles and Honor Blackman. He finished up his career by collaborating with Brauner and Jess Franco in Spain on such low-budget spectacles as *The Devil Came from Akasava* (1971, see also Chapter 17).

Throughout all of this, Fodor himself received billing under a variety of names, something almost de rigeuer for the men and women who made Dr. Mabuse films. Alternately credited as Laslo Fodor, Lazlo Fodor, and Ladislaus Fodor, the writer seemed almost to anticipate his importance to a film series principally concerned with the intangible qualities of identity.

Inspector Lohmann, Detective Voss, FBI agent (or not?) Joe Como and Lohmann's team of forensic scientists and psychiatrists have gathered to interrogate Alberto Sandro. The questions are obvious: how did he escape from prison, why did he kill the blind witness, who is he working for? But he will not answer—indeed, he *cannot*, says Dr. Griesinger; his mind has been destroyed. Sandro is now just a gigantic puppet, animated by the will of another, a zombie. The effect is probably caused by some kind of narcotic, Griesinger posits, and this very idea was described in a journal article not too long ago ... who wrote that article? What was that name?

As Griesinger tries to tease his memory, Sandro receives a message through a tiny earpiece, his final instructions. The killer breaks free of his handcuffs and throws his body through the window,

"I am confident I cannot be recognized," boasts Warden Wolff (Fausto Tozzi) to Inspector Lohmann (Gert Fröbe).

plummeting to his death on the sidewalk below. The cops race down to the bloody mess in the street, furious and frustrated that every lead is quashed before their eyes by Mabuse's operation. Every witness is killed, every clue erased, until nothing remains but the shadow of the phantom. Suddenly Griesinger remembers—*I've got it!*, he shouts. *The man who wrote that article was*—

Griesinger's body collapses. How apt that he should be shot dead with a silencer, as silence is exactly what Mabuse wants. The souvenir salesman replaces the weapon in his overcoat and slinks away unnoticed. Now the only hope Lohmann has is that Sandro's autopsy might reveal the chemical used to control his mind.

Those hopes are dashed when Lohmann arrives at the morgue to oversee the post mortem. Sandro's body is gone, disintegrated in a bath of acid.

Lohmann warns Warden Wolff that he may be next. Somehow a criminal enterprise is operating with impunity from within his prison's walls, using the prison's laundry service to transport convicts around the city on ruthless errands for some unidentified master. They can control people's minds and have racked up a horrific body count in their successful efforts to escape detection. Lohmann urges Wolff to take precautions to protect his life—but mere seconds after their meeting, Wolff is atomized by a car bomb.

The shadow of the phantom has all but blanketed the entire city…

"[*The Return of Dr. Mabuse*] is rather too graphic in its depiction of the various murders," writes esteemed genre historian William K. Everson in his indispensable survey *Classics of the Horror Film*, "When the menace is spelled out, and much of it is on a physical level, there is little room left for the mind to conjure its own fears and horrors." Despite this caveat, Everson, in what is one of the very rare critical assessments of this film ever to be written in America, recommends *Return of Dr. Mabuse* with strong praise. "It's Lang's world," he writes, "or a remarkable facsimile of it, and he wouldn't have been ashamed of it."

> Most of the post–Lang *Mabuse*s were carefully made but lacking in style, using the Mabuse character only as a framework and an excuse for gimmickry and action more properly belonging to the James Bond school.... But one film was an exception: *The Return of Dr. Mabuse* emerged as a kind of homage to Lang, and a *Mabuse* mosaic, although its trite title suggests that its producers were unaware of what a good film they had. Many of its characters and incidents are derived from specific Lang films: the opening sequence on a train is borrowed from both the original *Dr. Mabuse* and the later *Spies*. For the rest, it creates a typically Lang world, in which a church and an insane asylum are equally suspect as fronts for the crime empire, and in which originality and imagination on the part of the criminals (as well as reinstatement of Mabuse's genius for disguise) supplant the fancy gadgets of Bond's spy world.

Sadly, few U.S. critics shared Everson's view. Nor did many disagree with him, either. Few Americans ever saw the film, and the critical establishment decided that a Mabuse picture without Lang's provenance was unworthy of their attention. *Return of Dr. Mabuse* appeared in the States in 1966, destined for drive-ins and little else, and continued its life on late-night TV, far below the critical radar.

Lohmann is not about to let Mabuse get the better of him. If Mabuse wants a fight, he'll get one. Griesinger was killed to keep him from saying who wrote that journal article. Well, thinks Lohmann, there are other ways to get that information. At the local research library, Lohmann asks for all the back issues of the relevant chemical journals. The librarian chuckles to herself: For years no one has ever read that journal, and Lohmann's made the second request in an hour! Realizing he may already be too late, Lohmann races to the reading room where Maria Sabrehm already has the leather-bound volume, carefully slicing the article out with a razor blade. Lohmann stops her and takes the shred of paper. As he reads the byline for the name of the scientist, he feels a thrill run up his spine. This is it—the one clue that Mabuse could not erase.

She never was a photojournalist; that was just a ruse to give her an excuse to stay close to the investigation, a cover story to conceal her personal interest in the case. She is the link that connects it all, perhaps the key to the whole damned business. The time has come to pay a visit to the prison.

Meanwhile, Böhmler has taken over the prison following the murder of Warden Wolff. One of his first acts as warden was to report to Dr. Mabuse. But even to his inner retinue, Mabuse remains an insubstantial wraith: a disembodied voice, a silhouette on a curtain projected on a video screen, a threat from beyond the grave. "I shall sow confusion, dread and terror in this city!" rants the Voice. "Reinforce Cell Block D and prepare for battle! Our first act of aggression takes place on Friday the Thirteenth!"

But the Voice trembles with a barely concealed fear. Evidence can be erased, witnesses can be eliminated, cops can be bribed, but there is one risk of exposure he cannot remove, and her name is Maria Sabrehm. She is at once essential to his plans and a menace to his survival. And now, she and Inspector Lohmann have arrived at his front door with a warrant to see her father.

Dr. Julius Sabrehm was one of the greatest chemists of his generation. When he published his findings on a synthetic narcotic powerful enough to reduce a human being to a mindless automaton, Mabuse knew that he had to possess Sabrehm's drug. To that end Mabuse carefully engineered an elaborate plan to frame Sabrehm for treason, and have the falsely convicted man placed in *his* prison, easy prey to his influence. Driven half mad by the injustice, Dr. Sabrehm now maintains only a tenuous link to the land of the sane, spending his days in Mabuse's toil manufacturing enough narcotics to create an entire zombie army. Through it all, Sabrehm's one ray of hope was his daughter, making her useful leverage for Mabuse should the chemist try to disobey.

When her father was imprisoned, Maria sought out Pastor Briefenstein as her spiritual advisor. In his duties ministering to the prison, Briefenstein had cultivated a healthy fear of Mabuse's influence, so much so he had come to believe Mabuse was the devil incarnate. Terrified of Mabuse, Briefenstein had effectively kept Maria from seeing her father. But now that interfering fool Lohmann was bringing them together—if the scientist cracks upon seeing his daughter, if the old man starts saying inconvenient truths, Mabuse may have no choice but to kill her and Lohmann on the spot.

As it happens, Sabrehm seems unable to recognize Maria. Indeed, he seems only dimly aware of his surroundings. Raving like a madman, he mutters, "God gives us nuts but He doesn't crack them for us." Lohmann and Maria depart, another defeat in their pockets.

While Mabuse breathes a sigh of relief, in private Lohmann tells Maria that he didn't believe for a minute that her father was really insane. He knows the remark about the nuts was some kind of coded message, a way of telling her he still loved her while concealing his recognition from Mabuse. She admits it was a proverb he used to tell her when she was young. At last, thinks the detective, after being one step behind Mabuse all along I have at last gotten an edge—something I know that he doesn't know I know. To parlay that edge into a tactical advantage, though, will necessitate a risky gamble, and a dangerous leap of faith.

She was called Israel's answer to Brigitte Bardot. *Harper's Bazaar* once dubbed her "the most beautiful woman in films." As Maria Sabrehm, brunette bombshell Daliah Lavi gave *Return of Dr. Mabuse* an injection of sultry international sex appeal.

Born Daliah Levenbuch in 1942, she strangely enough started off as a soldier in the Israeli army, before she left to pursue a screen career. She starred with Peter Van Eyck in *No Time For Ecstasy* (1960) and Christopher Lee in *What?* (1963), co-starred with Lex Barker in *Old Shatterhand* and appeared in numerous spy flicks in the U.S., including Dean Martin's *The Silencers* (1965), the first of the Matt Helm spy thrillers. Perhaps her most famous performance was as the naked beauty menaced by Woody Allen in the James Bond parody *Casino Royale* (1967).

The Maria Sabrehm role was a transitional character for the Mabuse series. In reformulating the Mabuse concept as a running series, Ladislas Fodor and Harald Reinl had little interest in the kind of strong, heroic women that populated Fritz Lang's films and Norbert Jacques' books. Sexy damsels in distress, preferably in revealing costumes, were better box office fodder. Whatever threat Maria may pose to Mabuse's plans has nothing to do with what havoc she herself can cause, but how the men in the story will react to her—reactions all driven by patriarchal notions of protective males and vulnerable females. Daliah Lavi and the actresses who followed in her wake—Karin Dor, Senta Berger, Sabinne Bethmann, Yvonne Furneaux—were contracted for their ravishing looks, not their acting skills.

Maria dims the lights in her bedroom, and in her slinky nightgown prepares for bed. Much to her surprise, she discovers Joe Como standing in her room. Modestly she protest, "I never receive gentlemen in my bedroom." To this he replies by flipping her bed over into a couch—they are now in her living room, dilemma solved.

As Maria and Joe fall into one another's arms, Detective Voss bursts in and arrests Como. Voss checked the man's fingerprints and discovered they do not match the FBI records for the real Joe Como. Back at the police station, Lohmann explains he knows that Como is in fact Nick Scapio from the Chicago syndicate, but he needs Scapio's help anyway. Lohmann wants to send Scapio to prison, to get him locked up in Mabuse's cell block D as an inside informant to find out just what Mabuse has going on down there and how it's being orchestrated. Scapio agrees, and the trap is set.

How is it that Lohmann can place such faith in a mobster? Lohmann smiles benevolently at Voss and explains in the patient tone a father might takes with his child. "Someday you'll know the difference between a gangster and an FBI operative." The FBI has confirmed to the Inspector that they deliberately faked Como's identity papers to aid him in his deception. The real agent Como is only pretending to be Nick Scapio pretending to be Joe Como, who has just been sent to prison under the alias Bob Arko.

When you have a quadruple-agent in the cast, you know you're in Mabuse country. The sheer quantity of false fronts and deceptions put up in *Return of Dr. Mabuse* is enough to make the head spin. In addition to Como-Scapio-Como-Arko, there is Maria's ruse of being a reporter. The entire prison is a front for Mabuse's organization, who is maintaining at least two false identities of his own. Laundry trucks and souvenir salesmen are agents of evil, who may have also corrupted the local church. Poor Voss still innocently believes in the usefulness of such traditional methods of identification as, say, fingerprinting. The jaded Lohmann has discovered that in Mabuse's world, nothing like that can be trusted.

The Como/Scapio character is a holdover from *The 1000 Eyes of Dr. Mabuse*, Fodor's variation on the Heironymous Mitselzweig character played by Werner Peters in the previous picture. The Gert Fröbe character, Kras or Lohmann as the case may be, ostensibly heads up the investigation, but it's the undercover cop, so deep undercover that the audience cannot quite be sure which side he's on, who really cracks the case. (Fodor revamped the idea in his script for 1964's *Death Ray of Dr. Mabuse*, discussed in Chapter 15.) What is remarkable about Como/Scapio is that his disguise fools even Mabuse. For the first and only time in the cinema of Dr. Mabuse, the cops pull a fast one on the Great Unknown.

The Voice has warned Lohmann for the last time to back off or suffer the consequences. Recognizing the sound of a player piano tinkling in the background of the call, Lohmann realizes that the Voice is calling from the Bimbo Bar, where Mrs. Pisaro was killed. He races there in time to catch the silhouetted figure behind the desk. Has he at last captured the spider at the center of the web?

After a vain attempt to bribe Lohmann, the shadow draws his weapon. With swifter reflexes, Lohmann guns his assailant down dead in the blink of an eye. As Voss leaps up the stairs to his boss' aid, Lohmann peers down at his victim. Just another of Mabuse's agents, dressed up to play the patsy so the spider could escape detection and do away with another risk of exposure all at once.

Lohmann's one hope is "Bob Arko." No sooner has he arrived in his cell, though, he admits to Mabuse that he is not Arko at all, but Nick Scapio sent in by Lohmann as a spy. So much for his cover. But don't worry, says Scapio, I'm your man. I'm here to seal the deal with the Mafia for you.

Skeptical, Mabuse instructs Böhmler to inject Scapio with the zombie drug. Scapio is sent to the pharmacy, where he has a chance encounter with Dr. Sabrehm. When Como/Scapio repeats the proverb "God gives us nuts but doesn't crack them for us," the old scientist knows the young man must be a friend of Maria's. Placing his faith in Como, Sabrehm gives him a secret capsule to keep hidden in his mouth; when administered the injection by Bömmler, all he has to do is bite the capsule and he will be protected from the narcotic's effect.

Como's cover is nearly blown when Reverend Briefenstein recognizes him as Maria's friend, and blurts out that she has been kidnapped. Before Como can react to this news, Böhmler arrives, with what he calls a vaccination "against everything."

That night, Mabuse gives his instructions to his zombie army. On Friday the thirteenth, as a demonstration of his powers to the Mafia, he will stage an attack on the nuclear power plant. It is a meticulous, complex operation that will result in a nuclear explosion. Merely a demonstration.

As part of the zombie work crew preparing the way for the attack, Como—only pretending to be in Mabuse's control—manages to slip a warning note to the police. But when Lohmann's forces gear up to defend the nuclear plant, Mabuse realizes he has a traitor in his midst. He locks Como and Maria Sabrehm in a cell and begins to flood it—death is the punishment for betrayal.

So if Scapio was an FBI agent all along, then was a legitimate contact with the Mafia ever made? Suddenly unsure what in his world is true, the mad doctor decides to attack the nuclear plant immediately. He may go down, but he plans to take the entire city with him. The zombies of cell block D file out to begin the assault, herded by a recording that repeats, over and over again with hypnotic precision, "You have only one Lord and Master, Dr. Mabuse!"

In Fritz Lang's iteration, the Mabuse pictures had fallen into an uncomfortable and ill-defined mix of genres, straddling the fence between the conventions of film noir and detective fiction on the one hand and the genres of horror and fantasy on the other. Undoubtedly the most important and lasting contribution that Harald Reinl and Ladislas Fodor gave to the Mabuse franchise was to recast it with a decided science fictional bent. Dr. Julius Sabrehm is a mad scientist who has invented a method to chemically control men's minds. Dr. Mabuse needs this power, and orients his entire operation around exploiting Sabrehm and his discovery.

Almost without exception every Mabuse picture that followed adopted this scenario. *The Invisible Dr. Mabuse, Scotland Yard vs. Dr. Mabuse* and *Death Ray of Dr. Mabuse* all involve Mabuse trying to obtain some sci-fi gadget concocted by a mad scientist. In *Scream and Scream Again, The Vengeance of Dr. Mabuse* and *Club*

Lohmann confronts the phantom fiend at the climax of *Im Stahlnetz des Dr. Mabuse*.

Extinction, Mabuse is personally the mad scientist providing his own lunatic inventions. Only the 1962 remake of *The Testament of Dr. Mabuse* avoids the sci-fi trappings of mad science and presents a straightforward, *noir*-ish crime thriller. For better or worse, Fodor and Reinl left an indelible impression and forever redefined the public image of Norbert Jacques' creation.

Joe Como and Maria Sabrehm are trapped in a rapidly flooding room. There is no escape. In a few seconds they will be drowned. Such is the inevitable consequence of betraying Dr. Mabuse.

As an FBI agent, though, Como is not without survival skills. He breaks open the gas line running along the ceiling and whisks a cigarette lighter from his pocket. Como draws Maria close to him and raises the lighter to the pipe, already hissing with gas vapors. As the water level rises above them, he has just a fraction of a second before his hand will be submerged. In that instant he flicks the lighter, igniting the gas. The force of the explosion blows open the doors. They are free, and alive (thanks to a neat reversal of the escape scene from Lang's 1933 *Testament of Dr. Mabuse*).

Meanwhile, Lohmann and his troops are prepared for war. Mabuse's zombie army advances, driven inexorably by the incessant command: "You have only one Lord and Master, Dr. Mabuse!" As the mindless automatons open fire on the police, Lohmann spots an armored vehicle on the sidelines. Inside is the captive Dr. Sabrehm, his jailer Böhmler and a cloaked, masked figure who must be Dr. Mabuse. Leaping into action, the Inspector chases after the shadowy figure. Joe Como, arriving in the nick of time, captures Böhmler as Lohmann corners his prey at a railroad juncture.

In the moment of truth, Lohmann pulls aside the cloak to reveal the face of— Warden Wolff. He had faked his own death with that car bomb in order to put Lohmann off the trail. Or rather, Wolff had been killed long, long ago, before Lohmann was ever involved in the case, and ever since then Mabuse has been operating using Wolff's stolen identity. Lohmann rips off Wolff's mask to reveal the vague, almost intangible features of a man he saw drowned years earlier (Wolfgang Preiss). Sometimes the dead return.

While Lohmann is distracted by the stunning revelation, Mabuse manages to slip away and steal a rail car, speeding manically down the tracks to freedom. But he has made an error. In his haste, Mabuse has taken off in the wrong direction. As his car plunges at top speed into the tunnel, another train approaches from the other side. The tunnel erupts in a massive explosion, from which no one could possibly have survived.

Or at least, so thinks Detective Voss as he files away the case folder. "Wait," urges Lohmann. His voice is tentative. He almost cannot even bring himself to speak his fears aloud. That explosion must have killed everyone, certainly, but Mabuse's body was never recovered and he has cheated death in the past. Do they dare consider the case closed?

As the full horror of his realization dawns, Lohmann looks out the window. In the street below are thousands of people going about their lives—buying bread, reading the newspaper, hailing taxis, taking a walk, kissing their loved ones. But as innocent as this sunny tableaux might seem at first glance, Lohmann knows that any one of them might be Dr. Mabuse...

For approximately 90 minutes Reinl has unfolded a story that takes place at night, in the shadows, in dingy prison cells, in darkened hovels. The murky, chiaroscuro images are the stylistic hallmarks of the *film noir*, which this picture freely invokes. In its farewell scene, though, the setting switches to a sunny day, with an innocuous portrait of mundane daily life. Through its relationship with what has transpired before, aided by Gert Fröbe's nuanced and sensitive performance, Reinl manages to lend this otherwise benign shot a palpable air of menace and foreboding. It is perhaps the most chilling conclusion to any Mabuse film, and one of the most audacious and perverse conclusions in all horror cinema: *Return of Dr. Mabuse* has just articulated a compelling argument to be afraid of everyone.

The case is solved, Mabuse's web broken, Mabuse himself almost certainly killed, but Lohmann cannot bring himself to call the case closed. Instead he allows himself to succumb to paranoia. As we will see in future installments, both he and Joe Como will emerge from this encounter forever haunted by Mabuse, never again able to believe the evidence of their own eyes. It is Mabuse's greatest triumph to at once convince the world that he does not exist, and for those foolish few who do believe in him to drive them mad.

Unfortunately, the power of this strong, intelligent B-movie has been blunted and ignored in America. It was successful enough in Germany to justify yet four more sequels, but did not screen in the U.S. until five years later. When it did finally surface stateside in 1966, already two years after CCC had given up making Mabuse flicks, its already lackluster title *The Return of Dr. Mabuse* was rechristened *The Phantom Fiend* for drive-in runs and TV broadcasts. With the exception of William K. Everson's graceful review quoted above, it received virtually no attention from the press and disappeared like its phantom anti-hero.

The series would continue unabated in Germany for a few more years to come, but would never again boast such a congregation of talented artists and craftspeople.

CHAPTER 12

The Invisible Dr. Mabuse

The living dead, who write invisible letters?
—Commissioner Brahm

Despite its occasional charms and odd flashes of brilliance, *The Invisible Dr. Mabuse* (1962) feels like just what it is: the latest entry in a movie series now content to coast on the imagination of its predecessors.

With a title like *The Invisible Dr. Mabuse* (in German, *Die unsichtbaren Krallen des Dr. Mabuse*, "The Invisible Claws of Dr. Mabuse"), it is a given that at least one of the creative cabinets to be raided belongs to H. G. Wells. Wells' novel *The Invisible Man* was first published in 1897 and James Whale's 1933 film remains to this day the unsurpassed cinematic translation. In some respects, even, Whale's film outstrips the original book; it is a story about images, after all. As envisioned by Whale and his team of top-flight special effects pioneers, *The Invisible Man* became iconic.

But special effects cost money. Even with the improved filmmaking technology available to Harald Reinl in 1962, meeting the standard set by Whale a generation earlier—to say nothing of surpassing it—was out of the question. The best invisibility effects CCC's cash-strapped technicians could muster entailed dangling props on piano wire—the same crude puppeteering techniques that Universal Studios turned to when they cranked out a series of B-movie sequels to *The Invisible Man* in the 1940s.

Beyond the central conceit of an invisible man, though, *The Invisible Dr. Mabuse* borrows little from Wells, instead stealing its plot and ideas from the preceding CCC Mabuse flicks. Screenwriter Ladislas Fodor snatched a few scattered notions from *The 1000 Eyes of Dr. Mabuse*, but for the most part recapitulated his work on *The Return of Dr. Mabuse*. Having found a successful formula, Artur Brauner, Harald Reinl and Ladislas Fodor were loath to tamper with it.

As before, Dr. Mabuse (Wolfgang Preiss, naturally) is intent on stealing the invention of a mad scientist, and to this end manipulates the scientist's relationship with a woman. To put it in specifics, Mabuse wants Operation X, an invisibility process devised by Prof. Erasmus (Rudolf Furneau) of the improbably named Cosmographic Institute. In a nod to *The Phantom of the Opera*, Erasmus is deeply infatuated with Liane Martin (Karin Dor), star of the Metropol's equally improbably named operetta "The Dancer, the Executioner, and the Clown." She does not know of Erasmus—she has, of course, *never seen him*—but by menacing

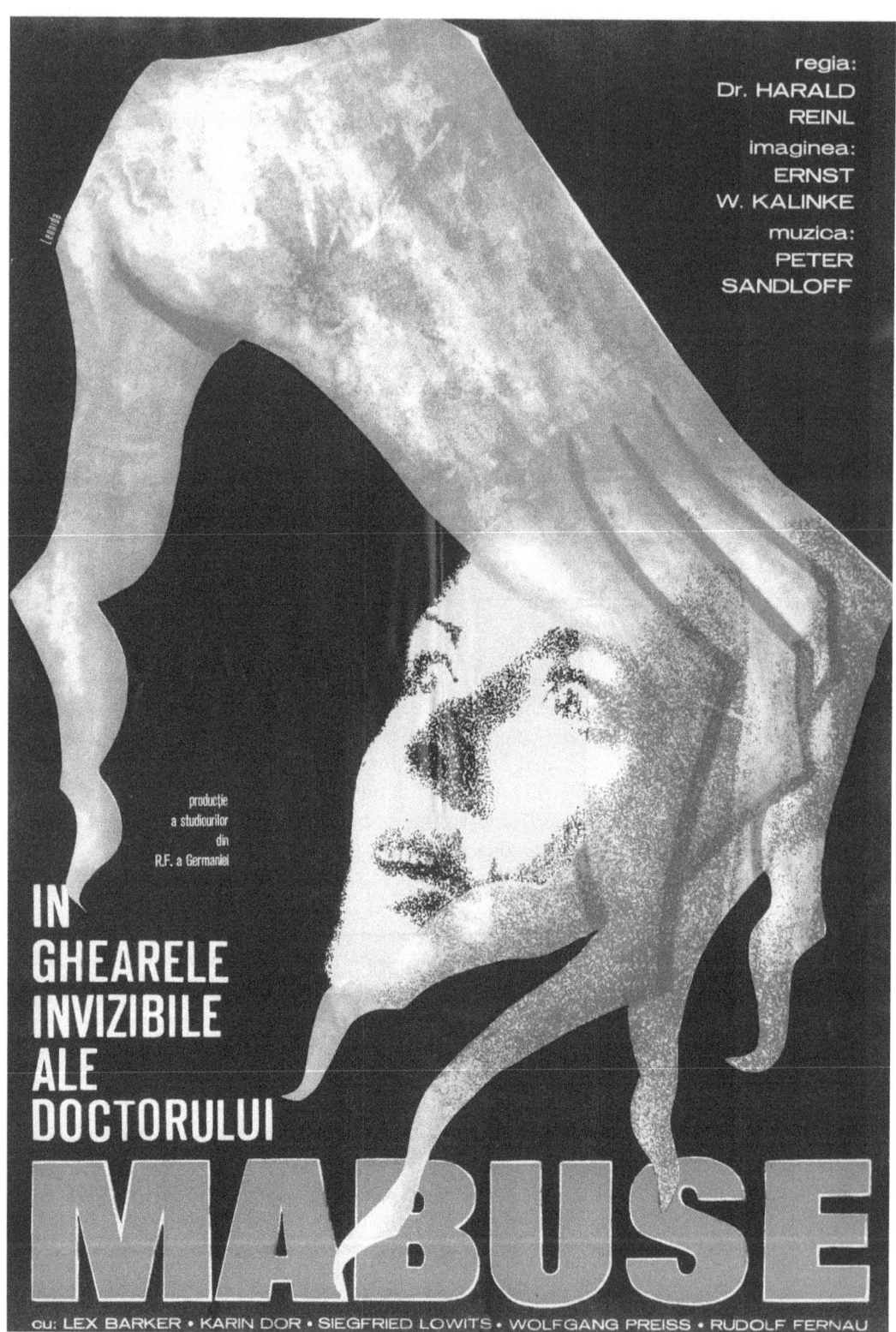

A ghostly hand menaces Karin Dor in this Romanian poster.

Ms. Martin, Mabuse can effectively blackmail Erasmus into compliance.

Mabuse's goal is to grant his loyal army of thugs the power of invisibility, and then send them forth to assassinate heads of state from around the world, and send the globe into chaos. The only genuine obstacle in his path is FBI agent Joe Como (Lex Barker reprising his role).

While Fodor played it safe by carefully remaking his earlier work, Reinl too chose the comfortable route, packing the cast with his friends and regulars. In addition to longtime Reinl standbys like Lex Barker and Rudolf Furneau, the director's wife Karin Dor took the female lead as Liane Martin. Born Kathe Rose Derr in Weisbaden, Germany in 1936, the red-headed star made a name for herself in numerous crime and horror thrillers, and by appearing in the James Bond picture *You Only Live Twice* (1967). Her most prestigious credit came as the Cuban resistance leader in *Topaz* (1969), Alfred Hitchcock's least prestigious production.

As the tormented Liane, haunted by phantoms and exploited by unseen enemies, Dor gives the film's best performance. She strikes just the right note of barely restrained hysteria. It is a shame that Reinl did not see fit to give his

This poster for a U.S. double-bill with *Das Testament des Dr. Mabuse* makes sure viewers catch the James Bond connection.

beloved any more screen time, to flesh out her character any better. Hers is the only really interesting character in the entire story.

While emotional resonance and character development are easily the film's weakest elements, its strong suit lies in Reinl's inventive and almost surreal imagery. The movie is always handsomely photographed, and its best sequence marvelously evokes old-school gothic chills:

Liane is at wit's end, certain that some spectral force is following her—

The cover to the German programme.

ghosts? Whatever it is, it has invaded her dressing room, and then her home. Like a hunted rabbit, she flees her home for a hotel, only to have *it* follow here there—and *touch* her. Under the advice of Dr. Krone (guess who—Wolfgang Preiss!), she retreats to a country inn to recuperate in peace and privacy.

She arrives at the gothic estate, having been followed all the way, both by the phantom and by that intrusive FBI agent Joe Como—is there no escape? The G-man wants to uncover Liane's secret. Whatever torment she is hiding may be the key to the case. Her opera house is ground zero for the crime wave, and his predecessor on the case, Agent Prado, was killed at the opera after watching her performance.

Ms. Martin manages to trap the invisible figure in the bathroom, and Como enters with his gun drawn. The lights are off; only the flickering glare from the fireplace dances across the walls. Thinking fast, Como turns on the hot water and fills the darkened room with steam. The swirling steam and the flickering fire light reveal the outline of the invisible man, and Como captures him. This sequence at the country estate is the highlight of the film, pitched at just the right emotional intensity, with high visual style and exciting well-choreographed action. For a film with no budget for special effects, the simple artistry of this scene is a case study in creative problem solving.

Much to Como's surprise, the man he has just caught is not Dr. Mabuse at all, but Prof. Erasmus. Badly disfigured in an accident, Erasmus has rendered himself invisible in order to observe Liane without frightening her with his scars (thank you, Gaston Leroux). Of course, though, this self-centered lunatic has instead terrified her by being a constant, unseen but always perceived presence.

Up until this point, Como has been operating on the theory that Erasmus is long dead, killed in the accident and replaced by Mabuse himself, who has thus already stolen Operation X. It is but one of many inaccurate suppositions Como makes over the course of the story. In so many sci-fi thrillers of the same period, the hero often jumps to wild and unsupported conclusions that turn out to be the correct answer, as in: this metal cannot be identified, so our opponents *must be* aliens from a planet in exactly our orbit on the other side of the sun. Fodor neatly turns the cliché on its head by making Como spout one inaccurate theory after another.

In all, Como's dialogue is a tangle of paranoid accusations. He variously alleges that the police are corrupted by Mabusian agents (no), that Erasmus and Mabuse have swapped places (not yet) and that Liane Martin is involved in the scheme (yes, but she knows nothing about it). Left to carry the film solo, though, Lex Barker is adrift without Gert Fröbe to play against. Fröbe was a natural at playing this kind of harassed paranoia, and Barker's cool calm made an effective contrast. Here, Barker is still unflappably cool, which is at odds with the manic characterization Fodor has written for him. Somehow between them, Barker and Reinl missed some of Fodor's point.

Prior experience with Mabuse has left psychological scars on Como. He now has difficulty distinguishing fact from fiction, because he has already seen how easily that line blurs. He's ready to believe in Liane's invisible man without skepticism because he no longer trusts the evidence of his own eyes anyway.

The talisman in his journey through fear is a blank piece of paper, an object with significance to him alone. He has just barely started his investigation when a courier pulls up alongside him on a motorcycle and hand-delivers a message from Dr. Mabuse:

A selection of newspaper ads from the brief U.S. run of *Die Unsichtbaren Krallen des Dr. Mabuse*.

"Stay away from dead people, Como. Death is contagious. There aren't many who survive it like I did—an old friend who wants to help you."

How did Mabuse know he was there? How did the courier find him so easily? Right away, Como is certain that he is being watched by unseen eyes. And naturally enough, the message turns out to be written in disappearing ink, leaving Como with nothing more substantial than a blank piece of paper.

As Como's colleagues in the police force ridicule his belief that he is getting messages from the supposedly deceased Dr. Mabuse, the FBI agent is learning a valuable lesson: in this shifty world, communication is an act of coded transmission, privately exchanged between two parties. If observed by outsiders, such transactions are as uninformative as a blank piece of paper.

The entire story revolves around the Metropol's production "The Dancer, the Executioner, and the Clown." To the average patron, who pays the ticket price and docilely take a seat, there is the entertaining performance of Liane Martin as a comely damsel in distress, victimized by an evil clown (Werner Peters). As the show ends morbidly with Liane's beheading, the crowd applauds politely, thrilled at the Grand Guignol spectacle of the stage guillotine, assured of its actual harmlessness. But for a select few in the audience, such as the invisible Erasmus or FBI agents Prado and Como, the show is more fact than fiction. Liane Martin really is a damsel in distress, and her real-life tormentors do include Clown Bobo, a.k.a. Martin Droste, Mabuse's right hand man du jour. And that guillotine sports a real blade, and can be wielded as a fatal instrument should the need arise to tip the

International star and former Tarzan Lex Barker takes the leading man role in *Die Unsichtbaren Krallen*.

balance of fact and fiction in the other direction.*

Primed to find the hidden meanings in public performances, Joe Como visits the planetarium. While ordinary folks—suckers!—sit and passively enjoy the show, Como is there to participate in cloak and dagger theatrics. He knows to take a specific seat and don the assisted listening device—his earpiece whispers instructions on how to meet Erasmus' assistant Dr. Bardof (Kurd Pieritz) and learn the secrets of Operation X.

Interestingly, the pseudoscientific mumbo-jumbo that Bardof provides concerning the technology behind Operation X—something about tinkering with the vibrations of matter to permit lightwaves to pass through—is actually much closer to H.G. Wells' literary *Invisible Man* than the chemically based approach of Whale's film.

When Como returns to the auditorium, he finds a corpse in his former seat. Some poor soul had the misfortune to take the wrong seat and, mistaken for Como, was murdered: Even the assassins are finding it hard to keep track of who is who.

---

*In the 1984 film The Image of Dorian Gray in the Yellow Press, *Ulrike Ottinger employed a very similar narrative device, with an elaborate opera that mirrored offstage intrigue. See Chapter 19 for more details.*

Rudolph Furneau as the Phantom of the Opera knock-off Professor Erasmus.

Architecture, for that matter, can be equally as deceptive. The bathroom where Como captures Erasmus was once a medieval torture chamber, now retrofitted to provide luxurious relaxation. The police HQ where Como reports to his German colleagues is disguised as a fully functional optometrist's. How ironic that these bumbling detectives, trailing an unseen enemy, profit from the sale of eyeglasses to a myopic public!

Harald Reinl concludes his film with his most audacious imagery: armies of transparent soldiers, a line-up of clowns, a severed head, a melting face, bodies floating in glass boxes, seeing-eye dogs yapping into the void, and the terrifying shriek of a madman finally losing what's left of his mind. The finale of the picture is a farrago of wild images, visual puns, duplications, impersonations, trap doors, false fronts and an astonishing spectacle of self-immolation. It begins and ends with Mabuse triumphant—but the manifestation of this triumph makes all the difference in the world.

He has kidnapped Liane, and through her Erasmus. Although the inventor put up a valiant attempt at resistance, by disguising himself as Bardof, Mabuse has finally taken possession of Erasmus' lab and all its fabulous contents. He has sent forth the first wave of his invisible army to inaugurate his reign of terror. And, for good measure, he has imprisoned Joe Como.

But Como is unwilling to concede defeat. In an extended and remarkably

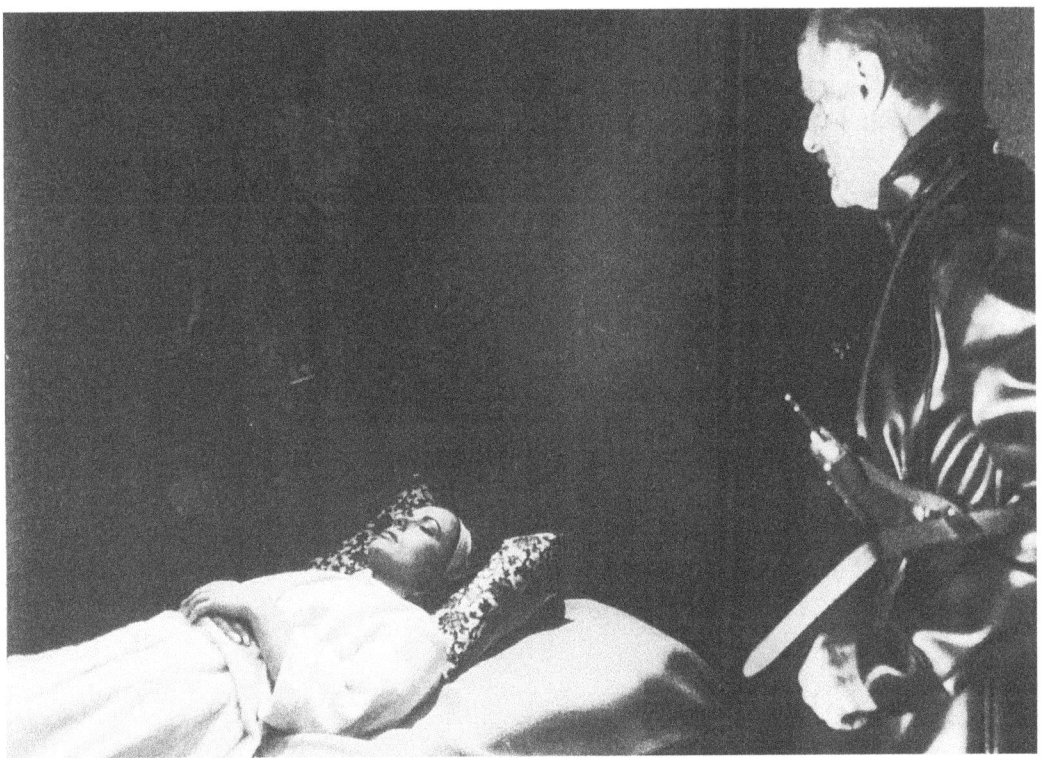

Director Harald Reinl's wife Karin Dor plays Liane Martin with the right note of harassed terror.

violent scene, Como breaks out of his cell, kills many of Mabuse's henchmen and pursues Droste back to the Metropol stage. Unfortunately, Droste has assumed his Bobo costume and slipped into a crowd of identical looking clowns. So, out come the dogs.

Dogs play a major role in this picture, and surface repeatedly in the Mabuse series. Dogs identify a person by a different set of clues—smell, body language and so on. Consequently, disguises designed to fool visually oriented human beings do not necessarily fool man's best friend. It was a dog that sensed Prado's corpse, hidden in a trunk on a pier—a delivery from one fictional party to another: the shortest distance between two non-existent points. It is a police bloodhound that picks Droste out of his clown line-up (recalling Werner Peters' encounter with a dog in *1000 Eyes*, at that). And it is dogs that will be called into service to locate Mabuse's invisible soldiers.

Discovered by the bloodhound, Droste tries once again to flee. But his end is nigh, and before long he will decapitate himself with the guillotine, an act of self-destruction that presages Mabuse's own destiny.

For all his technological advantage, Mabuse fails to found his empire of crime this time. Using decidedly low-tech defenses—trip wires, fire hoses and dogs—the cops roust and capture the invisible assassins. Mabuse beats a hasty retreat back to Erasmus' lab, but finds himself locked in when a fire breaks out. The police start to break through Erasmus' elaborate security measures, but the few minutes that Dr. Mabuse spends trapped in his literal Inferno of Crime are as good as an eternity.

When the lab door finally opens, the badly burned figure that staggers out is but the shell of a human being. With a terrifying laugh, he starts cackling: "I am victorious! Victorious!" In some parallel dimension, in the fantasy world of his own mind, Dr. Mabuse has finally achieved Eitopomar. In his dreamworld, he is Lord and Master at long last.

Like the figurative Inferno that climaxed Fritz Lang's 1922 silent film, this one has driven Mabuse out of his mind, setting the stage for Artur Brauner's dream project, *The Testament of Dr. Mabuse*.

Chapter 13

The Testament of Dr. Mabuse

With Dr. Mabuse, anything is possible.

—Inspector Lohmann

At last, Artur Brauner got his dearest wish. From the day that he, an impressionable teenager, first snuck out of his house to see Fritz Lang's controversial masterpiece against Father Brauner's wishes, he had been seized by *The Testament of Dr. Mabuse*. In his own way, Brauner had become possessed by the testament just like the asylum director in the story itself, compelled to carry Mabuse's legend onward. Lang's 1933 film inspired Brauner to become a filmmaker himself, and for decades he nurtured plans to stage his own version of the tale.

In 1954, with his CCC venture not yet ten years old, Brauner bought the rights to the character from the ailing Norbert Jacques. At about the same time, Brauner began a protracted campaign to woo Lang himself back to Germany. When at last he managed to hook Lang, Brauner almost immediately proposed a remake of *Testament of Dr. Mabuse*.

And why not? Brauner had built his CCC empire on a solid foundation of recalling the past glories of Germany's Golden Age. Remakes were good business, and what would be a better fit for the two men than a restaging of one of Lang's greatest hits, the very film responsible for Brauner's love of cinema?

Lang was disinterested in merely rehashing past successes, and instead persuaded Brauner to let him mount an entirely new production, one that bore precious little resemblance to his 1933 Mabuse film in either story or style. Once Lang left, however, Brauner was free to continue the Mabuse franchise as he saw fit. Naturally enough, producer Brauner had screenwriter Ladislas Fodor and director Harald Reinl make *The Return of Dr. Mabuse* a near clone of *The Testament of Dr. Mabuse*, borrowing heavily from both its broad story outline and many key scenes in specific. Immediately following that, *The Invisible Dr. Mabuse* was itself a near clone of *Return*.

Brauner could scarcely wait, however, to go all the way. Less than six months after *Invisible Dr. Mabuse* opened, Brauner unveiled a full-fledged remake of *Testament of Dr. Mabuse* (both pictures were released in the United States simultaneously in 1965). Although the resulting product was a modest enough commercial hit in Germany to justify the continuation of the Mabuse series, Brauner must have been disappointed by the overall critical reception. Lang's original had been hailed as a masterpiece, beloved around the world, an influential and groundbreaking classic of

A U.S. newspaper ad with comic book–like graphics.

modern horror. Brauner's remake, a high-profile release from the most successful studio in postwar Europe, benefiting from some 30 years worth of improved filmmaking technique, was just another B-movie thriller.

In the world of film criticism, sequels are an unloved lot, and remakes fare even worse. *Testament*, to its misfortune, is both at once, and thus is an easy target for critical disdain. Indeed, for many critics, it is a matter of principle to dismiss sequels and remakes as inferior, derivative products that reveal all the worst aspects of the commercial side of the film industry. Serious artists make original films, goes the thinking, while only hired hacks crank out such knock-offs.

In Hollywood at the dawn of the twenty-first century, an overwhelming trend towards remakes has taken hold. Major motion pictures are adapted from any preexisting source material with some minimal name recognition. Even unlikely sources with dubious popularity are raided by Hollywood in a desperate search for presold titles—from old TV shows like *The Wild Wild West* or *The Mod Squad*, to silent films like Buster Keaton's *Seven Chances*, to cult properties of questionable mass appeal like *Godzilla* or *The Avengers*. That many of these result in expensive bombs, while creations of more original vintage win the hearts of audiences and critics, has not in any way deterred Hollywood producers from their remake-obsession. The reason is that remakes offer, not the guarantee of success, but the illusion of that guarantee. In the fear-driven culture of studio executives, the staggering costs of film production coupled with the fickle and unpredictable audience tastes, a recognizable title offers reassurance to jittery bean counters. If that recognizable title does not in fact actually offer any greater likelihood of success, it at least appears to, and therein lies its perennial appeal to a risk-adverse culture like Hollywood.

However, Hollywood at the turn of the millennium is an economic juggernaut. Year after year box office records are set and broken, and "the industry" reigns as one of America's most powerful exports, its international hegemony unchallenged by any other country's films, no matter how good they may be. If such awesome prosperity can yet nurture a risk-adverse culture, the situation that Artur Brauner faced in the 1960s must have been fear itself.

Film historians now speak of the 1960s as a time of "crisis" for the German film industry, but the word crisis implies a solution, and to those experiencing the events first-hand, the words "calamity" and "apocalypse" would have been more apt. The 15–odd years after the end of the war had not been easy for German filmmakers, but now studios were closing their doors and disappearing into bankruptcy right and left, taking with them any banks that had been foolhardy enough to loan them money. The banks responded by refusing to issue credit to producers, who had to then rely on the profits of their own products to finance continued production. Those profits shrank, and with them shrank the already meager number of films being made in Germany. There was virtually no international market for German films, and audiences at home preferred Hollywood imports.

Furthermore, the domestic market had just been cut clean in half, as East and West Germany were severed by the erection of the Berlin Wall.

For years, the Communist government of East Germany had suffered the hemorrhaging exodus of many of their citizens to the West. Hundreds of people were crossing the border on a daily basis, never to return. It was not only a public relations disaster, an insult to their claims

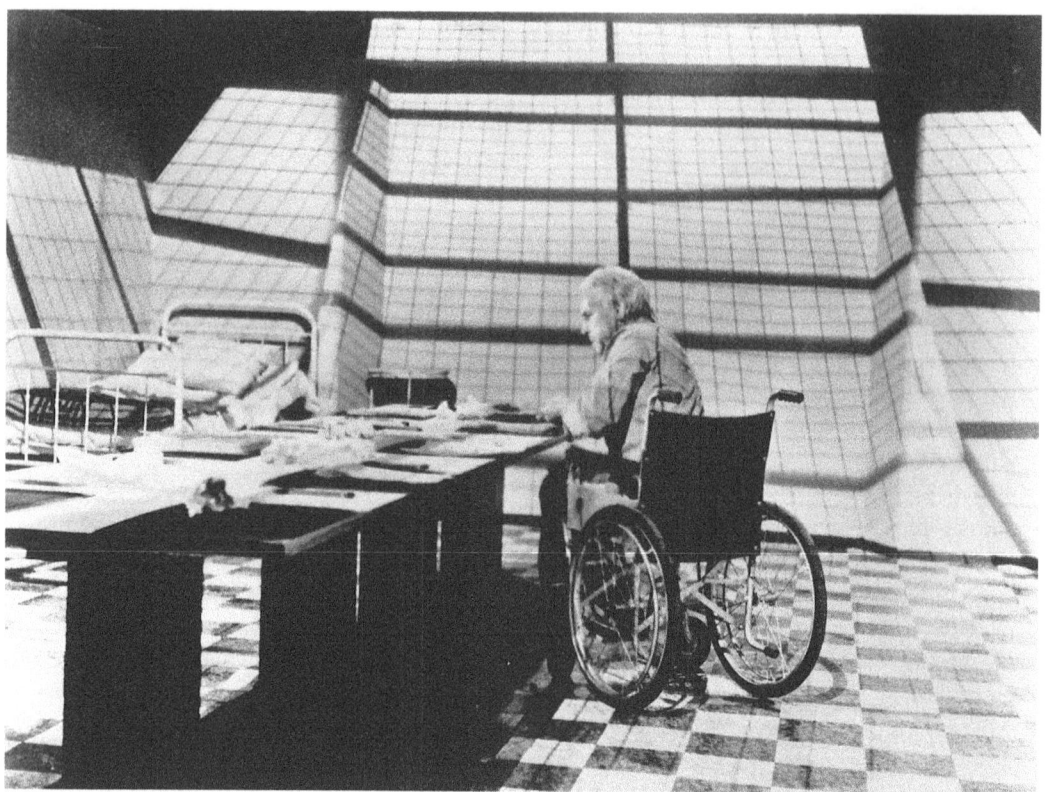

German Expressionism, 1960s style, heralds the start of the one of the best German thrillers of the decade.

of having created a perfect society in contrast to the decadent, exploitative ways of the capitalists in the West, but the exodus also sucked vital life-blood from the East German society.

On August 13, 1961, Walter Ulbricht put a stop to it. The Wall was called an "anti-fascist protective barrier," in the typically self-delusional party propaganda, but the 13-foot-high cement blocks topped with barbed wire were clearly designed not to keep Westerners out, but Easterners in. The guards with their machine guns aimed not over the wall, to the purported fascists outside, but at the 20-foot "death strip," covered by land mines, that led up to the Wall.

East Germans continued to try to escape, but what had once been a simple border crossing was now a deadly proposition. The guards were instructed to shoot to kill. Over the nearly 30-year life of the Wall, some 75 East Germans were killed in cold blood trying to cross the Wall. Ulbricht regretted his creation, and regarded it his worst public relations defeat. He once said that every bullet fired at a citizen trying to escape was a self-inflicted wound. But 75 dead in less than 30 years was nothing compared to the over 2.7 million who had fled in the years between the founding of the German Democratic Republic (GDR) and the construction of the Wall. In fact, 30,000 of those defectors had left in just one month, that July immediately before the Wall's installation.

What must be emphasized here, though, especially to those who may be unfamiliar with the geography of Germany, is that the city of Berlin lay in its entirety inside the boundaries of East Germany. In other words, the Wall was not a simple partition running down the middle of the country. Instead, Ulbricht's creation completely encircled West Berlin. From the standpoint, then, of the West, the Wall's principal threat was not the terrorism imposed on the East German people but the possibility that the population of West Germany might be cut off from the rest of the world altogether. The Berlin Wall could have been the flashpoint for World War III.

With their studios in West Berlin, the already beleaguered producers panicked. Driven by paranoid fears that borders would close, or that Berlin would soon be ground zero for a nuclear confrontation between the U.S. and the USSR, many of them simply fled. Brauner, ever the stubborn mule, stayed behind, committed as ever to his adoptive home. CCC, though, had few friends to whom they could turn for support. They were forced to severely curtail the number of films they would make, and the ambitions of those films to boot. To survive, Brauner would have to reduce risks in every possible way.

Brauner understood, however, that the strategies for risk-reduction took an inevitable artistic toll. Films were becoming stupider, more poorly made, duller, less interesting. No wonder audiences preferred American imports. So in 1962, Brauner announced that he was launching a new mini-studio, called CCC-Kunstfilm (CCC Art Films). The new branch was to produce three films a year on a set (low) budget reserved from the main studio's profits. In other words, CCC could and would continue in its time-honored rut of low-risk bottom-feeding, which would in turn give CCC-Kunstfilm the freedom to take risks. CCC-Kunstfilm could break new ground with nothing to lose: Their annual budget was guaranteed by the main studio's success. CCC-Kunstfilm's productions could fail without risking the future either of the branch or the main studio. It was a strategy that Hollywood would later mimic in the creation of classics divisions which would specialize in small art films and foreign imports while the main studios pursued traditional "mass market" blockbusters.

Nineteen sixty-two was, then, a perfect year for *The Testament of Dr. Mabuse*, as it was a perfect example of Artur Brauner's filmmaking. At once a sequel and a remake, a nostalgic repeat of Germany's past cinematic glories, an homage to Brauner's favorite director and Brauner's favorite movie character, the new and improved *Testament of Dr. Mabuse* was simultaneously a crassly commercial enterprise and one of CCC's greatest achievements. While the remake could never hope to compete with the best qualities of Lang's original, it did manage to improve on the original's weaknesses and take its place as a worthy, thoughtful, valid update.

Frozen in time and divorced from context, 1962 was a crowning year for Artur Brauner, as he survived the crisis that felled so many of his peers and competitors. While no one would mistake the new *Testament* for a classic, within the limited expectations Brauner had for the picture it was a solid success and a vindication of his overall philosophy: Films like this proved that risk-adverse did not have to be bad, and their box office victories could finance riskier, more innovative works. History would have the last laugh. Brauner kept the Mabuse series going, and going downhill at that. The individual merits of pictures like *Testament* would quickly be lost in the deluge of mediocrity that followed. As for CCC-Filmkunst, its initial stab at art film production was such a disaster that the branch lived out its life as a soft-porn factory, Brauner's grandiose dreams of a German New Wave long forgotten.

The remake focuses more on Mabuse's crime wave than Lang's version did.

The Testament of Dr. Mabuse was the last of Brauner's Mabuses to be released theatrically in the United States. The Mabuse films unfortunately fell between two stools. Their curious blend of horror, sci-fi and mystery genres made marketing a challenge. The foreign-language soundtracks posed an additional hurdle, American audiences being notoriously indifferent to non–English speaking films. While an audience existed (and exists) for subtitles, that niche crowd was more interested in brooding dramas, less so in lurid thrillers. Once dubbed in English, though, the Mabuse pictures were trapped in a cut-rate distribution cycle of drive-ins and double-bills, where the competition for the teenage audience's pocket cash was fierce. In terms of action, Brauner's Mabuses could not compete with the high-octane thrills of the James Bond pictures. In terms of horror, the garishly colorful Hammer films offered more gore and sex. Stylistically, Brauner's output best matched the work of American independents, whose low-budget, black-and-white sci-fi cheapies had the distinct advantage of being voiced in English. The Mabuse films were a genre unto themselves; and that fact all but denied them an audience. *Invisible Dr. Mabuse* and *Testament of Dr. Mabuse* made the rounds in 1965, dubbed in their original titles, and enjoyed a reissue in 1966 under the names *The Invisible Horror* and *Terror of the Mad Doctor*, respectively—the U.S. distributors obviously perceived no marquee value in the name "Mabuse." *Scotland Yard vs. Dr. Mabuse* and *The Death Ray of Dr. Mabuse* were fortunate to find TV bookings, and

The Vengeance of Dr. Mabuse never made it to the U.S. in any form.

The prevailing prejudice against remakes has long prevented a genuine appraisal of the 1962 *Testament of Dr. Mabuse*. What little has been written on the film goes no farther and no deeper than obvious and unnuanced unfavorable comparisons with Lang's original. Yet "Lang's original" is something of a misnomer. Sure, Brauner sought to remake a film first made by Fritz Lang, but Lang did not work alone, and his work resulted in more than one variant edition of the underlying narrative. Over the years, the involvement of novelist Norbert Jacques and screenwriter Thea von Harbou has been obscured, and the alternate French-language version and English recut version have disappeared, resulting in the illusion of Lang as a lone artist responsible for a classic 1933 film. In subsequent years, though, Lang struggled to rewrite his personal history and claim that the 1933 *Testament* was a project foist on him by his producer, something he made under protest and that he redeemed only by his subversive anti–Nazi subtext. That he had been scheming the project for years, collaborating with Jacques and von Harbou on it at a time when by his own admission his political views were naive and ill-formed, was shoved into the shadows.

If Lang struggled to disown the Mabuse legacy, Brauner struggled at least as much to lay claim to it. He purchased the rights from Jacques, which gave him an unassailable legal claim. That the original *Testament of Dr. Mabuse* had been the inspiration for Brauner's film career gave him something of a moral claim as well.

Four key sequences best illustrate the different approaches taken by the various versions of the story: Brauner's 1962 remake, Norbert Jacques' novel and Lang's 1933 film. (For the purposes of this discussion, the German, French, and English versions of Lang's film will be treated as a single entity.)

The first key sequence is the crime spree. Jacques spends little of his time describing the crimes, yet his novel contains one important element unique to his version. His Mabuse is planning a major nerve gas attack on Berlin, which is only averted at the last possible moment. His Mabuse was a specter of World War I, a monster who profited from the evils of that war. Naturally enough, his crimes invoked horrible memories of the Great War.

Lang did not include any such idea in his film. Neither does he spend much screen time on the various robberies and acts of terrorism being committed by Mabuse's gang. Instead, the crimes are described, referred to but never seen. Perhaps it was a budgetary issue that prevented Lang from visualizing these scenes, but it weakens the film. The audience is told that Mabuse's crimes are bringing the country to its knees, but since this is almost never directly shown, Mabuse's evil seems somewhat remote.

By contrast, the remake indulges in several memorable set pieces depicting in exacting detail the efficient, meticulous operation of Mabuse's gang. Led by the unctuously charming Mortimer (wonderfully played by Charles Regnier in a role unique to this version of the story), the gang pulls off a number of daring heists. These scenes are highlights of the film, and show with high style what Lang was content merely to describe. The remake is off to a good start.

Both Jacques and Lang begin their versions with the police informant Hofmeister having infiltrated Mabuse's counterfeiting plant. He is detected by the rest of the gang, and almost killed. In a moment that appears in all variations of

Testament, the thugs try to dispose of him with an exploding barrel of gasoline. Hofmeister escapes and attempts to phone Inspector Lohmann with his discovery. Lohmann refuses to talk to the disgraced ex-cop, and their argument costs Hofmeister precious time. Before he can utter the name "Mabuse" into the phone, he is driven mad by an agent of the master criminal. In examining the scene of the crime, Lohmann discovers that Hofmeister inscribed Mabuse's name backwards in a pane of glass using his diamond ring.

In detail, Jacques and Lang are telling the same story, but the effect is radically different. Jacques explains everything carefully for the reader: that Hofmeister was kicked off Lohmann's police force for accepting a bribe and is now trying to redeem himself by unauthorized undercover work; that Mabuse silences him with a drug that makes him appear insane, which in turn causes Hofmeister to be interred in Dr. Born's asylum, where he can be safely muzzled. In part because film is a medium ill-suited to that kind of detailed narrative exposition, but moreover because Lang is aiming for a queasier sense of ambiguity and mystery, his film's version of these events is baffling and disorienting.

Lang begins his film with an unknown man trying to escape some unknown place while other unknown figures try, for unknown reasons, to stop him. Not until later will the audience learn who Hofmeister is or what he was trying to do. At no point will Lang make any effort to explain just how Mabuse managed to drive a man out of his mind on cue. The resulting sequence is indeed fascinating, and arguably the 1933 film's best scene. It is pure cinema: Lang has strung together visuals and sounds that convey a palpable sense of terror and dread, but which cannot be easily translated into words because they create emotions without communicating any comprehensible narrative information.

The comparable sequence in the Brauner variant occurs quite late in the film, enabling the filmmakers to better approximate the effect in Jacques' book. By this point in the film, the audience knows that Flocke (Leon Askin, a familiar face to fans of the TV sitcom *Hogan's Heroes*) is an ex-cop who has infiltrated Mabuse's gang but intends to squeal to Lohmann (Fröbe again). The audience also understands what is at stake for Flocke, and to just what ruthless lengths Mortimer and the others will go to protect Mabuse's operation. Lang's approach is a triumph of pure cinema, but it is rather cold emotionally because the audience is confused. Brauner's approach milks greater drama out of the situation by placing it in context.

Additionally, director Werner Klinger stages the chase with a strong visual flair. As Flocke runs away, he steps in some white paint. His attempts to vanish into the crowd, or to evade his pursuers, are defeated by the tell-tale trail of white footprints he leaves. The idea resembles Lang's own *M*, when Peter Lorre was identified by a chalk M that enabled his pursuers to keep track of him in the crowd. Having paid due homage to Lang with this device, screenwriter Ladislas Fodor then tosses in something entirely of his own. Mortimer corners the frightened Flocke in a phone booth, interrupting his call to Lohmann before the informant can name Mabuse as the mastermind. Mortimer hands Flocke a gun and politely asks him to shoot himself, since Mortimer would rather not get blood on himself. Flocke aims the gun at Mortimer instead, and fires. The gun has been rigged to shoot backwards, and so Flocke has indeed shot himself. While the suicide-that-is-a-murder is a typically Langian touch, the particulars of the scene, from Mortimer's marvelously fey dialogue to the weapon that literally backfires on Flocke, are unique and memorable.

The invasion of Pohland: Wolfgang Preiss (middle) hands over the role of Mabuse to Germany's answer to Henry Fonda, Walter Rilla (left).

Then comes the topper. Lohmann investigates the scene of Flocke's murder (this Mabuse has no intention of letting his stool pigeon off with a wrist-slapping punishment like madness). Director Klingler places the camera outside the phone booth in just the right position so that we see the name "Mabuse" etched in the glass before Lohmann does. It is a revelatory moment. In terms of pure visual impact, this one shot by Klingler bests Lang's treatment of the same material.

By far the most telling difference between the various versions can be seen in the transformation of the asylum director into Dr. Mabuse. Of the three editions, Jacques' novel is the one most concerned with character psychology. Although in Jacques' telling of the story, the actual moment of transformation predates the events of the book, his emphasis is on the exploration of Dr. Born's mind. Somehow in the course of treating Mabuse's insanity, Born has lost control of his own identity and collapsed the distinction between therapist and patient.

In a detail unique to Jacques' rendition, Dr. Born had developed a split identity *prior* to his involvement with Mabuse. Born's first criminal alter ego is Rauschmann, a diabolical chemist who cooks up the poisons, nerve gases and psychoactive drugs to be used by Mabuse's underworld syndicate. Thus Born is already a psychologically unstable egotist fixated on the allure of authoritarianism, and predisposed to incognito criminal activity. When Mabuse is committed to his care, Born takes the opportunity to appropriate Mabuse's

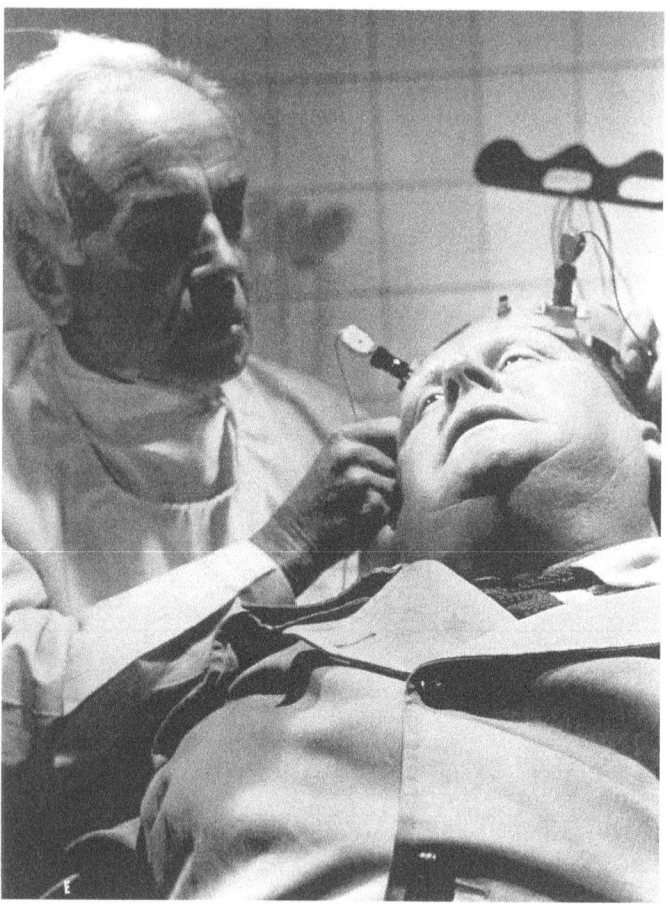

Walter Rilla affixes electrodes to Gert Fröbe's head for the final grudge match between Dr. Mabuse and Inspector Lohmann.

legacy and reputation as his own. Mabuse's mere physical presence awakens the worst aspects of Born's ugly soul.

Lang himself was less interested in that aspect of the story, and the 1933 film paints a more ambiguous picture of Baum's descent into madness. Two scenes in particular serve to illustrate Lang's approach.

In the first, Inspector Lohmann confronts Dr. Baum with the allegation that his star patient, Mabuse, is somehow directing a criminal enterprise from within the asylum. Baum responds by showing Lohmann the recently deceased corpse of Mabuse. As Lohmann stares at the toe-tagged body, yet another literal deadend in his investigations, Baum then proceeds to praise the late Dr. Mabuse as a genius, a god among men, a true Nietzschean superman. Baum not only envies Mabuse, he idolizes him. This psychiatrist is in no way suited to treat Mabuse's megalomania. If anything, Baum is rapidly succumbing to the same megalomania himself.

Shortly afterward, Lang looks in on Dr. Baum alone in his office at night. Like Ebenezer Scrooge, Baum is visited by a ghost. This Ghost of Crimes Past, Present and Future is none other than an apparition of the late Dr. Mabuse, come to claim that which is rightfully his— Baum's tainted soul. The Faustian bargain is sealed, and Baum trades his soul to Mabuse in exchange for Mabuse's fascist supremacy.

Lang later said that he regretted his visualization of this scene. After embracing strict realism during his Hollywood years, Lang looked back with some contempt on the more flamboyant symbolism of his German films. In other words, Lang always saw the supernatural aspects of this scene between Mabuse and Baum as a *symbolic* representation of Baum's corruption. He never intended a literal interpretation—that Mabuse's deathless spirit reaches out from beyond the grave to possess Baum's body—and had he to do it over again, he would have dropped the scene altogether.

So, although the presentation differs between Jacques' and Lang's iterations, both share the same basic message. Baum/Born is attracted to Mabuse's cult of personality, and when he takes Mabuse's name and mission as his own, it is not because of any faculty of Mabuse's per se but rather an expression of the corruption already present in the asylum director.

"Mabuse" no longer really exists at all—it's all Baum/Born. Even in Lang's film, Baum is seen to be acting as Mabuse, controlling the underworld organization, and singing Mabuse's praises to Lohmann *before* Mabuse's spirit appears to possess him.

The asylum director has become Mabuse not because Mabuse as a specific individual has any particular demonic power, but rather because—and here is the genuine horror of the story—Mabuse's evil personality is a dime a dozen, his cruel ideology prevalent. In early '30s Germany, this was the nightmare Jacques and Lang were living, and it made a natural choice of subject matter for their horror story. Adolf Hitler was a devil incarnate, but he was not alone. There were numberless petty Hitlers—the Himmlers, the Goebbelses, the Heydrichs—to say nothing of the armies of brownshirts, storm troopers and tag-alongs. What could be a more apt metaphor for Nazi Germany than an insane asylum taken over by its inmates? The world had indeed gone mad.

There is no reason to expect that the 1962 remake should follow the same subtext. If Brauner's remake had been the scene-for-scene remake some critics erroneously called it, it would have been a total misfire. Hitler was dead in his grave more than 15 years already, and the de–Nazification of Germany was no longer as pressing a concern. Brauner had already learned through his disastrous experience with *Morituri* (see Chapter 10) that German audiences wanted nothing less than to be reminded of their Nazi history. While Brauner had chosen to eschew overtly political themes, Ladislas Fodor had never shown interest in political issues at any point in his career. For his part, director Werner Klingler had remained an active director under Goebbels' regime and had no moral standing to wag his finger at the Nazis. Instead, Brauner, Fodor and Klingler would redirect the subtext of their remake to something more urgent to 1962 audiences, and they would do so by adapting the same two scenes used by Fritz Lang 30 years earlier.

The scene in which Prof. Pohland (Walter Rilla in the latest variation on the Born/Baum role) eulogizes Mabuse to Lohmann has been moved until *after* the scene in which Mabuse's spirit possesses Pohland's body. This chronological renovation has some significant consequences. By placing the transformation scene at a point before Mabuse's demise, the filmmakers have allowed the focus of that scene to be not on special effects (as in Lang's) but on the performance of the actors.

Wolfgang Preiss rises to the challenge. He gives arguably his finest appearance in the entire series—a run that, all told, adds up to only a few meager minutes of actual screen time.* Cool, calm and collected, Preiss' Mabuse proudly explains to a horrified Pohland that he has been used as Mabuse's tool. The arch-criminal then projects his will into Pohland's body. Only after this scene does Pohland lionize the late Dr. Mabuse to Lohmann. Thus, Pohland's pro–Mabuse speech does not reveal any latent corruption in his soul

---

*Preiss appears as Mabuse in only five of the six 1960s Mabuse films. Although credited in 1964's Death Ray of Dr. Mabuse, and prominently featured on the posters, Preiss was on vacation during filming and was surprised to find himself listed in the cast. "It sells better with your name," was Brauner's explanation.

Helmut Schmid as Johnny Briggs with Senta Berger as his girlfriend Nelly.

as in the earlier version, but instead reveals Mabuse's egotism expressed through Pohland's co-opted voice. Pohland is a puppet, animated by Mabuse's will. Previously, the asylum director was complicit in his own destruction, a willing acolyte of Mabuse. This time around, the asylum director is an unwitting stooge, an innocent victim, a good man forced to do bad things.

The casting of Walter Rilla reinforces the depiction of Pohland as a sympathetic victim. Rilla's extensive career began in 1923, when his talent was discovered by Prof. Eugen Robert, the esteemed director of the Berliner Tribune and the Theaters am Kurfurstendamm. Although he was entirely untrained, and placed on stage alongside many great, highly regarded actors, Rilla had found his destiny. He quickly became a star. Recognizing him as that rare gem, a natural, the film industry swooped in to claim him. Sure enough, Rilla found at least as much popularity on screen as on stage. He had an urbane charm, a refinement and cultivation that did not appear at all snobbish or distant, but genuine. It was said that he was a nobleman playing ordinary men. The analogous casting, had Brauner mounted his remake in Hollywood, would have been to cast James Stewart or Henry Fonda as Pohland. Far from the officious authoritarianism of Oscar Beregi in Lang's film, Rilla is clearly the decent man next door caught up in events outside his ken.

All of this reflects contemporary fears. If Lang and Jacques were responding to the dominant fear of their day (the fascism inherent in their fellow man), the new film touches a more modern nerve:

the threat from outside. From sci-fi parables like *The Invasion of the Body Snatchers* (1956) to *noir*-ish thrillers like *The Manchurian Candidate* (1962), filmmakers of all kinds made hay with the Cold War public's fear of mind control—a theme that Fodor had run through all of the CCC Mabuse pictures. Unlike Nazism, Communism was perceived as a totalitarianism imposed from without. During Hitler's reign, there were virtually no domestic attempts at resistance; contrast that with the daily imagery of the Berlin Wall, a concrete barrier erected to keep unhappy East Germans imprisoned in the Soviet system. As the face of German totalitarianism changed, with it changed the tactics of its metaphor, Dr. Mabuse.

Lastly, the role of the defector has been adapted. In both Jacques' and Lang's renderings, Thomas Kent is an ex-con unable to find honest work in the profoundly depressed economy. With no alternative option, he enlists with Mabuse's gang and finds his conscience torn. One the one hand, having clothes and food and a roof over his head are essential elements of one's self-esteem, but on the other hand the ruthless activities that bring him these creature comforts gnaw at his sense of morality. Thanks to the encouragement of his girlfriend (Born's daughter Helli in the book, a young woman named Lily in the film), Kent defects and reveals everything to Lohmann. Without his switch of loyalties, Lohmann would never have cracked the case. Indeed, in the book Lohmann cannot praise the turncoat enough for having saved Germany from Mabuse's planned gas attack.

In the remake, the economic commentary has been dropped. In the midst of an "economic miracle," German audiences would not have been as receptive. In fact for the English-dubbed recut of Lang's film that was prepared in Hollywood in 1950, all scenes relating to Kent's economic plight were deleted, with no resonance for 1950s America. Instead, Brauner and his team present Johnny Briggs (Helmut Schmid), a washed-up boxer who is recruited by Mabuse's enforcer Mortimer. Like Pohland, Briggs is at heart a good man forced to do bad.

As Briggs' girl Nelly, the lovely and talented Senta Berger is completely wasted. During the 1960s, Berger was considered the European answer to Raquel Welch—every bit as beautiful and a better actress to boot. In addition to her film career, Berger was a pop star as well. However, even at the best of times Fodor was unable to write well-developed female characters for the Mabuse pictures, and with the least female-centric work of Fritz Lang's entire filmography to work with, Fodor includes Nelly as nothing more than an afterthought. Like Daliah Lavi and Karin Dor before her, and Sabine Bethmann and Yvonne Furneaux to follow, poor Berger represents squandered potential personified.

As Briggs, Schmid gets more screen time but not much more in the way of characterization. His role is largely just to stand around and look strong, which Schmid does capably well. In the finale of the picture, Briggs comes to Lohmann's rescue in a sequence unique to the remake. As good as Lang's film was, it suffered from a pacing problem. After Kent's escape from Mabuse's lair, the emotional climax has passed, but the film still has some 30 minutes yet to unspool. For the remake, the filmmakers have substantially tightened things up. The revelation that Pohland has become Mabuse, Briggs' decision to defect, and the climactic chase as Lohmann and Briggs hunt Pohland down has all been compacted into a very few minutes.

In the course of this narrative compression, Fodor has added a personal

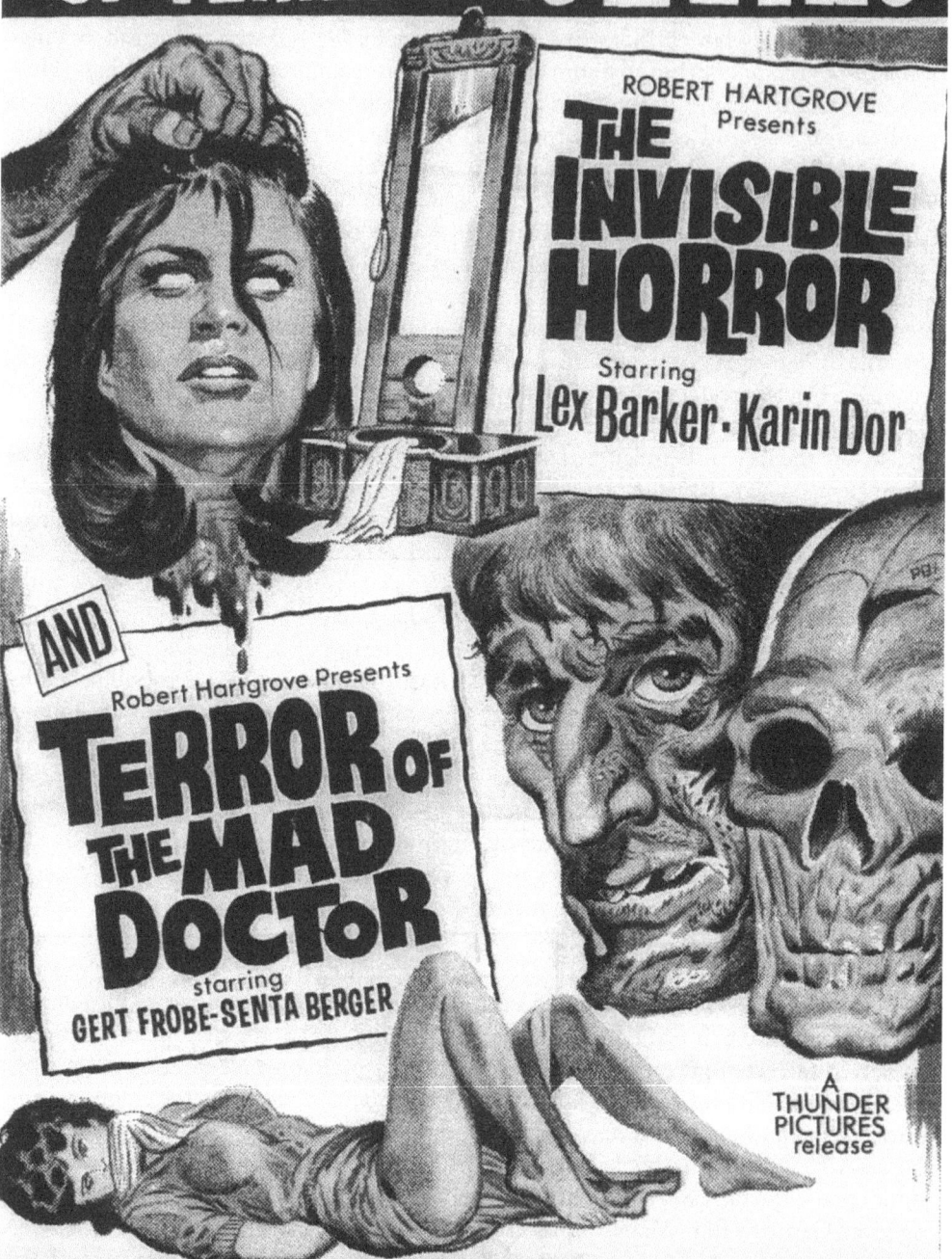

This ad from the U.S. double-bill amply demonstrates the mishandling these Gothic crime thrillers got from befuddled distributors.

confrontation between Pohland/Mabuse and Lohmann. Over the last four films, the police have methodically tracked the crime lord and thwarted his every nefarious scheme. For that Mabuse wants revenge. Since it would not be a Mabuse film without some kind of crazy gadget—unlike the James Bond series, in the world of Mabuse it is always the bad guys who have the coolest toys—Pohland/Mabuse straps his nemesis to a wild contraption intended to drive him insane.

He need not bother.

Pohland is not the only one who has lost track of the distinction between himself and Mabuse. Not in the sense of his being a criminal, though, since Lohmann remains an upstanding representative of the judicial system. Nevertheless, he has become obsessed with his quarry, such that he can no longer truly function in normal society. He sees evil conspiracies in every event, menace in every shadow. Even his assistant (Harald Juhnke) makes fun of his propensity to jump to theories straight out of pulpy comic books. In *The Return of Dr. Mabuse*, he stared out his window at a crowd of innocent people going about their business and wondered aloud which of them was Dr. Mabuse—at a time when everyone else was certain Mabuse was dead. To paraphrase a popular slogan, just because they really are after you doesn't mean you're not paranoid.

Johnny Briggs, captured by Mabuse's goons for his insubordination, happens to be in the asylum during Lohmann's torture and hears the man scream as his mind cracks. Briggs races to the rescue and frees Lohmann, but he can never free the detective from the memories of the nightmares he has witnessed first-hand over the years. Mabuse has laid claim to a small portion of Lohmann's mind and nothing will ever dislodge him.

It is tempting to think of Lohmann as checking himself into the asylum after the events of the film, perhaps even taking the cell right next to the one occupied by Pohland, the two of them trying together to exorcise the demons of their minds. Neither Gert Fröbe nor the name "Lohmann" would ever appear in the series again. There was much about the tone of *The Testament of Dr. Mabuse* that implied that those concerned considered it the finale of the series, the final confrontation between Lohmann and Mabuse, the end of the franchise. If this had been the thinking at CCC, the box office success of the picture put that notion to rest, and Brauner brought Rilla's tortured Pohland back for two more outings in the coming years.

The Testament of Dr. Mabuse could not beat Lang at his own game, but for what it was, this remake stands as a worthy, thoughtful update of a classic film. It is a solid achievement, and one of Brauner's finest creations.

Chapter 14

Dr. Mabuse vs. Scotland Yard

> It was exactly 3:35 on the afternoon of April 23rd when George Harry Cockston decided to conquer the world single-handed.
> —opening line of Bryan Edgar Wallace's *The Device**

With all the valedictory qualities of *The Testament of Dr. Mabuse*, for CCC to continue its Mabuse series some changes would have to be made. There was only so long they could have gone on raiding the works of Fritz Lang for ideas; new blood was needed. So, for 1963's entry *Dr. Mabuse vs. Scotland Yard*, screenwriter Ladislas Fodor chose to start raiding the works of Bryan Edgar Wallace.

To understand the role Wallace played in German horror cinema, one must first understand the role his father, Edgar Wallace, played. Born in 1875, Richard Horatio Edgar Wallace was an almost unfathomably prolific author, an unparalleled specialist in detective, horror and science-fiction thrillers. His parents were a pair of Greenwich actors, Polly Richards and Richard Horatio Edgar Marriott. To conceal the shame of the illegitimate birth, father Marriott used the pseudonym Walter Wallace on his son's birth records, and thus was Richard Horatio Edgar Wallace born. As the boy grew up in the adoptive home of Dick Freeman, a London fishporter, he applied all his faculties of dedication and hard work to claw his way up out of infamy and to a position not only of respectability, but overwhelming international acclaim.

Quitting school at the age of 12, Wallace served in the Royal West Kent Regiment from 1893 to 1896. Upon his discharge from the army, Wallace began a career as a foreign correspondent for *The Daily Mail* and other major newspapers. In 1905 he published his first novel, *The Four Just Men*, and by 1911 had established a solid literary reputation with *Sanders of the River*. During the course of his career, Wallace generated no less than 175 books, 23 plays and 957 short stories. This does not take into account his work as a practicing journalist (he was neither the first nor the last reporter-cum-novelist in the history of *Dr. Mabuse*). During the late 1920s, one out of every four books sold in England was by the hand of Wallace.

Or rather, by the voice of Wallace, for to maintain his prodigious output Wallace did not write his books so much as recite them. He would hole himself up with the necessary supplies—that is,

---

**Inexplicably, the dust jacket to* The Device *uses this line with different wording and even a different date: "At 3:35 on March 15th, George Harry Cockston decided to conquer the world single-handed."*

cigarettes and tea—and let his darkest imagination flow out from his soul through his lips and onto the recording spool of a Dictaphone. He could crank out an entire novel in about 72 hours. As the author collapsed in much-needed sleep, his loyal secretary Robert Curtis would take the wax cylinder from the Dictaphone and type up the manuscript. Aside from Curtis' mild proofreading—mainly to ensure Wallace was consistent in referring to characters by the same name throughout—there would be no editing. Wallace in fact flatly refused to look at the typed manuscripts, and would send them off to his publishers as soon as the ink had dried, turning his attention quickly to the next project. If a publisher had the gall to voice a word of concern during the process, no matter how deferentially the criticism might be couched, Wallace would discard the manuscript entirely and begin anew on a different story.

This technique lent his works a distinctive and punchy narrative "voice" that aided them immensely in appealing to readers. Whatever his works may have lacked in artistic ambition, they more than made up for in sensational thrills. He quickly became the most popular mystery writer in the English language. Some critics even credit him with inventing the modern thriller. For generations, the name Edgar Wallace was synonymous with mystery and horror; he was the Stephen King of his day.

His combined writings sold over 50,000,000 copies, and his books inspired 165 motion pictures. The first cycle of Wallace films were made in England, with a few of these silent pictures even directed

A typically stylish poster from Belgium.

by Wallace himself. Wallace took up original screenwriting as well, and when he died in 1932 he was furiously scribbling away on RKO's *King Kong* (1933).

The name Wallace, though, is largely unremembered today. His prolific catalog has fallen almost entirely out of print in the English speaking world. Like Norbert Jacques and so many others in the same situation, his success was its own curse. During his heyday, fellow writers looked upon his phenomenal popularity with envy, and critics objected that his prominence in the publishing trade was shoving aside far more worthy examples of true literature. It was an age-old attack: That which is popular cannot be artistically good. Luminaries such as Dorothy L. Sayers, George Orwell and Arnold Bennett joined Q. D. Leavis in a critical assault on Wallace's reputation, arguing that his very commercial success was proof of his literary worthlessness.

As it happened, the vast majority of the motion picture adaptations of Wallace's works were poorly made low-budget affairs that deviated substantially from Wallace's texts. The crude production values and sadistic violence that peppered the Edgar Wallace movie series only served to reinforce the idea that Wallace was a mere hack, and so the quickie exploitationist success of the movies also devalued the name Wallace, until his once-ubiquitous novels receded to the obscure shelves of second-hand bookshops.

When the Nazis took over Germany in the 1930s, Hitler and Goebbels banned the works of Edgar Wallace—not out of any regard for their relative artistic or literary merits but because they decreed these lurid thrillers to be politically subversive. Once on the Nazis' black list, the name Edgar Wallace suddenly gained a powerful cachet among German intellectuals, who defiantly read forbidden books as an act of cultural resistance. If Wallace's legacy was being tarnished back home, abroad in the Berlin underground he was becoming something of a *cause celèbre*. When the war ended and the censorship was lifted, Wallace reemerged from that underground with tremendous force. In many cases, it is easier to find his works now in German translations than as long out-of-print copies in English-speaking used bookstores.

Postwar Germany paid homage to Wallace with a new series of films based on his works. No better made nor more faithful than the earlier British-made series had been, the three dozen or so Wallace films made in 1960s Germany became a genre unto themselves. These violent, pulpy thrillers starred many faces familiar to fans of Dr. Mabuse: Wolfgang Preiss, Werner Peters, Klaus Kinski, Karin Dor.... The names were often the same behind the scenes, as well, since Artur Brauner's CCC cranked out Wallace films with the best of them. The Wallace films of the 1960s were bargain-basement items, set in a fantasy vision of fog-bound Londontown as constructed on Berlin soundstages, with the suggested shocks of Wallace's writings transformed into full-blown sadistic violence for maximum cinematic effect.

For all his prolific output, though, Wallace's catalogue had its limitations, and this is where his son fits into the picture. Bryan Edgar Wallace did not just share his father's name, but also his gift for top-notch thrillmaking. He was born in 1904 and, like his father, served in the Army. Later in his life he served as Diplomatic Secretary in Madrid for 12 years. Along with scholarly studies of international relations, the younger Wallace was a screenwriter for several British studios and a prolific novelist. With his experience as a diplomat and his academic interest in political science, Bryan Edgar gave his thrillers a distinct political bent, with espionage and sabotage updating his father's style of chills in a manner better suited to the Cold War age. As the 1960s wore on, German filmmakers decided that the works of the younger Wallace accorded with modern tastes better, and the Wallace cycle turned into a Bryan Edgar Wallace cycle—much the same Grand Guignol outrages as before, just with five extra letters appended.

In 1963, the year of *Dr. Mabuse vs. Scotland Yard*, CCC produced but seven films. Of these, five were based on Bryan Edgar Wallace's novels and a sixth sprang forth from one of papa Wallace's texts, leaving but one CCC feature for the entire year not of Wallace lineage (and *that* film, *Old Shatterhand*, was based instead on a Western novel by Karl May). CCC was already in full Bryan Edgar Wallace mode, and by fusing the Wallace traditions with the name Mabuse, Brauner got double the marketing bang for his buck.

How apt, too, that screenwriter Ladislas Fodor selected Wallace's 1962 novel *The Device* as his starting point, since it is not just a terrific specimen of pulp fiction but also easily takes its place alongside the works of Norbert Jacques—variously finished, unfinished or unpublished—as a prime example of Mabusian literature. That is, but for the omission of the name Mabuse itself. Instead, the antihero of Wallace's *The Device* is named George Harry Cockston, but he is Dr. Mabuse through and through. Here is how Wallace introduces his megalomaniac:

> To the many people who knew him, some as Cockston and some under other names, Cockston was many things: to the Professor he was a charming amateur anxious to sit at the feet of a great man and learn, but to Interpol, the great International Police Organisation, who knew him only as Cockston, he was a ruthless criminal who had never been caught, and his file was a frustrating combination of half-truths and dead-ends. In London, however, where he was known under a completely different name, he was accepted for what he claimed to be: a much-traveled man of the world, and he had made for himself a position of considerable influence. So well had he established himself in England that, later, when the name of George Harry Cockston became public property, some of the finest minds in London failed to connect his identity with the man they were seeking.

Like Mabuse, the book's Cockston is a Great Unknown. His name has become imbued with tremendous mythological baggage. Cockston goes about his nefarious dealings using a variety of aliases and alteregos, using the name "Cockston" only as a lightning rod to attract attention away from his other personae. Among the authorities there is controversy whether Cockston is dead; the crux of the debate is that while some believe the body is not Cockston's after all but merely a decoy, another equally vocal faction argue that Cockston cannot be dead since he never really existed. Through much of the book, the police are unsure if they are seeking a gang or just one man. Von Wenk would surely sympathize.

Cockston's similarity to Mabuse does not end with his malleable identity. He is also engaged in a very Mabusian agenda, to take over the world by co-opting a mind-control technique invented by a mad scientist. This mind-control apparatus, the Device of the title, requires making recordings of a human brain experiencing some thought or emotion—abject terror, for example, or the mental impulses involved in marching in formation—and broadcasting those brain waves into the heads of others, making them think, feel or behave likewise. Many of Cockston's victims are killed only after enduring several days of torture, during which time the arch-criminal sucks their skulls of all the relevant brain impulses he needs to manipulate people according to his master plan. In this way he recycles and reuses the minds of the dead, much as other Mabusian characters reanimate the bodies or body parts of the dead. *The Device* carries a running theme of resurrection: Cockston's body is discovered but he lives on, as "Dick Morton," a young poet whom he has murdered in order to assume his identity. The bodies, minds and names of the dead remain in circulation as the world grinds inexorably towards doom.

Cockston approaches the Communist Party of England with the proposition that he has a device that can take over the world, although he is cagey on the details of what this device is or how it functions. To back up his claims, he orchestrates a major demonstration at 11:30 on the

appointed day. The Communists gather outside Buckingham Palace to watch as the Queen's guards spin around, draw their weapons and implacably mow down the tourists gathered along the gate. In the chaos that ensues, the Communists realize Cockston means what he says, and the authorities scramble to figure out just what the hell is happening. The Communists issue a proclamation declaring their People's Soviet of Great Britain the new legal rulers and demand the existing government abdicate. The Prime Minister sends in a garrison of elite troops—thousands of soldiers with the most awesome artillery—to roust the Communists from their ramshackle hideaway, only to have the Army drop their guns and run away screaming when Cockston trains the device on them. The no-nonsense Brigadier in charge watches in horror as he realizes England has just lost, to an enemy who never showed his face and never fired a shot.

Dieter Borsche, a major German star in his day, made something of a half-hearted comeback with this film.

All in all, Cockston comes very close to succeeding. Inspired by a handful of mind-controlled incidents that Cockston and his cronies incite for effect, various unions go on strike and many people untouched by Cockston's tampering totter on the brink of full scale rioting. It is a hallmark of Mabuse that he can manipulate events such that people believing themselves to be acting of their own free will nevertheless choose to do exactly what he wants of them. Cockston actually deploys the device only a very few times, allowing the aftermath of his well-staged demonstrations to ripple outward and influence things on a grander scale than he, as just one solitary madman, can reach.

For all the terror he causes, Cockston appears only briefly in the book, which instead concentrates on the frustrating investigations of two agents of Scotland Yard into a series of bizarre murders. Inspector Quil is a typical hard-boiled detective, a somewhat colorless descendant of Inspector Lohmann. Working with Quil on the case is Bill Tern, a low-rent James Bond sent in to discover the connection between the murders and a mysterious

Opposite: Dr. Mabuse vs. Scotland Yard *was adapted from Bryan Edgar Wallace's well-crafted pot-boiler* The Device.

device enigmatically mentioned in a report by another spy, who was killed before he could elaborate. Between them, Tern and Quil realize that the shadowy and possibly deceased Cockston figures in the picture somehow, but just what the conspiracy is about and what the device is they do not learn until tragically too late.

True to the dictates of the Mabuse genre, Cockston's plan is not derailed by the police (alone) but rather by the betrayals of those close to him, specifically the women in his life. Like Dusy Told, Marion Menil and *The Big Heat*'s Debby before them (and women like Sonia Vogler yet to come), the strong women in *The Device* are the one who hold the power to halt Cockston's machinations and save the world. Three women share this narrative function. The first is May B. Good, Cockston's improbably named girlfriend who offers to tell Bill Tern who Cockston is, what he looks like, and everything she knows about the device—for a price. Unfortunately, while Tern tries to wrangle the cash from his superiors, Cockston has this risk of exposure eliminated, and poor Miss Good ends up with a toe tag instead of a reward. The second femme fatale in Cockston's inner circle is Jennifer Colles, Tern's beatnik love interest. Colles however does not know Cockston and therefore cannot pull back the curtain all the way on this little puppet show. Nevertheless she is the one who first puts Tern on the right track, albeit only by unwittingly revealing a key piece of evidence in her possession, the significance of which is unknown to her. Later, though, she does expose Cockston's right-hand man and principal agent, Ernest Hilliard. Lastly there is Nancy Masterson, niece of the spy who first reported the device, and current girlfriend of Cockston's, who comes to realize that the "Dick Morton" she's involved with is not the eponymous sensitive young poet at all but a ruthless international criminal bent on world domination.

Throughout the book, the reckless 007–wannabe Bill Tern must continually remind himself to rein in his womanizing impulses because women are trouble. For all his misogynist and sexist rhetoric, though, Tern's outlook does not quite match that of Wallace himself: Sure enough, women wield the greatest power in the world of the novel, but their threat is really directed against Cockston and not the cops. For all his fear of femmes fatale, Tern would surely have ended up as Cockston's slave if not for the inner conscience of May B. Good, Jennifer Colles and Nancy Masterson. Tern's fearful attitude is residue from Wallace's previous novel, *Death Packs a Suitcase*, which introduced the character of Bill Tern, a careless spy who nearly ends up in ruin after falling hard for the wrong woman. Although Ladislas Fodor elided all reference to *Death Packs a Suitcase* in his screenplay adaptation of *The Device*, producer Artur Brauner would later helm a film version (its title ultimately translated into English as *The Corpse Packs His Bags*). That film was one of a handful of Bryan Edgar Wallace films Brauner made in 1971, in Spain, with director Jess Franco—right after the two of them made *The Vengeance of Dr. Mabuse* (see Chapter 17).

Aside from deleting references to Bill Tern's prior adventures, and substituting references to Mabuse's prior adventures instead, Ladislas Fodor need not have done much to translate *The Device* into a solidly entertaining, and entirely typical entry in the Mabuse saga. Fodor had every right even to be flattered by Wallace's book, which so copiously followed the dictates of the genre he had been instrumental in creating. The dramatic scene in which Cockston demonstrates his mind-control technology to the Communists bears more than a passing resemblance to key scenes in Fodor's 1961 script for *The Return of Dr. Mabuse*, in which Mabuse

Walter Rilla returns as the latest villain to use the moniker Mabuse.

demonstrates his mind-control technology for the Chicago Mafia by sending an army of zombies out to raid an atomic plant as a dry run for larger scale maneuvers to come. Whether Wallace intended any homage is academic; clearly he and Fodor were playing with the same toys.

For whatever inscrutable purpose, though, Fodor elected to make pronounced changes to his screen adaptation of *The Device*. While it is true that the German Wallace films, from both father and son, displayed extreme artistic license in their adaptations, in this case Fodor has ironically tossed out those aspects of Wallace's book that most closely followed the Mabusian paradigm. While the character names have been retained (although with variant spellings), the characters' personalities, motivations and relationships to one another have been altered. Only the barest skeleton of *The Device*'s plot survives. If one were to read Wallace's book some time before seeing the film, long enough to forget the characters' names, it would be possible to miss the relationship between the two versions entirely.

Gone is any sense that Mabuse's grasp has exceeded his reach, that by exploiting the fears and prejudices and weaknesses of the human mind he can manipulate people otherwise untouched by his mind-control device. In the book, even at the height of his powers, George Harry Cockston can only exercise mental control over others for a brief spurt of time, and then only to the extent that he has predicted and prerecorded what he wants them to do. Yet the ripples of this effect spread across the country, seeding chaos and giving him his supreme advantage. By contrast, the film's Dr. Mabuse can control

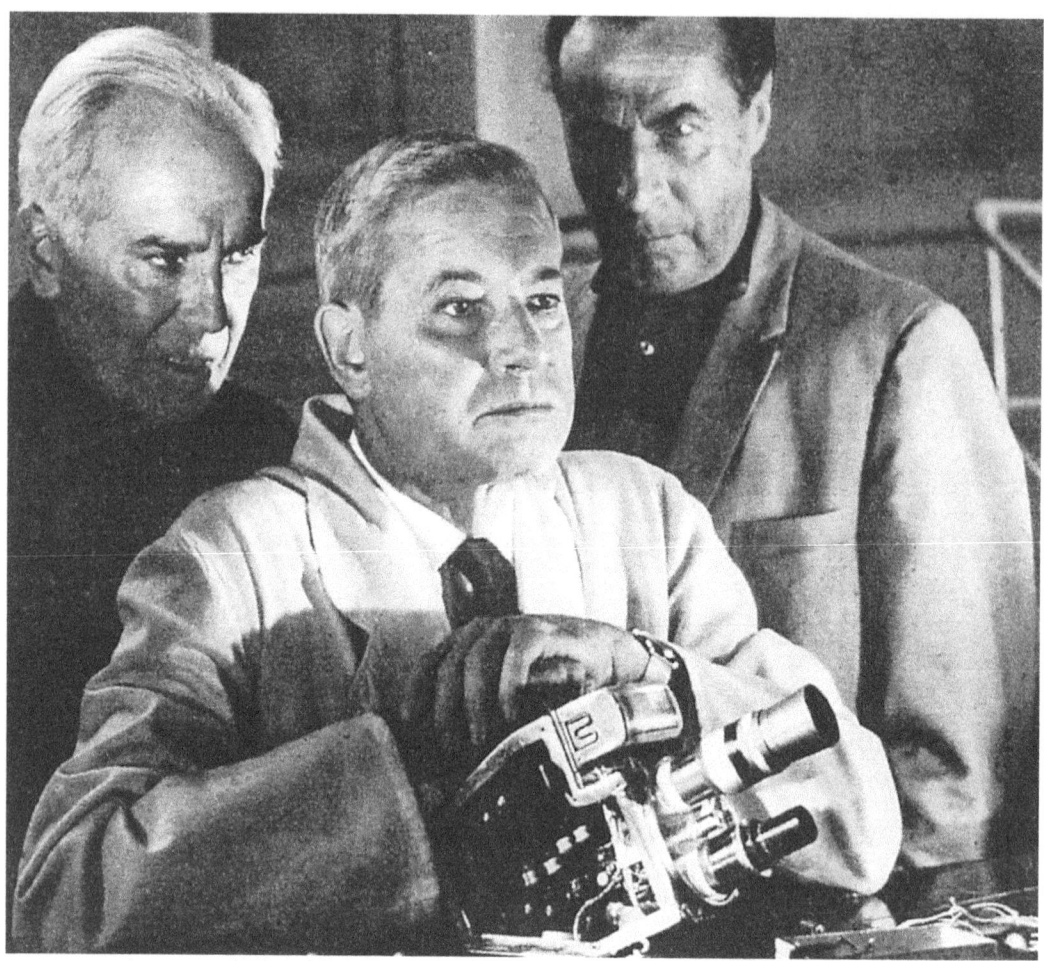

In the film, "the Device" is a mind-controlling camera.

any mind he wishes and command it to do anything. On one level, this gives him a greater and more impressive power than anything enjoyed by the book's Cockston, but in another sense it means he is only ever as powerful or as clever as his stolen technology permits. The police talk often of the "hand of a master" behind it all, but in fact any dumb sap with a mind-control device could pull off what Mabuse does.

The mechanics of that mind-control device have also been recast. Wallace took great pains to render his device plausible, and built his entire plot around the workings of the machine. Why these victims? Why the four-day lag between their disappearance and subsequent discovery as corpses? The answers to these questions only come through the revelation of the device's functioning: Cockston selected his victims based on what knowledge or experience he needed to record for future subliminal broadcasts, and he needed some four days apiece to sufficiently torture his victims to get all the brainscan tapes he desired. Fodor, however, has little interest in how his device works, and subscribes to Alfred Hitchcock's theory of the MacGuffin (that a plot device, a MacGuffin, need not be explained in detail so long as the audience buys enough of it to motivate the action, which is really what the film is about anyway).* Fodor's device is pure MacGuffin: Mabuse simply declares that it is an electronic thingamajig that controls people's brains, end of story. Aside from some vague references to "electronics," Fodor makes no effort to explain how it works.

Given the low budget of the film, and the different demands of cinematic drama against literary drama, Fodor's rethink makes sense. The novel builds its suspense around the threat of the device, which is left vague enough that the reader imagines horrors yet to come. Except for a few offhand allusions to prior tests of the contraption, only two instances of its use are directly depicted in the tale. The first is a show stopper of a scene, sadly absent from the film, as Cockston demonstrates its capabilities outside Buckingham Palace. Such a scene would surely have been too expensive for CCC's anemic budget to manage, and instead of one blowout scene the film indulges in numerous smaller moments as Mabuse's gang fans out across London issuing secret psychic commands. It is, though, a sign of the film's diminished expectations that when Mabuse asks for a "definitive test" of the technology, they decide on nothing so spectacular as the Buckingham Palace massacre but rather to coerce a hangman to hang himself.

The film begins with a quick recap of the end of *Testament of Dr. Mabuse*: The deceased Mabuse's evil spirit has possessed the body of his hapless psychiatrist, Prof. Pohland (Walter Rilla again). Evidently Mabuse has a subscription to the mad scientist newsletter, to stay on top of the latest developments in mind-control technology, and the latest innovation by England's Prof. Lawrence has caught his eye. Lawrence claims to have concocted an electrical gadget that projects the user's will into the bodies of others, rendering them little more than giant flesh-and-blood puppets. Recognizing the value of such a device, Mabuse decides to relocate his HQ to England, far from the eyes of the German cops, who by now have become all to good at recognizing his handiwork.

The first step in Mabuse's master plan is to engineer the escape of George Cockstone (now spelled with an "e") from the train bearing him to his German prison. Fodor pays thoughtful homage to Fritz Lang's *Spies* with this sequence, duplicating the Great Haghi's approach of conscripting agents by rescuing them from the gallows. The film's Cockstone is a former British Army doctor convicted of the theft of hi-tech electronics and illegal experimental surgery—just the kind of bad doctor to warm the cockles of Mabuse's heart. This Cockstone will play henchman to Mabuse's mastermind, just as the book's Ernest Hilliard was henchman to the elusive Cockston. An Ernest Hilyard (also respelled) does appear in the film, but instead of a Communist organizer this Hilyard is one of Mabuse's gang, and a former army buddy of Cockstone's. At first Cockstone does not recognize his old pal, since Hilyard has been given a new face by Mabuse's plastic surgeon. To throw the cops off the scent—as well as to satisfy Mabuse's passion for converted identities—Cockstone must also undergo cosmetic surgery to erase his old self.

Cockstone emerges from Mabuse's

---

*In Truffaut Hitchcock, *the Master of Suspense explains the MacGuffin: "It's the device, the gimmick, if you will, or the papers the spies are after.... [T]he 'MacGuffin' is the term we use to cover all that sort of thing: to steal plans or documents, or to uncover a secret, it doesn't matter what it is. And the logicians are wrong in trying to figure out the truth of a MacGuffin, since it's beside the point. The only thing that really matters is that in the picture the plans, documents, or secrets must seem to be of vital importance to the characters. To me, the narrator, they're of no importance whatever."*

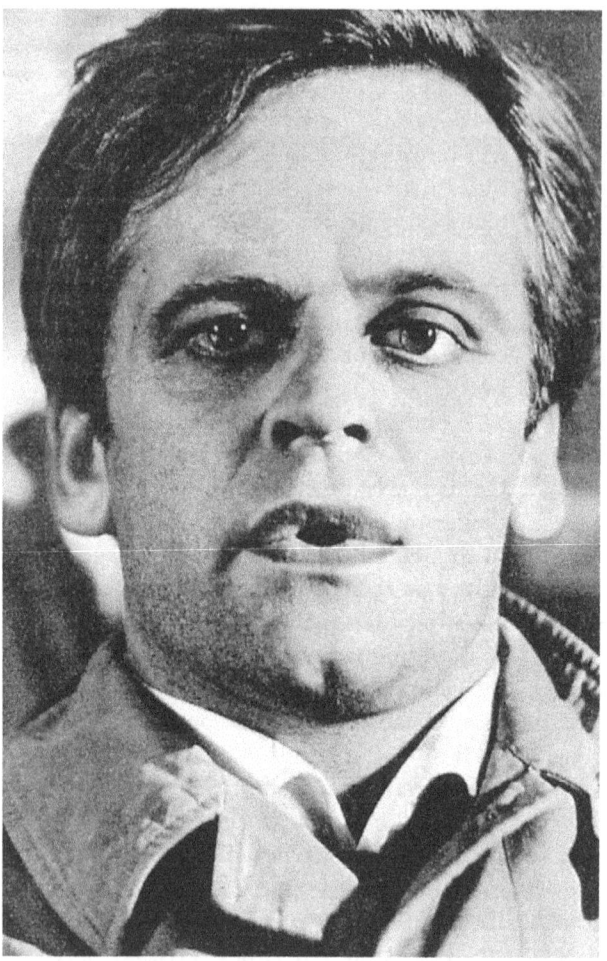

Klaus Kinski, a cult actor if there ever was one, has a small role as a zombified police detective.

bomb. For the next decade, Borsche retreated from films altogether, back to the German stage to lick his wounds and nurse back his reputation as a serious actor. Finally, in the mid–'60s he returned to the silver screen with a comeback performance as Cockstone in *Scotland Yard vs. Dr. Mabuse*! Or, at least that's how CCC's breathless press releases for the new Mabuse picture told the story, conveniently ignoring the two dozen films Borsche had made during his supposed absence from the cinema.

Using this new face, Cockstone weasels his way into Lawrence's confidence and gains access to the device. Meanwhile, Inspector Vulpius (Werner Peters in his fourth distinct role in the series) contacts Scotland Yard's Bill Tern (Peter Van Eyck in his second distinct role) to help investigate Cockstone's escape. They worry that maybe—just maybe—they sense the intervention of Dr. Mabuse in all this, but dare not speak such suspicions aloud because everybody knows Mabuse is dead.

surgery with the face of longtime German star Dieter Borsche. Thanks to director Harald Braun's 1949 hit *Die Nachtwache* (The Night Watch), Borsche leapt to stardom. The actor quickly became an icon of German film. Playing nobility, aristocracy, authority and heroes, he embodied all the finest qualities audiences wanted to associate with Germanness. When Borsche wanted to vary his repertoire a bit and took the role of an Arab thief in *Ali Baba and the Forty Thieves* (1954), he crashed and burned. Not only had he violated the public's trust by playing a villain, he did so in an unmitigated artistic and commercial

Well, Dr. Mabuse is dead and well and living in England's verdant countryside. His sinister evil has crept into the shadows and left poor Prof. Lawrence dead. This is one of Fodor's better embellishments, since in the book Cockston does nothing more interesting than smother the old man with a pillow. Never one to use a simple method for murder when an overcomplicated scheme would do as well, Dr. Mabuse uses the prototype device to compel a kindly mailman to bludgeon Lawrence to death, and then go on about his rounds as if nothing had happened. In a terrific scene, Vulpius and Tern interrogate the poor mailman, the last person to see Lawrence alive.

Perhaps he can provide a clue as to "who done it." He gives them more than that, and a great deal less besides: "I was the last to see him alive," the poor sap admits, "because when I handed him the letter he was alive, but when I left he was dead." As Vulpius and Tern puzzle over this odd remark, the mailman fills in the gap. "I killed him, you see." Of course, he cannot offer any explanation of *why* he did such a thing. Someone else's will compelled him, somehow.

With Hilyard and Cockstone's help, Mabuse has concealed Lawrence's device in a camera. There are those who believe that having one's picture taken robs the subject of his soul; for Dr. Mabuse's mind-control camera, this is literally true.

Before long, Dr. Mabuse comes as close as he ever would to winning. With his minions swarming across London disguised as paparazzi, snapping pictures that wipe away free will and create mindless slaves to Mabuse's will, he quickly establishes his own government. Thanks to the mind-control cameras, even members of the Royal Family happily confer legal legitimacy on Mabuse's phantom regime. Whatever threat Vulpius and Tern may pose is quickly extinguished when Mabuse takes over the mind of their boss, Joe Rank of the Secret Service.

Although Rank's role in the film is slight, he is the only character from Wallace's book to survive the translation in anything resembling his original character. The part is played with wild-eyed inten-

Sabine Bethmann's role was almost entirely cut from the U.S. version.

sity by Klaus Kinski, one of cinema's hardest-working and most bizarre actors. Born Nikolaus Günther Nakszynski in 1926 Poland, Kinski grew up in Berlin. He was drafted into the German Army during World War II, but spent most of the war as a POW in England. At war's end, he began acting, first on stage but soon in the newly resurrected German film industry. Over the decades to come until his death in 1991, Kinski kept busy in so many films that it is virtually impossible to accurately list them all. His best and best-known work was with Werner Herzog (himself quite an eccentric character), over the course of a 15-year collaboration. During the 1960s, in the early days of his screen career, Kinski played in a number of the Edgar Wallace and Bryan Edgar Wallace films, including *The Daffodil Killer* (1961), *The Door with Seven Locks* (1962), *The Squeaker* (1963) and *Psycho-Circus* (1966). In *Dr. Mabuse vs. Scotland Yard*, though, Kinski's talents are wasted in a supporting part, while Werner Peters and Peter Van Eyck are expected to carry the show.

There are three means of defense against Mabuse's mind-control cameras. First, Lawrence's colleague Masterson has invented a counteractive apparatus which, inexplicably enough, is worn in the user's shoe. In the book, such a contraption existed but involved grounding the subject to prevent reception of the transmitted commands. Neither was Wallace's Masterson a scientist, but a secret service agent, whose murder first put Bill Tern on the case.

The second line of defense is a natural one, as the effect of the subliminal influence wears off with sleep. This embellishment by Fodor is a nice touch. So much of the Mabusian genre takes place in a surreal world of dream logic, the landscape of Caligari's somnambulist. That escape from Mabuse's dominion would come by waking from the nightmare is quite apt indeed.

Third, it turns out that wearing a certain brand of hearing aid cancels out the device's effectiveness. Mabuse does not know this, and the heroes only discover it by serendipity. *Dr. Mabuse vs. Scotland Yard* is probably the only thriller of its kind to climax with the hero's mom riding to the rescue with a briefcase full of hearing aids.

Ah, the hero's mom. This is where Fodor's adaptation diverges from Wallace in toto. The deadly serious tone of the book has given way to a goofball silliness in the film, thanks to Mrs. Gwendoline Tern (Agnes Windeck), a Hitchcockian matron providing plentiful comic relief. Her obsession with mystery novels is at once a holdover from Harald Juhnke's character in the previous year's *Testament of Dr. Mabuse* and a sly in-joke, since her favorite pastime is with Wallace-style thrillers about "The Gorilla" or "The Strangler." Whereas Juhnke's Inspector Krüger could never quite grasp the case at hand because his head was filled with fantastical exaggerations from pulp fiction, Mother Tern's hobby has given her an insight her son lacks. She alone sees the connections that reveal the truth of Mabuse's plans; she has the good sense to show up at Mabuse's hideaway with enough hearing aids to give the government troops a fighting chance against the device.

There is no analogue of Mrs. Gwendoline Tern in the book, and her straight-laced son is related to the book's Bill Tern in name only. Wallace's Bill Tern is a cavalier youth who spends too much time thinking with his crotch and not enough thinking with his brain, a failing that more than once risks the fate of the entire world. The film's Tern is a dullard, devoid of distinction. Actor Peter Van Eyck is at his best when cast as a dangerous, hardened man who is revealed to be a softy at heart. With his clean-cut good looks but slightly menacing twinge in his expression, he shines in such films as *Wages of Fear* or *The Spy Who Came In from the Cold*. CCC, however, stubbornly cast him time and again in heroic leading man roles that inverted these characteristics: Called upon to play a good man with a hint of danger under the surface, Van Eyck is not quite up to the task. The blandness of his performance in *The 1000 Eyes of Dr. Mabuse* was no liability because his role as Henry Travers was but one pawn among many in Fritz Lang's complex chess match. Here, and in the subsequent *Death Ray of Dr. Mabuse*, Van Eyck's limp stage presence

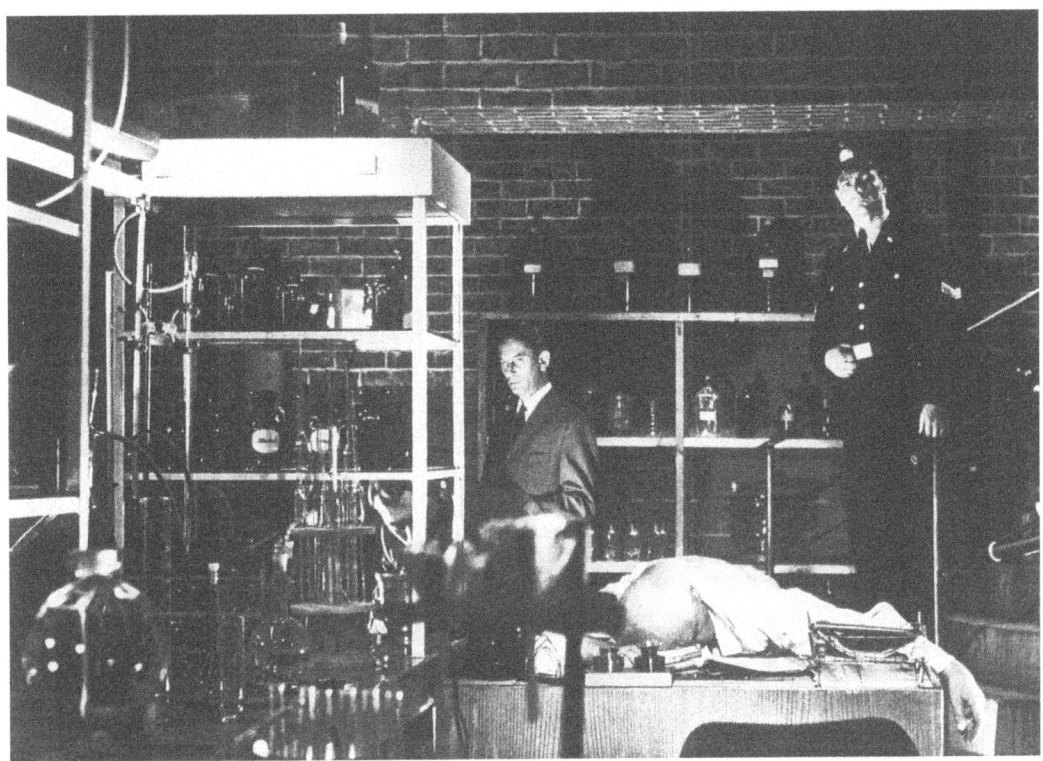

Scotland Yard vs. Dr. Mabuse is an odd blend of tongue-in-cheek humor and high Gothic style.

cannot compensate for his underwritten role.

This Bill Tern has nothing to fear from his libido since the three femmes fatale of the book have been all but banished from the screen. May B. Good has disappeared entirely, and the least interesting aspects of Jennifer Colles and Nancy Masterson have been fused together into one character, who retains the name Nancy Masterson but threatens neither Tern nor Mabuse in any way. This Nancy Masterson is a frightened damsel in distress, a helpless little girl in her nightie. The most attentive viewers might just perceive a connection between Miss Masterson and the "Masterson" that Lawrence says invented the counteractive slip-heels Mabuse uses to avoid mind-controlling himself. This connection has been blurred to the point of incomprehensibility for American audiences, since the English-dubbed edition of the film has shed nine minutes from its already trim 90 minute running time, removing almost the entirety of Sabine Bethmann's performance as Nancy. (She stills gets second billing, but only a few fleeting minutes of her screen time remain.)

In the closing moments of the film, Vulpius and Tern corner Mabuse in his lair. The spirit of Wolfgang Preiss' Mabuse slinks out of Walter Rilla's body, like a fighter pilot ejecting from a plummeting plane. As the cops grab Pohland's dazed form, they realize he is no longer the criminal they are after: Dr. Mabuse has left the building. For all their frustration and disappointment, they should not be so surprised. Mabuse vanished long ago, when Ladislas Fodor first got hold of *The Device* and set to bleaching out all the qualities that would have made this project a legitimate fusion of Bryan Edgar Wallace and Norbert Jacques.

In the United States, *Dr. Mabuse vs. Scotland Yard* would miss even the lackluster theatrical outings that CCC's previous Mabuse entries enjoyed—although, for some reason, the American print inverted the German title *Scotland Yard jagt Dr. Mabuse* ("Scotland Yard hunts Dr. Mabuse") to give Mabuse top billing, a curious choice given the lengths distributors had gone to in order to eclipse all reference to the name Mabuse in the previous four pictures. Columbia Pictures' Screen Gems arm picked up *Scotland Yard*, dubbed into English and shorn of nine minutes' worth of romantic interludes, and leased it out for late-night TV screenings. If Mabuse was ever going to penetrate American pop culture, it would not be through second-rate B-movie claptrap like this.

Nor would it be through the third-rate B-movie claptrap yet to come.

CHAPTER 15

The Death Ray of Dr. Mabuse

> Terror, world enslavement—the dream of Dr. Mabuse.... He's the embodiment of evil.
>
> —Major Bob Anders

Two men stand alone in a darkened room, waiting for the world to end. British secret agent Bob Anders (Peter Van Eyck, of course) and his colleague, the even more secret secret agent Dr. Krishna (Valerij Inkijinoff), stand on opposite sides of the massive steel door, their weapons drawn. Any minute now, that door will swing open and they will be face to face with their enemy.

Inside the room is the most dangerous weapon ever devised. Whoever stands at these simple controls wields the power to destroy entire nations. It is a doomsday weapon, a death ray, and *he* wants it.

But who is *he*? Until recently, Anders suspected Krishna of being in league with *him*. Now that Anders knows that he and Krishna are playing for the same team, an even greater fear looms. When that door opens and the face of the enemy is finally revealed, will it be someone Anders trusted even more, someone whose treachery would be even more devastating?

Then it starts. There is activity on the other side of the door; the gears in the lock start to turn. The secret combination, stolen from the helpless professor's mind by a master hypnotist, is being keyed in. Soon they will see his face, the face of the man who can pilfer the very thoughts out of your brain, the face of the man who has eluded the finest detectives the world has to offer. The face of Dr. Mabuse.

This is the climax of *The Death Ray of Dr. Mabuse* (1964). Or, the closest approximation to a climax this herky-jerky mess of a movie can muster. As the vault door opens and Mabuse's latest incarnation steps into the light, for a brief moment the film's overpopulated and overcomplicated narrative makes sense. That moment passes quickly. The film soon hurtles onward breathlessly, like a hyperactive toddler in a toy store, towards the next sensational revelation, and the next, and the next after that, until so many masks have been yanked away that there is nothing left but a naked projector bulb's light flickering away on a blank screen. *The Death Ray of Dr. Mabuse* does not end its story with any narrative closure, but instead stops abruptly as if screenwriter Ladislas Fodor ran out of ink, or director Hugo Fregonese ran out of film stock. All of a sudden, everything just chokes to a stop.

With it, the film series too ran aground. This was the last of CCC's Mabuse pictures, the last Mabuse film in black-and-white, the last one to follow in the loose continuity that had linked all of the movies from 1922 onwards. Producer Artur Brauner and his minions had mined the territory so fiercely over the last five years that the ground caved in around them.

The desperation behind the scenes was evident in the scenario. No longer would Langian *film noir* cinescapes suffice, with their hard-boiled cops, femmes fatale and sinister underworld conspiracies. Apparently convinced that the Mabuse genre had played itself out, Brauner's last installment is little more than a cheapjack James Bond knock-off, with some half-hearted Mabusian touches tossed in to the mix.

The everything-but-the-kitchen-sink story covers long-familiar territory: A mysterious international organization of criminals is working to gain access to some new scientific marvel that will help them take over the world. But the devil is in the details, and on closer inspection the fabric of *Death Ray* unravels completely.

The Death Ray itself is the brainchild of a misanthrope named Larsen (O.E. Hasse), who has built an undersea bunker in Malta near an island he affectionately calls "Projection Island." From the lab in this submarine installation, he can manipulate a massive orbiting mirror to reflect his Death Ray onto any point on the planet. Whoever controls the Death Ray controls the world.

Naturally enough, the British are worried lest Larsen's invention fall into unscrupulous hands. This matter could easily have been resolved had they taken the simple step of paying Larsen—the mercenary mad scientist built his contraption for no better reason than to make a boatload of cash. Rather than fund his research, however, the Brits have decided the best course of action is to acquire the device through espionage. To this end, they have populated Projection Island with spies. In fact, it seems as if there are more British spies there than genuine inhabitants.

The principal industry of the village is gossip, so it is well known that there are spies afoot, rendering the term "secret agent" a misnomer. Nevertheless, Her Majesty's Government asks Major Bob Anders (inexplicably renamed from Ken Anders, as the German version calls him) to take a girlfriend along to Malta as a cover, pretending to be newlyweds so no one will suspect his true mission. This is a pointless enterprise since from the moment Anders arrives, everyone he meets knows who and what he is.

So why ask him to drag girlfriend Judy (Rika Dialina) along? Once on Projection Island she is "rescued" from an off-screen, and possibly bogus, bomb threat by the local branch of the Secret Service, which is operating out of a sham pharmacy (their secret password—carefully selected to maintain the highest level of security—is to walk in and say you have a prescription for aspirin). The cloak-and-dagger types now announce poor Judy knows too much for her safety, so they can either kill her, or she can join them. Unsurprisingly she opts for choice number two and thereby becomes a spy. No *La Femme Nikita*-style training for her, though. She is assigned to a brothel (another facade) where she and other British spy-whores hope to worm classified information out of their johns' mouths during the throes of passion. Bob Anders is morally outraged at the fate of his cohort, but she assures him that she is quite happy with her new job. "Don't worry," she purrs. "*You* don't have to pay."

Judy may be a willing prostitute, but a bad spy. She enjoys putting on the airs of an international woman of mystery, carrying a revolver in her cleavage and purring her code number 996 (hmm, not so far off from 007, is it?), but she overlooks important information and treats the mission like a child's game.

Not that her moronic companion Bob Anders is any better. Unlike the gentleman hero James Bond, Anders is a frumpy killjoy who has little interest in sex but equally little intelligence-gathering skill. Anders' colleagues operating the phony pharmacy once remark on the many willing nymphets throwing themselves at his feet. "A beautiful girl," says the spymaster. "So what?" is Anders' oh-so-witty retort.

Anders does allow his libido to get the better of him on occasion. Since he is an idiot, he chooses to bed the wrong women. While investigating the mysterious Kaspar Botoni (Dieter Eppler), one of many suspicious characters on Projection Island, he is seduced by Botoni's beautiful secretary Mercedes (Yoko Tani). Right in the middle of foreplay, she whips a revolver out of the bed pillows and plugs him in the chest. Miraculously he survives, because he had the presence of mind to wear a bullet-proof vest (pressed so close to him, she couldn't tell?). He doesn't, though, have enough presence of mind to prevent Mabuse from instantly assassinating his agent Mercedes to foreclose any risk of exposure.

Anders also carries on a loveless sexual affair with Gilda Larsen (Yvonne Furneaux), who just happens to be Prof. Larsen's niece. She is also a Champion Female Sharpshooter, but don't expect this slapdash script to ever use that character detail for anything meaningful, it's just another random idea introduced and abandoned in the same breath, like prescient dreams and killer sharks; the expert marksmanship of a major character just vanishes into the ether.

Aside from sexually servicing our jackass hero, Gilda Larsen's principal narrative function is to have a birthday party. And for reasons that make perfect sense to the characters but remain totally oblique to the audience, Dr. Mabuse has decided that his bid for world domination will coincide with this party. Mabuse calls this plan Operation 13. So as not to have an operation gap, the British spies have dubbed their meandering endeavors Operation Archimedes.

To gain access to the Death Ray, though, Mabuse will first have to get into the lab, and to do that he will need the combination to the vault door. This combination is so secret, nobody knows it. Nobody. Not even Prof. Larsen himself, who has managed a form of self-induced posthypnotic suggestion to conceal the keycode in a visual image of a famous chess game. For the better part of the film, Larsen keeps his secret from all interested parties. But as the heat piles on, he decides to divulge the chess-game trick to his favorite niece Gilda.

In a true-to-form Mabuse picture, there would have been a femme fatale to break rank from Mabuse's organization and re-ally herself with the good guys. Mercedes does not fit this bill, since she is murdered immediately after failing Mabuse's instructed task. Gilda Larsen comes closer to filling that narrative function, in that it is through her character that Bob Anders acquires the secret entrance code to the lab and can thereby block Mabuse's access to the deadly invention. Gilda is unaware of having done this, though, since Anders was secretly eavesdropping on her private tête-à-tête with Prof. Larsen. She knows nothing of Mabuse, never switches sides, and only contributes to the cause by simply standing around and looking pretty. And, yes, hosting a birthday party.

Since the essential step in acquiring the Death Ray is to get the entrance code for the lab door, Anders is understandably suspicious of anyone—other than him—trying to weasel such information from the Prof.. This makes Larsen's assistant Dr.

O.E. Hasse (right) was the top-billed star of *Die Todesstrahlen des Dr. Mabuse*.

Krishna a prime suspect. It would be just like Mabuse to plant an agent in such a close confidential rapport with his victim—for example, Cockstone's relationship with Prof. Lawrence in *Dr. Mabuse vs. Scotland Yard*. And what to make of Krishna's adept hypnotic skill, or his inscrutable claim to have "five or six thousand years" experience with telepathy?

Such suspicions are baseless: Krishna is not a plant for Mabuse's Operation 13. Instead he's the key player in the British Operation Archimedes. The Secret Service has always intended that Bob and Judy would be such obvious "secret agents" precisely to attract attention away from their true operative, quietly going about his business deep in the background. The hope is that Mabuse will squander his energies combating the decoy Anders while Krishna weasels his way into Larsen's mind, extracts the secret code and steals the Death Ray before Mabuse can.

It's a tall order, because in his lust for the Death Ray, Mabuse has cooked up a very sensible and elegant three-prong strategy, in sharp contrast to the disorganized Brits. First, he has an army of frogmen spying on Projection Island. To smuggle his agents in past the English-controlled borders, Mabuse conceals them in coffins and drives them around in his hearse; Mabuse himself remains hidden in a confessional inside a long-forgotten crypt. Mabuse's desecration of the Hall of the Archbishops has just the right measure of mystery and sacrilege.

The second component in Mabuse's strategy is to use one of the region's wealthiest men to do what the British should have done in the first place. Through Mario Malta (Gustavo Rojo), he is going to buy the Death Ray legitimately. Contracts are drawn up, and Larsen is readying to sign them at, you guessed it, Gilda's birthday party.

Thirdly, and most impressively, Mabuse has usurped the identity of the commanding officer of the Secret Service's operations on Projection Island, Admiral Quency (Leo Genn). This is by far his best trick, because it makes him privy not only to Anders' activities but Krishna's as well; it no longer matters which of the two spies gets Larsen's code first, either way Mabuse gets it by default. He doesn't have to squander his energies combating anyone, merely sit back and let the spies do their work—and his—for him.

Or rather, that is one possible explanation. When the vault door opens and Mabuse enters, that is to say Admiral Quency enters, the story falls neatly into place. Throughout the picture, the filmmakers have feverishly pointed fingers of suspicion at Quency: Anders was surprised to learn that Quency was neither dead nor retired, but heading up Operation Archimedes. Wouldn't it be just like Mabuse to have assumed the man's identity after his death? And the explosion that apparently failed to kill Quency left him scarred and crippled, distracting physical traits that Mabuse could hide behind to better conceal the deception. Longtime Mabuse buffs would also recall the sinister portrayals of the differently abled in these pre–PC era flicks (the clubfoot in *1000 Eyes of Dr. Mabuse* or the peg-leg in *Return of Dr. Mabuse*).

Quency instructs his agents to call him "Chief," the same moniker Mabuse insists his frogmen call him. Quency discounts and discredits all of Anders' theories regarding Mabuse's involvement, and sends his spy on a mission that drops him straight into the clutches of Mabuse's agents. So when Mabuse appears as Quency, Anders is not surprised and neither is the audience. The master criminal has once again manipulated people without their knowledge, coopting the British secret service into working against themselves.

However, the real Admiral Quency then walks in to confront his evil doppleganger. How can this be? If Mabuse was impersonating Quency all along, where did the real one come from? And if the real Quency had been administering Operation Archimedes all along, then why was he acting so suspiciously? Did the fake Quency slink in and out of the pharmacy HQ only on occasion, somehow miraculously avoiding his authentic counterpart? Or did Mabuse just put on his Quency disguise now, for this one single moment?

But wait, there's more. Quency unmasks his double, revealing poor old Kaspar Botoni, the lonely widower who runs the local history museum. Botoni was Dr. Mabuse—his secretary did try to kill Anders, and his library was conveniently missing the documents showing the whereabouts of Mabuse's Hall of the Archbishops—but just how did Mabuse's spirit jump all the way from Pohland's body to Botoni's? As the last frames of film unspool and the whole enterprise crashes to a halt, Botoni's dog Pluto senses that Mabuse's spirit has left Botoni's body, and wanders away. As in *1000 Eyes* or *Invisible Dr. Mabuse*, dogs can sense things humans cannot, and this dog knows that Botoni is no longer his evil master. As this strange, unsatisfying movie fades out, Mabuse has been fully transformed from the flesh-and-blood man of 1922 into a supernatural wraith that body-jumps at will, deathlessly pursuing its megalomaniacal goal.

Fans of James Bond may be forgiven for seeing *Death Ray of Dr. Mabuse* as a low-rent take-off of *Thunderball* (1965). With its emphasis on spies, stunts and sex, *Death Ray* is clearly more inspired by the

Despite prominent billing and his glassy-eyed face staring out from the poster, ex-Mabuse Wolfgang Preiss was not in any way involved in the making of this film.

Bond films than the Mabuse films it supposedly follows. Both *Thunderball* and *Death Ray* take place in an island paradise befouled by a madman's attempts to ransom the world with the threat of annihilation. As the eye-patched Quency, Leo Genn is a dead ringer for Adolfo Celi's villainous Largo in *Thunderball*. Both pictures spend much screen time underwater; both pictures conclude with a climactic battle of frogmen, furiously spearing each other with harpoons. Taking into account that *Death Ray*'s budget was a mere fraction of blockbuster Bond's extraordinary expenses, the scrappy little Mabuse film even manages to copy some of the underwater scenes fairly faithfully.

Which is more than a little odd, because *Death Ray* was filmed in the spring of 1964, exactly one year *before* production began on *Thunderball*. Can it possibly be that the producers of the James Bond series actually stole ideas from the B-movie realm of *Death Ray of Dr. Mabuse*?

The James Bond movie franchise officially began in 1962 with the release of *Dr. No*, but the story of *Thunderball* precedes even that. Back in 1959, long before Sean Connery was even considered for his starmaking role, Ian Fleming first toyed with the idea of adapting his popular Bond novels into films. He joined forces with filmmaker Kevin McClory to develop an original James Bond screenplay—*Thunderball*. When the project did not bring instant gratification, Fleming grew impatient and turned his attentions back to novel writing. Naturally enough, his next book was *Thunderball*, incorporating the story ideas from the unfinished screenplay.

Ah, there's the rub. McClory argued that as he had co-authored that script with Fleming, Fleming had no right to go publishing it under his own name without McClory's cooperation. A suit resulted, and after years of legal wrangling Fleming settled with McClory, granting the filmmaker all screen rights to the *Thunderball* story.

Then, in the early '60s, producers Harry Saltzman and Albert Broccoli approached Fleming for the rights to make James Bond movies—with *Thunderball* their desired first choice. Since *Thunderball* was still tied up in the lawsuit, they chose instead to begin the film series with *Dr. No*, and a phenomenon was born. When they came to make the fourth installment in 1965, Saltzman and Broccoli joined with McClory to produce the first film version of *Thunderball*.

This was the film that really turned up the heat on the burgeoning spy genre and turned James Bond into a veritable pop culture juggernaut. *Thunderball* was the quintessential Bond story, hence the various efforts to make it the first Bond movie, so it would be natural to assume that any efforts to mimic Bond's success would look to *Thunderball* for inspiration. It was for this reason that the makers of *Austin Powers: International Man of Mystery* (1997) chose *Thunderball* as their primary inspiration; like *Death Ray*, they copied even small details from *Thunderball* like Number 2's eye-patch. For a time, it even seemed that a Bond movie franchise would be inaugurated that relied exclusively on the raw material of *Thunderball*: McClory produced a later remake, titled *Never Say Never Again* (1983), separate from MGM's Bond series. McClory threatened to continue his own parallel Bond movies indefinitely, to be made entirely of successive *Thunderball* remakes.

Although production did not begin on the original *Thunderball* movie until May of 1965, eight months after *Death Ray*'s theatrical release in Germany, the content of the movie was to a degree public knowledge since the book's publication in 1961. Having chosen to pay homage to (and parody) the Bond films with *Death Ray of Dr. Mabuse*, Brauner's team might have been inspired to consult Fleming's novel *Thunderball* for ideas. Not only is it the obvious starting point for all things Bond, but upon hearing *Thunderball* announced as the upcoming sequel to *Goldfinger* (1964), the opportunity was there to steal a bit of Bond's thunder and beat it to theaters.

However, this cannot entirely explain the similarities between the two films. Most troubling of all is the fact that in Fleming's novel, as in McClory's 1983 film version, Emile Largo is presented as an athletic villain, suave and physically imposing. It is only in the 1965 film *Thunderball* (and the *Austin Powers* take-off) that the character is shown as an eye-patched survivor of some ambiguous past adventure—a dead ringer for *Death Ray*'s Admiral Quency/Dr. Mabuse.

In other words, either the makers of filmdom's biggest, most successful and most enduring movie franchise cribbed ideas from the last gasp of CCC's dwindling Mabuse series—which itself was desperately bolstering its flagging appeal by borrowing from the 007 films—or else it was just a remarkable coincidence.

Although longtime CCC star Peter Van Eyck was once again playing the hero, the headlining star of the film was actually O. E. Hasse as Prof. Larsen. Given Larsen's relatively brief screen time and his prickly, unpleasant characterization, this may surprise some American viewers. Nevertheless, Hasse's face and name are prominently featured in the advertising, and the theatrical program book focused entirely on his contributions. Otto Eduard Hasse was born in 1903 in what is now Poland, and was a student of the great Max Reinhardt. His career spanned almost 50 features, from 1934 to 1977. American audiences likely know him best from his role as the killer in Alfred Hitchcock's *I Confess* (1952).

Despite Hasse's star billing and Van Eyck's star turn, the real highlight in the cast is Yvonne Furneaux, an accomplished actress clearly slumming as Gilda Larsen, birthday girl. Horror movie fans may remember her from Hammer's 1959 remake of *The Mummy*, Fellini fans may know her from *La Dolce Vita* (1960), Polanski fans may remember her from *Repulsion* (1965), and fans of Claude Chabrol (see Chapter 20) may recall her role in *The Champagne Murders* (1966). Her chiseled beauty and regal bearing bring a level of class that the rest of the production simply cannot justify.

Financed jointly by Brauner's CCC, the British company Franco London Film, the French Criterion Film Company and Italians Serena Film and Anglo Italia Film, *The Death Ray of Dr. Mabuse* may not have been the first foreign co-production in the series but it did boast the first foreign director. For once, it was not a German calling the shots, but Argentinian Hugo Fregonese. Born in 1908 in Mendoza, Argentina, Fregonese directed a handful of forgettable low-budget films including 1969's *Dracula vs. Frankenstein* (not to be confused with Jess Franco's film of the same name, nor Al Adamson's film for that matter). Also known as *Assignment Terror*, *Dracula vs. Frankenstein* shared with *Death Ray* the dubious distinction of wasting great actors in a cast full of B-movie stalwarts. Onetime Mabuse starlet Karin Dor and Spanish horror flick avatar Paul Naschy (who also penned the script) starred alongside none other than *Day the Earth Stood Still*'s Michael Rennie in a ludicrous story about space aliens reviving classic gothic monsters like Dracula and Frankenstein as part of a plot to take of the world. Fregonese was also responsible for a 1953 remake of Alfred Hitchcock's *The Lodger*, *The Man in the Attic*, with Jack Palance in the title role.

Fregonese was the third child of immigrants from Northern Italy. When he was just four years old, his father was shot and killed in a dispute over a card game. Soon after this tragedy, the family upped and moved to Buenos Aires. Fregonese went to accountancy school, and after graduation worked as an accountant for a meat cutting firm in Buenos Aires in the late 1920s.

With a friend, Fregonese leased a ranch in the Pampas region and earned enough money to emigrate to America in 1935. He settled in Los Angeles, mostly for the climate, and found himself taking jobs as an extra in films. Feeling the allure of the motion picture world, he realized his true calling.

But it would be back in Argentina that he really learned the craft. In 1940, he returned to Argentina and began as a film cutter. Within a few years he got the chance to direct. His second film, *Donde Mueren Las Palabras* ("Where Words Die," 1944) won him a contract at MGM.

In 1947, Fregonese married American actress Faith Domergue, best known for her role in the sci-fi picture *This Island Earth* (1955). At the time, he was helming B-grade Westerns and gangster flicks for MGM. The studio bosses assigned him to a Frank Sinatra picture called *The Kissing Bandit* (1948), but Fregonese balked. The studio bosses were perplexed. Here was a no-name director with no meaningful films to his name, employed by one of Hollywood's most esteemed production houses, assigned as a matter of contract to not just any job, but one starring one of the world's most beloved celebrities. By what right did Fregonese refuse? Reckoning the Argentinian upstart to be a Grade-A nutjob, MGM's administration hastily canceled his contract.

"As to why he did that," recalls his daughter Diana, "I can only say there was a very self-destructive streak in his nature. After having worked hard for many years to be in just such a coveted position, he refused to comply because he didn't like the script and was disillusioned with the Hollywood power structure. I have this second-hand from my mother who thought it was a bad decision on his part and I have to agree. We knew Lazlo Benedek, the director who wound up doing *The Kissing Bandit*, for many years and he certainly had a respectable career. If Dad had played the power game, he later could have had more clout in choosing his projects, but he was always rebellious."

Set loose, Fregonese took his new wife back with him to Argentina, where he launched a career as a directorial gun-for-hire. He was now free from Hollywood's studio politics, free from the tyranny that assigned great artists to make films starring Frank Sinatra. However, he had delivered himself into a new form of tyranny.

"Dad went back to Argentina sometime after Easter 1948," remembers Diana "DeDe" Fregonese, "and Mother left later in May of that year. My maternal grandmother followed in a couple of months and they all suffered an uncomfortable winter of shortages due to the Peronista regime's allocation problems. Additionally, acquaintances sometimes failed to show up for appointments, due to the police's sudden need to question them about public remarks interpreted as criticism, i.e., the Perons were your typical paranoid dictatorship, times two! My parents realized that they would have to leave once my father's picture and Mother's pregnancy were completed."

Domergue was happy to take a hiatus from the pressures of Hollywood, and in 1950 gave birth to their daughter Diana. Hiding her pregnancy as well as she could, Domergue took a bit part in Fregonese's film *Hardly a Criminal* (1949), his first outside Hollywood. Soon thereafter, though, she returned to Hollywood. Meanwhile, as an itinerant director, Fregonese's career took him all over the globe, which put considerable strain on their relationship. They divorced in 1961.

Fregonese then began forging a relationship with Artur Brauner, the 800-pound gorilla of European cinema. Fregonese directed CCC's only non–Edgar Wallace–related picture of 1963, *Old Shatterhand*, from the famed Western novel by Karl May. One of CCC's biggest successes of the 1960s, *Old Shatterhand* launched a series of Karl May Westerns and made a bona fide European star out of Lex Barker, who was reunited with *Return of Dr. Mabuse* co-star Daliah Lavi with a script by Mabuse scribe Ladislas Fodor. Thrilled at the success of the Western, Brauner quickly assigned Fregonese to his ailing Mabuse franchise, which Fregonese promptly put out of its misery.

Following his work on *Death Ray*, Fregonese directed only four more films before his death, and of these only *Dracula vs. Frankenstein* received any meaningful distribution. He had once taken a taste of Hollywood's apple only to exile himself from the promised land.

"He truly disliked Hollywood society and was ever conscious of what a stranger he was in their midst," says his daughter. "I believe this was two-sided—Dad's own personal discontent added to the fact that Hollywood is indeed a rather strange town. One has to inure oneself to this in order to make the best of it, but Dad failed to see this, and I don't think he ever understood his own sensitivity. And that is the story of his life."

He died in Buenos Aires in 1987, a forgotten journeyman director of bad movies.

CHAPTER 16

Scream and Scream Again

> You've turned every scientific advance into a weapon!
> —Dr. Browning to Konratz

Reconciling *Scream and Scream Again* with the Mabuse features that precede it presents a challenging exercise. The film does not follow in the loose continuity that had been developed from 1922's *Dr. Mabuse the Gambler* through 1964's *Death Ray of Dr. Mabuse*. At the same time, *Scream and Scream Again* does not dispute that prior continuity in any direct way, and can be seen as a logical progression of the events of *Scotland Yard* and *Death Ray*. No, the biggest problem is that this Mabuse film does not include a Dr. Mabuse, at least not directly by name.

There is no Dr. Mabuse in *Scream and Scream Again* because, quite simply, *Scream and Scream Again* is not a Dr. Mabuse film.

American International Pictures (AIP) and Amicus Films undertook this project (with the working title *Screamers*) as an adaptation of the 1966 novel *The Disoriented Man*. Producer Milton Subotsky adapted the book into a screenplay without any regard for the Mabuse series, and the film was staged, produced and released without any larger motive beyond providing the casting coup of uniting horror superstars Vincent Price, Christopher Lee, and Peter Cushing. It was only after the fact that the German distributors retitled the picture *Die lebenden Leichen des Dr. Mabuse* ("The Living Corpses of Dr. Mabuse") to cash in on the marketability of the Mabuse name. This was a marketing decision that mirrored the way in which the American distributors often stripped off the Mabuse name from the U.S. editions of series entries: Americans took the name off the real thing, Germans tacked it on to wannabes.

This is not to say that *Scream and Scream Again*'s only claim to Mabuse-dom is the German release title. In the late 1960s, AIP began planning a lavish production of the life of Marquis de Sade, to be filmed in Germany at facilities provided by Artur Brauner and the CCC Studios. Independent producer Gordon Hessler and director Michael Reeves flew out to Munich and Berlin to scout the locations for this multi-million dollar shoot. As they did so, however, AIP's top brass began to fret that their most expensive and prestigious undertaking to date was to be helmed by an outside contractor rather than an in-house AIP producer, and maneuvered to remove Hessler from the project. Artur Brauner successfully lobbied AIP to hand *Marquis de Sade* over to him to produce under CCC's banner at a fraction of Hessler's budget. As a consolation

Despite enormous fidelity to the pulp novel on which it was based, the film Scream and Scream Again turned the book's severe flaws into thrilling cinema.

prize, AIP sent Hessler and Reeves to Ireland to film *The Oblong Box* (1969)—a much lower-budgeted project, but an auspicious one that quickly led to Hessler's being assigned *Scream and Scream Again*.*

Distributor Ufa duly recognized the film's very strong thematic and stylistic similarity that warranted the Mabuse brand name, even if the American filmmakers had not consciously intended the parallels. *Scream and Scream Again* presents a very paranoid scenario, bubbling over with spy planes, hidden television cameras, radio-transmitting shoes, military dictatorships, inexplicable crimes, the destruction of evidence and mad conspiracies to take over the world.

The story of *Scream and Scream Again* not only resembles the Mabuse pattern in its on-screen content, but in its off-screen circumstances as well. The story behind *Scream and Scream Again* is rife with false names, suicides and deceptions.

---

*File under "Doppelganger": AIP's De Sade *(1969) came out just one year after* Marquis de Sade: Justine *by director Jess Franco, whom Artur Brauner would hire in the aftermath of* Scream and Scream Again *to helm the next legitimate Mabuse series entry. Franco's* de Sade *stars Klaus Kinski, who appeared in* Scotland Yard vs. Dr. Mabuse, *and Gustavo Re, who would appear in Franco's* Vengeance of Dr. Mabuse.

While the screenplay is credited as an adaptation of the novel *The Disorientated Man* by Peter Saxon, there is no such person as Peter Saxon. Originally, that pen name had been adopted by Irish author W. Howard Baker (who, like Norbert Jacques, was also a journalist) for a series of pulpy mystery novels he wrote for Amalgamated Press. The bulk of these works were the continuing adventures of the Sherlock Holmes–like Sexton Blake, a series that ran under the Amalgamated banner up until 1963. Then, in 1965, Baker joined with publisher Mayflower Books to revive and continue the Sexton Blake series. Mayflower's Sexton Blake books continued to credit author "Peter Saxon," although Baker was but one of several authors now working on the series. The Saxon name had been adopted by Mayflower as an all-purpose *nom de plume*. Thus, the 1966 novel *The Disorientated Man*, credited to Peter Saxon, had been edited by Baker, but principally authored by Stephen Frances using Baker's erstwhile appellation.

That book caught the eye of producer Milton Subotsky, whose company Amicus Films had been attempting to compete with Hammer Films in the field of gothic horror. In partnership with Max J. Rosenberg, Subotsky had raided the Hammer lot for stars and technical personnel for Amicus' productions. Many of their best (and best-known) works such as *Dr. Terror's House of Horrors* (1965) followed an anthology format, with several short stories linked together by some framing device. Whereas Hammer's horrors took place in a gothic past, Amicus generally located their movies in much less expensive modern-day settings. Subotsky thought the ghastly storyline of *The Disorientated Man* was ideal for Amicus, and bought the rights.

Initially, Subotsky worked on the screenplay adaptation himself. The book featured an extraterrestrial menace as the force responsible for animating creatures stitched together from bits of corpses, and Subotsky wisely dropped that element. What was left still constituted a complex web of Cold War political intrigue, old-style gothic chills and cops 'n' robbers police procedurals.

Meanwhile, American International Pictures (AIP) had built itself up as the preeminent force in low-budget thrillers. AIP produced and distributed some of the best and most commercially successful horror and science-fiction genre pictures ever screened in the U.S. In 1968, AIP had teamed with another Hammer rival, Tigon Pictures, for a controversial and very adult-themed film called *Witchfinder General*, starring Vincent Price. Louis M. "Deke" Heyward, AIP's English production chief, had been the mover and the shaker behind the AIP-Tigon pairing. He renamed the film *Conqueror Worm* for the American market, adding a recording of Price reading Edgar Allan Poe's poem of the same name in order to reclassify the picture as part of AIP's hugely successful Vincent Price-Edgar Allan Poe series. When Subotsky approached Heyward with the *Disorientated Man* project, Heyward sensed the possibility to repeat his earlier success.

One of Heyward's first decisions was to remove Subotsky and Rosenberg from the day-to-day duties of production. They retained producer credits for their financial participation, but Heyward took over supervision of the project, which he felt was too much of a demanding, big-budget endeavor for the Amicus team.

Almost immediately, AIP announced that the newly retitled *Screamer*, "a super-suspense mystery feature," was slated to begin filming in 1969. Given that AIP had been making money hand over fist from a series of Edgar Allan Poe adaptations starring Vincent Price, there was never any

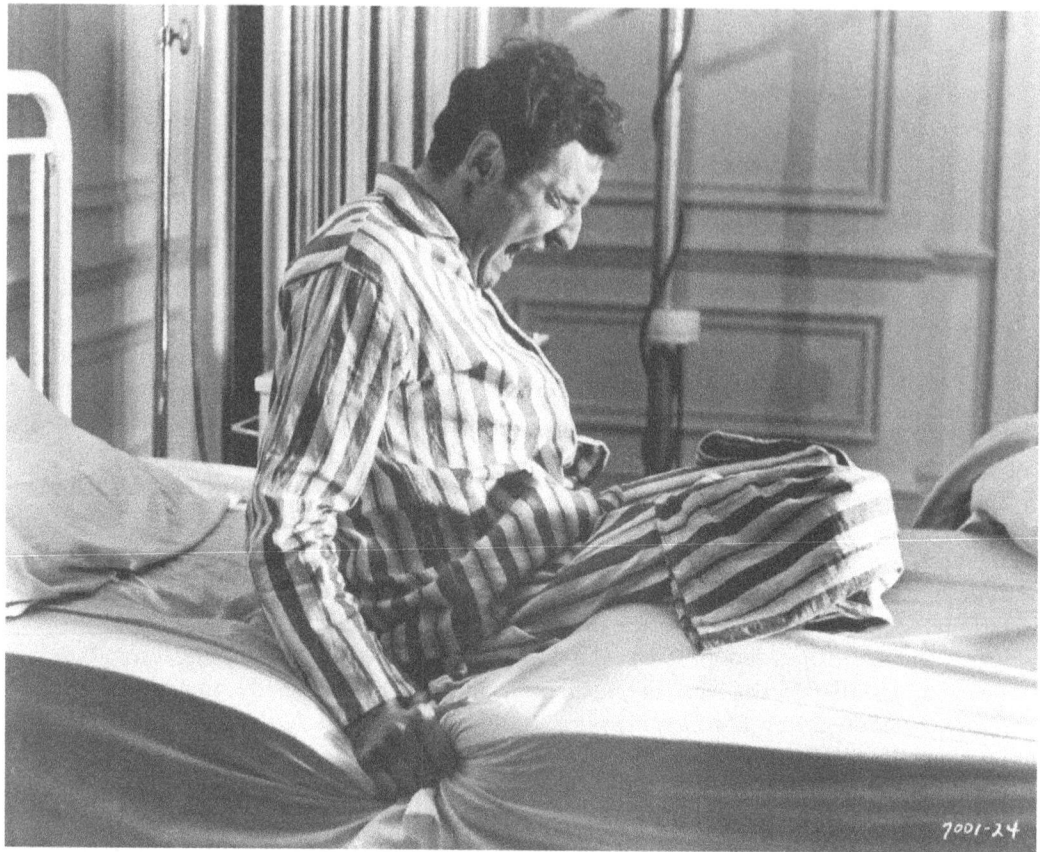

Nigel Lambert as the disorientated man.

question that Heyward would see his contracted star Price headline in *Screamer*. The AIP producer had even grander ambitions, though. Having already teamed horror legends Boris Karloff, Christopher Lee and Barbara Steele in the 1968 production *The Crimson Cult*, Heyward was scouting for new opportunities for all-star promotional vehicles. In 1969, Heyward paired Christopher Lee with Vincent Price in *The Oblong Box*, again reaping box office rewards. Never one to tamper with a winning strategy, Heyward decreed that *Screamer* would co-star Price with Lee (again) and Peter Cushing. However this decision was made at a fairly late stage in development, by which time the film could not so easily accommodate its three headliners.

In the early stages of preparation, Heyward and Subotsky planned to give the picture to the young and upcoming director Michael Reeves to helm. Reeves had distinguished himself as a very gifted, if tortured and temperamental, artist on *Conqueror Worm*. That film boasts one of Price's most accomplished, if atypical, performances. As Price was known to ham his roles up, Reeves bitterly resented having the actor forced onto his film as a fait accompli. Reeves wanted Donald Pleasence for the lead role in *Conqueror Worm*, but Heyward insisted that AIP's box office king Vincent Price was a non-negotiable item. The director and his star fought throughout the production, with Reeves baffling Price with almost incomprehensible directions. The finished product was

Including Vincent Price was a non-negotiable item for the U.S. producers.

sublime, though, and even Price had to admit that the mercurial director knew what he was doing. "I realized only after I saw the finished film how talented [Reeves] was."

Although they had gotten off to a rocky start, Heyward decided that Reeves and Price should collaborate again, on 1969's *The Oblong Box*, which teamed Price with Hammer's icon Christopher Lee. Following that, it was planned, Reeves, Price and Lee would add Peter Cushing to the mix and proceed with what had by now been retitled *Scream and Scream Again*, with the U.S. edition of the "Peter Saxon" novel duly renamed to match. None of this came to pass, for Michael Reeves passed away in early 1969 at the very young age of 25.

"It was a great loss to the cinema," Vincent Price told Lawrence French in an interview years later. The director had died of an overdose of barbiturates and alcohol, but whether he had taken his own life on purpose or by accident remains unknown to this day. What is certain is that Reeves had made several previous suicide attempts, and had recently been abandoned by his girlfriend, who found his self-destructive persona too much to bear.

In the wake of Reeves' untimely death, *The Oblong Box* passed to producer Gordon Hessler, who also inherited Reeves' director of photography from *Conqueror Worm*, John Coquillon. "He was so talented," Hessler recalled of his cinematographer, "He was just 19 or 20 years old, but he could hand-hold a camera and move it around in the most impossible shots to do…. He was an extraordinary cameraman."

The inestimable Peter Cushing made the most of his minor role.

Hessler was born in Germany in 1930, when Fritz Lang, Thea von Harbou and Norbert Jacques were first developing ideas for *The Testament of Dr. Mabuse*. Hessler worked with the Master of Thrillers himself, Alfred Hitchcock, first as a story editor on the television series *Alfred Hitchcock Presents* and later as a producer and director on *The Alfred Hitchcock Hour*. With this kind of training, his first concern on *Scream and Scream Again* was Subotsky's script, which Hessler felt was a disorientated mess all on its own.

On the previous AIP-Price project *The Oblong Box*, Michael Reeves had brought in screenwriter Christopher Wicking to improve the dialogue. Hessler and Wicking became something of a team, working together on several consecutive films. Naturally, then, Hessler asked if Wicking could have a go at fixing Subotsky's script, too. Wicking explained later that Hessler "wanted to do a Don Siegel-style horror film, *Coogan's Bluff* meets *Invasion of the Body Snatchers*. This does serve Peter Saxon's [sic] novel *The Disorientated Man* rather well on some cosmic level."

"This became the script where the true genius of Chris Wicking comes out," Hessler told *Filmfax* magazine in 1997. "If you read *The Disorientated Man*, it's a really bad piece of pulp fiction. Chris turned it into something much more extraordinary because he gave it a political influence that wasn't there. In thematic content, Chris stayed closely to the book, which Milton hadn't done."

In terms of incident and action, Wicking's script is almost slavishly faithful to

Many Mabuses, none genuine: Marshall Jones (left) as Konratz and Christopher Lee (right) as Fremont.

the book. The principal difference between the two is in the question of style. The book is badly written, the kind of "literature" in which the various characters are always referred to by their full names by a pseudonymous author evidently unconvinced that the reader could otherwise discern one underdeveloped stock character from another. Although recounting the same events in the same chronology, Wicking's screenplay is exciting, thrilling and mesmerizing. Like Subotsky's earlier adaptation, Wicking has dropped all reference to space aliens (a decidedly silly idea in the book), opting instead to render the bizarre Frankensteinian experiments creating artificial humanoids as the work of an international conspiracy—a Mabusian plot, as it were.

The book clearly stages much of its action in Communist East Germany: Mabuse's interconnectedness with the troubled political history of Germany is never very far away. However, this theme is suppressed somewhat by Wicking, who renders these scenes in a vaguely defined Eastern European Bloc nation, sort of a cross between Nazi Germany and the GDR. The idea of Communists colluding with gangsters and megalomaniacal madmen that fueled such written works as Bryan Edgar Wallace's *The Device* and the ghost-written *Disorientated Man* would be elided from their respective screen adaptations. Not until Claude Chabrol's *Club Extinction* would a Mabuse picture tackle the GDR as the next evolution of Hitler's evil, but by 1989 it would be too late to be relevant (see Chapter 21).

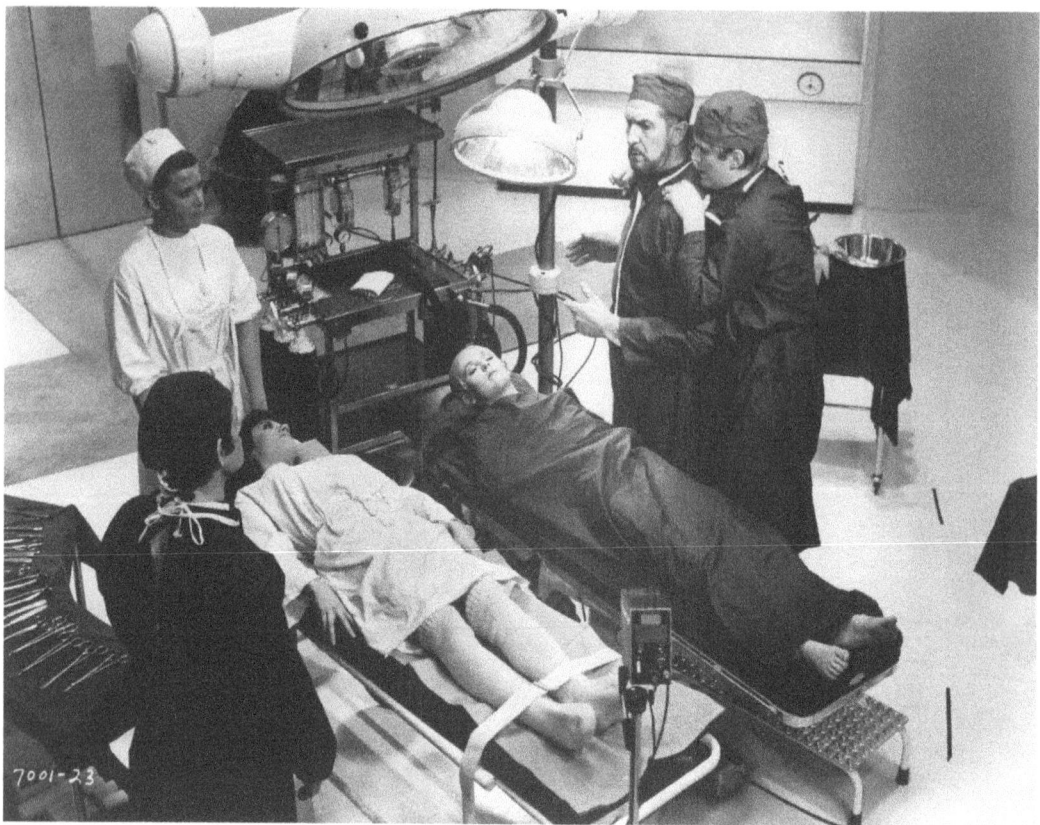

Dr. David Soren (Christopher Matthews, far right) confronts D. Browning/Dr. Mabuse (Vincent Price) in his secret lab.

By the time it became clear that Heyward intended to cast the trio of Vincent Price, Christopher Lee and Peter Cushing in the picture, though, Wicking's screenplay had limited options on how to best use their acting talents. Fans of these great horror stars were destined to be disappointed by the end result, since between them Price, Lee and Cushing get precious little screen time, and with one minor exception no two of them appear on-screen together. Cushing appears in only one scene, and is immediately killed. Lee gets four scenes, and while his role is a pivotal one, his scenes are extremely brief. Price fares only slightly better, and nearly a full hour elapses between his first and second screen appearances.

Instead, *Scream and Scream Again* gives the lion's share of attention to its second-billed players as it presents a number of seemingly unconnected events: In one story thread, an unnamed man suffers an unidentified injury and is taken to a mystery hospital, where, under the "care" of a silent nurse, he is dismembered limb by limb. Story strand number two takes place in the aforementioned Eastern European military dictatorship where Konratz (Marshall Jones), a member of the Secret Police, tortures and kills his way up the ranks of power. Story thread three follows the London police as Inspector Bellaver (Alfred Marks) and coroner's assistant Dr. Sorel (Christopher Matthews) investigate the serial murders of the so-called "Vampire Killer," who mutilates young women and somehow bleeds their corpses dry. How these disparate episodes relate to each other is reserved for the final climactic moments, as the few surviving characters converge to discover their world is crashing in on them. In the grand tradition of *The 1000 Eyes of Dr. Mabuse*, it's confusion as entertainment: confusatainment.

Cushing's cameo amply demonstrates why the actor maintained such a high reputation. He may have only a few fleeting minutes of screen time, but he gives the part his full respect, imbuing the character with a palpable dignity. Cushing plays Major Benedek, one of the top military strongmen in the unidentified fascist/Communist nation. He knows that torturers like Konratz are essential for keeping order in a totalitarian state. Admiring how Konratz has remained "always anonymous—a non-entity," Benedek has to admit that recently Konratz has rendered himself a liability. Having tortured and killed a young couple whose crime was trying to flee to the West, Konratz has stirred up a public relations problem. What Benedek does not know is his errant enforcer is only in such a powerful position because he has murdered everyone who gets in his way. No sooner has Benedek started criticizing his underling than the sinister madman digs his fingers into Benedek's shoulder blades and removes another inconvenient obstacle to his ambitions.

In the role of Konratz, actor Marshall Jones may not have been one of the top-billed stars but he provides an important and fully developed villainous performance. A diabolical schemer who works behind the scenes in anonymity on a plan of world domination, Konratz is almost a Mabuse figure himself, and is only dethroned from this position in the final seconds of the picture by Fremont, Konratz's counterpart at the head of the British intelligence agency.

As Fremont, Christopher Lee gets more footage, but he does less with it. Apparently of the opinion that this glorified cameo did not warrant his serious attention, Lee delivers a lifeless performance. Hessler remarked later, "I was not impressed with Christopher Lee as an actor. He always seemed to have this bland, stoic face. But I saw him do pictures much later where he was quite extraordinary. I had no idea of his talent." Unfortunately, Lee's Fremont is a critical character, and the essential link between the various plot fragments. As it happens, Fremont is the ultimate Machiavellian mastermind, orchestrating a massive yet silent takeover of the world by a new race of artificially engineered supermen composites, of which he and Konratz are examples.

The "composites" are so named because they are stitched together from the bits and pieces of cadavers, and animated by mad scientists such as Dr. Browning. As Browning, Vincent Price plays his role with a subdued dignity, as if in deference to the late Michael Reeves who had originally been picked to direct. Always capable of making even the most despicable monster somehow sympathetic, Price gives Browning the perfect blend of terrifying selfishness and childlike innocence. When Browning unveils the full scope of the nightmare to Dr. Sorel, demonstrating his surgical technology with the obvious intention of transplanting Sorel's girlfriend's brain into a composite body, he does so with such sincere, naive enthusiasm, he comes across as so much more menacing than the usual gloating megalomaniac. This poor soul genuinely believes that the world will be better off once the human race has been supplanted by man-made cyborgs. He rattles off the evils of the modern world, from world hunger to the threat of nuclear annihilation, and pities the human beast: "What future do they have?" he asks disdainfully. Ironically,

Browning's justifications sound very much like the explanations offered up by Dr. M for his program of mass suicides in Claude Chabrol's *Club Extinction*. More interesting still, Browning predicts that the composites will have assumed control in 20 years, and 20 years from *Scream and Scream Again*'s 1969 release date coincides with *Club Extinction*'s 1989 release date.

What brings these various characters together is the case of London's "vampire killer," played by Michael Gothard. Film historian David Del Valle remarked that Gothard was once seen as "a cross between Mick Jagger and Klaus Kinski." He gave a star-making appearance in Ken Russell's 1971 picture *The Devils* and played the bad guy in the 1981 James Bond entry *For Your Eyes Only*. While great things were expected from Gothard, he too committed suicide, hanging himself in 1993. His character here is quite the ladykiller, lounging around clubs like the Busted Pot Disco, literally preying on the vulnerable young lasses drawn to his good looks.

That a psychopath is racking up a body count is alone problem enough for Inspector Bellaver (the latest model in the line of von Wenk/Lohmann substitutes) and Dr. David Sorel (played by the young Peter Van Eyck–lookalike Christopher Matthews). That he is mutilating their bodies and somehow exsanguinating them too is a more troubling mystery. They trap the killer, but he manages to beat off a gaggle of burly cops and survive an impossible fall off a cliff before being handcuffed to a car bumper. Bellaver realizes he has a monster on his hands when his prisoner escapes by simply breaking off his hand and running away. Dutifully the police give chase yet again, only to be foiled when the vampire retreats to Browning's estate and dissolves himself in a hidden vat of acid; in the world of Mabuse, the bad guys rarely allow themselves to be caught when they can do themselves in instead. Suicide is the ultimate manifestation of *je m'abuse*: the abuse I do to myself.

The case garners enough press attention to pull Konratz away from his busy schedule of slaughtering his way up the ranks. Konratz knows that the composite conspiracy is too small to survive any significant attention from the authorities, and he guesses correctly that the "Vampire Killer" is one of Browning's composites gone wrong. Unless somebody cleans up the mess properly, the wrong people might start asking the right questions. He travels to England to shut down Dr. Browning's secret composite factory. Once Fremont realizes what Konratz is planning, he also heads to Browning's lab to see to it that *all* incriminating evidence is destroyed—such as Browning himself. As the film unspools its final frames, Browning dumps Konratz in the acid bath only to face Fremont. The mastermind does not even have to raise a finger, only stare with his burning all-seeing eyes, for Browning to sacrifice himself in the acid. *Je m'abuse*.

"In horror films the odds are always heavily against me," said Price in an on-set interview quoted in David H. Smith's essay on *Scream and Scream Again* in the book *Vincent Price*. Unfortunately, in filming this death scene, Price did not wear nose plugs as he dipped his face into the yellow liquid, and he inhaled enough of the goo to suffer respiratory problems for the rest of his life.

In these final moments, David Sorel has quickly (and wisely) escaped the operating theater with his girlfriend's brain still intact. His hasty exit means that the only investigator who came close to figuring out the dastardly plot (and asking those questions Konratz was so desperate to keep unasked), departs before learning that Fremont is behind it all. Although actors Christopher Matthews and Christopher Lee scarcely share a second of screen time here, they would square off

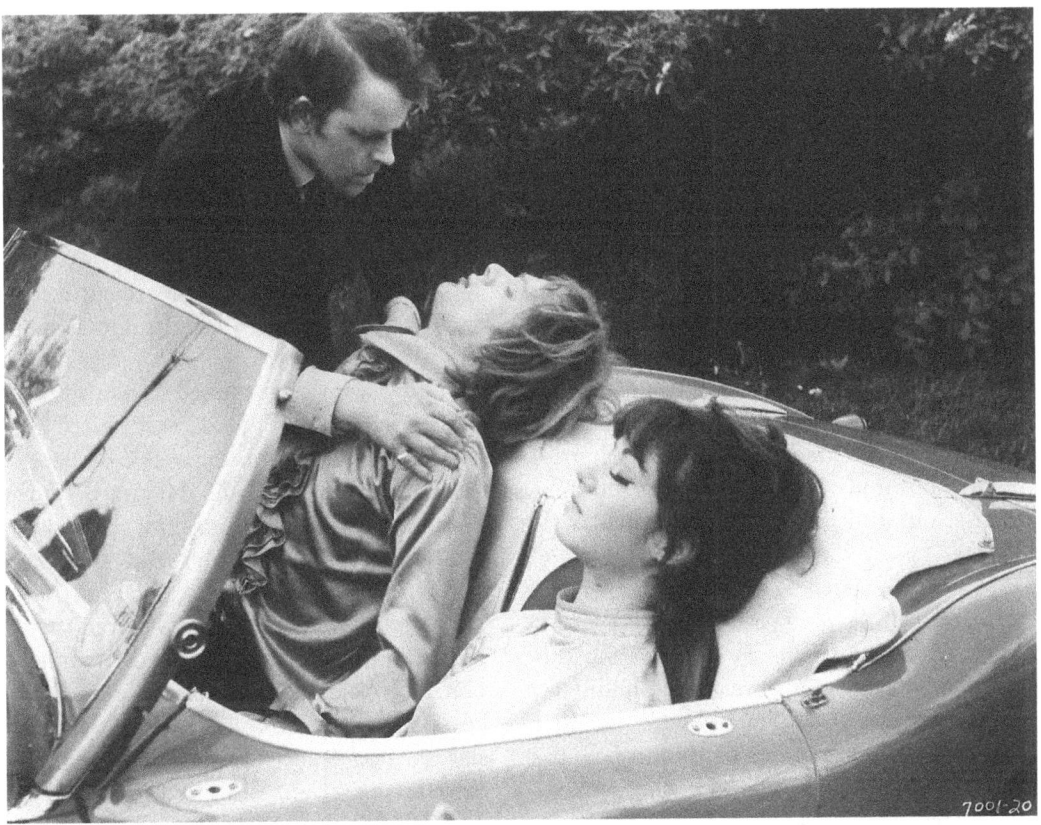

Michael Gothard (middle) became a minor star thanks to this performance.

against one another more substantially in Hammer's *Scars of Dracula* the following year.

Also a card-carrying member of Hammer's film vampire club, Yutte Stensgaard appears briefly in *Scream and Scream Again* as an ill-fated lodger in Konratz's torture dungeon before going on to B-movie stardom as the vampire Mircalla in *Lust for a Vampire* (1971), which Heyward produced as part of a much-ballyhooed but brief-lived partnership between AIP and Hammer.

In a slightly more substantial guest spot, Heyward featured the British pop group The Amen Corner as the band playing in the Busted Pot Disco where Gothard's vampire does his trawling. The Amen Corner had a few Top 10 hits in the U.K. before proving themselves a mere flash in the pan. For many viewers, though, the two songs they perform here ("Scream and Scream Again" and "When We Make Love") are the only fragments left of the original movie's soundtrack. The incidental score had been composed by David Whitaker, who also scored a number of Hammer's later pictures. Appropriately, he chose a musical homage to the jazzy soundtracks of German crime thrillers, and his music sounds like a close twin of Peter Sandloff's backing tracks from films like *Return of Dr. Mabuse*. Unfortunately, AIP neglected to think ahead, failing to secure the rights to this music for other media. When the video age dawned and films like *Scream and Scream Again* found renewed life on tape, AIP had to replace Whitaker's soundtrack with new synthesizer recordings. Hessler rues this turn of events, and believes that the atmosphere of his film is substantially altered by the modified soundtrack.

Some of *Scream and Scream Again*'s contributors did not even have to wait that long for their work to be excised from the picture. Heyward asked Monty Python's Terry Gilliam to animate the opening titles. "They were full of humor and violence—and even better than the James Bond titles," Heyward reminisced to interviewer Christopher Koetting in 1997. "He did it as a favor to me for practically nothing. Then [AIP executive James] Nicholson just took all of Terry's animation out and replaced it with regular titles."

Gilliam repeated the favor for Heyward the following year for AIP's Vincent Price vehicle *Cry of the Banshee*, and this time Nicholson left the animation intact. *Banshee* was also scripted by Christopher Wicking, photographer by John Coquillon, directed by Gordon Hessler, and co-starred Marshall Jones. However, while Gilliam's titles survived, this time around Hessler chosen soundtrack was discarded even before the picture hit theaters. The score Hessler commissioned from Wilfred Joseph was axed by the AIP brass in favor of a generic one by Les Baxter. While Hessler had been relieved that his quirky take on *Scream and Scream Again* had been passed on to screen virtually intact, his subsequent work with AIP would meet with increasing interference from the producers. After only a few more pictures fraught with such frustration, Hessler left AIP, and later directed *The Golden Voyage of Sinbad* (1974) for famed animator Ray Harryhausen. "I was never in a position to afford a personal vision," Hessler concluded. "I was just sort of a journeyman and tried to do the best with what I had."

Scream and Scream Again opened to quite good box office showings. Hessler explained in *Filmfax*, "Everybody was very worried about the picture but, when it came out, I'd never gotten such universally positive reviews! What it had, I think, was a style that was different from the standard horror picture. It had a fluid excitement and it all jelled. All those disjointed scenes add to the mystery, with everything eventually coming together."

"We were young," Hessler reminisced in 1999, "and we had a lot of fun making it."

Few were as surprised at the film's success than the man who got it started in the first place, Milton Subotsky. Perhaps smarting at how Louis Heyward had taken the reins away from him, Subotsky grumbled that "it was a bit of a cheat to advertise [Price, Lee, and Cushing] as 'stars' rather than 'guest stars,'" given that the second-billed players really carried the film. As it happened, Gothard received the best reviews of all the cast anyway. Subotsky did not expect the film to be a hit, since he felt "it wasn't all that good." Acknowledging that the three star names had to have helped, he also felt that the title was an important asset. On this point, Christopher Lee disagreed. He thought the title was "dreadful" and feared audiences would laugh at it.

In fact, the title would be substantially altered as the film made its route across Europe. In France, the theatrical release was named *Lachez les Monstres!* ("Free the Monsters!"), and the video title was *Dr. Diabolic*. In Germany, *Scream and Scream Again* became *Die lebenden Leichen des Dr. Mabuse* ("The Living Corpses of Dr. Mabuse"), and thus, only after the fact, did Hessler's picture join the ranks of the cinematic incarnations of Norbert Jacques' errant creation.

Mabuse not only appears in the picture's title, but thanks to the German dubbing in the cast as well. However, the choice of which character to rechristen as Mabuse may not seem so obvious at first

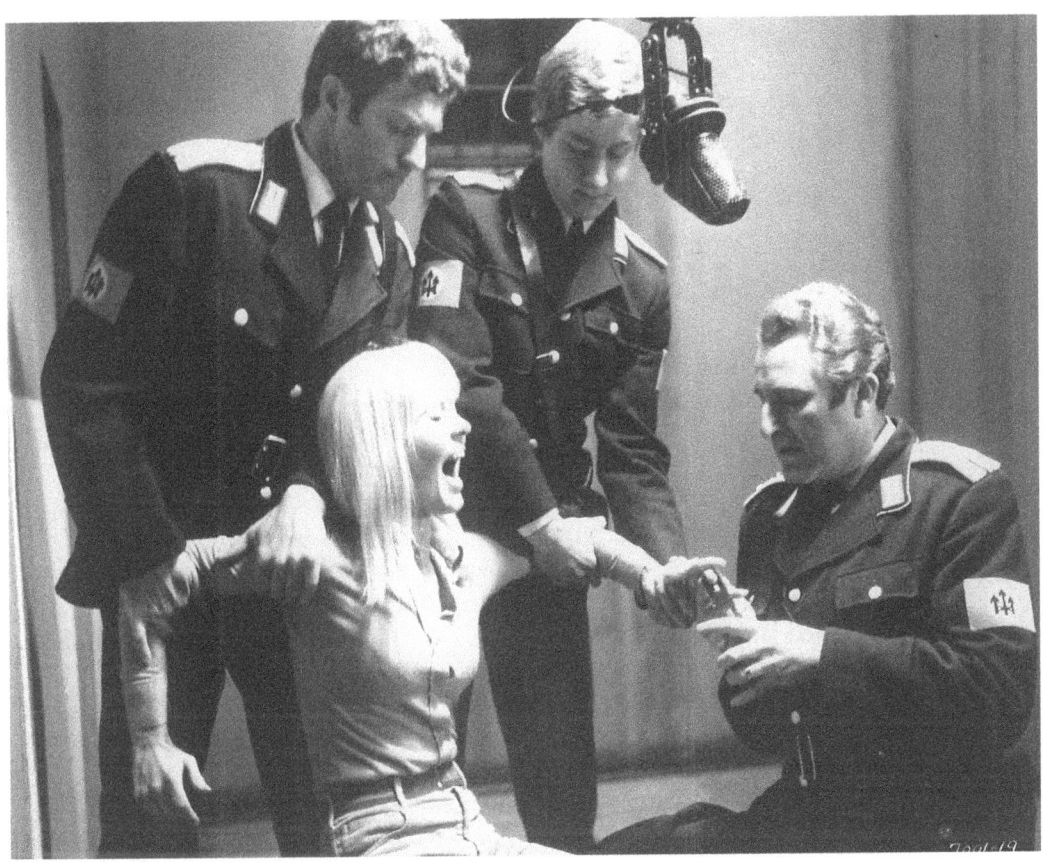

Yutte Stensgaard screams and screams again in the clutches of Marshall Jones.

blush. Characters like Konratz and Fremont are decidedly old-school Mabusian figures, power-mad conspirators using terror, mad science and deception to take over the world in secret, one step at a time. Today the GDR, 20 years from now, the world. The book even describes Konratz with words all but cribbed from Norbert Jacques:

> He was a man of vaunting ambition, grim purposefulness and deadly menace.
> Konratz had amassed astounding information about the lives of all important political personages. He knew every whim, superstition, and habit of every official of any importance whatsoever. He had harnessed political power for his own purposes. He had a thousand spies, agents provocateurs, hirelings, thieves and killers ready to obey his orders at a moment's notice. The Police Chiefs of all the provinces were in the palm of his hand...
> Without people knowing it, Konratz was now the true leader of the German Democratic Republic! ...
> Sitting like a spider at his desk, Konratz had woven an enormous web of power throughout the entire country...
> [He] had a thousand ears that listened for him, a thousand tongues that reported to him, ten thousand fingers to condense those reports.

Nonetheless, the German edition tags Vincent Price's character as the new "Doktor Mabuse."

German film critic Hans Schmidt in his essay "Kino als Sabotage" ("Cinema as sabotage") notes that "Mabuse always had a little bit of Frankenstein in him." Traditionally, Mabuse enslaves his victims with hypnotism and mind control, remaking people with disguise, plastic surgery and fake names. In *Die lebenden Leichen des Dr. Mabuse*, he has simply taken this program to its extreme, making an army of will-less zombies out of the parts of other people. And if one of his manufactured soldiers turns out to be rather ungrateful dead, full of bloodthirst and rebellion, that's just the price of progress. Of course, those responsible for orchestrating the conspiracy cannot be expected to be as tolerant of such attention-grabbing shenanigans, and so like any good Mabuse scenario, the whole thing dissolves into fractious infighting and internecine bloodshed: the snake swallowing its own tail.

For Schmidt, the key image of the film is the ill-fated jogger whose plight is stretched out in horrific vignettes across the picture. The jogger first appears during the opening titles, suffering some kind of injury on his morning run. He awakens in a silent hospital, attended by a silent nurse. The only sound is his own screams, as he realizes he is being slowly dismembered. First a leg is gone, then the other. The next time he appears, all that remains is his head and trunk. In the closing sequence, Dr. Sorel discovers the poor man's head in a freezer cabinet, spare parts for Browning/Mabuse's mad science. "*Scream and Scream Again* is about the destruction of identity," writes Schmidt. That, and the creation of artificial identity, built up from scratch.

Among those to recognize the heritage of Mabuse in Hessler's film was none other than Fritz Lang himself. Price told *Cinefantastique* in 1973, "Fritz really loved it." Lang became so smitten with the film that he sought out Christopher Wicking to tell him that it was a marvelous political thriller, "suspensefully developed."

Die lebenden Leichen des Dr. Mabuse opened in Germany in February 1971, by which time Artur Brauner had already produced the legitimate, authorized return of Dr. Mabuse. That this production, *The Vengeance of Dr. Mabuse*, would be an even more idiosyncratic interpretation of the Mabuse legend than *Scream and Scream Again* would be less a criticism of *Vengeance* than a testament to the sincere and respectful treatment director Gordon Hessler had given the material. Under any title, *Scream and Scream Again* stands a worthy installment in this provocative and enduring franchise.

CHAPTER 17

The Life and Times of Jess Franco

> Franco is a born rule breaker, a man driven to make his own brand of sex soaked cinema, a maverick trailblazer who personifies the untapped potential of film.
> —Cathall Tohill and Pete Tombs, *Immoral Tales*

M, the motion picture Fritz Lang believed to be the pinnacle of his directorial career, marked the auspicious debut of actor Peter Lorre, whose subsequent credits are both numerous and impressive. With his bug-like eyes and raspy, unctuous voice, Lorre came to epitomize creepiness in countless classic horror films and *noir*-ish thrillers. Lorre was both a truly gifted performer and a movie icon. After his death, an American producer hatched the arguably ill-advised plan of remaking several of Lorre's classic vehicles, including *The Man Who Knew Too Much* (1934), with a Lorre lookalike.

This bizarre notion was ultimately abandoned, in large measure because the lookalike had little time for acting since he was busy as one of filmdom's most prolific, if notorious, directors. To date, Jess Franco has directed over 160 films over the span of four decades, acting in and composing the soundtracks for many of them, as well as assisting in the production of other films by other filmmakers. Of course, quantity and quality are distinct issues, and the quality of Franco's output has sparked lively debate among *cineastes*.

Franco's enormous *curriculum vitae* includes such luridly titled creations as *Sadisterotica* (1968), *A Virgin Among the Living Dead* (1971), *The Bare Breasted Countess* (1973) and *The Killer Barbys* (1996), not to mention his authentically pornographic films. Franco has worked with a variety of producers of questionable reputation, some of whom financed films while dodging arrest. Franco once made a feature with money he won from the lottery. Despite his advanced age, Franco is still a busy filmmaker, and remains one of the most iconic representatives of the independent spirit in world cinema.

As befits a man who would navigate the tricky Mabusian landscape of false fronts and multiple identities, Franco has gone under a bewildering number of aliases in the course of his extensive career, including Joan Almiral, Clifford Brown, Betty Carter, Terry De Corsia, Chuck Evans, Dennis Farnon, Jeff Frank, James Gardner, Manfred Gregor, Jack Griffin, Lennie Hayden, Frank Hollman, James Lee Johnson, Peter Kerr, David Khune, Marius Lasouer, Lulu Laverne, John A.

Lazer, A.L. Malriaux, Roland Marceignac, Tawer Nero, John O'Hara, Preston Quaid, Dan Simon, Michael Thomas, Dave Tough, Michael Thomas and Pablo Villa.

In some cases, the multi-talented Franco would work under various names on the same project, credited separately for his contributions as screenwriter, director, soundtrack composer and actor. More often, the numerous pseudonyms allowed Franco to seek production financing across Europe from countries that offered backing only under conditions that local directors be used; Franco's wily producers would register him under an appropriately French-sounding name, for example, for a film made with French money. Nowadays, though, Franco has achieved enough success under his own name to no longer need to or want to play that game, and he insists on being called either by his given name of Jesús Franco Manera or his official cinematic name Jess Franco.

The Lorre connection is but one of many coincidences and linkages between Franco and Fritz Lang. Like so many of these coincidences, it raises the recurring Mabusian theme of identity and disguise, and points to the polarized disparity between Lang's and Franco's professional reputations. The Lorre anecdote suggests that Franco is a wannabe, a lookalike, an impostor, traveling in the cinematic underworld of low budgets and even lower artistic standards, while Lang is the struggling artist battling the forces of commerce to maintain his creative integrity. But this is a fiction, and to examine the life and times of Jesús Franco Manera is to discover the similarity between these two men, underneath their masks.

Franco was born on May 12, 1930, to a well-educated family that included philosophers, musicologists, writers, critics and other luminaries. "My grandfather from my mother's side was a real Cuban composer, and renowned poet," Franco told *Psychotronic Video* in 1999. "Mainly I grew up between people talking about literature, music and cinema." Franco showed prodigious gifts at an early age, learning the piano as a youth and playing in jazz bands as a teen.

He had been groomed for a career as a diplomat, but just as Lang never followed through with his education, Franco dropped his legal studies to pursue artistic passions instead. Lang had paid the rent working at cabarets and selling sketches; Franco wrote pulp novels and played in jazz bands. Franco wrote over 100 crime and horror stories (the kind of fiction that so inspired Lang), while hoping to join the film business.

"That period was fantastic," Franco recalls of going to the movies in his youth, "Because it was before [Generalissimo] Franco's censorship arrived.* Franco was already there, but he had more important things to do ... killing people, you know, so he was not thinking about cinema."

He enrolled in the Spanish film school, importantly designated the Institute of Cinematographic Research and Experience. After two years, though, he transferred to the French film school at the Sorbonne in Paris. The move to France not only anticipated how the renegade director would have to seek backing from the French time and again when his Spanish homeland rejected his excesses, but also mirrored Lang's youthful relocation to Paris in the years before World War I. But now, after World War II, Franco reveled in a new set of creative influences, the same cultural climate that nurtured the French New Wave of Godard and Truffaut.

---

*No relation to Jess Franco, Generalissimo Franco was a Mabusian tyrant who ruled Spain with an iron fist from 1939 to 1975.

Franco attended the Cinémathèque so frequently that they started admitting him for free, and even held special screenings for him; Lang had also been a frequent attendee of the Cinémathèque, and had deposited his papers there upon his death.

While Lang only claimed to be a world traveler, Franco was the real thing, fluent in at least six languages. This facility would serve him well once he began his career making low-budget films underwritten by a motley collection of international investors. When Franco returned to Spain to start that career, he had an uphill road ahead of him.

Generalissimo Franco held the country in a tight thrall. All forms of cultural and creative expression were subject to strict governmental censorship. The prevailing mode of cinema at the time was realism: the style of safe, uplifting historical dramas and religious stories. Creative expression had to take a back seat to the propaganda needs of the government.

As the young Jess Franco returned to Spain, a move was underfoot to open up the country to international tourism, partly to promote the image of Spain in the world community and partly to court much-wanted foreign cash. As Spain became a playground for Continental tourists, the Spanish locals became increasingly exposed to the more liberal attitudes and tastes of their neighbors. Spanish cinema seemed increasingly anachronistic in the '50s, a time when the rest of Western Europe was reveling in wild, trashy films full of sex and horror.

In 1962, Manuel Fraga was appointed the new Minister of Information and Tourism (a job title that acknowledged the link between film and tourism that was so pointedly true in Spain's experience). Fraga loosened censorship, hoping to encourage the film industry to become more competitive in the international market. It was against this background of cultural battles over the content of motion pictures, a battle between governmental regulators and artists, between Spain and the world, between art and commerce, that Jess Franco made his indelible mark.

He had been working up to a feature film for some time, exercising his cinematic muscles in short subjects and documentaries. Beginning in 1953, Franco started composing soundtracks. Within a year he was serving as an assistant director as well, working on 14 pictures in four years. At the same time, he scored six films, scripted four others, and acted in several more. He was demonstrating his prolific tirelessness even at this early stage. In 1957, he helmed his first solo work, a short documentary about olives. By 1959, he was ready to direct a full-length feature: *We Are 18*.

Franco had aspired to unite his interest in film with his interest in jazz, to develop his own free-wheeling expressionistic style in contrast to the dominant mode of realism. From his very first feature, Franco proved himself a director who would choose the path least traveled; while the usual first-time director might opt to play it safe, Franco established an anarchic working style and narrative approach that defied all existing conventions. *We Are 18* has no story to speak of, just a rambling connection of episodes exploring Franco's interests. The censors had little idea what to make of this experimental concoction, and all but banned it.

Such a setback did not derail Franco. He simply plowed ahead with another film, *Red Lips* (1960), hoping that someone might step forward to pay his rapidly mounting production bills. Indeed, a producer did ultimately back *Red Lips*, and the experience taught the emerging filmmaker a lesson he would keep close at heart: that he should always keep filming (something, anything), and the money would (he hoped) come later. It was a lesson

With a face like Peter Lorre and a filmmaker's mind like nobody else, Jess Franco has made an improbable career out of low-budget oddities (courtesy Kevin Collins).

learned in much the same way by Fritz Lang some 33 years earlier when Ufa gave him the boot.

Red Lips caught the eye of producer Serge Newman, who signed Franco to a three-picture deal. At first, they collaborated on musicals, taking advantage of Franco's extensive musical knowledge. It was their third picture that established Franco's reputation and gave Spanish cinema a bona fide international hit.

Franco had been interested in horror for some time; his early writings had included many horror stories, and *We Are 18* included a pastiche of horror clichés. Spain had never produced a real horror film as yet, and this fact in and of itself was an attraction to a trailblazing iconoclast like Franco. Newman had never really seen a horror film, though. So Franco took Newman to a screening of the British film *The Brides of Dracula* (1960) in Nice (such stuff being unavailable in Spain). *Brides* was part of a revival of Gothic horror then underway by England's Hammer Films, which was updating their fright flicks with bosomy women and bright red gore. Impressed by what they saw, Franco and Newman set their sights on one-upping Hammer, with outright nudity and graphic violence that would have scandalized the gentlemanly filmmakers of Hammer. (In the end, they succeeded all too well, and their film was edited by censors for screenings in Spain, England and the U.S. Only France saw Franco's sexy shocker uncut.)

Of perhaps more direct influence than Hammer's output, though, was the 1958 French film *Eyes Without a Face* (originally released in the United States as *The Horror Chamber of Dr. Faustus*) by Novelle Vague filmmaker Georges Franju. Combining expert cinematic craftsmanship with a luridly grisly story, *Eyes Without a Face* set audiences around the world reeling. Franju's picture concerned a surgeon whose beautiful young daughter is facially disfigured in an accident. Obsessed with restoring her looks, the doctor proceeds to kidnap young women and graft their faces (unsuccessfully) onto his daughter's. Among its many notable qualities, *Eyes*' most notorious achievement was a gut-churning sequence in which the mad doctor actually peels away a woman's face, revealing the bloody grue underneath.

Eyes Without a Face opened at the same time that Artur Brauner and Fritz

Lang were remaking *The Indian Tomb*; while the European film industry was still looking backward, Franju broke new ground and discovered an untapped audience hungry for sensation. Suddenly, an entire genre of European exploitation horror films was born.

Franco's *The Awful Dr. Orlof* (1962) revisits Franju's territory. Again, a mad doctor kidnaps and kills young ladies in his quest to restore the beauty of his disfigured daughter. However, the somber, serious horror of *Eyes* has been replaced here with a demented, daft loopiness. Slathered over with a jaunty jazz soundtrack, and packed with quirky humor, *Orlof* makes the material seem brand new. Of course, the originality of the work would be ultimately blunted by the many official and unofficial sequels and remakes Franco would make of *Orlof*.

Franco's cinematic style would continue to be a visual adaptation of the unrestrained and unpredictable qualities of jazz, but topping those visuals with the music itself made the connection complete. Franco composed many of these scores himself (often under aliases), but also collaborated extensively with jazz musician Daniel White (although Franco sometimes used White's name as one of his pseudonyms). The Scottish-born White narrowly escaped death in World War II, and left the experience with a promise to pursue what mattered most to him in life: music. He composed his first soundtrack in 1947, and first joined forces with Franco in 1962. He has composed over 160 features, including all of Franco's works for the French production company Eurociné. White has been a close associate of Franco's, serving as actor or production assistant as the demand arises. Like his friend, White has adopted aliases of his own, such as Guy Forlaine, Virginie Morgane and Emile Doryphore.

Franco's fascination with nightclubs (a modern update of Lang's fascination with cabarets) had translated into a recurring cinematic signature. Nearly every Franco film includes a nightclub scene, whether it fits into the narrative or not. Franco carefully hired real strippers for these scenes, choreographing these scenes using a knowledge of stripping gleaned from years of patronage of night clubs across Europe.

The women in Franco's filmography occupy a more important place than mere sexual objects (although they are indeed that). Women are the true stars of Franco's canon. They are the intelligent ones, the actors, the brave ones, the force that drives and resolves the story. By contrast, the stalwart male hero is a buffoon, ineffectual and silly. In *The Awful Dr. Orlof*, the ballerina played by Diana Lorys is hardly a damsel in distress, despite the threat posed by Orlof's insane ambitions, and it is she who defeats the madman. Her boyfriend, a police inspector investigating the killings, wastes his effort fruitlessly.

As played by the late Howard Vernon, Dr. Orlof is a prototypical Franco villain: a lunatic driven by intense personal obsessions. Vernon was born in 1914 to a Swiss father and an American mother. He cast off his true name Mario Lipert to assume the stage name Howard Vernon for his acting career. During the Nazi occupation of Paris, he gave dancing lessons. In 1945, he made his film debut in the French Resistance picture *Un Ami Viendra ce Soir*. This led, however, to a disappointing period where he was typecast as a Nazi, until director Jean-Pierre Melville gave him a breakthrough role in 1949's *Le Silence de la Mer*.

Fritz Lang cast him in *The 1000 Eyes of Dr. Mabuse*, and the two became fast friends. Lang helped Vernon win another supporting role alongside Richard Widmark in *The Secret Ways* (1961). It was Franco, though, who gave Vernon the leading role

Jess Franco's wild and woolly career has crossed paths with both Fritz Lang and Orson Welles (courtesy Kevin Collins).

in a hit picture, *The Awful Dr. Orlof*. Vernon became friends with Franco, too. Although Vernon has worked with some of the giants of world cinema, including Lang, Woody Allen, Jean-Luc Godard and Michael Powell, his loyalty to Franco is profound. Franco has cast Vernon in no fewer than 35 films over 25 years.

Vernon had nothing but praise for Franco, and the director has repaid the sentiment. Calling Vernon "a sensational actor," Franco explained in an interview in *Filmfax* magazine that Vernon chose his marginality in order to retain control over the kind of parts he played.

Despite the unprecedented popularity of *Dr. Orlof*, the low-budget production was such a slapdash affair that its distributors could not afford to make more than a couple of prints. Limited by the number of showings that could be scheduled with so few prints, *Orlof* took some two years to generate a profit. But Franco had proved himself, and it was at this time that he adopted the screen name Jess Franco to make him a more exportable quantity for the international market.

Like Lang, Franco would spend his career moving about from producer to producer. However, while Lang's peripatetic journey would be driven by his personal strife with producers, Franco's was motivated by the quest for money in a starved market. The European exploitation film business was a world of fly-by-nighters and hacks. The key to success was to crank out images of sex and horror and cheaply as possible. It was not an industry designed for artistry. Yet Franco chose this seamy cinematic underworld because it offered him the freedom to pursue his interests (which conveniently overlapped the tastes of the exploitation audience) and to work in an anarchic, experimental style that would never have been acceptable in the professional mainstream. Franco understood that this creative freedom would come at a price; he would never have the kind of budgets of someone like Lang, nor the actors and production values those budgets could buy. Instead, Franco's world would be populated by actors and craftspeople who were misfits like himself.

Having seen his well run dry in France, Franco *had* moved on to Germany in search of backers and hooked up with Karl-Heinz Mannchen, a colleague of Artur Brauner's. Mannchen helped Franco win the support of the millionaire Pierre Caminecci, and together they made what has become Franco's biggest-budgeted, best-known production, *Succubus* (1967, also known as *Necronomicon*). Even with relatively more money with which to work, Franco still chose to experiment. He never wrote a script, but instead improvised with his actors as he filmed. The result was impressive enough to win friends and influence people, and *Succubus* was invited to the Festival of Berlin.

Fritz Lang, who admitted to disliking erotic films, attended a showing of *Succubus* simply to see his friend Howard Vernon again on the screen. Lang was pleasantly surprised by what he saw, and told Franco that he was touched by "the beauty and the dark nature of the film," which he considered a work of "Spanish Expressionism." Franco took such compliments to heart, since he had long been a fan of Lang's work, cherishing such pictures as *Dr. Mabuse*, *Metropolis*, *M* and *The Big Heat* as cinematic classics. Even this level of recognition and respect, though, was limited by the B-movie milieu Franco had chosen for himself. *Succubus* may have been his biggest-budgeted work, but it was still an extremely low-budget creation.

In America, *Succubus* was billed as "THE sensual experience of '69." Some theaters refrained from advertising the title, asking patrons to call the box office for a definition of the word "so that you will not be surprised by the sophisticated subject matter of this film."

When American B-movie legend Roger Corman saw *Succubus*, he was greatly impressed. Corman suggested to Samuel Z. Arkoff, of the equally legendary American International Pictures (AIP), that he hire Franco to make low-budget films in Hollywood. Arkoff would distribute Franco's *Venus in Furs* (1969) in America, but Franco declined his offer for a job. On the European continent, Franco had a measure of creative autonomy to pursue whatever demented subject matter he pleased in whatever unlikely style he chose, a freedom he feared would be withdrawn by Hollywood producers. Franco chose obscurity in order to slake his cinematic thirst for the weird, the perverse, the anarchic.

By this point, Franco's films were increasingly fixated on softcore eroticism. As Franco's softcore films evolved, though, the iron hand of Spanish censorship was once again lowering. The liberal attitudes of Manuel Fraga left when Fraga himself was ousted and Generalissimo Franco's regime attempted to reimpose the kind of monolithic cultural standards that had existed in the 1950s. The connection between film and tourism became once again distinct, but now at Spain's expense. Under Fraga's reign of tolerance, foreign tourists expected racier imagery on Spanish screens. With Fraga gone, Spanish film buffs began to flock across the border to France in search of cinematic thrills denied them at home. Savvy French theaters began advertising in Spanish newspapers for special "Spanish Weeks," in which subtitled prints of risqué films would be screened almost around the clock in French border towns.

However, the real fear of the Spanish authorities was not so much the corrupting influence of exploitation pictures as the flow of Spanish money outside the borders. Many of these European horror and sex films were financed by international consortiums (hence Franco's list of noms de plume), which meant that Spanish audiences watching purportedly Spanish films in Spanish theaters were spending money that went to French, Italian and German entrepreneurs. So, even as the fist of censorship tightened, there would still be a place for horror films, which were usually cheaply made by domestic filmmakers who understood that there was an international audience hungry for gory thrills, no matter what the country of origin. Horror filmmakers like Paul Naschy and Armando De Ossorio had the advantage that their productions brought foreign ticket sale revenue into Spain. Franco's erotic fixations, though, would drive him ever farther away from Spanish censors, and towards the very international financing deals Spain wanted to discourage.

Following the success of *Succubus*, Franco continued to work with its co-producer Adrian Hoven on two semi-sequels to *Red Lips* (*Kiss Me Monster* and *Sadisterotica*, both 1968) before moving on to Harry Alan Towers. Towers is a British-born producer with a colorful history of notoriety and adventure; the films he made with Franco were produced while Towers was on the run, having skipped bail in the United States after being caught running a prostitution ring. Towers had enough capital to give Franco entry into a slightly more reputable and professional circle than he had heretofore achieved.

It was during their brief collaboration that Franco wooed the famed horror star Christopher Lee away from Hammer to star in *Count Dracula* (1969). Lee had already appeared in two *Dracula* features for Hammer, which had won worldwide legions of fans but had left Lee frustrated with what he felt were juvenile scripts and crude productions. He tried to quit, but found his agent had contractually bound him to a third, *Taste the Blood of Dracula* (1969). Lee unsuccessfully tried to escape the agreement, and Warner Brothers (then Hammer's American partner) objected, "If you don't do this film, think of all the people you'll be putting out of work."

Lee was especially fond of Bram Stoker's original novel, and resentful that despite being typecast as Dracula he had been unable to persuade any director to helm a faithful restaging of the book. Hammer's closest attempt, *Horror of Dracula* (1958), although an acknowledged classic of horror cinema, was a significant deviation from the novel, using little more than character names and settings. When Jess Franco and Harry Alan Towers approached Lee with the idea of doing Stoker's book faithfully, Lee happily jumped at the chance. The actor even sneered at his Hammer colleagues that at last he was going to be doing Dracula right, and show them up.

Lee wrote to his Hammer producers on September 23, 1969, that *Taste the Blood* would be his final Dracula picture for them:

> I have long wanted, as you know, to do Bram Stoker's *Dracula*, as he wrote it. I have now agreed to do this, for three weeks on location starting on October 13th. So I will be playing the role twice in the space of two months. In order to forestall the outraged howls of protest, let me say in my defence that I was committed to one film which I could not avoid, when I had already decided that I would do the other and attempt to re-create the original novel once and for all. I hope never to have to play this part again for two reasons. First, because Hammer has never made the film of the book and secondly because when I will have finally done this, that will be the end of it. This will mean that will have played the part of Dracula five times in all and only once as Stoker wrote it. And it will be with the latter that I will be content.

Franco's *Count Dracula* was indeed the most faithful adaptation for its time, and with stars like Lee and Herbert Lom and Klaus Kinski in the cast, it was one of Franco's most respectable productions. But being one of Franco's more respectable works is not the same thing as being the definitive treatment of Stoker's novel, and so Lee returned to Hammer with his tail between his legs to star in another three more Dracula features, each less like Stoker than the last.

This was not Franco's first intersection with a long-running film franchise.

European B-movie makers understood that the easiest way to promote a low-budget picture is to confuse the audience into expecting something better. Recognizable names, like Dracula, make that possible. Franco directed a few Fu Manchu films, some pictures with "Frankenstein" in the title, and a number of adaptations of Edgar Wallace and Bryan Edgar Wallace stories.

And, of course, he remade his own *Awful Dr. Orlof* countless times, both with and without the Orlof name. One of these unofficial Orlof remakes was 1970's *The Vengeance of Dr. Mabuse*, produced for Artur Brauner and starring *Succubus* star Jack Taylor.

Franco had left Towers shortly after *Count Dracula* and joined forces with Brauner. The two had first become acquainted through mediation of *Succubus* producer Karl-Heinz Mannchen. After producing Franco's *Lucky the Inscrutable*, Mannchen offered Franco the chance to work for CCC. Franco attended his first meeting with Brauner with an eight-page script (not an eight-page outline, but an eight-page final script), and Brauner responded by sketching out a budget on a napkin. A low-budget allegiance was forged. The result was *She Kills In Ecstasy* (1970, also known as *Mrs. Hyde*).

The years 1970–1971 turned out to be quite busy for Franco and Brauner, as they churned out *Vampyros Lesbos*, *Dracula vs. Frankenstein* (aka *The Erotic Rites of Frankenstein*), *The Corpse Packs His Bags* (written by erstwhile Mabuse screenwriter Ladislas Fodor, from the Bryan Edgar Wallace novel), *The Devil Came From Akasava* (another Wallace entry) and *X-312 Flight to Hell*. Under Brauner's suggestion, Franco directed *The Vengeance of Dr. Mabuse*, and their collaboration was concluded shortly thereafter.

It was also during 1970 that Franco met Lina Romay, who was to become his Thea von Harbou. Up until that point, Franco's recurring female star and point of cinematic sexual fixation was the lovely actress Soledad Miranda. In a tragic accident, Miranda died in a car crash after finishing work on *The Devil Came from Akasava* for Franco and Brauner in 1970. Although he would be forever haunted by Miranda's memory, Franco found an almost spiritual replacement in Lina Romay. They met on a shoot in Madeira, and Franco was struck by what he felt was a sort of reincarnation of Miranda. They became friends, lovers and partners. In addition to acting in his films, Romay has been a script advisor and assistant director—a creative collaborator.

Franco left Brauner, joining up with Swiss producer Erwin C. Dietrich for a few "women in prison" movies, remaking *Orlof* a few more times (including one in 1976 titled *Jack the Ripper*, starring Klaus Kinski, whose own extensive CV includes *Scotland Yard vs. Dr. Mabuse*) and even remaking Franju's *Eyes Without a Face*, the basis for *Orlof*, as *Faceless* in 1988.

The period following Generalissimo Franco's 1975 death brought tremendous cultural upheaval and uncertainty, as well as an unprecedented relaxation of censorship. A flood of softcore pictures washed over Spanish screens, crowding out Franco's personal and unusual productions. By the 1980s, outright hardcore was legalized and the softcore film was no more, its audience co-opted. This spelled the end of a large part of Franco's specialized market niche, but Franco himself helped drive the nails in the coffin, with the dubious honor of having made the first true Spanish porn flick, 1983's *Lilian the Perverted Virgin*.

In 1979, a Socialist government was elected. Pilar Miró became the Director General of Cinematography (her job title no longer reflecting a link to tourism), and she promised substantial government backing for an approved list of filmmakers of

Jess Franco in the late 1990s, still making movies (courtesy Kevin Collins).

"artistic merit." Although the move was intended to (and did) support the Spanish film industry, it also served to further marginalize Jess Franco's place in that industry.

While Fritz Lang slipped into an undesired retirement, frustrated at his perceived inability to find adequate support for his creative visions, Franco did not let the changes in the marketplace end his career. He has remained productive at least until the time of this writing. As a man pushing 80, he still outlasts his youthful producers, stars and collaborators with his boundless energy and enthusiasm for film. His works may not have won awards or the accolades of critics, but Franco has always been concerned first and foremost with satisfying his own desires. In their book *Immoral Tales*, "Franco-philes" Cathall Tohill and Pete Tombs quote him as saying, "It never occurs to me that I'm making a film for a large audience." They conclude that his films "aren't designed for mass market consumption, they're too personal to be truly commercial."

At first glance this would seem a deep contradiction. Exploitation movies are, by definition, commercial products manufactured to "exploit" audience tastes. However, the term "exploitation movies" is a pejorative designation often handed out by critics and members of the cinematic mainstream as a way of defining the good from the bad, the art from the commercial. In the real world of film production, artists like Fritz Lang could feel themselves constricted by commercial demands while others like Jess Franco, supposedly working in an idiom that precludes artistry, could find a true freedom of creative expression.

In the final analysis, however, the respected artist to whom Franco would wish to be compared is not Lang at all, but rather Orson Welles. Both Franco and

Welles are mavericks whose single-minded pursuit of cinematic expression exiled them from the film industry mainstream of their time. While history has been kind to Welles, during his life he found a cold reception in Hollywood. In fact, during the 1960s, Welles was virtually unable to find production backing in Hollywood, his *wunderkind* reputation having made him a pariah. So Welles sought financing abroad. In Spain, Welles worked on *Mr. Arkadin* (1955), *Don Quixote* (unfinished), *Treasure Island* (1972, produced by Artur Brauner) and *Chimes at Midnight* (1965).

In this way, he crossed paths with Franco in a fairly substantial way. Jess Franco served as Welles' second unit director on *Chimes at Midnight*, and the two reportedly became (temporary) friends. How this unlikely pairing of high and low cinematic art came to pass has entered into legend, with at least three different versions of what transpired.

According to Story Number One, Welles' assistant Juan Cobos knew Franco, and recommended him for the job as Welles put together his Spanish team.

Story Number Two is slightly more sinister, and more flattering to Franco. According to this version of the tale, Welles had seen Franco's *Death Whistles a Blues* (1962), liked it and asked Franco to join the crew. Welles' producer Emelio Piedra thought this was a bad idea, given Franco's somewhat sleazy reputation, and decided to persuade Welles to change his mind. Piedra told the director to screen *Rififi in the City* (1963), figuring it to be Franco's very worst film and thereby the perfect way to demonstrate to Welles his mistake. *Rififi in the City* had been designed as a tribute to Welles and an homage to *Citizen Kane*, and Welles was both flattered and encouraged by Franco's technical experimentation. Far from dissuading him, the plan backfired and Welles was more certain than ever that Franco was the man for the job.

Story Number Three adds a personal twist, with the same facts as Story Two but with the producer's motive being to exclude Franco from the shoot in order to give the job to a friend.

Their pairing was brief. Welles started to run out of money on the shoot (a common occurrence in his Spanish productions), so Franco stepped in to help. He sent a rough cut of the project to producer Harry Saltzman to entice him to put up funds. Saltzman liked what he saw, and agreed to invest. Welles was furious that Franco had done this behind his back. Although he accepted Saltzman's money, Welles reportedly attacked Franco physically and had his credit removed from the picture.

Nevertheless, Franco never forgot his experience with the master and continued to idolize him. Many years later, Franco found an opportunity to help Welles again, even if it was once again without Welles' knowledge. Welles had never finished his version of *Don Quixote*; money ran out and he had to move on to other projects. In 1992, with the softcore exploitation market gone, Franco was seeking scarce money, too. Franco was hired to complete Welles' project. It opened to decidedly mixed reviews, but the finished product represented the train-wreck fusion of two of cinema's most uncontrollable artists.

Not even Franco's most ardent defenders would suggest he is in the same league as Welles (or Lang) in terms of talent. His determination to work with low budgets has denied him the chance to learn from the experience of other professionals. His experimental approaches could have achieved more polished and revolutionary effects had he been able to build upon the successes of others, rather than be saddled with the limited talents of actors and technicians rejected by the mainstream industry. Nevertheless, Franco is a true auteur, a filmmaker possessed of a distinctive and recognizable style that suffuses every project he makes.

His rendition of the Mabuse saga is nothing like the films that precede it, and owes little if anything to Norbert Jacques' literary contributions. The directors who followed in Lang's footsteps in the 1960s were deeply indebted to Lang for creating the style that they mimicked and recreated faithfully. William K. Everson even called Harald Reinl's *Return of Dr. Mabuse* "an homage to Lang." The films, from *Return* to *Death Ray of Dr. Mabuse* on, all inhabit the same cinematic world; even *Scream and Scream Again*, not quite a full-blooded Mabuse movie, follows in Lang's style. But Franco's *Vengeance of Dr. Mabuse* is a new animal, and undeniably a Jess Franco film.

For better or worse, Franco was the first director in the Mabuse series with a strong enough personal vision to finally escape the legacy of Fritz Lang.

CHAPTER 18

The Vengeance of Dr. Mabuse

> No one will discover me. No one imagines that Dr. Mabuse lives.
> —Prof. Farkas

The names Jess Franco and Fritz Lang have rarely been spoken together in the same breath. In terms of artistic reputation, they seemingly occupy two different worlds. To the extent that the name Dr. Mabuse means anything in America, it is a sign of the great Fritz Lang, a recurring character in the cinema of one of filmdom's most acclaimed auteurs. For the Mabuse franchise to have devolved from the hands of Lang to those of Franco is unexpected to say the least.

The many intersections of the lives and careers of Franco and Lang, and the history of Artur Brauner's collaboration with Franco (discussed in the previous chapter), may explain the mechanics of how this came to pass, but does little to excuse it. Even Brauner himself seemed a trifle scandalized by the whole affair; of the eight films he produced with Jess Franco, *La Venganza del Dr. Mabuse* ("The Vengeance of Dr. Mabuse," 1970) is the *only one* not listed in CCC's official catalogue of films. When the picture opened in Germany, it was given the German title *Der Mann, der sich Mabuse nannte*—"The Man Who Called Himself Mabuse." It was as if Artur Brauner, faced with the finished product of his labors with Franco, just could not bring himself to grant true Mabuse-dom to it. Spanish audiences may have been fooled, but Germans know from Mabuse.*

While they were at it, both Brauner and Franco granted themselves pseudonyms. Brauner billed himself as "Art Bern," and Franco adopted a screen name of Frank Manero (in other CCC jobs, Franco sometimes billed himself as Frank Hollmann). Some critics have occasionally suggested that the rampant practice of pseudonymous work in low budget films like this exposed the filmmakers' unwillingness to take full credit for their work; it was in fact a dodge by cunning filmmakers to exploit international financing rules (see also Chapter 17).

Brauner and Franco had already collaborated successfully on a number of pictures: *Vampyros Lesbos*, *The Devil Came from Akasava* and *She Kills in Ecstasy* (all 1970). "Then Brauner gave me a Mabuse script that he had on file with the intentions of making one day," remembers Franco. "I worked on it and then we made

---

On subsequent reissue, the German version was again retitled to Dr. M schlagt zu *("Dr. M Strikes Back"), further suppressing the name Mabuse.*

This lurid image would be at home on any vintage pulp novel or comic book cover.

the film. I suppose that Brauner wrote the script that he gave me."

As Art Bern, Brauner certainly takes credit for the story, such as it is. Mabuse has survived his past exploits and taken up residence in Spain under the assumed name of Prof. Farkas (so many pseudonyms), where he launches a new bid on world domination. He orchestrates the theft of a set of radioactive Moon rocks, which provide the key ingredient in an elaborate contraption that allows him to project his will into his chosen victims. Although the basic idea recalls the zombie army in *Return of Dr. Mabuse,* Farkas is limited by the buggy prototype of his mind-control apparatus. Still in the beta-testing stage, it kills people more effectively than it renders them his slaves. So rather than embark on his much-vaunted revenge—the title of the movie no less—Mabuse spends most of the film kidnapping young women to experiment on in his efforts to improve his zombie-making technique.

Those three kidnapped women and their fate not only provide the only genuine manifestation of Mabuse's cruel vengeance, but also allow director Franco to take the reins away from Brauner and steer this, CCC's final Mabuse picture, headlong into Franco's personal brand of sleazy cinema. Once Brauner's script, full of radioactive rays and mind control and technogadgetry, landed on Franco's desk, the Spaniard took to rewriting it into a virtual remake of his 1962 horror opus *The Awful Dr. Orlof.*

In its own way, *Dr. Orlof* had been a remake of the landmark 1958 horror film *Eyes Without a Face.* That earlier picture, directed by French New Wave director George Franju, told the story of a doctor whose daughter had been disfigured in a car accident. Desperate to restore her beauty, and driven to madness by his obsession, the doctor kidnaps and kills local girls in abortive attempts to graft their faces onto his daughter. Franju's film, innovative for its use of on-screen gore, inspired many imitators.

For his 1962 take on the story, Franco also took inspiration from the classic Edgar Wallace film *The Dark Eyes of London* (1939).* He cast Howard Vernon (*1000 Eyes*' assassin) as the titular Dr. Orlof, borrowing the name from Bela Lugosi's character in *Dark Eyes*. As Orlof's daughter Melissa has been disfigured in an accident, the mad doctor needs his blind, brutish assistant Morpho (doubly inspired by Alida Valli's role in Franju's film and Wilfred Walter's ruthless Jake in the 1939 film) to kidnap local women to supply the raw skin for his experiments. Where Pierre Brasseur's performance in *Eyes Without a Face* is tinged with sympathy, Howard Vernon's Orlof is pure sadism.

To various degrees, much of Franco's work in the ensuing decades drew inspiration from this early success. Franco helmed four sequels and a few outright remakes—such as 1976's *Jack the Ripper*, starring Klaus Kinski in the Howard Vernon role. Or, for that matter, *The Vengeance of Dr. Mabuse*.

Franco even copied some scenes down to their tiniest details. In *Awful Dr. Orlof*, a drunken tramp fishes out of the river a bracelet from one of the victims, delivers it to the inspector in charge of the case and gauges, from his fishing experience, how long the bracelet has been underwater. In *Vengeance of Dr. Mabuse*, a drunken tramp fishes out a pair of panties from one of the victims, delivers it to Inspector Thomas (Fred Williams) and gauges how long he thinks it has been submerged.

In *Awful Dr. Orlof*, the last victim, Wanda (Diana Lorys), escapes from her cell to discover the scarred, terrified shell of her predecessor. Suddenly, the freak Morpho (Ricardo Valle) bursts in on her and drags her towards her hideous fate. Before the nightmare can play out, though, Morpho turns on Orlof and kills his former master. As the laboratory goes up in flames, Morpho carries Wanda out to safety. For this, he is shot in the back by the inspector—her boyfriend—who has arrived just after the nick of time. In *Vengeance of Dr. Mabuse*, the last victim (Eva Garden) escapes from her cell to find the remains of her predecessor Wanda (Eva Strömberg). Suddenly, the freak Andros (Moises Rocha) bursts in and drags her towards her hideous fate. Before the nightmare plays out, though, Andros turns on Dr. Mabuse (Jack Taylor) and kills his former master. As the laboratory goes up in flames, Andros carries the young woman to safety. For this, he is shot in the back by the inspector—her boyfriend—who has arrived just after the nick of time.

Fully conscious of how much he was borrowing from himself, Franco included an in-joke as well. While Inspector Thomas is a sort of Spanish Inspector Clouseau, and the police pose no real threat to Mabuse's operation, another investigation does have the evil genius worried: Dr. Orlof (Friedrich Joloff) of the Physics Institute knows the power of the Moon rocks and is capable of tracing them to Mabuse. Mabuse sends Andros and his

---

Although the film Dark Eyes of London *has no connection to the Mabuse genre, save through extension, the original novel by Edgar Wallace is quite Mabusian: blind men real and fake, split identities and pseudonyms, murderous laundry trucks, a spider's web of a gang whose members do not even know how they are being manipulated, the ruthless elimination of witnesses and evidence, false fronts, hidden doors, secret passageways and a sinister theater complete with guillotine. It is no surprise that CCC's perennial screenwriter Ladislas Fodor was simultaneously penning adaptations of Wallace's novels as he devised Mabuse's diabolical world.*

Jack Taylor (left) plays the latest Dr. Mabuse.

world. Like his erstwhile boss, Taylor got used to pseudonyms: He was born George Brown Randall in 1936, and also worked at times under the moniker Greg Martin. By any name, he lacked both Vernon's Continental allure and his innate talent. Instead, Taylor was a man who would stand on his chalk mark and say his lines, enough to serve Franco's most basic needs but not enough to lift the material above its increasingly disreputable level. Taylor occasionally surfaced in more mainstream genre fare, such as *The Trollenberg Terror* (1958) or Hammer's *Paranoiac* (1963), but it was in Spain that he found regular employment in sex and horror flicks—*Dr. Jekyll vs. the Wolfman* (1971), *Ghost Ships of the Blind Dead* (1974), *Vengeance of the Mummy* (1973). Naturally, working in Spanish sex and horror movies meant working often with Jess Franco—*Succubus* (1967), *Count Dracula* (1970), *The Black Countess* (1973). In *Vengeance of Dr. Mabuse*, his vacant blue eyes with their icy stare, usually photographed in distorted extreme closeups, have a haunting elegance.

Nazi dominatrix Leslie (Monica Swinn) to do away with the pesky Dr. Orlof. "Brauner didn't know about the connections with *The Awful Dr. Orlof*," admits Franco. "And of course the Dr. Orlof character was just a private joke."

If Franco was having his fun at Brauner's expense, it was only in the most good-natured of ways. "Brauner is a curious mixture of a producer-creator on the one hand and a cheap filmmaker on the other," says Franco. "He is very clever and has great knowledge of actors, editing and sound. He never came to the shooting of any of our films, though. He was never interested in the shooting."

Left to his own devices, Franco naturally stocked the production with his mainstays. As Dr. Mabuse, the star of the show, Franco cast longtime stalwart Jack Taylor. Since Howard Vernon had moved on to other, better things, Jack Taylor had stepped in to take his place in Franco's

Another Franco regular, Eva Strömberg, plays Wanda, the nightclub stripper. Much like her namesake in *Awful Dr. Orlof*, Wanda is a willful young dancer. Where the original Wanda was a bang-up detective, though, cracking the Orlof case for her idiot inspector boyfriend, this

Wanda is simply victimized. Having been used as Mabuse's remote-controlled puppet and discarded like a wet rag, she is left to rot in her cell. Interestingly, the actress had previously worked with Brauner as well, starring in the epic *Fight for Rome* (1969) directed by Robert Siodmak.

Franco even gave himself a cameo role. The detective genre conventions demand a scene where the grumpy lieutenant dresses down the inspector heroes for failing to catch the bad guy, a set-up for the exciting climax when the cops finally get their man. Franco enjoys turning such genre conventions on their head, and essayed the clichéd role of the grumpy lieutenant to draw audience attention to the genre rules he was violating. The cops are indeed inept fools—in the middle of a chase scene, their car overheats and breaks down—and they do not, in the end, get their man. Dr. Mabuse's own underlings turn on him and blow his empire to smithereens before Inspector Thomas arrives on the scene.

As if to emphasize the misfit between the sinister doings at Mabuse's HQ and the ineffectual police, all scenes with the cops are played for laughs. As Franco cuts between the two opposing sides, he switches wildly from a colorful hi-tech sci-fi setting to something out of a spaghetti Western. Dr. Mabuse and Inspector Thomas look as if they live in entirely different movies.

Mabuse's HQ, situated in a remote lighthouse, a phallic structure of moldy

Moises A. Racha (right) plays an essential role in the climax of this unofficial remake of *The Awful Dr. Orlof*.

stone surrounded by crashing waves, was Franco's greatest disappointment in the film. "I'm only sorry that we didn't have more money for the laboratory set. Brauner never said anything to me but I'm sure he felt the same. It was a nice film, I think, even if it wasn't a gothic *Mabuse*."

After the perpetual grousing of Fritz Lang, ever unhappy with his artistic compromises, Franco's satisfaction with his creation is refreshing—even if it is weirdly incongruous, given the high artistic achievements of Lang and the scandalous results of Franco's work. This was Franco's baby, though, and he was proud of it. Sadly, especially for Franco's many fans, his contribution to the Mabuse legend would be quickly forgotten. It was screened in Germany in 1974, under various titles, in an 88-minute version that would seem to have been complete. Meanwhile, in Spain the film was censored down to a trim 63 minutes. It is this truncated version that has been issued on video in Spain, while the film has essentially vanished everywhere else; it has

 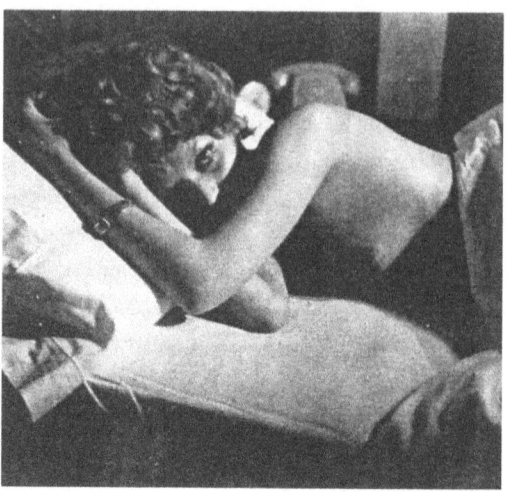

Left: Fred Williams plays the bumbling Inspector Thomas, a sort of live action Dudley Do-Right. *Right:* This publicity still features a glimpse of nudity, now lost from the censored videocassette.

never been shown in America under any title.*

It was an ignominious end for one of cinema's most enduring and fascinating icons. Dr. Mabuse rose in 1922 as a symbol of twentieth century turmoil and German fears. His many cinematic adventures had marked major innovations in the history of filmmaking technique, the rise and fall and rise of the German film industry, and the careers of some of Europe's most interesting film personalities. Now, in 1970, the character had met his demise in Spain, far from home and left behind by a modern world no longer interested in the specters of the past.

Or so it seemed. Dr. Mabuse, though, would rise from the grave again…

---

*The edited video version was the only edition that Mr. Franco was able to make available for review; this author has not seen the unexpurgated 88 minute cut.

CHAPTER 19

The Image of Dorian Gray in the Yellow Press

> We shall create a person. Gentlemen, Dorian Gray, a beautiful and somewhat dull and inexperienced young man, is to be our creation! Naturally, without his knowledge or consent. Young, rich, beautiful—we shall build him up, seduce him, annihilate him!
>
> —Dr. Mabuse

Dr. Mabuse has a problem. She is the head of a major multinational media empire, one of the richest and most influential people in the world. Her tabloid papers and tawdry magazines are top sellers across the globe. But profits simply are not growing fast enough for her voracious tastes.

How tedious and wasteful it is to pay reporters and photographers to seek out the scandals and gossip and celebrity-tinted sensationalism needed to keep her printing presses engaged. How much more efficient and elegant it would be to manufacture the scandals from the outset, by manipulating the life of a celebrity of her own making.

Ah, there's the answer! And what a ready-made victim she has found in Dorian Gray, a vapid pretty boy, a worthless fop, a self-absorbed upper-class twit of the year unable even to comprehend how he has become Mabuse's puppet. Everything that Dorian Gray experiences will be observed, catalogued and recorded by Mabuse's thousand eyes and ears. From this day forth, Dorian Gray's world is thoroughly tricked out with hidden cameras and bugs. Every detail of his life is foreordained by Mabuse according to the dictates of the tabloid marketplace.

As she presents code name Operation Mirror to the editors of her many papers, the yes-men nod in submissive approval. That is, save for one lone voice of dissent: The Little Doctor, scrupulous editor of *Der Spiegelwelt*. While the other editors in Mabuse's employ have long ago sold their souls, locked in a desperate and degrading chase after lurid sensationalism, the Little Doctor clings to his archaic values.

This ethical, principled man still believes that the newspaper business has to do with informing the public about important and complex issues. Confronted with Mabuse's plan to corrupt and ultimately destroy an innocent man's soul merely to exploit it as a living soap opera, he decrees the idea abhorrent. It will be some time before the Little Doctor discovers Mabuse's weakness and seizes a weapon by which to effect his defiance of this abomination. And by then, it may well be too late.

Ulrike Ottinger's *Dorian Gray im Spiegel der Boulevardpresse* ("The Image of Dorian Gray in the Yellow Press," 1984) is a strange beast. Aggressively *avant garde*, off-putting in the extreme, unpredictable and mystifying, this motion picture owes precious little to Oscar Wilde's infamous novel; in this version, the picture that keeps Dorian Gray alive is not a supernatural portrait of Gray, but a photograph of Dr. Mabuse. Ah, but what is Dr. Mabuse doing in a film about Dorian Gray? That is, of course, the question.

This particular Dr. Mabuse is a vampish, bitchy and drag-queen cool *femme fatale* as played by the late, great Delphine Seyrig (think Joan Crawford playing Rupert Murdoch). Frau Dr. Mabuse is the true centerpiece of the picture, despite the title. She is a pill-popping control freak who carries on multiple conversations at once, in several different languages, while barking commands to her underlings through the microphones woven into the very fabric of her outrageous clothes. (Only Claude Chabrol's Dr. M goes farther, implanting a camera inside his own body.) Coming from a filmmaker like Ottinger, whose works are driven by a highly-charged, woman-positive, often lesbian aesthetic, such images of female transgression and power are only to be expected. It is however unfortunate that it took more than half a century to finally realize a female incarnation of Mabuse, especially given the women heroes that populate so many of Fritz Lang's films (or Jess Franco's, for that matter).

In a letter dated September 17, 1930, Norbert Jacques wrote to Lang:

> Years ago I was offered the chance to compose a film drama for one of the German actresses, I no longer remember if it was Lia de Putti-Futzi or not, to give her a female Dr. Mabuse role. At the time I declined, but I've thought about it a lot since then and I don't find the idea at all unappealing. Now that we're discussing *The Testament of Dr. Mabuse,* the notion is popping back into my head.

He went on to outline his concept for *Mabuses Kolonie,* in which an international woman of mystery, Frau Kristina, sought Mabuse's final will and testament as part of her diabolical master plan. Jacques gave up on the *Kolonie* book before finishing it, and turned his attention instead to developing the script for *The Testament of Dr. Mabuse.* Jacques still clung to the idea of a female villain, and included one in his book version; Lang, however, discarded the dancer Laura from the screenplay, keeping the film's villains exclusively male. The idea of a female Mabuse was essentially lost.

When Ottinger arrived on the Mabuse scene in 1984, she was not directly inspired by either Jacques or Lang. Ulrike Ottinger is essentially a cinematic collage artist. She does not adapt literary sources into films so much as she appropriates familiar characters and story elements to recombine in her own original ways, with ironic and unexpected juxtapositions. Reviewer Laura Pierce described Ottinger's films as "short on plot but filled with allegorical and political references that would boggle any semiotician." Her cinema is densely packed with all manner of cultural references: fairy tales, famous literature (both classic and pulp), cinematic forms and historical figures all stirred up in one big pot.

In the case of *Dorian Gray,* Ottinger is making an acerbic commentary on mass media, sampling characters and ideas from the Mabuse films and Wilde's notorious novel. Despite the names of the two main characters, we cannot view this as an adaptation in the commonly accepted sense of the word. Nevertheless, to fully appreciate Ottinger's intentions, some background on Wilde's *Dorian Gray* is in order.

19. The Image of Dorian Gray in the Yellow Press

Model Veruschka stars as the androgynous Dorian Gray (courtesy Women Make Movies).

Oscar Wilde's 1891 novel *The Picture of Dorian Gray* scandalized Victorian society twice over. The story deals with a vapid youth, Dorian Gray, who has astonishing physical beauty but whose personality is something of a blank slate. His two closest friends write much of themselves on that slate: Lord Henry Wotton, an obvious stand-in for Wilde himself, indoctrinates the pretty boy with his own poisonous philosophy, all selfishness and hedonism. Meanwhile, artist Basil Hallward is madly in love with Dorian—a homosexual love—and paints Dorian's portrait to express all his pent-up passions. Somehow, although on the precise mechanics of this Wilde remains circumspect, the portrait has a supernatural link to Dorian's soul. Dorian never ages—his picture, walled away in a secret closet, bears the burdens of age on his behalf. Moreover, the portrait also reveals visually the ugliness of Dorian's inner self. While his "real" self continues in perpetual youth and resplendence, his tawdry sins and venal crimes, the products of Lord Henry's evil philosophy, etch themselves into his painting.

Wilde deliberately concocted *Dorian Gray* as a metaphor for the hypocrisy of Victoriana, a culture that prized appearances over substance at every turn. No one suspects Dorian's cruelty, because he looks good:

> Even those who had heard the most evil things against him, and from time to time strange rumors about his mode of life crept through London and became the chatter of the clubs, could not believe anything to his dishonour when they saw him.

But it was Wilde's own homosexuality, and the scarcely concealed homoerotic content of the book, that created the real brouhaha. Wilde was tried for his sexual orientation, and sentenced to prison for his so-called crime. The proceedings provided the nineteenth century equivalent of the O.J. Simpson trial. Thereafter the pejorative "Cult of Wilde" was coined to refer to homosexuals, and Wilde's notorious book became a touchstone by which social outcasts could identify kindred spirits.

And it must be said that Ulrike Ottinger is one of those kindred spirits. In her inscrutable avant garde take, she has preserved much of Wilde's subtext: an obsession with style over substance, Dorian's corruption concealed by a pretty face, homosexual overtones and even the doppelganger portrait—albeit substantially transformed. The plot of her film, such as it is, is hard to summarize:

Mabuse (Delphine Seyrig) approaches Dorian (model Veruschka von Lehndorff, cross-dressing to play a man) with a proposition. She wants to publish Dorian's life story as serial form in her papers. The young man is surprised, since his wealthy playboy lifestyle is actually quite dull. In her seductive, manipulative fashion, Mabuse steamrolls over Dorian's opposition, and invites him to the premiere of a new, modern opera.

The opera stars the beautiful (and mostly nude) Andamana (Tabea Blumenschein, Ottinger's ex-lover and recurring star). Dorian promptly falls in love with Andamana, oblivious to the fact that the actress is employed by Operation Mirror. Harking back to *Dr. Mabuse the Gambler* and *1000 Eyes*, Frau Mabuse has engineered a love affair. Dorian's romantic turmoils with Andamana will provide the scandal she craves.

If Dorian were only paying attention, he would see his current predicament reflected back at him through the opera, in which Seyrig and von Lehndorff play dual roles. Dorian's operatic double, the Lucky Prince of Spain, falls in love with the Amazon-like savage queen Andamana (Ottinger makes no differentiation in name between Blumenschein's on- and off-stage roles). Appropriately, Mabuse's alter ego is the Grand Inquisitor, who invades Andamana's island, slays the warrior queen and enslaves the Lucky Prince for his having fallen behind on paying his taxes. Both on and off the stage, Mabuse's various persona have an exclusively mercenary interest in Dorian's fate.

The fact that Dorian, in the audience, completely misses the portentous content of the opera (and at no time remarks on seeing his and Mabuse's doppelgangers on stage) may seem to conventional eyes a hole in the story. Ottinger the filmmaker is contemptuous of the narrative experience and principally concerned with the striking visuals she can build around her loose narrative structures. The opera, which consumes fully 30 minutes of the film's endurance-testing 150 minutes, is allegorical, not literal. The unexplained and unacknowledged duplication of Mabuse and Dorian on "stage" is overshadowed by the "stage" itself: Although framed by a traditional proscenium arch, the opera takes place on miles of open beach. And despite the sound effects of hundreds of unseen viewers applauding, the "audience" consists of Mabuse and Dorian alone in a scraggly cave.

This sequence presents by far the most obvious and recognizable Dorian Gray doppelganger, but of the many mirror images Ottinger has inserted into the film it is the most superficial.

Mabuse takes Dorian along to the press ball celebrating the opening of the opera (any similarities between this scene and Jacques' short story *Dr. Mabuse at the Press Ball* are in name only). At this event, everything—the walls, the glasses of champagne, the waiters' clothes—are draped in

19. The Image of Dorian Gray in the Yellow Press

Dr. Mabuse (Delphine Seyrig) escorts Dorian (Veruschka) to the Press Ball (courtesy Women Make Movies).

newspaper. And, what luck, Dorian meets up with Andamana there. As Mabuse watches with satisfaction, Dorian walks blithely into her trap.

While Mabuse's editors and their guests enjoy a punk cabaret backed by wind-up children's toys, Andamana admits to Dorian that her opera "is too crazy for the conservative audience. The staging and music are too *avant garde*. I'm afraid it won't run very long." The two lovebirds skip out for a night on the town, end up in bed together and discover every facet of their private, intimate evening splayed across every paper the next morning.

Impressed by Operation Mirror's success, Mabuse ratchets her plan up a notch. She takes Dorian on a wild tour of Berlin's seedy underground, full of hedonism, sexual perversion and drug abuse. Wilde's Dorian Gray became corrupted by what he did, but Ottinger's Dorian is utterly passive. This is not about what Dorian does, but what Dorian sees—and what Mabuse's readers see Dorian seeing. He silently follows Mabuse like a trained puppy until he has become nothing more than a spectator to his own existence.

One of the bizarre scenes of depravity on the Mabuse Studio Tour is an old man, an ex-civil servant, seated in a bathtub, with a goat, carefully cataloguing the insults heaped upon him. With great disappointment, he reveals that although his ledger can accommodate 894 insults a day, no one comes around to insult him any more. Then, a man in a flowing cape strides up and urinates on him. Naturally, Dr. Mabuse has taken pains to highlight spectacles of self-destruction.

Dorian was supposed to spend the evening with Andamana. Thanks to Mabuse, he has stood her up, and the debauchery of his evening's activities are indiscreetly reported in the morning editions. When Dorian tries to make up with her, Mabuse's secret army of reporters and photographers sate themselves on the lovers' spat. Of course, they created the spat—by dictating Dorian's activities and then by broadcasting them—and in any event, Andamana is a paid participant in the whole scheme. The result is that Dorian's life is no longer his own; a separate Dorian Gray, a doppelganger, has been created in the press, one who is apparently living a life of licentiousness and doing so in public. The flesh-and-blood Dorian Gray cannot extricate his identity from the mirror image Mabuse has created in print. A fly caught in a web, Dorian struggles to defend his honor to the women he loves, but it is a battle he is destined to lose.

Except...

Accidentally, one of Mabuse's photographers has snapped a picture of the media baron herself orchestrating Dorian Gray's long strange trip through the Berlin subculture. The photo represents a severe risk of exposure, its existence threatens not only Operation Mirror but her whole empire by extension. In time-honored Mabuse tradition, she has tripped herself up: It is her own spies acting on her instructions who have created positive proof of her misdeeds. And in time-honored Mabuse tradition, she responds by having her underlings put to death.

The Little Doctor, however, has acquired the negative and slips it to Dorian, who in turn confronts Andamana with it, and she confesses to being in on the arrangement.

To protect herself from exposure, Mabuse disposes of the Little Doctor (a fake suicide, of course) and Andamana (stabbed in the opera with a real, not prop, knife) and steals the photo back from Dorian. He knows that he will now be killed, too. Indeed, was the breakfast he just ate poisoned?

It is at this point that any residual pretense to narrative logic flies out the window. The film barrels ahead into a series of mutually contradictory conclusions, which can only be reconciled with one another depending upon one's interpretation of the film's message.

In the first climactic sequence, one of Mabuse's gang manages to secret yet another copy of the incriminating photo to Dorian. She then assists him in breaking into Mabuse's underground lair. Brandishing the same knife that killed his beloved Andamana, he attacks and kills Mabuse and her editors (all of whom are wearing rooster masks for no readily apparent reason).

Suddenly, the film negates the preceding sequence and veers off in the opposite direction. Dorian Gray cannot have killed Dr. Mabuse, since it is Mabuse we see laying Dorian's earthly remains to rest in a solemn ceremony witnessed by her editors. Perhaps the previous sequence with its wish-fulfillment revenge fantasy was nothing more than a hallucination of Dorian's dying mind, a delusional flight of fancy as his body succumbed to Mabuse's poison.

Scarcely has this new version of the ending begun than the film negates it as well. That cannot be Dorian Gray's body in Dorian Gray's tomb because the real Dorian Gray is alive and well and maniacally steering the red sportster Mabuse gave him. He ruthlessly runs down Mabuse and every one of her henchmen—an orgy of violence that is quite literally overkill, since everyone in this scene has been killed at least once in the immediately preceding minutes.

Who has killed who? Dorian kills

Tabea Blumenschein, usually nude, was director Ulrike Ottinger's lover (courtesy Women Make Movies).

Mabuse kills Dorian kills Mabuse ... the serpent swallowing its own tail. Both are true, in a sense, because while Dorian kills Mabuse (which happens in both versions of the climax), Mabuse has killed Dorian—the real Dorian, Dorian's identity, that is. As the final rendition of the climax reveals, Dorian Gray is now Dr. Mabuse: As the credits roll, we see that Dorian has now replaced Mabuse as head of the media empire, and intends to continue his/her sensational exploitation of self-manufactured "news."

"We have new headlines," says Dorian/Mabuse, "more sensational than the old."

Like Mabuse's invasion of Doctors Born, Baum, and Pohland in the various manifestations of *The Testament of Dr. Mabuse*, to be Dr. Mabuse's victim is the same thing as being Dr. Mabuse's heir. The merging of male and female personas in Dorian's body, too, has been prefigured by the casting of female von Lehndorff in male drag.

However, on a strictly literal level—on the customary level of narrative appreciation—*Dorian Gray*'s finale is incomprehensible and nonsensical. Ottinger's characters are for the most part ciphers, whose function is to strike poses and bear meaningful names. Dorian Gray is hardly a sympathetic victim; he is an idiot playboy who deserves his fate. Andamana is somewhat more sympathetic, an actress hired to play a part. She is simply unfortunate to have been hired by the Forces of Evil, but despite being played by Ottinger's erstwhile lover she is almost without exception photographed only in long shot; it is hard to identify with an indistinct figure on the distant horizon. While the Little Doctor plays a critical role in the narrative flow and espouses Ottinger's own opinions, she considers his character insignificant enough to not even credit the actor in question in the titles.

As for Mabuse, Seyrig's distinguished performance merely enlivens a fairly dull role. Her sinister activities do not threaten the safety of the world or lives of millions. Instead she is polluting the integrity of the news media; to the extent that Ottinger's film plays as a media critique, its satirical barbs have been long since overtaken by the real-life media scandals of the end of the twentieth century. From Internet gossip-monger Matt Drudge, to the many high profile columnists and documentary filmmakers exposed for fabricating their stories, to the tawdry stuff of "reality" programs like *Cops* and *The Real World* that populate the dial, to accusations of paparazzi hounding Princess Di to her death, Mabuse's Operation Mirror seems awfully tame by comparison.

Instead, *The Image of Dorian Gray in the Yellow Press*' strength is its bold visuals, which Ottinger delivers in spades. Working with a spare budget that makes Jess Franco's finances seem generous by contrast, Ottinger's inventive mind has filled her screen with memorable and frequently disquieting imagery. Ulrike Ottinger's film is playing by a completely different set of rules than any of the other films discussed in this book.

Motion pictures are the most absurdly expensive form of artistic expression ever devised, and this fact has been the source of unending strife. Movies are so consumptive of technological and personnel resources that filmmakers are obliged to temper their visions with respect for the commercial marketplace. That is, in order to make a movie, vast sums of money must somehow be raised. The investors and corporations that are in a position to supply this production financing are naturally disinclined to lose it. To recoup these expenses and return a profit, the motion picture in question must be sold to consumers. Films that are likely to alienate audiences are therefore notoriously hard to finance, while the marketplace overindulges products that are easily marketed to mass tastes. Thus is born the constant struggle between art and commerce, a struggle present in all artistic endeavors but writ especially large in the history of film.

In the microcosm of the Mabuse genre, filmmakers like Fritz Lang or Claude Chabrol worried that they had made too many compromises, but history has judged them as great artists. These filmmakers are like the Little Doctor, men of principle who have made essential concessions to the marketplace without selling out.

The Harald Reinls and Gordon Hesslers of the world are professionals. They go to work and do their job with no pretensions to art, but nevertheless manage to turn out very personal pictures of superb craftsmanship. Theirs may not be art, but it is quite respectable.

Then there are the Artur Brauners and the Jess Francos, filmmakers who aspire to art but who have at least appeared to cave in to commercial concerns too often. Despite the genuine personal touch their work exhibits, their creations cannot be seriously considered art.

On the next level down are directors like Hugo Fregonese and Paul May, commercial hacks with neither the aspiration to art nor the subsequent critical reappraisal. Their work is factory-grade assembly line work, devoid of anything personal.

Ulrike Ottinger, however, operates in a separate sphere altogether. Her uncompromisingly personal visions are produced and exhibited independent from the commercial film industry. Her primary audience, especially here in the United States, is in art museums and film festivals. *Dorian Gray* has not received any commercial distribution in America, and is available only through the efforts of the non-profit organization Women Make Movies.

Yet Ottinger is not quite the outsider she at time appears. She is a highly acclaimed director of multifarious skills. She writes her own screenplays, which she directs and produces, while also serving as cinematographer, set designer and more, as the need and occasion arises. She is one of the rarefied few female directors in Europe to be known internationally, and although her works are relegated to art house screenings, they are enthusiastically received in that limited venue.

The magazine *Artforum* raves, "There is no other filmmaker." *The Village Voice* writes, "Watching her films is like traveling through an undiscovered country of marvels, a journey alternately dazzling, infuriating, hilarious, and rewarding." *The Boston Globe* says, "Ottinger's films are marked by their wild imagery; celebrations of misfit characters, narrative looseness and sometimes infuriating length." *The New York Blade* admires that "Ottinger has succeeded in crossing nearly every cultural line." *The Los Angeles Times* calls her works "the personal vision personified."

Ulrike Ottinger was born in 1942, and launched her artistic career as a painter in Paris. After enjoying some modest success at painting, she returned to Germany in 1971 to direct her first film, a short feature entitled *Laocoon and Sons*, the first of her cinematic collaborations with Tabea Blumenschein. She settled in Berlin and redirected her energies into filmmaking full-time, directing her first feature-length project *Madame X: An Absolute Ruler* in 1977.

From the very beginning, her fascination with outsider cultures and minority voices defined her unique outlook. She has called herself an "ethnographer," a term which seems best to apply to her work in documentaries, epic-length excursions into foreign landscapes. Nevertheless, her fiction work too obsessively explores the margins, the underworlds, the outcasts. Ottinger is still busy today, but her spirit now has also been taken up by more modern filmmakers like Monika Treut, who cites Ottinger as her primary influence.

For every critic who lavishes such words as "sumptuous" and "transgressive" on Ottinger, though, the words "difficult" and "elitist" are not far behind. When *Dorian Gray* was first shown at the Berlin Film Fest in February 1984, *Variety* acknowledged Ottinger's strengths and recognized the complex cultural and artistic traditions feeding into the film, but the otherwise sympathetic reviewer nevertheless concluded, "After two-and-a-half hours of static pictures and operatic poses, one assumes he has seen a collection of rushes—and waits for the film to be cut for commercial release. But no, Ottinger apparently cannot part with images of her own creation, and thus as a filmmaker overtaxes the patience of her audience."

Her contempt for the commercial film industry and refusal to compromise so much as a single frame to appeal to wider audiences has kept her works, the best and the worst alike, from being seen by any wider numbers than a tight circle of intellectuals and art theorists. Her ethnography can have little effect on mainstream society when she merely preaches to the converted. Ottinger makes films for herself.

"In Germany also they don't understand my films so well," she lamented in a 1989 *LA Weekly* interview, "but yet she resists changing her approach in any way to

Frau Dr. Mabuse's newspaper is the central motif for this poster for *Dorian Gray Im Spiegel der Boulevardpresse*.

make her ideas better understood. "I think my audiences could be bigger," she complained in a 1991 interview in *Cineaste*, grumpily voicing her frustration that her films only play in museums and special retrospectives in major cities like New York. However, one of the stumbling blocks to finding mainstream commercial distribution for her films is their patience-straining length, and she will neither cut down her finished films nor agree to rein in her indulgence on future projects.

Instead of accepting any responsibility for limiting her own audience, she finds fault with the distributors for their blinkered bottom-line mentality. But why should the distributors bear sole responsibility in that regard? Why should they shoulder such immense financial risks on behalf of a defiant filmmaker unwilling to concede even slightly to audience tastes?

"When I negotiate with producers for funding," she continued in the *Cineaste* interview, "I usually end up saying I won't do what you want, but I would nevertheless like to delight you with my own concept of the film."

In a 1983 essay entitled *The Pressure to Make Genre Films*, Ottinger relates an anecdote she apparently believes best illustrates the intransigence of distributors.

A potential French co-producer recently recommended that I make my films technically as elaborate and also as realistic in their detail and story as a James Bond film. The audience is simply used to things being like this.... And with my imagination and my powers of emotion it surely would be possible for me to come up with an identification figure for a very large audience, a person who could then go on to experience all kinds of bizarre things, because it goes without saying that she didn't want to impose any further limits on me. I told her that I might be able to agree [to] the final point, but in no case could I accept the other ones. The co-production fell through.

To Ottinger, the incident reveals the narrow-mindedness of the mainstream industry, and the virtual impossibility of working in an original idiom, such as she does. At the same time, in her own words Ottinger depicts herself as equally intransigent and narrow-minded, but on her own separate track. Were she happy working on the extreme periphery of the film world, crafting her unique products without any strings attached but understanding that her freedom and her poverty were two sides of the same coin (basically the scenario with which Jess Franco has contented himself), there would be no problem. But Ottinger deeply resents her exile from the film community, and is quick to identify her enemies.

In addition to blaming the distributors for their bourgeois tastes, she also criticizes the German government for not supporting artists. Or rather, for not supporting true artists, as she defines the term. "They work with stars, not artists," she says of government subsidies.

She blames feminism and other minority movements for their "lobbyism," defining minorities by their difference from the majority and thereby relegating them to a "self-chosen ghetto."

She finds little support from other directors of the German New Wave. "I have nothing in common with Schlöndorff and his conventional, conservative literary adaptations," she proclaims.

She blames, too, the audience, for its ignorant tastes: "The daily regimen of many hours of TV training limits the visual habits of most people so sharply to television conventions that they are effectively unable to understand any other visual and aural language," she writes in her 1983 essay. "If one tries to use different possibilities ... to reach a general audience, one is almost bound to fail. The resistance is absolute."

In other words, everyone is wrong but

her, and everyone is ganging up on her to force unacceptable artistic compromises: "A lively gauntlet consisting of TV editors, program directors, producers, distributors, exhibitors, film subsidy committees, all of these await the unconventional film that cannot be readily cubbyholed."

In the film of her own life, Ottinger casts herself in the unenviable position of permanent outcast. She is the angry voice outside the studio gates, her fist raised insolently in the air as she rails against the injustice of her exile. She has been unable, or unwilling, to accept her marginality, as Jess Franco has done, or to cleave a middle path of compromise and artistic innovation, as Fritz Lang and Claude Chabrol have done.

Ulrike Ottinger is her own worst enemy, and her career-long spectacle of self-destruction provides yet another conjugation of Norbert Jacques' reflexive verb: *je m'abuse.*

CHAPTER 20

The Story of Chabrol

> He is the craftsman par excellence of the New Wave.... When he is at his best Chabrol has no peers as a manipulator of the medium.
> —James Monaco

They say it began with an argument over movies.

The fighting, that is. The summer of riots and mass protests that rent Paris apart at the seams. Students versus police, a melee of tear gas and violence that sent shock waves across the French political landscape.

It was as if the world was finally coming undone. The year was 1968, and the entire globe was succumbing to the bloodbath. Right wing coups in Greece, the North Vietnamese Tet offensive, the Russian tanks that rolled into Czechoslovakia and rolled over Czechoslovakians—this kind of violence was distant, foreign, remote. These were the places where the power-mad Mabusian dictators had taken over; it made sense that their empires of crime would descend into barbarity. But the West was supposed to be safe, and stable. It was the place of democracy and freedom, societies that had faced down and expelled the demons of fascism and Communism. In the West, it was supposed to be better. But in 1968, that lie was exposed. In the United States, Martin Luther King and Robert Kennedy joined that increasingly long list of world leaders tragically cut down by an assassin's bullet. Israeli forces waged a preemptive war on their Arab neighbors, American troops massacred innocent civilians in My Lai, and French students launched a virtual civil war in the streets of Paris. It was a truly global spectacle of corruption, cruelty and self-destruction: the final triumph of Dr. Mabuse.

What would, in France, ultimately result in a general strike began in its first embryonic stages as a very noisy controversy over the leadership of the Cinematheque. For years that post had been held by Henri Langlois, whose eclectic tastes in movies had made the Cinematheque the hip meeting place for French youths. Not only that, but his programming selections had been instrumental in inspiring the movement known as the Nouvelle Vague—the New Wave. So when, in early 1968, De Gaulle's Minister of Culture André Malraux decided to oust Langlois, the filmmakers of the French New Wave rallied to Langlois' defense. In the opinion of many historians, those rowdy demonstrations in February 1968 helped set the stage for the more virulent and chaotic riots that followed in May. The New Wavers had already led a bloodless revolution within the ranks of the

French film industry, so why not take to the streets in a real-life revolution over the things that mattered most in life—art, culture, movies?

Now, looking back many decades later, the force of the New Wave has been blunted. Their most aggressively innovative filmmaking techniques have been absorbed into the Hollywood mainstream, their fresh-faced crop of actors have become respected grand old ladies and gentlemen, their films—once revolutionary indictments—have now become classics, pored over by film students. The New Wave has become old-school.

For many, the term Nouvelle Vague is virtually synonymous with its twin axes, its most famous practitioners, François Truffaut and Jean-Luc Godard. But Truffaut and Godard were not alone. In its day, the Nouvelle Vague was a vast groundswell of young talent, with many filmmakers involved in some peripheral manner or another. At its core was a group of five young men who had met in the darkened theater of Langlois' Cinemathèque, who had learned the craft of film by watching carefully and dissecting their experiences in the printed pages of the film journal *Cahiers du Cinema*. This core group was Truffaut, Godard, Eric Rohmer, Jacques Rivette and Claude Chabrol. And if Truffaut and Godard were destined to become the famous names of the lot, Chabrol was there first.

It was his 1958 film *Le Beau Serge* ("Handsome Serge") that launched the movement, and it was he who financed much of the early New Wave productions. This revolution in cinema depended on many individuals—Langlois for his brilliant administration of the Cinemathèque, Andre Bazin for founding *Cahiers du Cinema* and giving the New Wavers the chance to find their voices, Alexandre Astruc for first articulating the theory of a personal approach to cinema ... and Claude Chabrol for cleaving the path into the once unattainable halls of the waning French film industry. The story of the Nouvelle Vague is in no small part the story of Claude Chabrol.

Claude Chabrol was born on June 24, 1930, in Paris. Important to the ultimate development of his artistic sensibilities, though, he was not raised in the cosmopolitan capitol, but rather grew up in a parochial little village named Sardent, situated some 150 miles to the south. It was there, amid the quaint trappings of a rural existence essentially untouched by the passage of time, that Chabrol fell in love with a very modern form of technology, an undeniably twentieth century form of entertainment: the movies. "I was seized by the demon of cinema," says Chabrol.

When he was but ten years old, he started a local film club, screening movies in a barn. It may have been a crude manifestation, but even reeking of horse manure the setting was essentially Chabrolian—a darkened screening room, the most romantic place in the world. Not so many years later, in the comparatively pristine environs of the Cinematheque, Chabrol would meet his soulmates: Truffaut, Godard, Rohmer. Chabrol was supposed to be studying pharmacy, but like Fritz Lang and Jess Franco he was far more interested in hanging out in a movie theater than genuinely pursuing such a traditional, bourgeois career. Even when Chabrol was packed off for military service, he saw to it he was assigned as a movie projectionist in Germany.

After his stint in the military, Chabrol returned to his old haunts at the Cinemathèque and rediscovered the old crowd. He took a job working in the publicity department at 20th Century–Fox's Paris branch, the better to learn the world of moviemaking from the inside. When he

Claude Chabrol was one of the essential pioneers of the French New Wave (courtesy Photofest).

left the job a few years later, Godard took his place—Chabrol was always first.

It was around this time that André Bazin was rounding up the likes of Chabrol and Truffaut and Godard and Rohmer and Rivette to write for *Cahiers du Cinema*. Like many of his peers, Chabrol also wrote for other journals, such as *Arts*, but it was in the pages of *Cahiers* that he made his mark.

At that moment in time, French film criticism was the very epitome of cool. For one thing, motion pictures were only just beginning to be taken seriously as an art form, and the French were among the first to grant the new medium that respect. Secondly, French critics were unique in their willingness not simply to accord artistic respectability to heavy, pretentious dramas, but also to films whose principal aim was mere entertainment. Lastly, and most importantly, these French critics rallied their voices in support of, more often than not, American B-movies at a time when the French film industry was increasingly irrelevant and exclusionary. The French industry was a dinosaur, staffed with old fogeys who cranked out unimaginative and derivative pictures for a rapidly diminishing audience. French critics pointed to directors like Alfred Hitchcock, Fritz Lang, Don Siegel, Samuel Fuller, Robert Aldrich, Edgar Ulmer, Jacques Tourneur, and Howard Hawks as proof that one could make films that were simultaneously personal artistic statements and commercially viable entertainment. They had fallen in love with these films in the Cinematheque, and rightfully wondered why the hell France couldn't come up with anything that could compete.

In 1948, critic Alexandre Astruc put the basic idea on paper for the first time. In his essay "Le Caméra Stylo" ("The Camera Pen"), he derided the assembly line flavorlessness of most films, and argued that the true filmmaker ought to be able to wield the camera the same way as a writer does a pen, to "write" a personal statement in the language of cinema. Astruc identified Orson Welles, Jean Renoir and Robert Bresson as filmmakers who in his opinion fit the bill. To prove his point, Astruc then set down his pen and took up a camera to make a film of his own. Though the results were awkward and ineffective, Astruc had nevertheless articulated the basic idea of what would come to be known as auteur theory.

The *Cahiers du Cinema* crowd took Astruc's notion and ran with it. Their fascination with American genre films marked the first time that anyone had ever suggested that a filmmaker's personality could emerge recognizably from within the rigid structures of the Hollywood studio system. Hollywood's best efforts to stamp out all traces of individuality in its creations could not suppress the innate artistry of certain visionary directors. In a 1957 essay, André Bazin first coined the term *auteurs* to describe this category of filmmaker.

Astruc had already shown the natural path for these writers to follow—to put down their pens, pick up cameras and put their theories into practice. Some important technological developments had occurred that would make this transition easier: the creation of faster, more sensitive film stocks and the manufacture of lighter-weight cameras capable of being handheld by a single operator meant that, all of a sudden, motion pictures could be made with smaller crews working faster—that is to say, they could be made cheaper. It naturally flowed from this low-budget technique that the aesthetics of such films would also be transformed—films made under such limited conditions would be rawer, more realistic, less polished, more earthy. This *cinema verité* aesthetic would therefore become a hallmark of the Nouvelle Vague.

But before anyone could follow Astruc's example and start making films, one last, and quite daunting, hurdle remained. The existing French film industry, the recipient of so much of *Cahiers du Cinema*'s scorn, had no use for these insolent young men and no desire to finance their risky projects.

Claude Chabrol's first wife, a young lady who otherwise plays no meaningful part either in the rest of this story or in the rest of Chabrol's life, inherited a significant sum of money. So, not unlike Artur Brauner hocking his mother-in-law's fur coat to finance his first film, Chabrol blew the entire inheritance on making a movie. It was possibly the best decision Chabrol made in his entire life.

In December 1957, Chabrol headed back to his childhood home of Sardent with a tiny crew and a handful of unknown actors to spend three months shooting *Le Beau Serge*. The story of a young man's return from his new urban life to his childhood home Sardent, only to discover the seething corruption beneath the surface of the small town, obviously echoes aspects of Chabrol's own life. It was a personal film, small and simple, with documentary-like black-and-white photography, and an uplifting and deeply Catholic message about redemption, forgiveness and salvation—in short, it was a perfect inauguration for the New Wave. But it was not quite as perfect an inauguration to Chabrol's own career, for reasons that were not immediately clear.

What was immediately clear was that the earth had moved. *Le Beau Serge* took home a prize at the 1958 Locarno film festival, but it was the picture's popular and commercial success that truly spelled the start of something big. André Bazin died of a heart attack in 1958, his work done. The core writers of *Cahiers du Cinema* were ready to graduate.

In 1959, François Truffaut won the Cannes Best Direction prize for his landmark creation *The 400 Blows*, which was an especially piquant success for Truffaut since he had previously been banned from attending the festival as a critic for his defamatory remarks about the state of French filmmaking. By the end of the year, no less than 40 new directors had made their first films—and it was Chabrol who financed much of this prodigious output.

Through the auspices of his then-production company AJYM Films, Chabrol paid for short films by both Rivette and Rohmer, Rohmer's maiden film *The Sign of Leo* (1959), Philippe de Broca's *The Games of Love* (1960), and helped fund Rivette's *Paris is Ours* (1960). Although AJYM was not long for the world, Chabrol's generosity and business savvy provided vital resources to the New Wave at its seminal hour.

In some ways, it was that business savvy, that real-world understanding, that tarnished Chabrol's critical reputation, if only by a bit. Despite his inestimable contributions to the New Wave movement, Chabrol would be denied the stature of Truffaut and Godard. Despite his incredibly prolific output, which continues unabated to this day, Chabrol would suffer from a certain critical disdain, regarded

Chabrol is known for his keen eye for human foibles (courtesy Photofest).

as the most commercial, and therefore the least interesting, of his New Wave peers.

There are several reasons for this unfortunate and undeserved reputation. For one thing, Chabrol is an unpretentious man given to self-deprecating humor. It is hard to spin an image of the tortured artist around a man who says things like, "[*Les Godelureaux*, 1960] would only have made any sort of sense if it had lasted five hours and people had walked out all the way through so that there was no one left at the end. If the film had been a complete success there would have been three hundred people in the cinema at the beginning and only three at the end. But you can't make films on that principle, so it should never have been made at all."

Additionally, Chabrol has made perhaps more than his share of clinkers. Working on his 1990 adaptation of Gustave Flaubert's famous novel *Madame Bovary*, Chabrol found the American press talking about his "comeback." He looked back on three decades' worth of almost continuous film production and marveled at the idea. "Every film is a comeback because between films you disappear," he laughed to Andrea Vaucher for *American Film Magazine*. "Americans think I'm making a comeback because in the past ten years I've made two bad films and those are the ones they saw."

It is not surprising, given the enormous quantity of films Chabrol has produced over the years, that some would be better than others. But in addition to those that were through and through Chabrol's own fault, there was a period in the 1960s when he was obliged to sacrifice creative control over his product. AJYM's well had run dry and producers were unwilling to bank on his ideas, so simply in order to pay the bills Chabrol accepted some director-for-hire assignments on conventional genre films. So it came to pass that Chabrol helmed a handful of spy spoofs: *Le Tigre aime la chair fraîche* ("The Tiger Likes Fresh Blood," 1964), *Marie-Chantal contre le Dr. Khâ* ("The Blue Panther," 1965), *Le Tigre se parfume à la dynamite* ("An Orchid for the Tiger," 1965) and *La Route de Corinth* ("The Road to Corinth," 1967). He also directed *Le Scandale* ("The Champagne Murders," 1965) and *La Ligne de démarcation* ("The Line of Demarcation," 1966) during this period. None were well received in France, and they were scarcely screened elsewhere.

In a 1970 interview for *Movie*, Chabrol explained his attitude towards these films, with all his customary self-effacing wit: "In drivel like the *Tiger* series, I really wanted to get the full extent of the drivel. They were drivel, so OK, let's get into it up to our necks and even beyond if necessary, but let's not do things by halves. In the spy stories the silliness was more important than the spying, so they had to fall into the genre of drivel, rather than the spy genre."

For a man who had learned to love the merits of B-movies, he understood what the assignment required and did his job admirably. That the results were no better than they were certainly should not have been held against Chabrol, though it was. It was a sacrifice of creative integrity that none of his peers endured. And since these films came out under Chabrol's name, he was first in line for the critical drubbing that ensued. The irony was not lost on Chabrol, that he was now making the very kind of commercial dreck that he had made a name for himself by deriding. It also was not lost on Chabrol that he had been painted into a corner by his former peers—the critics. Chabrol had been forced to accept these assignments because his own personal films had been losing money—a consequence of having been harshly treated by French critics at the time. Chabrol called his critics "wicked criminals," and resented the fact that they had robbed him of his audiences in such a way that he had to take on the *Tiger* films simply to pay the rent, only to be slammed all over again by the very same critics. "*Merde!*" Chabrol is quoted by Robin Wood as saying. "It was because of them!"

Chabrol's trouble with the critics began shortly after the success of *Le Beau Serge*, as it became clear that he was marching to the beat of a very different drummer than his New Wave peers. When asked why he seemed so apart from the rest of the Nouvelle Vague, Chabrol brushed off the question with a tart, "There are no waves, only the ocean."

Much of the appeal of the Nouvelle

Vague was its sense of a generational shift, a political and cultural awareness of the power of cinema. "The New Wave films," wrote Florence Jacobowitz and Richard Lippe for *CineAction*, "portrayed a sense of immediacy and the quality of a direct recording of a social moment." They drew influence from Rossellini and the neo-realist movement, using *cinema verite* techniques to rebuild the broken values of a world falling to pieces around them.

Chabrol's *Le Beau Serge* certainly fit that bill, but as he began to take the earnings from that film and funnel them into making more ambitious, more expensive films, he began to demonstrate that *his* personal statement was a caustic and vitriolic screed on the French middle class. The quiet earthiness of *Le Beau Serge* was more a consequence of Chabrol's inexperience technically and his low budget than a deliberate stylistic choice. Once he was in a position to make a deliberate stylistic choice, he would opt for classical technical proficiency, creating slick, colorful films as adept as Hollywood's. His spiritual dimension, too, soon displayed a shocking, and indeed quite alienating, sense of cynicism and misanthropy. Chabrol's cinematic world is populated by cheats and liars, murderers and criminals, and a pervasive sense of corruption and decadence so inevitable that any personal interaction or relationship is liable to erupt in homicide.

"His great problem as an artist has been the difficulty of affirming belief in anything," writes Robin Wood. "Rejecting the bourgeois world for its materialism, pretensions and repressiveness, but finding the various alternatives to this world either self-destructive or completely arid."

"The Chabrolian aesthetic," according to Julien Lapointe, "[is] an interest in socially contextual tragic narratives, and an underlying moral attitude that is often ambivalent and at times ambiguous."

"Claude Chabrol is a son of the bourgeoisie who has made it his life's work to expose the lies of the bourgeoisie," says Chabrol's friend Gabriel Desdoits of Gades Films.

Chabrol was fascinated with *film noir* and pulp fiction, and a committed fan of both Alfred Hitchcock and Fritz Lang, so it came as no surprise that he would tend to make crime thrillers as his chosen specialty. However, his monomaniacal fixation on the thriller genre was a two-edged sword: If he became known as France's Hitchcock, he was also seen as somewhat lesser in stature to those, like Truffaut and Godard, who freely explored a wide variety of genres. In his simple focus, though, Chabrol perfected his art, and became the modern, European heir to the legacy of Hitchcock and Lang.

Chabrol, along with Eric Rohmer, in fact wrote the very first serious book on the films of Alfred Hitchcock, in 1957. One can catch in Chabrol's writings on Hitchcock the ideas that he would carry into practice in his own work. Robin Wood even suggests that Chabrol's book "tells us more about his films than about Hitchcock's." One passage in particular might just as well be about Chabrol himself:

> From now on, the two poles of his future work—because we can now talk of a body of *work*—are clear. One is fascination, moral captation—in other words, depersonalization, schism: in psychoanalytic terms, schizophrenia; in philosophical terms, amoralism; in Baudelairean terms, the assumption of evil, damnation. The other pole is its opposite: knowledge—or more exactly, reknowledge—of self, unity of being, acceptance, confession, absolute communion.

It was Fritz Lang, however, whose work would most greatly influence Chabrol. Indeed, Chabrol's moral compass seems

Claude Chabrol looking *very* comfortable as a bourgeois husband and father, pictured here with wife and recurring star Stephane Audran in 1970 (courtesy Photofest).

Although a visionary auteur, Chabrol was not always in control of his films (courtesy Photofest).

much more in alignment with Lang than Hitchcock. In Hitchcock's cinema, an innocent party is often on the run from the law, wrongfully accused and desperately pursuing the real evil while trying to also stay alive. Chabrol, though, like Lang depicts a world where everyone is guilty, where the guilty parties often escape punishment from an ineffectual legal system. James Monaco notes that "Chabrol himself ... has not missed an opportunity to suggest that Fritz Lang's films might be more important referents than Hitchcock's." Monaco goes on to explain that Chabrol's interest lies in exploring those dark psychologies of guilt and self-destruction, rather than the superficial cops vs. robbers approach of traditional crime thrillers. "It is not ratiocination that fascinates Chabrol, but guilt, psychopathy, and violent passion."

Curiously, though, Chabrol does this without exploring very deeply into his characters. In fact, Chabrol has admitted that he is far more interested in the color schemes of his set design and photography than he is with his characters. This profound contempt for his characters, who are almost uniformly depicted as cruel, loathsome idiots, has its obvious consequences for audience identification.

"People have said that I don't like the people I was showing, because they believe that you have to ennoble them to like them," Chabrol told Andrew Sarris, defensive about the criticism of his trademark cynicism. "Quite the opposite: only the types who don't like their fellows have to ennoble them."

"Chabrol does not ... encourage audience identification as unambiguously as the Hitchcock of, say, *Vertigo* and *Psycho*," writes Robin Wood:

> Hitchcock involves us with his protagonists to the extent that we *live* the film with them emotionally, and then abruptly, through some sudden shock, shatters this identification so that we are forced to construct a new, more complex relationship to the action. Chabrol at times constructs and shoots his films so that they appear to be setting up precisely an audience identification of this kind, but counterbalances this effect by arousing greater sympathy for the watched than for the watcher.... The result is a subtly disturbing divided viewpoint, as if we were reacting against a part of ourselves.... The inscrutability of human motivation has always been a leading Chabrol theme.... One becomes aware ... of the difficulty of being even *reasonably* sure about the motivation behind key acts.

In many Chabrol films, his aloof distance from the characters is so extreme that he reuses the same character names time and again, to emphasize that we should view these people as he does: nothing more than generic character types. In film after film we are introduced to variations on the same basic trio of Chabrolian types: Helene, Charles and Paul. That these films invoke the same generic characters, take place in the same bourgeois social milieu, attack the same corrupt value system, and revolve again and again around the subject of murder causes Chabrol's filmography to appear as a gigantic whole—each film is but a subset of the larger work. Each film is a riff on the same theme, to be understood best in the context of the rest of Chabrol's work than on its own.

That context has been steadily growing over the years. Chabrol is as busy as ever, and his filmography numbers over 70 pictures. He has also contributed shorts to a number of compilation films, and dabbles occasionally in television—such as his episodes of the 1979 television mini-series reviving *Fantômas*. He has produced numerous films by other New Wave directors, and was a technical consultant on Godard's landmark *Breathless* (1959). As a writer, producer, director and actor, Chabrol has immersed himself in the world of cinema as fully as any person can.

His love of film—specifically *genre* film—is absolute. The thrillers of Claude Chabrol are at once off-putting yet mesmerizing, artistically brilliant yet commercially slick, critically acclaimed yet also underrated, influential yet also marginalized. In the cinema of Dr. Mabuse, dominated as it has been by the difficult balance between art and commerce, Claude Chabrol has found perhaps the best and most viable equilibrium.

And so it was apt that he was the one to bring the series to a close, all wrapped up in one astonishingly complete package.

Chapter 21

Club Extinction

> I'm a travel agent, nothing more. I sold them the ticket they were born to buy.... I am the Wall.
>
> —Dr. M

Berlin is gripped by panic. Hundreds of citizens lie dead, seemingly by their own hands. The city is now the suicide capital of the world. The suicide victims come from all walks of life: anonymous masses and celebrities alike, old and young, rich and poor, the depressed and the healthy.

As rumor spreads of a suicide virus, some kind of contagion that drives ordinary people to their doom, the official line is put out that these deaths are unrelated to one other, simply a rash of unfortunate accidents.

The most recent "unfortunate accident" involved a truck driver who crashed his rig into a stash of deadly nerve gas stacked alongside the Berlin Wall, taking hundreds of innocent lives along with his own. As the news of this horrifying tragedy rivets the citizens of Berlin to the CNN-like broadcasts of Mater Media, the mayors of East and West Berlin converge to discuss strategy.

Police Lt. Klaus Hartmann (Jan Niklas) believes otherwise. Somehow—perhaps the virus idea is not so far-fetched after all?—these deaths are indeed suicides. His is a dangerous theory, one likely to inflame the already anxious public.

The East German delegation is also not so easily mollified by talk of "accidents." The suicides have occurred in both East and West, and now the most horrifying incident has happened at the Wall itself. That Hartmann has spoken his mind so forthrightly, heedless of politics, has aroused East German operative Moser (Hanns Zischler). While keeping an eye on Hartmann's investigation into the deaths themselves, Moser pursues a separate line of inquiry, focusing on the head of Mater Media, Dr. Heinrich Marsfeldt (Alan Bates).

Mater Media is naturally making ratings hay out of the crisis, and Marsfeldt's unctuous persona seems tailor-made to hide something ugly underneath. Can Marsfeldt actually be involved, and if so by what mechanism?

Hartmann discovers that simultaneous with the nerve gas explosion—down to the exact minute—two other suicides also took place. One was Reimar von Geldern (Michael Degen), Germany's most popular TV talk show host, whose elaborate self-destruction almost concealed that it was a suicide at all. At the moment that the drugged von Geldern drowned in his own indoor pool as his apartment went up in flames, the same moment that Martin Sehr exploded the nerve gas at the Berlin Wall, a young lady named Ana Sednick threw herself under a passing train. Surely the coincidence of these three deaths cannot be just a coincidence?

To their surprise, Hartmann and his partner Sgt. Stieglitz (Benoit Régent) determine that these poor souls did not want to die—none of them did. The city's morgue is piling up with the bodies of people who wanted to live, yet died by their own hands. That is not the only curious connection between the cases, either—the victims are all connected through spokesmodel Sonja Vogler (Jennifer Beals) and her employers, the vacation club Theratos.

Hartmann confronts Vogler with a ghastly fact: The homes of the dead are each filled with pictures of her. This is, in itself, not so surprising. She is after all a beloved supermodel, the embodiment of all that is beautiful. Her image is the most ubiquitous icon in the city, calling out from video-billboards the slogan of Club Theratos: "Escape. Escape to a better life. Time to go." But the pictures that adorn the walls of the victims have been altered, defaced, distorted. What obsession with Sonja's face grips these people with the urge to destroy themselves?

"What are you to these people, the Angel of Death?" asks Hartmann. With that, he tells the poor woman of an ambulance driver whose suicidal crash killed three bystanders, his final act committed with a hologram of Sonja's face dangling from the ambulance's dashboard.

If Hartmann has linked the deaths, somehow through some occult connection to Sonja Vogler's face, he has yet to make the next essential discovery—a critical fact that Sonja, unwilling to accept the full horror of the truth, is keeping to herself. The dead had all been recent visitors to Club Theratos' vacation paradise in Corfu.

Their experiences while on vacation, conflated in some way with the image of Theratos' spokesmodel, is compelling the rash of self-destruction.

Agent Moser has discovered this for himself, and more: Theratos is owned by Marsfeldt's Mater Media. Like a nuclear explosion in which the atomic reaction generates the fuel that keeps itself blazing, Marsfeldt is sitting pretty on a recursive catastrophe. The more people commit suicide, the more desperate the citizens become to escape the city, the more they mob the Theratos offices to book vacations. The more people visit Theratos, the more people commit suicide. And as the cycle consumes more and more unwitting Berliners, Marsfeldt's companies—Mater Media and Theratos—make gargantuan profits.

Back at the gathering of the East-West Berlin administrations, Marsfeldt had joked that the suicide-panic was inspiring greater attendance at the vacation clubs. "If there's a conspiracy," he had said, "perhaps we should be investigating all the vacation clubs and travel agents. Should we?" It had gotten a laugh, but Moser now realizes that Marsfeldt was deviously defusing the only genuine threat of exposure, by making the proper path of investigation seem ridiculous.

Marsfeldt's master plan is not, however, going off without a hitch. Both Moser and Hartmann are getting too close to the truth—if they were ever to share notes, the whole scheme could be exposed at once. And Sonja Vogler, the unwitting key to it all, is growing suspicious. Now that she knows that the victims are obsessed with her image, how much longer can she stay unwitting? Furthermore, Sgt. Stieglitz has learned that Sonja is an orphan, adopted and raised by Marsfeldt. She is not only a dangerous risk of exposure now, but she is falling in love with Lt. Hartmann. Something must be

Claude Chabrol in 1990, with the pipe Jennifer Beals gave him during production on *Club Extinction* (courtesy The Everett Collection).

done to get the matter under control once again.

Marsfeldt's desperate actions, though, do not have quite their desired effects. An assassination attempt on Moser's life fails. Although Marsfeldt refuses to authorize an attack on Sonja—family ties do count for something, even among pathological mass murderers—his subordinates send an assassin (Andrew McCarthy, in little more than a cameo appearance) anyway. Hartmann manages to kill the hit man before any harm is done, which only serves to strengthen the bond between Vogler and Hartmann. Stieglitz is found dead by suicide, but his death only spurs Hartmann on ever more towards his obscure goal. Lastly, Marsfeldt's efforts to curb the investigation through his turncoat agent in the force, Capt. Engler (Alexander Radszun), do nothing to slow the efforts of either Hartmann or Moser.

Now allied in their pursuit of the truth, Hartmann and Vogler follow the trail to its logical destination—Club Theratos. There they uncover the mechanism of the holocaust: the vacationers are subjected to cult-like suppressions of their individuality, omnipresent video surveillance to expose their most secret weaknesses, and a healthy dose of hypnotic suggestions linking Theratos' advertising slogan—"Time to go"—with the act of self-destruction. Upon returning from their vacation, the poor saps are primed to seek out their own demise upon hearing that trigger phrase, which Vogler's face announces laconically from every street corner video board.

As Hartmann and Vogler race back to Germany with their discovery, Moser has uncovered the final horror. Marsfeldt has arranged an East German TV broadcast to send Sonja's ad out to millions of viewers. On November 17, the better part of Berlin's citizenry will end their lives in a single act of mass suicide to put Jonestown to shame. Although Moser is mortally wounded in the course of discovering this fact, he survives long enough to warn Hartmann and Vogler.

The broadcast begins. All across Berlin, East and West Germans alike measure their rope, sharpen their knives, count out their bullets. The apocalypse is now.

But it does not happen. Instead, Sonja Vogler takes her place before the cameras to issue a live plea: "Time to come home. No more vacations." As the ranks of the almost-dead step out of their trances and shudder at the realization of what nearly happened, Sonja and Hartmann confront Marsfeldt in his secret lair. He is a frail old man, hooked up to a bank of life support systems and video monitors that keep him calm—with footage of nuclear explosions, war atrocities and natural disasters, of course. They prepare to mete out the final judgment.

"Go ahead, Lieutenant," screeches Marsfeldt in defiance. "I've been married to life support too long. Grant me my divorce."

Hartmann stops. He realizes that there is no punishment severe enough for the gravity of Marsfeldt's crimes. What can they do to compensate for the thousands of lives destroyed by this bastard? Sonja and her lover walk away, abandoning the evil Dr. M to his own conscience, a punishment he cannot bear. Marsfeldt yanks out his own life support tube, and the city awakes to a bright new day.

According to the closing titles of *Dr. M* (released on video in the United States under the far less interesting title *Club Extinction*, 1989), Norbert Jacques' novel *Dr. Mabuse der Spieler* provided the inspiration for the film. Certainly, as adaptations go, Fritz Lang's 1922 silent epic is by far the more faithful, but Claude Chabrol's 1989 film is a free-wheeling, all-purpose, come-one-come-all homage to all things Mabuse, and a spirited tribute to Lang as well.

The diabolical Dr. M, Heinrich Marsfeldt as he likes to be called in this latest outing, is a media mogul much like Ulrike Ottinger's take on the character (see also Chapter 19). Like Ottinger's Frau Dr. Mabuse, Marsfeldt is manufacturing the news his network reports. If the body count has increased since 1984, Mabuse has simply realized that if killing three people sells so many papers, why not multiply that by a factor of a thousand? Like his predecessors in the CCC series of the '60s, Marsfeldt communicates with his underlings through distorted video screens, his identity scrupulously concealed from even his most trusted followers.

Marsfeldt has also learned the benefits of a close association with the police. Like his forerunners in *Dr. Mabuse the Gambler* and *The 1000 Eyes of Dr. Mabuse*, he feeds misinformation to the cops while scoring valuable insider information on the status of their investigations. And, like his precursors in *The Big Heat, Scotland Yard vs. Dr. Mabuse* and *Scream and Scream Again*, he has placed a double agent within the police force (Capt. Engler) to harass the detective hero and derail any line of inquiry that hits too close to home. His ultimate demise, destroyed by his own guilty conscience, is far closer to the denouement of Lang's 1922 *Dr. Mabuse* than Jacques' novel.

The two-way mirrors and pervasive video surveillance at Theratos have obviously taken their cue from the Hotel Luxor, that voyeur's paradise in *The 1000 Eyes of Dr. Mabuse*. Marsfeldt's black-clad entourage have apparently acquired their kinky fashion sense from the cast of *The Vengeance of Dr. Mabuse*, and a rigged roulette wheel in Marsfeldt's private club Extinction (which lends the U.S. version its title) is a nod to the secret gambling dens of the original *Dr. Mabuse*.

Beyond that, Extinction (the club, not the film) also recalls similar nightclubs like The Busted Pot (*Scream and Scream Again*), The Red Garter (*The Vengeance of Dr. Mabuse*) and the punk club where Dorian Gray and Andamana initiate their arranged romance.

In 1979, writer Lester Bangs identified the link between punk music and Mabusian-style tyranny:

> The punk stance is riddled with self-hate, which is always reflexive, and any time you conclude that life stinks and the human race mostly amounts to a pile of shit, you've got the perfect breeding ground for fascism.

It does Marsfeldt's heart proud to witness all these youths so eagerly embracing nihilism. Agent Moser sums up the inherent corruption of (capitalist) youth culture: "Disposable—the ultimate consumer product. When they've used themselves up, they throw their lives away." Moser is on to something here: Dr. Marsfeldt is treating death as merchandise, using the tools of mass marketing to sell the concept of self-annihilation to a city full of reluctant customers. It is this aspect of Marsfeldt's master plan that most scathingly indicts the media; it is this edge that was lacking from Ulrike Ottinger's fairly softball critique of Big Media (see Chapter 19). As the public increasingly cedes power to the media elite, becoming passive couch potatoes easily manipulated by the boob tube, the power of that media elite becomes a form of tyranny, a form of fascism.

For his part, Moser is a suave and efficient secret agent, nothing less than an East German James Bond. As such he follows in that proud tradition of 007–inspired spy heroes in *Scotland Yard vs. Dr. Mabuse* and *Death Ray of Dr. Mabuse*, with the GDR connection forming a link to the East German spies (good, bad and indifferent) in *Scream and Scream Again*.

While there is no overt affiliation between Chabrol's film and Jacques' original story, the basic structure of the stories are the same. The detective hero is investigating what appears to be a generalized social phenomenon, but one that is so sinister he suspects there is a criminal conspiracy behind it; that conspiracy turns out to be directed in secret by an evil genius who is manipulating events on a grand scale; the hero and the villain are each united through their love for the same woman. However, Sonja Vogler's role in the plot is a pivotal one, and therefore has less to do with the Countess Told from Jacques' story and far more in common with Marion Menil of *1000 Eyes*. Indeed, her final rebellion—in which the assertion of her independence and individuality disable the criminal plot—parallels the defiant heroines of Lang's *1000 Eyes*, *The Big Heat* and *Spies*. Sonja Vogler's name even mirrors that of Agent Sonia from *Spies*.

Certainly Chabrol and writers Thomas Bauermeister (original story), Wolfgang Hundhammer and Sollace Mitchell (screenplay) cannot have intended all of these references—many, if not most, are just coincidence. But there is no coincidence to the conspicuous casting of Wolfgang Preiss as

Police Commissioner Kessler—a casting coup given additional emphasis by a special opening title credit identifying the former Dr. Mabuse as a "Special Guest Star." During the course of the film, there is also a passing in-joke about a truck driver named "Klein-Rogge," the original Dr. Mabuse himself.

Not all of *Club Extinction*'s referents are from the Mabuse series. Chabrol also draws from more ordinary genre sources. Fans of detective thrillers will find much about *Club Extinction* to be familiar, even to the point of cliché: the cop hero is on the outs with his bosses for political reasons; his partner is killed which spurs his investigation onward, even after he is suspended; and he falls in love with a woman who is, for a time, the prime suspect.

In taking the role of Sonja Vogler, Jennifer Beals carried with her a certain degree of subtextual baggage. While her best known work remains *Flashdance* (1983), for the purposes of this discussion it was her role in the 1984 horror flick *The Bride* that is germane. In Franc Roddam's poorly received update of *Bride of Frankenstein*, Beals plays Eva, an artificial being created by Dr. Frankenstein (Sting).* In educating her, Frankenstein wants to indoctrinate her with his own ideas and ideology, to create a perfect mate for himself, a female doppelganger. The already complex psychological and sexual problems inherent in such an act of narcissism are only further complicated by Frankenstein's decision to convince Eva that she was an orphan, whose parentage is unknown. He raises her like a daughter, adding incestual lust to his litany of moral transgressions. Just a few years after this film, Chabrol cast the same actress as a woman who, if genuinely human flesh and blood, is nonetheless also a creation of a mad scientist. Marsfeldt molds Sonja's mind and manipulates her fate to use her as a tool in his machinations. Marsfeldt's egotism is of a different stripe than Frankenstein's—Marsfeldt cannot bear to go on living, and because he holds such a high opinion of himself, he needs to destroy the world with him—but he is equally dependent on his adopted daughter, an orphan whose true parentage in unknown, to realize his selfish dreams. And, like Frankenstein, Marsfeldt is incestuously obsessed with his ward. In both films, Beals' character undoes the schemes of her father figure by falling in love with another man and asserting her independence from the man who "made" her.

Chabrol is also firing off references to his own body of work. In his 1972 film *Dr. Popaul*, Chabrol explored the Langian theme of suicide-as-murder. In that film, Mia Farrow plays a woman who carefully manipulates the titular Dr. Popaul (Jean-Paul Belmondo), a serial killer, into committing suicide. Although Popaul does not, in the end, take his own life, Chabrol was already prefiguring the various uses of suicide that would surface in *Club Extinction*.

The character of Klaus Hartmann, haunted by guilt over the suicide of his wife Nina, alludes to a character named Andreas Hartmann from Chabrol's earlier film *L'Oeil du malin* ("The Evil Eye"). In that 1962 film, "Hartmann" is a suicidal man who murders his wife Hélène in a jealous rage. As a filmmaker, Chabrol was in the habit of reusing character names as a way to establish recurring character types—that is, different characters with the same name are supposed to share some personality traits as well. "Hélène" was unquestionably one of the most frequently recurring such character types. Perhaps by

---

*Coincidentally, one of Beals' co-stars in *The Bride* was Veruschka von Lehndorff, ex–Dorian Gray herself.

linking *Club Extinction*'s detective hero with *The Evil Eye*'s guilty murderer, Chabrol means to imply a shared degree of culpability in their deceased wives, too. For Chabrol fans capable of catching the reference, it opens up levels of meaning not wholly contained in the text of *Club Extinction* itself.

To make such an offhanded and subtle allusion to past works, though, presupposes that the audience for *Club Extinction* would be in a position to recognize and appreciate such obscure levels of meaning. Chabrol himself considered *Club Extinction* as a part of his overall canon. Like any Chabrol film, he treated it as an opportunity to explore his favorite themes and character types.

If Chabrol saw *Club Extinction* as a full-blooded Chabrol film, his audience did not feel the same. In the end, Chabrol's take on Dr. Mabuse fell uncomfortably between two stools, alienating both the art-house cognoscenti and science fiction fans alike. When fellow New Wavers François Truffaut and Jean-Luc Godard tried their hands at sci-fi, they fashioned oblique, arty, intellectual exercises like *Fahrenheit 451* (1966) or *Alphaville* (1965)—ever so much more palatable to the cultural elite, whose distrust of the sci-fi genre sometimes borders on contempt. Reportedly, Fritz Lang's reaction to *Alphaville* was a bewildered, "What is it about Godard that is afraid to show action on the screen?"

Chabrol's concerns have always been more commercial and populist, and unsurprisingly he embraced the pulp traditions of his chosen subject without inhibition. Shot in English and unflinchingly violent, *Club Extinction* seeks a mass international audience, and appears to want nothing more than to genuinely terrorize them. That it does so while maintaining its intellectual sophistication is a testament to Chabrol's brilliance. In a decade otherwise starved of thoughtful sci-fi fare, *Club Extinction* stands as one of the finest genre films of the 1980s, albeit one that precious few have ever actually seen.

Fans of science fiction, who might conceivably have rescued Chabrol's picture from oblivion and turned it into something of a cult favorite, turned out to be just as unmoved as Chabrol's art-house viewers, but for entirely the opposite reasons. The intellectuals who fell in love with the Chabrol of *Les Bonnes Femmes* (1966), *Les Biches* (1968) or *Le Boucher* (1969) were turned off by the trappings of *Club Extinction*'s unsavory genre. Meanwhile, the adherents of that particular genre were left cold by precisely those elements of Chabrol's style his highbrow devotees most admired: his distanced and alienating tone, his cynicism towards his characters, his skill at depicting personal anguish and self-destruction, his unwillingness to explore his characters' motivation. Like the best Dr. Mabuse films, *Club Extinction* requires multiple viewings to figure out just what the hell is going on; but even after multiple viewings some aspects of Chabrol's story remain forever clouded in mystery.

Even its U.S. distributor, Cori Film, seemed at a loss as to how to handle such a singular motion picture. Since American audiences were unlikely to appreciate its relationship to the Dr. Mabuse series, they changed the title from the evocative *Dr. M* to the blandly exploitative *Club Extinction*. This alteration was accomplished in the crudest of ways: During the opening titles, the name "Dr. M" comes careening out of the nerve gas explosion to fill the screen, with "Club Extinction" half-heartedly superimposed on top in crude lettering.

Cori made no effort to sell the name "Chabrol," either. Instead, Cori focused on the names they considered most commercial in the U.S. market: Jennifer "Flashdance" Beals and brat-packer Andrew McCarthy. While McCarthy had starred as Henry Miller in Chabrol's concurrent *Quiet Days in Clichy* (1990), here he has but a few seconds of screen time in a cameo role that is fairly inconsequential to the plot. To compensate, Cori's publicists mendaciously distorted that plot:

> An epidemic of bizarre deaths is sweeping through the future-shocked city. From thousands of giant monitors, Sonja (Jennifer Beals) issues a steady stream of hypnotic propaganda. In a hidden fortress above Club Extinction, media tycoon Dr. M (Alan Bates) directs the subliminal madness. His disembodied heart beats faster as the deaths increase and the panic builds. The Assassin (Andrew McCarthy) is the wall between freedom and mass destruction. Chaos descends as the world rushes to oblivion in this relentless sci-fi thriller.

Reading such a summary on the back of the video box, those handful of viewers who did rent *Club Extinction* were sure to end up even more disoriented by Chabrol's already challenging flick. If any character deserves to be called a "wall between freedom and mass-destruction," it is not McCarthy's don't-blink-or-you-missed-him assassin, but Dr. M. Marsfeldt openly compares himself to the Berlin Wall in the film's finale, and that speech has come to symbolize one of *Club Extinction*'s main difficulties in reaching its audience: immediately upon its release, history had rendered Chabrol's tale out of date.

Most of Chabrol's films take place in the small cities and provincial towns of France. Indeed his precise rendering of the details of provincial life is one of the things for which he is celebrated. By stark contrast, *Club Extinction* plays out in a future version of Berlin, as urban and modern a metropolis as one will find in continental Europe. The exact date of the story is left vague, but it is clearly one of those not-too-distant futures. There are laser beams, video phones, holograms and gigantic video boards à la *Blade Runner* (1982), but the clothes and scenery seem otherwise familiar. Cori's already suspect publicity places the film in the twenty-first century, and there is a fleeting and ambiguous reference to "the millennium" which could lend arguable support to such a claim. Nevertheless, the presence—and prominence—of the Berlin Wall in the story grounds the events firmly in 1989 and no later.

On November 9, 1989, the 13-foot high concrete wall dividing West Berlin from the rest of East Germany was finally toppled. For decades, East Germans had risked their lives attempting to cross that barrier. Some 75 people had died in the act over the years, shot in the back by their own "democratic" government. Now that government was allowing free and unfettered travel and emigration to the West; talk would soon be abuzz with the reunification of Germany. Twenty-eight years of real-life horror had come to an end on November 9.

In *Club Extinction*, the final act of Marsfeldt's plan is scheduled to take place in a TV studio in East Berlin, on the other side of the Wall, on November 17. The film opens with an explosion at the Wall; after Marsfeldt's speech in which he hisses, "I am the Wall," the film concludes with a shot of the Wall as Hartmann and Vogler stroll off into the distance. The entire scheme to kill tourists cruelly mocks the way that the Berlin Wall had always equated travel with death. The symbolism of the Wall is woven deep into the fabric of the story.

Club Extinction opened in Paris in November 1989, just in time to see its chief symbol yanked out from underneath it. The U.S. first saw it in January 1990, when *Variety* remarked, "The Berlin Wall is used throughout ... as a metaphor for modern malaise, its presence contaminating the story's Berliners in a way now hopelessly dated since the wall was torn down." By the time of its late May 1990 premiere in Germany, the reunification process was already underway.

Chabrol can certainly be forgiven for not foreseeing such a momentous historical event. No one saw it coming. Not long before the Wall was dismantled, East German authorities had busily reinforced its most lethal features—such as the automatic weapons designed to indiscriminately shoot would-be escapees when the human guards suffered an untimely attack of conscience. When the unthinkable finally happened, more than a few on both sides of the border were reluctant to believe the news. Erich Honecker, the Mabusian dictator who ruled East Germany with an iron fist from 1971 to 1989, had not so long ago pronounced that the Wall would last "another 100 years"—this on January 29, 1989.

By May 1989, though, the situation had changed. For it was then, on the occasion of Soviet leader Mikhail Gorbachev's first official visit to West Germany, that the Iron Curtain began to lift. Gorbachev publicly disavowed the old order, by which military force and state-sponsored terror was used to keep its satellite states in line. Since it was precisely the application of Soviet-backed state-sponsored terror that kept Honecker's Germany discrete from the West, it was now only a matter of time before the arbitrary division of Germany dissolved.

Of the Eastern Bloc states, Hungary was the first to respond, quickly opening its border with Austria. This meant that not only could Hungarians now freely travel to the West through Austria, but any other East Bloc citizen could bypass their own nation's restricted borders by traveling via Hungary's open port. Within six months, some 220,000 East Germans had poured through Hungary to the West, a worse exodus than the one that had first inspired the creation of the Wall (see Chapter 10). East Germany was in dire peril of total collapse unless something could be done to stem the tide. A hardline crackdown would be tricky if not outright impossible, given the political thaw the USSR had signaled. There were not many options open.

When Honecker had first taken office, one of his early triumphs was a "Basic Treaty" with West Germany that had markedly increased traffic across the border. However, on close analysis, most of the border crossings were from West to East, while Honecker held a rigid line limiting Easterners access to the West. Public relations successes notwithstanding, his was a brutal regime that preferred to shoot its citizens in the back rather than let them leave. The ruling Communist party realized that Honecker was exactly the wrong kind of man to respond to the crisis of 1989 and forced him out.

In his place, the party installed Egon Krenz. Krenz had one virtue, if only one. He understood that the best way to keep East Germans at home was to let them leave. Once the opportunity to travel was restored to them, the vast majority took it—in order to visit the West, and then return. The solution to the exodus was not a totalitarian crackdown, but a liberal policy of open borders. Of the hundreds of thousands of East Germans who flocked to West Berlin on November 9, only a small fraction stayed. The rest went back home.

As Sonja Vogler says in the climax of *Club Extinction*, "Time to come home. No more vacations." Travel does not have to equal death.

Chabrol's love of Lang is absolute. He has spent his entire career revisiting the themes of Lang's films. He explicitly dedicated *Alice, ou le dernier Fugue* ("Alice or the Last Escapade," 1976) to Fritz Lang. Nineteen eighty-seven's *La Cri du Hibou* ("Cry of the Owl") was a direct homage to Lang's *Fury*. And Chabrol once said that, not unlike Artur Brauner, he was inspired to become a filmmaker after seeing *The Testament of Dr. Mabuse*.

As Brauner's Mabuse series wound down, Chabrol first began thinking about helming his own installment. It was to be called *Le Dernier Mabuse* ("The Last Mabuse"), and Chabrol even considered filming it silent with intertitles, a la *Dr. Mabuse the Gambler*. But the late 1960s were not good to Chabrol (see Chapter 20) and the project never got off the ground.

Over the next two decades, Chabrol continued to pay homage to Mabuse in little ways here and there. Echoes of Mabuse can be perceived even in his cheap and trashy spy thrillers of the 1960s, such as *Marie Chantal contre Le Dr. Kha* (1965), with Akim Tamiroff as the Mabusian Kha. Orson Welles' role in Chabrol's 1972 *Ten Days' Wonder* was a distinctly Mabusian puppetmaster, even if his reach was domestic rather than criminal. Immediately after *Ten Days' Wonder*, Chabrol planned to team again with Welles on a spy thriller called *Atrox*, conceived as a two-part film like Lang's monumental silents. Marc Behm's script for *Atrox*, originally to have lensed in Germany by Robert Siodmak, cast Welles as a master criminal in a decidedly Mabusian mold. Unfortunately, this too did not come to pass. However, in 1976 Chabrol did direct *Les Magiciens* ("The Magicians"), starring Gert Fröbe as a magician named Vestar. Commenting on the film, Christian Blanchet wrote that "Vestar, the German magician, is a figure symbolic of Mabuse (much like many other films by Chabrol)." Then in the early 1980s, Chabrol was tapped for the *Fantômas* TV mini-series. He directed two of the four episodes, including its first episode, which owed perhaps more to Lang for its imagery than to Feuillade.

Finally, in the late 1980s, opportunity knocked for the real Mabuse project, although without the name Mabuse. To use the name would mean working with Artur Brauner, something Chabrol had already done back in 1976 on *Folies Bourgeosies* ("The Twist"), starring Bruce Dern and Ann-Margret. The two were an "ill fit" from the start, with Brauner's cheapskate antics and self-appointed auteurship certain to collide with Chabrol's goofball nature and determination not to cede artistic control ever again. Chabrol never worked with Brauner again, and the last Mabuse would hence be named Marsfeldt.

In preparing the story, Chabrol had a number of ideas kicking around his head. Long ago, Fritz Lang himself had suggested the notion of a ruthless, powerful man with a literal iron heart. Also of influence was an unfilmed project Nicholas Ray had been trying to launch back in the late 1960s, called *Only Lovers Left Alive*. Ray's story concerned an apocalyptic future where everyone over the age of 25 has died, thanks to an epidemic of suicides that overtakes England. Set to star Mick Jagger and Keith Richards, Ray was unable to find financial backing, and the Rolling Stones stars lacked confidence in Ray, and the whole matter dissolved. Chabrol, an admirer of Ray's, almost certainly took a cue from this script.

Chabrol began work on the screenplay with Odile Barski (who had also collaborated with him on *La Cri du Hibou*). The producers however, wanted an American writer involved, and persuaded Chabrol to hire Sollace Mitchell, an undistinguished scribe whose only credential was that he was a fan of Lang's. Mitchell's principal task was to provide the English dialogue, as Chabrol had decreed that the film had to filmed in

Germany (on the same soundstages that Lang had used for *1000 Eyes*, no less), in either German or English. The producers, naturally, selected English as the more commercially appropriate choice.

It has been said of Chabrol that he can be out of his depth when working in a foreign language. His English productions like *The Champagne Murders* (1966) and *Ten Days' Wonder* have lost something in the translation. This criticism is not entirely true of *Club Extinction*; Chabrol's English has improved over the years. Chabrol's choice to work in English on this picture acknowledged what Fritz Lang understood back in 1960—that a picture like this cannot reach a mass audience in America with subtitles. He deserves credit for rendering Jennifer Beals' finest performance, something not even her erstwhile husband, director Alexandre Rockwell, was able to do. At the conclusion of the project, Beals gave Chabrol a pipe inscribed with the words "Master of the Universe." As Sonja, she delivers a heady blend of innocence and worldliness, of self-confidence and near hysteria. And in Alan Bates, one of the greatest Shakespearean actors of his generation, Chabrol has found the most charismatic Dr. Mabuse save for Vincent Price (David Lynch, Richard Attenborough and Max von Sydow were all considered for the role). Among the non-native English speakers in the cast, Hanns Zischler has a pitch-perfect performance virtually untouched by any accent. Yet the other actors do seem uncomfortable with the English dialogue, which is at time unduly distracting. Try as he might, poor Jan Niklas as Klaus Hartmann cannot quite get his mouth around some of his more colloquial dialogue. He cannot quite nail the right inflection on such highly idiomatic lines as "Inquiring minds wanna know."

The larger question, though, is to what extent the entire choice of subject matter is outside Chabrol's vernacular. The typical Chabrol film is small in scale, focused on prosaic domestic squabbles that lead inexorably to murder. *Club Extinction* is a sprawling futuristic epic about nothing less than the end of the world. To a casual observer, *Club Extinction* does not look like a Chabrol film at all—even if it was photographed by Jean Rabier, the ace cinematographer whose collaboration with Chabrol dates all the way back to 1958 and *Le Beau Serge*. How can the dichotomy of style be reconciled?

At first glance, the difference in tone seems severe, but on closer examination the epic scope of *Club Extinction* is deeply connected to the cramped world of, say, *L'Enfer* (1994) or *Le Boucher* (1969). Chabrol himself provided the key, in a seminal essay he wrote for *Cahiers du Cinema* in 1959. This article, titled "Little Themes," has been the Rosetta Stone for many a critic seeking to comprehend Chabrol's cinema. In his study of Chabrol's films, writer James Monaco summarized the essay:

> Little Themes ("Le Petits Sujets") is the shortest and most succinct defense of genre films ever published in [*Cahiers du Cinema*]. Chabrol sets up two potential scenarios: "The Apocalypse of Our Time," obviously a "Big Theme," and "The Quarrel Between Neighbors," a little one.... As he has set them up, there is no essential structural difference between "The Apocalypse of Our Time" and "The Quarrel Between Neighbors": each offers the same thematic possibilities, but whereas the Big Theme film does so inductively, the Little Theme film proceeds by deduction and is grounded in concrete, experiential reality. Chabrol's films are marked by an insistent—at times obsessive—structural restriction because, as he concludes, "the smaller the theme is, the more one can give it a big treatment.

By his own analysis, then, Chabrol sees the Big Theme of *Club Extinction* as the twin brother of the Little Themes that usually populate his films.

The typical Chabrol film, with its Little Theme, obsesses over the family unit. As a filmmaker, Chabrol claims to be singularly interested in "the mundane rituals of everyday life." Where best to view such rituals, and the violence he sees simmering beneath them, than the family, the basic building block of bourgeois society? "The bourgeois family is a farce," Chabrol told *Sight and Sound* in 1970. "It doesn't exist. But a *real* family, that is something wonderful."

Underneath its Big Theme, *Club Extinction* is also just a story about family—as well as a story about a love triangle, another recurrent Chabrolian obsession. Dr. Marsfeldt incestuously lusts after his adoptive daughter Sonja. Although like all good Mabuses he keeps his emotions rigorously in check and never acts on that incestuous impulse, the desire does drive his jealousy for Klaus Hartmann. Indeed, the viewer gets the feeling that Marsfeldt perceives a greater threat from Hartmann's relationship with Sonja than from Hartmann's investigation. The entire set-up recalls Chabrol's very first film, *Le Beau Serge*, which also revolved around an incestuous father-daughter liaison.

Critic Robin Wood, writing about *Les Biches*, remarked that "one reaches a fundamental aspect of Chabrol's films: the *complicity* of the protagonists in the machinations of one another." In a Langian world of universal guilt, Chabrol indicts everyone. Obviously, Dr. Marsfeldt is a guilty sinner, as the evil genius behind it all, but he has help—from his opponents and prey. The victims of his scheme do indeed die by their own hands. Sonja is his tool, the trigger for all these acts of self-destruction, and she blindly refuses to step down from that role. As long as she refuses to acknowledge the truth about her complicity in the crime, she will continue to sound her siren's call leading Berliners to their doom. Only once she recognizes the hypnotic influence she wields can she break free of Marsfeldt's control.

Sonja's unwillingness to believe anything bad about dear old dad, no matter how blatant the evidence, plays directly into Dr. M's hand. He knows that Sonja's natural psychological defense mechanisms will help shield his operation from scrutiny. It is only through Hartmann's persistence that Sonja is ultimately forced to accept the horrible reality that her whole life has been a sham. She asks Hartmann to respect the distinction between her appearance and her self; but like Dorian Gray that distinction is being used against her, as her appearance has taken on an inimical life of its own.

The underlying message of *Club Extinction* holds that the salvation of the world depends on the heroes' recognition of their own corruption. We have seen how this applies to Sonja; Moser is a special case. He has no illusions to start with, and therefore no disillusionment is called for. He begins his assignment with the healthy skepticism that the "suicide virus" might just turn out to be a biological weapon designed by his own government. Harboring no self-deception about who or what he is, Moser has the integrity of character to be able to play the undercover game. And as von Wenk, Mistelzweig, Joe Como and Bob Anders know, the best way to defeat a Dr. Mabuse is to go undercover.

Hartmann's personal corruption, though, is far more subtle and insidious, and his eventual recognition of it the most painful. As we have seen, the name "Hartmann" carries, within the context of Chabrol's filmmaking, some connotation that he is responsible for his wife Nina's suicide. This is an important point and deserves careful analysis. Hartmann definitely still smarts from her death. The mere mention of her name exposes raw nerves, induces painful winces. He still wears her watch on his wrist, and maintains a miniature shrine to her in his home.

When it is suggested that Nina's suicide might have been a part of the current crisis, Hartmann bitterly rejects the notion. That she died months before the mass suicides began is but one reason to see her death as apart from the others. More relevant, though, is Hartmann's realization that the dominant characteristic of the current rash of suicides is that the victims have no desire to die, none of the customary psychological markers that accompany "true" suicides. Unspoken, of course, is the obvious corollary: Nina did have a reason to kill herself.

Although Hartmann cannot plumb the depths of Nina's mind to identify that reason, he knows that she was driven by despair to take her own life rather than face another day—with him. To add to his pain, he learned, only after her death, that she had been pregnant. Something in his relationship with her precipitated her self-destruction. In some way, left ambiguous, he drove her to her suicide. "Death beat me once, took away half my life," Hartmann reflects. "But half a life is better than none."

Nina's is not the only blood on his hands, either, since Hartmann also played a role in the death of his partner Stieglitz. Unlike Nina, Stieglitz' suicide is caught up in Dr. M's intrigue. Stieglitz did go to Theratos, and his demise was specifically triggered by Sonja Vogler's subliminal commands. But there is more at work here. Unlike the other ex–Theratos suicides, Stieglitz was profoundly depressed. All throughout the film he had been jumpy; one got the feeling he was likely to shoot himself at any moment. At one point he said, "The place for me is the morgue." He actually means he would prefer to *work* in the morgue, so as not to have to interview victims' families, but the ambiguity of his chosen words is intentional; Chabrol signals right away that there is a secret death wish in this man. While at Club Theratos, Hartmann watches the secret videotapes taken of Stieglitz during his stay. In the footage, Stieglitz reveals that he wants to retire from the force, but cannot for fear that Hartmann would ridicule his cowardice. By bullying his friend into a job for which he was not suited, Hartmann pushed Stieglitz into the depression that sent him to Theratos and all the finality that came with it.

Just as Sonja needed to acknowledge her relationship with Dr. M, Hartmann needs to recognize his too. Like his nemesis, Hartmann has driven other people to suicide. Once he accepts that dark side of his own soul, he is finally in a position to turn that personal corruption to good measure. He kills Engler in cold blood and, along with Sonja, motivates Marsfeldt's self-annihilation. These murders save the world.

The ostensible purpose of Club Theratos is to remake its visitors as better people, to send them away renewed and purified. Only in the case of Vogler and Hartmann is this actually true. In the final analysis, although *Club Extinction* appears to be about the Biggest of Big Themes, the Apocalypse of Our Time, it is actually an epic exploration of Chabrol's Little Themes, of dysfunctional incestuous families, love triangles and the corruption of the individual soul.

Claude Chabrol made a name for himself advancing a theory of film criticism that demanded that movies be evaluated simultaneously as products of their genre and of their creator(s). The poor reception that greeted *Club Extinction* is due, ironically, to the failure of audiences and critics to follow Chabrol's advice and chart this film at once as a sci-fi thriller, an homage to the diabolical cinema of Dr.

Mabuse, and a Chabrolian work of art. Seen for what it is, *Club Extinction* is long overdue for a reappraisal. It is not only one of Chabrol's tautest and most ambitious endeavors, but one of the finest and most nuanced entries in this long-running film franchise.

CHAPTER 22

The Legacy of Dr. Mabuse

> In fact, when we talk about Mabuse as the force of disruption and destruction, the nihilist agent of chaos and anarchy, we are probably limiting him unduly by definition: in Lang's work what he and his kind represent is something much more basic and inescapable—the Power of Darkness itself.
> —John Russell Taylor, *The Nine Lives of Dr. Mabuse*

> What becomes clear is how the name "Mabuse" does not finally designate a fictional character that Lang returned to several times (let alone a character that fits Kracauer's "Caligari to Hitler" hypothesis). Rather Mabuse is the name of a system—a system of spectacular power whose strategies are continually changing but whose aim of producing "docile" subjects remains relatively constant.
> —Jonathan Crary, *Dr. Mabuse and Mr. Edison*

Full of self-importance and pride, the makers of *Dr. Mabuse the Gambler* celebrated the 1922 opening of the film with a program stating:

> [D]irector Fritz Lang has set his sights on making not a blockbuster film, not a detective story, not even a social film, but rather following the suggestion of the novel to forge a picture of the time, in which the year of its creation is every bit as important a performer as the actors, the set designers, the photography. Every epoch has had its epic dramatic works in which the spirit of the age in which it was made is vital and evident. This film stands as a new dispatch, powered by characteristic directness, intended as a picture of the times, a document for future generations. The world of this film is the world in which we all live.... This *Dr. Mabuse, the Gambler*, was not possible in 1910, and perhaps—you might say hopefully—will not be possible by 1930. But for the 1920's, he is a larger than life likeness—almost a concept, at least a sign.

Of course, it was willful shortsightedness not to acknowledge the early twentieth century literary and filmic traditions in whose arch-villainous footsteps Mabuse so confidently tread; fans of Fantômas and Dr. Fu Manchu knew otherwise. Additionally, the claim that Mabuse could not be possible in 1930 would also fall apart, when the bad doctor returned for his first sequel in 1932.

Dr. Mabuse has since starred in 11 sequels, two additional books and a handful of short stories. His name has become an icon of horror, invoked by rock groups and car advertisers alike. The publishers of *Heavy Metal* printed a graphic novel of *Dr. Mabuse* featuring a very Langian Mabuse (complete with monocle!) terrorizing a city that can only be described as Metropolis. The Teutonic dance group Propaganda's biggest single was 1985's *Dr. Mabuse*. In the 1990s, 2001 Publishing reissued Jacques' three novels and assorted other Mabusian writings in a handsomely bound set bearing George Grosz-like Dadaist cover art, and illustrated with reprints of the film programs and production artwork.

A poll of German teenagers conducted in the mid-1980s found a remarkable 95 percent of them recognized the name Mabuse, and even if they had not seen any of the films or read any of the books they still connected his name with fear, paranoia, mind control, tyranny, totalitarianism.

Although the character never achieved the kind of name recognition in the US that he did in Germany, American journalists nevertheless have found him a valuable metaphor, a handy if unflattering way of describing such figures as investment wizard George Soros or software tycoon Bill Gates. Echoes of Mabuse reverberate through such modern Hollywood films as *The Usual Suspects* (1995), *Conspiracy Theory* (1997) and *The Game* (1997).

For a character supposedly defined and limited by the contemporary concerns of 1922, he has had a remarkable shelf life.

When it came time for Hollywood to ballyhoo their release of the dubbed and edited version of *Testament of Dr. Mabuse* (now retitled *Crimes of Dr. Mabuse*) in 1952, rather than make any portentous claims that the now almost 20-year-old picture was a unique document of its time, they instead invoked some more commercially recognizable references:

> More frightening than Frankenstein! Deadlier than Dracula! More hideous than Mr. Hyde! Madman? Monster? Murderer? Scientist?

By 1952, Fritz Lang's efforts to promote the film as an anti-Nazi parable had taken firm hold, and the English dubbed *Crimes of Dr. Mabuse* dutifully opens with narration placing its horrors in 1938, in the full grip of Hitler's reign of terror. The Mexican version of the film became titled *Titans of War*, and was advertised with exciting but misleading images of Luftwaffe bombers strafing cities and guerrilla soldiers sabotaging bridges. From this point onward, the preferred reading of the film held Mabuse as a stand-in for the Führer, a mad criminal bent on destroying the world. *The Testament of Dr. Mabuse* was accepted by film critics the world over as cinema's first anti-Nazi motion picture, a film so politically charged that Lang had to flee Germany. This is the reading actively endorsed by Lang himself, the reading preferred by the author of this book. However, it is not the only possible reading of the Mabuse legend. Dr. Mabuse is like that classic optical illusion, which seen one way depicts a young lady in a fur coat, but viewed another way appears as an older woman. Depending on one's set of assumptions, two different viewers confronting the cinema of Dr. Mabuse can come to radically different conclusions about what it all means. So far this book has presented only one view, but before we proceed any farther it is necessary to step back, and see Mabuse through the eyes of Dr. Joseph Goebbels.

Undoubtedly, the encounter between Fritz Lang and Joseph Goebbels in early 1933 did not happen quite as Lang later portrayed it. Nevertheless, there is no reason to doubt that on at least one occasion they met to discuss the fate of *The Testament of Dr. Mabuse*. Goebbels did indeed ban the film, and so Lang most likely later exaggerated Goebbels' reaction to the film rather than inventing it wholecloth.

"There was nothing wrong with [the

film]," Lang quoted Goebbels to John Russell Taylor, "only it needed a Führer to defeat Dr. Mabuse in the end and save the world order from those who would destroy it by perverting the true ideals."

Taking Lang at his word regarding Goebbels' complaint, we are left with a conundrum. Apparently Goebbels failed to recognize the Mabuse-Hitler symbolism that Lang so proudly trumpeted. Given that Goebbels enjoyed the film greatly and would screen it, uncensored, for himself at such occasions as his own birthday, it would seem highly unlikely that he saw the insane villain Dr. Mabuse as having any connection with his Nazi Führer. What, then, were his reasons for banning the picture?

Goebbels felt that the flaw was the absence of a Führer; he did not equate Mabuse with the Führer. The Nazi Minister of Propaganda saw no link between Mabuse's evil schemes and the program of his own party because, to him, Mabuse was a Jew.

Not just any Jew, but the Eternal Jew. The cause of Germany's (and the world's) troubles. The sinister phantom who works in secret behind the scenes to promote his own agenda at the expense of the ordinary, upstanding, Christian, Aryan citizens.

Goebbels could see this in Mabuse, because whether they intended it or not the creators of the character had played into the ugliest racial politics of the day. Enlightened modern viewers might easily miss the stereotypes at work, but for German audiences at the time there were several aspects of Mabuse's characterization that invoked anti–Semitic imagery. For one thing, as a psychiatrist, Dr. Mabuse was a successor to Freud and his Jewish profession.

In fact, four of the nine Mabuse figures from these 12 films claimed to be psychiatrists (although whether any of them actually held legitimate degrees or maintained practices is a matter for debate). Norbert Jacques does not appear to have held any specific animus towards the profession: Mabuse's evil is in the ends to which he puts his knowledge, not the means by which he acquired it. Moreover, his psychiatric practice is as much another of his many false fronts as it is a core aspect of his personality. Mabuse knows that his doctoral title commands a measure of respect, a peculiar facet of human nature Mabuse exploits to deflect suspicion. Thanks to his respectable standing as a healer, a scientist, an educated man, people like the Count and Countess Told consult him for advice while simultaneously trying to escape or defeat the Great Unknown. His prey deliver themselves into his clutches thanks to that handy little title, Herr Doktor.

For his part, Fritz Lang was fascinated by psychiatry, and made a point of accumulating psychiatrists as acquaintances, such that he could pick their brains for ideas and details with which to pepper his films. Not everyone in that day shared Lang's boyish curiosity. There was considerable fear of this new science, and its claims of insight into the mysteries of the soul which for so long had been the sole province of religious leaders. Psychiatrists dared to explore forbidden territory, to commit blasphemy in the name of science. They were seen as real-life Frankensteins. Who better than a psychiatrist to exploit the fault lines of the human mind, to transgress the boundaries of identity?

The character which could easily be seen as the archetypal template for Dr. Mabuse, Dr. Caligari, or *Metropolis'* Rotwang, was George du Maurier's Svengali, a sinister Jew with hypnotic powers. A film version had been very popular in Germany during World War I, just a few years before the creation of Mabuse. Anti-Semites at the time often accused Jews of practicing magic, or of using science as a

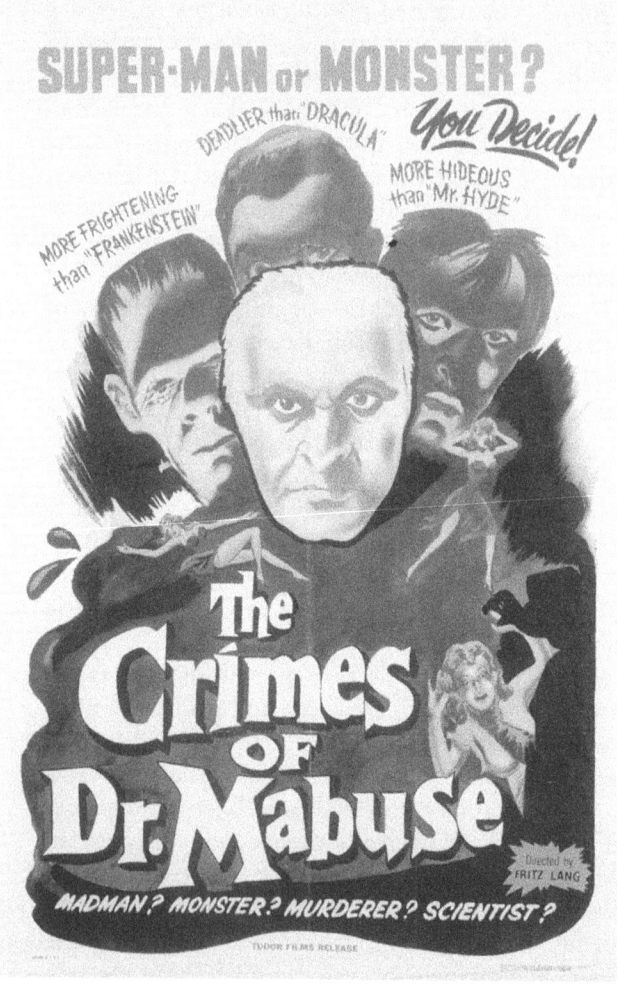

The unholy trio of Frankenstein, Dracula, and Dr. Mabuse adorn this poster to the American version of *Das Testament des Dr. Mabuse*.

form of magic. Mabuse's hypnotic skill and seemingly paranormal powers were traits that in this stereotype would mark him as a diabolical Jew.

Furthermore, one of Mabuse's real-life antecedents was Jewish. Adam Worth was a genuine archcriminal who directed a massive international underworld network from London during the 1870s. For years he orchestrated headline-grabbing thefts that remained unsolved for decades. Scotland Yard dubbed him "The Napoleon of Crime," but he often called himself "Henry Jarvis Raymond," an identity he borrowed from the founder of *The New York Times*. Worth was born in 1844 to a pair of German Jews who had immigrated to Massachusetts. He began his life of crime early, defrauding the Union army of several thousand dollars during the Civil War. After stealing several hundred thousand dollars from the Boyleston Bank in Boston, he fled the American police to relocate his activities to London. There he launched a major counterfeiting ring, stole over a half-million dollars worth of diamonds from South Africa and, in his most celebrated crime, managed to remove Thomas Gainsborough's painting "The Duchess of Devonshire" from the gallery of its owner William Agnew, who had just paid a record sum for the portrait at a Christie's of London auction. Worth briefly served time in a Belgian prison under the pseudonym Edouard Grau, but largely managed to evade capture and punishment for his many crimes. American detective William Pinkerton, who chased Worth for many a decade, declared him "the most remarkable criminal of all." Sir Arthur Conan Doyle was so impressed by Worth's deeds that he modeled his sinister mastermind Prof. Moriarty after him; and in this way, the little American Jew Adam Worth became a forefather for such fictional characters as Fantômas and Dr. Mabuse.

Mabuse's mastery of disguise was seen by racists as still another Jewish trait, since the Nazis believed that Jews disguised themselves as ordinary Germans in order to infiltrate and advance their own racial agenda. Hitler accused Jews of being hidden masterminds, phantoms working in secret to destroy the world. To Hitler and those who agreed with him, the character of Dr. Mabuse was the embodiment of any number of anti–Semitic stereotypes.

In his last will and testament, Hitler still railed against what he saw as the threat of the Eternal Jew, the all-pervasive force corrupting the world. Even in his dying moments, he refused to acknowledge any responsibility for the horrors he had wrought, instead blaming the Holocaust on its victims. In that last will and testament, Hitler dictated his instructions for continuing the battle against the Eternal Jew, his program for the future world of terror. And then he took his own life— although his body was never found, leading to speculation that he had escaped and assumed a new identity in South America, to continue his evil schemes there.

We have of course seen all this before. This is what happened in *The Testament of Dr. Mabuse* in 1932, some 14 years earlier. Goebbels and Hitler and the Nazi ideologues in their thrall looked into the fantasy world of Dr. Mabuse and saw what they wanted to see, a reflection of their hateful philosophy. Of course they saw it— partly because Norbert Jacques and Fritz Lang and Thea von Harbou had unthinkingly perpetuated cruel stereotypes current in their culture, but much more importantly they saw it because the world of Dr. Mabuse was a funhouse mirror reflecting them and everything about them, twisted and distorted but complete all the same. Narrow-minded by hate, people like Goebbels could look into that mirror and focus on a small part of the image, satisfied to see their anti–Semitic prejudices reflected back. But other viewers, standing farther back with the proper perspective, could see the whole image: an image of fascism and totalitarianism, of the apocalypse, of the end of the world.

Seen from the proper perspective, the mirror reflected everything—not just who monsters like Hitler were at the moment, but who they would yet be in the future. The most striking parallels in the Mabuse films predate their real-life analogues. Sure, the Mabuse's last will and testament can be seen as a parody of Hitler's *Mein Kampf*, but how odd indeed that Hitler would 14 years later pen his own last will and testament with the same ambition and approach. How odd that in *Mabuses Kolonie*, Frau Kristina wants to reclaim Germany's lost money for the glory of the Fatherland just as the Nazis would later reclaim Germany's lost land for the glory of the Fatherland. How odd that Mabuse scampers off to South America to establish his new life, where the Nazis would self-exile themselves at the end of the war. How odd that Hitler, like Mabuse, would kill himself before the Forces of Justice could get at him.

Ask anyone engaged in finding eerie parallels between Abraham Lincoln and John F. Kennedy and they will tell you how easily one can find coincidences of this sort when one goes looking for them. But the coincidences between Mabuse and the Nazis belie something deeper, and more disquieting. We find meaning in these weird coincidences because they help to justify something we already suspected, that Mabuse and Hitler are kindred spirits. That Mabuse and Hitler are different manifestations of the same persona.

The history of pop culture is rife with examples of social ills or issues too raw to be discussed openly, but which find expression coded into the "safe" environs of fantasy. No Hollywood filmmaker would dare have made a picture with the Watts rioters as its heroes, but in 1972's *Conquest of the Planet of the Apes* such taboo ideas could be addressed indirectly. Japanese filmmakers found in *Godzilla* an opportunity to revisit the trauma of the atomic bombings of Hiroshima and Nagasaki, and the H-bomb tests in the Bikini Islands, in a fictional context that blunted the taboo. So, when Artur Brauner, a survivor of the Holocaust, found his direct anti–Nazi films like *Morituri* foundering, he used the Mabuse films as a means of translating his anti-fascist sentiments into more acceptable forms. Were this the beginning and the end of the Mabuse-Hitler connection, we would be on familiar ground. What gives the Mabuse series its troubling edge is that the most memorable Mabuse-Hitler connections predate Hitler's rise to power, and thus as a matter of simple chronology prevent any such simple analysis. How then to account for such connections?

By and large, history often gets boiled down to a contest of individual personalities: World War II as a battle between Hitler, Churchill and Roosevelt, for example. The Great Man Theory of History, with its emphasis on individual personalities, lends itself well to this popularization of historical events. Many science fiction writers, subscribing to this interpretation of history, have posed the question: What if you could go back in time and kill Hitler's parents before he was born? The Mabuse films, though, fly in the face of this worldview, and suggest that if one did manage to retreat through time and prevent Hitler's birth, nothing would change.

The Mabuse series is not about character. These 12 films do not involve a recurring set of characters that audiences returned time and again to watch, as with almost any other movie series. Instead, they offer a recurring set of narrative themes, a constant struggle between the pervasive corruption of evil and the ineffective forces of law and order. The hook that keeps the series going is that each film ends with an incomplete, insufficient resolution of the underlying conflict. Mabuse may be held at bay, but he is never defeated. Good wins the battles, Evil wins the war.

There is no Dr. Mabuse, which is another way of saying anyone can be Dr. Mabuse. The films discussed in this book feature a number of villains, many of whom have adopted the name Mabuse but none of whom are related in any direct way to one another. Mabuse is not a man at all, but a deathless spirit of evil that transcends individual personalities. No matter how often any given manifestation of Mabuse is imprisoned or blown up or drowned or dissolved in acid or in some other way disposed of, the evil reappears in some other body. Inspector Lohmann stares out the window at the end of *The Return of Dr. Mabuse* and wonders aloud which of countless seemingly innocent people is the new Dr. Mabuse.

In *The Testament of Dr. Mabuse*, a previous Lohmann has been stumped by the case at hand. All clues point to "Dr. Mabuse" as the cause of Berlin's crime wave, but yet Lohmann knows Mabuse to be dead. One of Mabuse's lackeys, Thomas Kent, has turned himself in seeking police protection from his ex-employer and tries to convince the Inspector that indeed Dr. Mabuse is the culprit. Kent shows Lohmann one of Mabuse's written directives, duly signed "Dr. Mabuse." Lohmann is unimpressed; the note is typewritten, and thus proves nothing. Anyone can have written it.... And in that moment he achieves clarity, but uncovers a terrifying secret. Anyone can be Dr. Mabuse. It answers the riddle, but poses an altogether worse challenge. The essence of police work is to seek out and identify whodunit. If identity is a mutable, inconstant quality, then his job loses its meaning. The strange case of Dr. Mabuse is solved with circular logic: The question is who has committed these crimes, and the answer is Dr. Mabuse. To the question who is Dr.

Mabuse, the answer is the person who committed these crimes. It is the serpent swallowing its own tail, a Moebius strip of identity. What good does it do to pose the question "Who is behind it all?" if the answer changes with time?

Lohmann is on the hunt for a person, but it is not really a person he seeks. Instead he seeks the force of evil that drives people to act on its will. Yet that force cannot be captured, because it cannot be fixed in space. Kent thinks he has it cornered behind a curtain, but there is no one there. Lohmann thinks he has it on the run, but all he ends up with is a broken shell of a man who imprisons himself in his own asylum. The force of evil escapes, to continue its ill will in future episodes. There will always be others to take on the name "Mabuse."

When Norbert Jacques, Fritz Lang and Thea von Harbou first invented Dr. Mabuse in the early 1920s, they had no crystal ball to see into the future. Hitler was still a local problem for the citizens of Bavaria, and the idea that he would eventually take over much of Europe would have been laughable to many people. What enabled these three people to so accurately forecast the rise of Nazi Germany had nothing to do with any specific analysis of Hitler himself, but rather with their concern with the more general social ills of Weimar Germany. They attempted to honestly depict their world, and since their world actually was careening towards fascism, their depiction is of a world careening towards fascism. It is a troubling realization, that such paranoid misanthropes like Fritz Lang would be right after all, that the world really was a corrupt and diseased place. The world of Dr. Mabuse was a set of circumstances ripe for the arrival of a tyrant. If not Hitler, then someone else—*anyone* else—could have exploited the same set of circumstances to similar effect.

The Mabuse series rails loudly and forcibly against the Great Man Theory of History. These films insist that if Hitler had not been there, someone else would have. Mabuse can leave behind his testament as a detailed set of instructions because he knows someone will pick up where he left off—Dr. Baum, and if not Dr. Baum then Dr. Jordan, and if not Dr. Jordan then Dr. Pohland, and if not Dr. Pohland then.... These films warn us not to be complacent, not to think that we have triumphed over the forces of evil. Mabuse is still out there because there is no Dr. Mabuse because anyone can be Dr. Mabuse.

If the price of freedom is vigilance, then the price of vigilance is insanity. The law enforcement heroes like von Wenk and Lohmann and Hartmann emerge from their experiences with battle scars. They can never again rejoin the company of the innocent, those who foolishly believe that the world makes sense. Those who have fought Mabuse come away forever frightened of their own shadows, always seeking the phantom conspiracy, unable to sleep at night without worrying where or when the hand of Mabuse will reveal itself next. These few, though, are our only line defense against Mabuse.

This, then, is the message of the series. It is a warning, shouted by a paranoid little wretch on a street corner with a sign saying "The End is Nigh." He stops you as you try to pass by, and he starts ranting. He tells you about a man who isn't there. Propaganda called him the man without a shadow, but that is all he *is*, shadow. Pull away the curtain and there's nothing there. His name is Mabuse, the man rants on. I know, he says, because there is no Mabuse—I checked. I shot him once, but it was just a wooden prop. A dummy. I saw him dead, toe tag and everything, dissected, his brain in a jar. But he's still out there. He'll get you, too. He's controlling everything. The stock market, traffic accidents, suicides. It's mind control, you see, and he makes his own people from scratch. He's out there, you've got to listen to me, he's still out there—

You walk away. It's all nonsense, you tell yourself, just a lunatic's ravings and nothing more. There were evil men, once, with names like Hitler and Goebbels and Himmler and Honecker, but they're all dead now. We fought them and killed them and that's all in the past.

Isn't it?

The cinema of Dr. Mabuse indulges the belief that the game of life has been rigged by secret and powerful cabals. And it must be said that one need not be a paranoid crank to agree that, in many ways, the game is rigged—if not by real-life Mabusian conspiracies, then by the forces of selfishness and corruption for which Mabuse is a metaphor.

The directors of these films—outcasts, mavericks, pioneers, misanthropes and misfits, visionaries and hacks—return time and again to the character of Dr. Mabuse in order to illustrate the essential and universal corruption of the world. They take us to the precipice and warn, *This is the future. The coming apocalypse may not kill you, but there is no escaping it. There is nothing the authorities can do to stop it. The best you can hope for is that before we all plunge over the cliff, we may find an answer to the question, "Why is this happening?"*

From the viewpoint of these films, evil is such a pervasive and nearly omnipotent force that the countervailing forces of law and order are ineffective, even incompetent. In Norbert Jacques' original novel, von Wenk only slowly, agonizingly slowly, comes to the harrowing realization that he has delivered himself into Mabuse's hands and been the fiend's prisoner now, unwittingly, for quite some time. If not for the timely intervention of the Countess Told—the damsel in distress who von Wenk was supposed to be rescuing—von Wenk would have been killed.

Von Wenk's successor, Inspector Lohmann, finally manages to figure out how asylum director Baum has assumed Mabuse's identity and perpetuated his criminal organization, but he fails to capture the man. Instead, Baum goes out of his own mind and locks himself in a cell in his own institution.

In *Scream and Scream Again*, neither Dr. Sorel nor Inspector Bellaver ever learns the whole truth behind the bizarre plot to take over the world with artificial humans. Sorel learns some of the facts behind Browning's operation, but is unconscious during the final confrontation between Browning and his colleagues Konratz and Fremont. For his part, Bellaver is killed without ever receiving any satisfactory explanation.

With little of use coming from the cops, the only way evil can be vanquished is if it vanquishes itself: The Mabuse Principle. Dr. Browning dips himself into his own acid tank; Dr. Marsfeldt yanks out his own life support; Dr. Jordan drives his car into the river; Doctors Mabuse and Baum and Pohland go mad before being arrested; Georg hangs himself in his cell; Mortimer blows his own brains out; Haghi ends his own life.

The work of Fritz Lang is rife with self-destruction and suicide. Biographers have speculated that the circumstances of his own personal life, such as the mysterious fate of his first wife, are the driving forces behind such themes. There is more to it than that, though, more to his cinema than simply the ruminations of his own guilty conscience. There it is in his fixation on the character of Debby in *The Big Heat*, there it is in his controversy with Bertolt Brecht over *Hangmen Also Die!*, there it is in the project that almost wooed him away from Hollywood and into Artur Brauner's stable: *Der 20 Juli*.

Der 20 Juli represented something deeply resonant to Lang. He had once called for Germany to be razed by nuclear bombs, to wipe away all trace of the Nazi mentality and start anew. But the story behind *Der 20 Juli* was the shining ray of hope that forbore the need for a nuclear Noah's flood: During the height of Hitler's reign of terror, members of his own inner circle attempted to assassinate him. Although unsuccessful, the mere attempt proved that totalitarianism is never truly total.

Lang was a pessimist, and a misanthrope. To him, the People was just a nice way of saying the Mob. In films like *Metropolis* and *Fury*, he showed the ugly antics of mob behavior, masses of people who act together and surrender their humanity. It was this deep, abiding distrust of the people that prevented Lang and Brecht from seeing eye-to-eye on *Hangmen Also Die!* Brecht's idealization of the people and his Communist faith in their ultimate political triumph was irreconcilable with Lang's contempt. As far as Lang was concerned, democracy was a dead letter concept from the outset, inherently doomed by its reliance on the masses.

However, since absolute power corrupts, Lang was also opposed to tyranny, as can be seen in his Mabuse films, *Hangmen Also Die!*, *Cloak and Dagger* and other works. If democratic institutions were fundamentally incapable of combating fascism, though, Lang found hope in one alternative solution—defection. Evil, for all its strengths, could never hope to control everyone at all times. In the case of *Hangmen Also Die!*, there would remain within a fascist state some irreducible quantity of resistance. As *Der 20 Juli* showed, even Hitler's own generals might turn against him. In *The Big Heat*, Debby, a gangster's moll long ignored, much abused and greatly underrated, might one day take gun in hand and bring the entire world crashing down around the crooks. In *Spies*, Agent Sonia goes from being Haghi's most valued ally to his most dangerous enemy.

This idea recurs in each of Lang's Mabuse pictures. In *Dr. Mabuse the Gambler*, the master criminal is worried that Cara Carozza will rat him out to von Wenk, and so has her eliminated, but she is in fact the least of his worries. As the stakes rise, he will find that others in his ranks, like the coke-addicted Spoerri or the cowardly Pesch, are not as loyal as he hopes. In *The Testament of Dr. Mabuse*, Thomas Kent defects from his gang and hands Inspector Lohmann all the evidence he needs to solve the case. In *The 1000 Eyes of Dr. Mabuse*, Mabuse has arrogantly assumed that he can control Marion Menil's every emotion. Too late, he learns that she has escaped his influence and revealed the entire plot to its intended victim, Henry Travers.

Not everyone is susceptible to Mabuse's mind control. To varying degrees, characters like von Wenk, Volpius and Joe Como all reveal themselves to be resistant. The bloodthirsty human composite Keith, mute henchman Andros and Dr. M's adoptive daughter Sonja Vogler all defy the roles their masters have prescribed for them; they all reveal individuality at precisely the moment that Mabuse's plans assume total conformity from his subjects. Evil may be omnipresent, even omniscient, but it is not in the end omnipotent. And defiance, even in small doses, is a disruptive element of unpredictability that can derail the villain's dastardly schemes.

After World War II ended, the so-called de–Nazification of Germany had to confront the vast numbers of people like Thea von Harbou and Gert Fröbe, people who had gone along with the program, been good little Nazis, but insisted they had nothing to do with what Nazism stood for. Hordes of soldiers argued in

Something is wrong here: This cast and this director worked together only on *Testament of Dr. Mabuse*, yet this Mexican poster certainly does not suggest that film—even as it cites their names.

their own defense that they had simply followed orders, did what they had to protect their lives and their families, and that the real culpability belonged to the ideologues who gave the orders. Short of letting Fritz Lang loose with an A-bomb, there was no choice but to accept this reasoning simply in order to move onward and let Germany rebuild itself. But there had been those who had resisted, who did not follow orders, who did not go along with the program. Like the unlucky conspirators of *Der 20 Juli*, they generally paid for dissension with their lives. But neither were these conspirators martyrs to the cause of truth and justice—they were Nazi generals, high-ranking officers in a totalitarian state committing some of the gravest crimes against humanity ever recorded by history. Their misfired conspiracy against Hitler was an act of redemption by the damned; such too are the acts of Debby, Marion, Sonia, Sonja and the other defectors of the Mabusian genre. These are tainted heroines (heroes among them, too, but mostly women). Satan is a fallen angel who rejects God to try to destroy Creation; Mabuse's defectors are fallen devils who reject the Great Unknown to try to destroy Hell.

That defiance should be so highly prized, such a cherished rarity in a world doomed by its sheepish obedience to the madman's master plan, speaks to the essential Germanness of this particular myth. As Reverend Briefenstein notes in

The Return of Dr. Mabuse, Mabuse is a myth, a modern myth created in Germany in the twentieth century to articulate twentieth century German fears. Mabuse never achieved the pop culture penetration in the U.S. that he did in Germany because American fears have largely been different. Our country never threatened to slip into fascism. During the century, we experienced a few severe economic disruptions, most powerfully during the 1930s, but our democratic institutions were strong enough to weather them. Only briefly, in 1973, when all three of Lang's Mabuse pictures were reissued to great critical acclaim, was the U.S. properly primed to understand: in the aftermath of Kent State and Vietnam and Watergate, Lang's metaphor started to make sense.

Moreover, much of Mabuse's terror in German culture stems from his shifting of identity, be it by disguise, assumed name or supernatural leaps of spirit from body to body. American culture prides itself on classlessness, on the ease with which one can move up the social strata. Ours is a so-called melting pot of cultures from around the globe, where diversity is an asset and nothing is ever entirely foreign. With the (arguable) exception of Native American tribes, all Americans are immigrants. Conversely, Germany is a place where you must seek governmental approval of the name you give your child, and laws govern when you may wash your clothes or mow your lawn. Conformity is such a ubiquitous goal of German society, even minor deviations from the norm are considered significant. When the Berlin Wall was dismantled and plans moved forward to reunite East and West Germany, many feared that such a reunification was impossible given the cultural differences between the two halves. Mind you, these two halves spoke the same language and had been divided for only a few decades, yet it was seriously debated that this short-lived political separation had created an insurmountable cultural divergence.

It was within this mentality that a man with no name and no fixed appearance began moving effortlessly between the class divisions, stealing from the rich to give to himself. He exposed all that was ugly and loathsome about his society, and proved himself virtually indomitable while the institutions of public safety and order collapsed before him. He survived while the government imploded; he survived and grew stronger because he understood an essential fact of human nature: People are cattle.

It was a nightmare, made all the more potent by the nightmare of history it reflected and anticipated. Germany has made some of the finest nightmare cinema the world has ever seen, and while the nightmare cinema of Dr. Mabuse has not yet earned its due in the American marketplace, there is yet time. Now at the turn of the millennium, paranoia is in vogue. The world is still a chaotic, dangerous place. Humankind has cooked up a myriad ways to do ourselves in. From nuclear holocaust to global warming to biological catastrophe to overpopulation to mass extinction, the twentieth century has been marked by a pathological compulsion towards self-destruction. What better metaphor for the history of the twentieth century than Dr. Mabuse?

As the century closes, there is one simple sentence that sums it all up, that encapsulates the catalogue of horrors wrought by humanity on itself in just two simple words:

Je m'abuse.

Bibliography

Allain, Marcel, and Pierre Souvestre, *Fantômas*, William and Morrow, New York, 1986.

Ambrose, Stephen E., *Citizen Soldiers*, Touchstone Books, New York, 1997.

Ashbery, John, "Introduction," *Fantômas*, William and Morrow, New York, 1986.

Bergan, Ronald, *Eisenstein: A Life in Conflict*, Little, Brown, New York, 1998.

Blanchet, Christian, *Claude Chabrol*, Rivages, Paris, 1989.

Bogdanovich, Peter, *Who the Devil Made It: Conversations with Legendary Film Directors*, Ballantine Books, New York, 1997.

Bronfen, Elisabeth, "Die tödliche Schrift des Dr. Mabuse," edited by Günter Scholdt, *Das Testament des Dr. Mabuse*, Rogner & Bernhard GmbH, Hamburg, Germany, 1994.

Burch, Noel, *In and Out of Synch: The Awakening of a Cine-Dreamer*, Scholar Press, Aldershot, England, 1991.

Cambi, Leslie, "The Films of Ulrike Ottinger," *The Village Voice*, January 27, 1999.

Chabrol, Claude, "The Evolution of the Crime Film," *Film Noir Reader 2*, edited by Alain Silver and James Ursini, Limelight Editions, New York, 1999.

Chatten, Richard, "Howard Vernon: Obituary," *The Independent*, September 5, 1996.

Crary, Jonathan, "Dr. Mabuse and Mr. Edison," *Art and Film Since 1945: Hall of Mirrors*, The Museum of Contemporary Art, Los Angeles, 1996.

"The Crooked Hypnotist," *New York Times*, August 9, 1927.

Crowther, Bosley, "*The Last Will of Dr. Mabuse*," *New York Times*, March 20, 1943.

Daniel, Dennis, "Jesus Franco," *Psychotronic Video* Issue 28 (Psychotronic Video, Narrowsburg, NY, 1999).

de Mendoza, Javier Gonzalez and Javiera Figueroa, "Expressionist by Vocation: an Interview with Jesus Franco," *Filmfax* Issue 67 (Filmfax, Inc., Evanston, IL, 1998).

Dillman-Kühn, Claudia, *Artur Brauner und die CCC*, Deutsches Filmmuseum, Frankfurt am Main, Germany, 1990.

Dixon, Wheeler Winston, "The Colonial Vision of Edgar Wallace," *Journal of Popular Culture* Volume 32 Issue 1 (UMI Company, England, 1998).

"*Dr. M/Club Extinction*," *Variety*, February 18, 1991.

Dolgenos, Peter, "The star on C.A. Rotwang's door: Turning Kracauer on its head," *Journal of Popular Film and Television* Volume 25 Issue 2 (Helen Dwight Reid Educational Foundation, New York, 1997).

"*Dorian Gray Im Spiegel der Boulevardpresse*," *Variety*, March 28, 1984.

Eisner, Lotte, *Fritz Lang*, Da Capo Press, New York, 1976.

Elsaesser, Thomas, "Fritz Lang: The Illusion of Masters," *Sight and Sound* Volume 10 Issue 1 (British Film Institute, London, 2000).

Everson, William K., *Classics of the Horror Film*, Citadel Press, Secaucus, NJ, 1974.

Farin, Michael, "Tsi Nan Fu, oder die auslöschung des Augenblicks," edited by Günter Scholdt, *Das Testament des Dr. Mabuse*, Rogner & Bernhard GmbH, Hamburg, Germany, 1994.

Ferber, Lawrence, "Think Globally: Ulrike Ottinger brings cultures together on film," *New York Blade*, January 29, 1999.

Fischer, Klaus P., *Nazi Germany: A New History*, Continuum, New York, 1995.

Fleming, Ian, *Thunderball*, Viking Press, New York, 1961.

Gablik, Suzi, *Magritte*, Thames and Hudson, New York, 1985.

Garnham, Nicholas, English translation and description of *M: A Film by Fritz Lang*, Classic Film Scripts, Simon and Schuster, New York, 1968.

Gordon, Richard, letter to the editor, *Midnight Marquee* Issue 60 (Midnight Marquee Press, Baltimore, MD, 1999).

Göttler, Fritz, "Eine Mona Lisa des Verbrechens," edited by Günter Scholdt, *Das Testament des Dr. Mabuse*, Rogner & Bernhard GmbH, Hamburg, Germany, 1994.

Greenspun, Roger, "*The 1000 Eyes of Dr. Mabuse*," *Film Comment* Volume 9 Issue 2 (Film Comment Publishing Corp., Boston, MA 1973).

Grundman, Roy, and Judith Shulevitz, "Minorities and the Majority: An Interview with Ulrike Ottinger," *Cineaste* Volume 18 Issue 3 (1991).

Hallenbeck, Bruce G., "*Taste the Blood of Dracula*: The making of an underrated shocker," *Little Shoppe of Horrors* Issue 13 (Elmer Valo Appreciation Society, Des Moines, IA, 1996).

Haller, Robert, ed., *Fritz Lang 2000*, Anthology Film Archives, New York, 2000.

Hoare, Philip, *Oscar Wilde's Last Stand*, Arcade, New York, 1998.

Jacobowitz, Florence, and Richard Lippe, "French New Wave 40th Anniversary," *CineAction* Issue 48 (CineAction Collective, Canada, 1998).

Jacques, Norbert, "Dr. Mabuse," *Dr. Mabuse, der Spieler*, Rogner & Bernhard GmbH, Hamburg, Germany, 1994.

Jacques, Norbert, "Dr. Mabuse, I Presume," *Dr. Mabuse, der Spieler*, Rogner & Bernhard GmbH, Hamburg, Germany, 1994.

Jacques, Norbert, "Wenn man sein Werk im Film sieht," *Dr. Mabuse, der Spieler*, Rogner & Bernhard GmbH, Hamburg, Germany, 1994.

James, Caryn, "This Time Around the Mongol Hordes Are Women," *New York Times*, May 15, 1992.

Jensen, Paul M., *The Cinema of Fritz Lang*, A.S. Barnes, New York, 1969.

Kaplan, E. Ann, "Fritz Lang and German Expressionism: A Reading of *Dr. Mabuse der Spieler*," *Passion and Rebellion: The Expressionist Heritage*, J.F. Bergin Publishers, South Hadley, MA, 1983.

Katz, Ephraim, *The Film Encyclopedia*, Thomas Y. Crowell, New York, 1979.

Kirkup, James, "To prove a villain, Obituary: Howard Vernon," *The Guardian*, August 8, 1996.

Koetting, Christopher, "AIP's Third Man: Part Two: The Other Guy, Deke Heyward," *Filmfax* Issue 62 (Filmfax, Evanston, IL, 1997).

Koetting, Christopher, "The Golden Voyage of Gordon Hessler," *Filmfax* Issue 62 (Filmfax, Evanston, Illinois, 1997).

"Korrespondenz: Jacques-Harbou-Lang (12.6. 1930—8.9.1959)," edited by Günter Scholdt, *Das Testament des Dr. Mabuse*, Rogner & Bernhard GmbH, Hamburg, Germany, 1994.

Kracauer, Siegfried, *From Caligari to Hitler: A Psychological History of the German Film*, Princeton University Press, Princeton, NJ, 1947.

Lapointe, Julien, "Pre '59 New Wave," *CineAction* Issue 48 (CineAction Collective, Canada, 1998).

McArthur, Colin, *BFI Classics: The Big Heat*, British Film Institute, London, 1992.

McGilligan, Patrick, *Fritz Lang: The Nature of the Beast*, St. Martin's Press, New York, NY 1997.

Marcus, Greil, *Lipstick Traces: A Secret History of the Twentieth Century*, Harvard University Press, Cambridge, MA, 1990.

Mars-Jones, Adam, "Russian hide and seek," *The Daily Telegraph*, January 10, 1998.

Monaco, James, *The New Wave*, Oxford University Press, New York, 1976.

O'Dalby, Albert, "Finally... The *Flesh* Hits the Fan," *Draculina* Issue 30 (Draculina Publishing, Glen Carbon, IL, 1997).

Ottinger, Ulrike, "The Pressure to Make Genre Films: About the Endangered *Autorenkino*," *West German Filmmakers on Film: Visions and Voices*, Holmes & Meier, New York, 1988.

Parla, Paul, and Donna Parla, "Newfound Faith: Rediscovering the Reclusive Faith Domergue," *Filmfax* Issue 59 (Filmfax, Evanston, IL, 1997).

Pierce, Laura, "The World According to Ulrike Ottinger," *Gay Community News*, January 21, 1991.

Read, Piers Paul, *The Train Robbers*, J.B. Lippincott, New York, 1978.

"Reinl, Harald," *Cinegraph: Lexicon zum deutschsprachigen Film*, Hamburg.

Riefenstahl, Leni, *Leni Riefenstahl: A Memoir*, Picador Press, New York, 1995.

Robinson, David, *BFI Classics: Das Cabinet des Dr. Caligari*, British Film Institute, London, 1997.

Rohmer, Eric, and Claude Chabrol, *Hitchcock: The First Forty-Five Films*, Frederick Ungar Publishing, New York, 1979.

Sarris, Andrew, *Interviews with Film Directors*, Howard M. Sans, New York, 1967.

Sayre, Nora, "Film Festival: Lang's *Doktor Mabuse*," *New York Times*, October 15, 1973.

Sayre, Nora, "Lang's *Testament of Dr. Mabuse* at Cultural Center Tomorrow, *New York Times*, December 6, 1973.

Schmid, Hans, "Herrschaft des Verbrechens," edited by Günter Scholdt, *Das Testament des Dr. Mabuse*, Rogner & Bernhard GmbH, Hamburg, Germany, 1994.

Schmid, Hans, "Mabuses Kino: Kino als Sabotage," edited by Günter Scholdt, *Das Testament des Dr. Mabuse*, Rogner & Bernhard GmbH, Hamburg, Germany, 1994.

Scholdt, Günter, "Dr. Mabuse der Spieler: Eine Bestandsaufnahme,", *Dr. Mabuse: Roman Film Dokumente*, Werner J. Röhrig Verlag, St. Ingbert, Germany, 1987.

Scholdt, Günter, "Fritz Lang: Aus, Tableau (1924–1968)," *Das Testament des Dr. Mabuse*, Rogner & Bernhard GmbH, Hamburg, Germany, 1994.

Scholdt, Günter, "Mabuse, ein deutscher Mythos," *Dr. Mabuse, der Spieler*, Rogner & Bernhard GmbH, Hamburg, Germany, 1994.

Scholdt, Günter, "Norbert Jacques—der Autor des Mabuse,"*Mabuses Kolonie*, Rogner & Bernhard GmbH, Hamburg, Germany, 1994.

Scholdt, Günter, "Das Phänomen Mabuse (1962)," *Das Testament des Dr. Mabuse*, Rogner & Bernhard GmbH, Hamburg, Germany, 1994.

Scuerman, Matthew L., "The East German Film Library Survives," *German Life*, September 30, 1998.

Senn, Bryan, *Golden Horrors: An Illustrated Critical Filmography 1931–1939*, McFarland, Jefferson, NC, 1996.

Senn, Bryan, "Witchfinder General," *Vincent Price*, edited by Gary J. Svehla and Susan Svehla, Midnight Marquee Press, Baltimore, Maryland, 1998.

Sherman, Betsy, "Retrospective for German Director," *The Boston Globe*, January 21, 1991.

Shirer, William L., *The Rise and Fall of the Third Reich*, Touchstone, New York, updated 1990.

Smith, David H., "Scream and Scream Again," *Vincent Price*, edited by Gary J. Svehla and Susan Svehla, Midnight Marquee Press, Baltimore, Maryland, 1998.

Sorel, Nancy Caldwell, "When Fritz Lang met Joseph Goebbels," *The Independent*, May 25, 1996.

Stevens, Dana, "Writing, Scratching, and Politics," *Qui Parle*, University of California at Berkeley, Fall/Winter 1993.

Sturm, Georges, "Mabuse: Ein Bild der Zeit, Ein Spiel mit dem Bild," edited by Günter Scholdt, *Das Testament des Dr. Mabuse*, Rogner & Bernhard GmbH, Hamburg, Germany, 1994.

Taylor, Ella, "Kulturkampf: West meets East in the Films of Ulrike Ottinger," *LA Weekly*, November 3, 1989.

Taylor, John Russell, "The Nine Lives of Dr. Mabuse," *Sight and Sound* Volume 31 Issue 1 (British Film Institute, London, 1961).

Thomas, Kevin, "Ottinger's *Dorian Gray* a Surreal Adventure," *Los Angeles Times*, November 14, 1990.

Tohill, Cathall, and Pete Tombs, *Immoral Tales: European Sex and Horror Movies 1956–1984*, St. Martin's Griffin, New York, NY, 1995.

Vaucher, Andrea R., "Madame Bovary, C'est Moi!" *American Film* Volume 16 Issue 9 (BPI Communications, New York, 1991).

Weber, Otto, "Matejkos Mabuse," edited by Günter Scholdt, *Dr. Mabuse, der Spieler*, Rogner & Bernhard GmbH, Hamburg, Germany, 1994.

Weldon, Michael, *The Psychotronic Encyclopedia of Film*, Ballantine Books, NY, 1983.

Werner, Gösta, "Fritz Lang and Goebbels: Myth and Facts," *Film Quarterly* Spring Issue (University of California, Berkeley, CA, 1990).

Wood, Robin, and Michael Walker, *Claude Chabrol*, Praeger, New York, 1970.

Zacks, Richard, *An Underground Education*, Anchor Books, New York, 1997.

"Zeitgenössische Stimmen zum Film (mit Zeichnungen von Theo Matejko)," edited by Günter Scholdt, *Dr. Mabuse, der Spieler*, Rogner & Bernhard GmbH, Hamburg, Germany, 1994.

The Books

Jacques, Norbert, "Chemiker Null," *Mabuses Kolonie*, Rogner & Bernhard GmbH, Hamburg, Germany, 1994.

Jacques, Norbert, "Dr. Mabuse auf dem Presseball," *Mabuses Kolonie*, Rogner & Bernhard GmbH, Hamburg, Germany, 1994.

Jacques, Norbert, *Dr. Mabuse, der Spieler*, Rogner & Bernhard GmbH, Hamburg, Germany, 1994.

Jacques, Norbert, *Dr. Mabuse, Master of Mystery*, authorized translation by Lilian A. Clare, George Allen & Unwin Ltd., London, 1923.

Jacques, Norbert, "Ingenieur Mars," *Mabuses Kolonie*, Rogner & Bernhard GmbH, Hamburg, Germany, 1994.

Jacques, Norbert, *Mabuses Kolonie, oder N.J. sucht Kristina*, Rogner & Bernhard GmbH, Hamburg, Germany, 1994.

Jacques, Norbert, *Das Testament des Dr. Mabuse*, Rogner & Bernhard GmbH, Hamburg, Germany, 1994.

Jacques, Norbert, *Das Testament des Dr. Mabuse*, Virgilio Iafrate Verlag, München, Germany, 1986.

McGivern, William, *The Big Heat*, Dodd Mead, New York, 1953.

Wallace, Bryan Edgar, *The Device*, Hoddler & Stoughton, Suffolk, England, 1962.

Wilde, Oscar, *The Picture of Dorian Gray*, Barnes & Noble, New York, 1995.

Internet Sources

http://mars.acnet.wnec.edu/~grempel/courses/germany/lectures.html (History of Modern Germany Lectures by Prof. Gerhard Rempel of Western New England College)

http://www.fantomas-lives.com (Fantômas Lives)

http://www.german-way.com/cinema/rief.html (Leni Riefenstahl Bio)

http:///www.imdb.com (The Internet Movie Database)

Motion Picture Presskits

The Image of Dorian Gray in the Yellow Press, Women Make Movies (US).

Invisible Horror and *The Terror of the Mad Doctor* (1962), Ajay Films (US).

Scotland Yard yagt Dr. Mabuse, CCC Films (Germany).

Im Stahlnetz des Dr. Mabuse CCC Films (Germany).

Die Tausend Augen des Dr. Mabuse CCC Films (Germany).

Das Testament des Dr. Mabuse Nero Films (Germany).

The 1000 Eyes of Dr. Mabuse and *The Return of Dr. Mabuse* Ajay Films (US).

Die Todesstrahlen des Dr. Mabuse CCC Films (Germany).

Die Unsichtbaren Krallen des Dr. Mabuse CCC Films (Germany).

Interviews by Author

Ackerman, Forrest J. Conducted January 13, 2000.

Franco, Jesus Manera. Conducted April 27, 1999.

Fregonese, Dorothy. Conducted February 3, 2000.

Gordon, Richard. Conducted March 18, 2000.

Hessler, Gordon. Conducted February 16, 1999.

Mandelik, Gilbert. Conducted January 13, 2000.

Schnauber, Cornelius. Conducted January 14, 2000.

Thomas, Kevin. Conducted January 14, 2000.

Other Interviews

Brauner, Artur. Conducted by Jorge Dana and Hubert Niogret for the documentary *Fritz Lang: The Circle of Destiny*, 1998.

Filmography

Dr. Mabuse, the Gambler, Parts 1 and 2

Credits: Alternate Titles: *Dr. Mabuse, der Spieler: Der große Spieler—Ein Bild der Zeit* (Part 1), *Dr. Mabuse, der Spieler: Inferno—Ein Spiel von Menschen unserer Zeit* (Part 2), *Dr. Mabuse the Gambler: The Great Gambler* (Part 1), *Dr. Mabuse the Gambler: King of Crime* (Part 2), *The Fatal Passions of Dr. Mabuse* (U.S. edited version); Director: Fritz Lang; Producer: Erich Pommer; Screenplay: Fritz Lang and Thea Von Harbou, from the story by Norbert Jaques; Director of Photography: Carl Hoffman; Art Direction: Otto Hunte and Stahl-Urach; Produced by Uco-Film for Decla-Bioscop AG; B&W; length 10 reels: 11,470 feet for Part 1, 8310 feet for Part 2, approximately 4.5 hours depending on projection speed. Premiered in Berlin on April 27, 1922 (Part 1) and May 26, 1922 (Part 2).

Cast: Rudolf Klein-Rogge (Dr. Mabuse), Bernhard Goetzke (Inspector Von Wenk), Aud Egede Nissen (Cara Carozza), Gertrude Welcker (Countess Tolst), Alfred Abel (Count Tolst), Paul Richter (Edgar Hull), Robert Forster-Larrinaga (Spoerri), Hans Adalbert Sclettow (Georg), Georg John (Pesch), Karl Huszar (Hawasch), Grete Berger (Fine), Julius Falkenstein (Karsten), Lydia Potechina (The Russian), Julius Hermann (Emil Schramm)

The Testament of Dr. Mabuse

Credits: Alternate Titles: *Das Testament des Dr. Mabuse*, *The Crimes of Dr. Mabuse* (U.S. edited version), *The Last Will of Dr. Mabuse*; Director: Fritz Lang; Producer: Seymour Nebenzal; Screenplay: Fritz Lang and Thea Von Harbou; Director of Photography: Fritz Arno Wagner; Art Direction: Karl Vollbrecht and Emil Hassler; Music: Hans Erdman; Produced by Nero-Film; B&W; length 122 minutes (*Crimes of Dr. Mabuse*: 76 minutes). Premiered in Budapest in April 1933.

Cast: Rudolf Klein-Rogge (Dr. Mabuse), Otto Wernicke (Inspector Lohmann), Oscar Beregi, Sr. (Dr. Baum), Gustav Diessel (Thomas Kent), Wera Liessen (Lily), Karl Meixner (Hofmeister), A.E. Licho (Dr. Hauser), Theo Lingen (Karetzky), Klaus Pohl (Mueller), Theodor Loos (Dr. Kramm), Camilla Spira (Anna), Rudolph Schündler (Hardy), Oskar Höcker (Bredow), Georg Jahn (Baum's assistant)

Le Testament du Dr. Mabuse

Credits: Alternate Title: *The Last Will of Dr. Mabuse*; Director: Fritz Lang; Producer: Seymour Nebenzal; French language screenplay adapted by René Sti from the script by Fritz Lang and Thea Von Harbou; Director of Photography: Fritz Arno Wagner; Assistant Director: Saul C. Colin; Art Direction: Karl Vollbrecht and Emil Hassler; Music: Hans Erdman; Produced by Nero-Film; B&W; length 95 minutes. Premiered in Paris in April 1933.

Cast: Rudolf Klein-Rogge (Dr. Mabuse), Jim Gèrald (Inspector Lohmann), Thomy Bourdelle (Dr. Baum), Maurice Maillot (Thomas Kent), Monique Rolland (Lily), Karl Meixner (Hofmeister), Ginette Gaubert (Anna), René Ferté (Hardy), Raymond Cordy (Karetzky), Daniel Mendaille (Bredow)

The 1000 Eyes of Dr. Mabuse

Credits: Alternate Titles: *Die Tausend Augen des Dr. Mabuse*, *The Diabolical Dr. Mabuse*, *Eyes of Evil*, *The Shadow vs. the 1000 Eyes*

of Dr. Mabuse; Director: Fritz Lang; Producer: Artur Brauner; Executive Producer: Alfred Bittins; Screenplay: Fritz Lang, Heinz Oskar Wuttig and Jan Fethge; Director of Photography: Karl Loeb; Art Direction: Erich Kettelhut and Johannes Ott; Music: Gerhard Becker and Bert Grund; Produced by CCC Filmkunst; B&W; length 105 minutes. Premiered in Stuttgart on September 14, 1960.

Cast: Wolfgang Preiss (Dr. Mabuse), Gert Fröbe (Inspector Kras), Peter Van Eyck (Henry Travers), Dawn Addams (Marion Menil), Werner Peters (Heironymous B. Mistelzweig), Reinhard Kolldehoff (The Clubfoot), Howard Vernon (Number 12), Nico Pepe (Hotel Manager), Andrea Checci (Hotel Detective Berg), Reinhold Koldehoff (Roberto), David Camerone (Parker), Wolfgang Völz (Bartender), Marieluise Nagel ("The Blond Luck"), Werner Buttler (Number 11), Linda Sini (Corinna), Christiane Maybach (Blonde)

The Return of Dr. Mabuse

Credits: Alternate Titles: *Im Stahlnetz des Dr. Mabuse, FBI vs. Dr. Mabuse, The Phantom Fiend, The Phantom vs. The Return of Dr. Mabuse*; Director: Harald Reinl; Producer: Artur Brauner; Executive Producer: Wolf Brauner; Screenplay: Ladislas Fodor; Director of Photography: Karl Loeb; Art Direction: Otto Erdmann and Hans Juergen Kiebach; Music: Peter Sandloff; Produced by CCC Films with SPA Cinematografica and Criterion Productions; B&W; length 89 minutes. Premiered in Munich on October 13, 1961.

Cast: Wolfgang Preiss (Dr. Mabuse), Gert Fröbe (Inspector Lohmann), Lex Barker (Joe Como), Daliah Lavi (Maria Sabrehm), Fausto Tozzi (Warden Wolff), Werner Peters (Bömmler), Rudolf Forster (Dr. Julius Sabrehm), Rudolf Fernau (Reverend Briefenstein), Ady Berber (Alberto Sandro), Joachim Mock (Voss)

The Invisible Dr. Mabuse

Credits: Alternate Titles: *Die Unsichtbaren Krallen des Dr. Mabuse, The Invisible Horror*; Director: Harald Reinl; Producer: Artur Brauner; Executive Producer: Wolf Brauner; Screenplay: Ladislas Fodor; Director of Photography: Ernst W. Kalinke; Art Direction: Gabriel Pellon and Oskar Pietsch; Music: Peter Sandloff; Produced by CCC Films; B&W; length 86 minutes. Premiered in Hannover on March 30, 1962.

Cast: Wolfgang Preiss (Dr. Mabuse/Primarius Krone), Lex Barker (Joe Como), Karin Dor (Liane Martin), Siegfried Lowitz (Commissioner Brahm), Rudolf Fernau (Prof. Erasmus), Werner Peters (Bobo the Clown/Martin Droste), Kurt Pieritz (Dr. Bordoff), Walo Lüönd (Hase), Heinrich Gies (Optician)

The Testament of Dr. Mabuse

Credits: Alternate Titles: *Das Testament des Dr. Mabuse, The Terror of the Mad Doctor, The Terror of Dr. Mabuse*; Director: Werner Klingler; Producer: Artur Brauner; Executive Producer: Wolf Brauner; Screenplay: Ladislas Fodor, based on the screenplay by Fritz Lang and Thea Von Harbou; Director of Photography: Albert Benitz; Art Direction: Paul Markwitz and Helmut Nentwig; Music: Raimund Rosenberger; Produced by CCC Films; B&W; length 87 minutes. Premiered on September 7, 1961.

Cast: Wolfgang Preiss (Dr. Mabuse), Gert Fröbe (Inspector Lohmann), Walter Rilla (Prof. Pohland), Helmut Schmid (Johnny Briggs), Charles Regnier (Mortimer), Senta Berger (Nelly), Harald Juhnke (Krueger), Leon Askin (Flocke), Ann Savo (Wackel-Heidi), Claus Tinney (Jack), Albert Bessler (Joe), Rolf Eden (Eddie)

Scotland Yard vs. Dr. Mabuse

Credits: Alternate Titles: *Scotland Yard jagt Dr. Mabuse*; Director: Paul May; Producer: Artur Brauner; Screenplay: Ladislas Fodor, based on "The Device" by Bryan Edgar Wallace; Director of Photography: Nenad Jovicic; Art Direction: Hanns H. Kuhnert and Albrecht Hennings; Music: Rolf Wilhelm; Produced by CCC Films; B&W; length 90 minutes. Premiered on September 20, 1963.

Cast: Walter Rilla (Prof. Pohland/Dr. Mabuse), Peter Van Eyck (Major Bill Turn), Werner Peters (Inspector Volpius), Klaus Kinski (Joe Rank), Sabine Bethmann (Nancy Masters), Agnes Windeck (Mrs. Turn), Dieter Borsche (George Cockstone), Hans Nielsen (Scotland Yard Chief), Wolfgang Lukschy (Hilyard), Albrecht Schoenhals (Sir Robert Allingham), Ruth Wilbert (Princess Diana), Gerd Wiedenhofen (Kloppe), Anneliese Würtz (Rose), Sigurd Lohde (Postman), Wolfgang Preiss (Dr. Mabuse)

The Death Ray of Dr. Mabuse

Credits: Alternate Titles: *Die Todesstrahlen des Dr. Mabuse*, *The Death Ray Mirror of Dr. Mabuse*; Director: Hugo Fregonese; Producer: Artur Brauner; Screenplay: Ladislas Fodor; Director of Photography: Riccardo Pallottini; Music: Carlos Diernhammer and Oskar Sala; Produced by CCC Films and Franco-London Films; B&W; length 91 minutes. Premiered on September 18, 1964.

Cast: Peter Van Eyck (Major Bob Anders), Walter Rilla (Prof. Pohland), Yvonne Furneaux (Gilda Larsen), Yoko Tani (Mercedes), O.E. Hasse (Prof. Larsen), Rika Dialina (Judy), Dieter Eppler (Kaspar Botoni), Leo Glenn (Admiral Quency), Ernst Schroeder (Doctor), Valerij Inkijinoff (Krishna), Gustavo Rojo (Mario Monta)

NOTE: Although Wolfgang Preiss is listed in the credits and prominently mentioned in all posters and advertising, he does not actually appear in the film.

Scream and Scream Again

Credits: Alternate Titles: *Die Lebenden Leichen des Dr. Mabuse*; Director: Gordon Hessler; Producer: Max J. Rosenberg, Milton Subotsky and Louis M. Heyward; Screenplay: Christopher Wicking, based on "The Disorientated Man" by Peter Saxon; Director of Photography: John Coquillon; Art Direction: Bill Constable and Don Mingaye; Music: David Whitaker; Produced by American International Pictures and Amicus; color; length 95 minutes. Premiered on September 17, 1969.

Cast: Vincent Price (Dr. Browning), Christopher Lee (Fremont), Peter Cushing (Benedek), Alfred Marks (Inspector Bellaver), Christopher Matthews (Dr. David Soren), Marshall Jones (Konratz), Michael Gothard (Keith, the Vampire Killer)

The Vengeance of Dr. Mabuse

Credits: Alternate Titles: *La Venganza del Dr. Mabuse*, *Der Mann der sich Mabuse nannte*, *Dr. M. schlägt zu*; Director: Jess Franco; Producer: Artur Brauner; Screenplay: Jess Franco and Artur Brauner (as Art Bernd); Director of Photography: Manuel Merino; Art Direction: Karl Meyerberg; Music: Jess Franco (as David Khune; Produced by Copercines, Telecine, and Rosa Films; color, length 88 minutes. Premiered in 1970.

Cast: Jack Taylor (Prof. Farkas), Fred Williams (Inspector Thomas), Ewa Stronberg (Wanda), Moises A. Racha (Andros), Gustavo Re, Ava Garden, Angel Melendez, Friedrich Joloff, Roberto Camardiel, Linda Hastreiter, W. Kieling, G. Mendez, Jesus Franco

The Image of Dorian Gray in the Yellow Press

Credits: Alternate Titles: *Dorian Gray im Spiegel der Boulevardpresse*; Director: Ulrike Ottinger; Screenplay: Ulrike Ottinger; Director of Photography: Ulrike Ottinger; Art Direction: Ulrike Ottinger; Music: Peer Raben; Produced by Ulrike Ottinger with WDR and SFB; Represented in the United States by Women Make Movies; color; length 150 minutes. Premiered in Berlin on February 20, 1984.

Cast: Delphine Seyrig (Dr. Mabuse), Veruschka von Lehndorff (Dorian Gray), Tabea Blumenschein (Andamana), Toyo Tanaka (Hollywood), Irm Hermann (Passat), Magdalena Montezuma (Golem), Barbara Valentin (Susy), Else Nabu (Singer), Hanno Jochimson (Man of the World), Fritz Ewert (Mr. Charles Chronicle), Joachim v. Ulmann (Alexander Baron von Regenbogen), Horst Benzrath (Mr. Standard Telegraph)

Club Extinction

Credits: Alternate Titles: *Dr. M*; Director: Claude Chabrol; Producer: Francois Duplat and Hans Brockmann; Screenplay: Sollace Mitchell, Thomas Bauermeister, and Claude Chabrol, inspired by "Dr. Mabuse der Spieler" by Norbert Jacques; Director of Photography: Jean Rabier; Art Direction: Wolfgang Hundhammer and Dante Ferretti; Music: Paul Hindemith and Mekong Delta; Produced by NEF, Ellipti Film, and ZDF; color; length 116 minutes. Premiered on May 24, 1990.

Cast: Alan Bates (Dr. Marsfeldt), Jennifer Beals (Sonja Vogler), Jan Niklas (Inspector Hartmann), Hanns Zischler (Moser), Benoit Regent (Stieglitz), Alexander Radszun (Engler), Wolfgang Preiss (Police Chief), Micheal Degen (Reimar von Geldern), Andrew McCarthy (Assassin), Peter Fitz (Veidt), Daniela Poggi (Kathi), William Berger (Penck), Isolde Barth (Mrs. Sehr), Tobia Hösl (Achim), Bêatrice Macola (Anna)

Index

Numbers in **boldface** indicate pages with photographs.

Abel, Alfred 46, **53**
Addams, Dawn 118, **119**, **120**, **121**, 125
AJYM Films 261–262
Albert, Maria Therese 134
Ali Baba and the Forty Thieves 198
Alice, ou le Dernier Fugue 276
Allain, Marcel 9
Allen, Woody 157, 232
Alphaville 125, 273
Alraune 151
American International Pictures (AIP) 116, 127, 153, 213–215, 223–224, 233
Amicus 213, 215
Ann-Margret 276
Arkoff, Samuel Z. 233
As Long as You Live 147
Askin, Leon 180
Attenborough, Richard 277
Audran, Stephane 264
Austin Powers International Man of Mystery 209–210
Austruc, Alexandre 258, 260
The Awful Dr. Orlof 126, 231–232, 235, 240–243

Baker, W. Howard 215
The Bare Breasted Countess 227
Barker, Lex 148, 150–151, 157, 165, 167, **169**, 212
Barrymore, Ethyl 154
Barski, Odile 276
Bates, Alan 267, 274, 277
Batman 89
Bauermeister, Thomas 271
Baxter, Les 224
Bazin, Andre 258–261
Beals, Jennifer 268–269, 272–274, 277
Le Beau Serge 258, 260–263, 277–278
Behm, Marc 276

Belmondo, Jean-Paul 272
Bennett, Arnold 189–190
Bennett, Joan 85, 96–97, 99–102
Beregi, Oskar 184
Berger, Senta 158, **184**, 185
Berlichingen, Götz von 57
Berlin Wall 3, 6, 141, 175–177, 185, 267, 274–275, 291
Berliner Illustrierten 16, 27, 46, 103
La Bête Humaine 108
Bethmann, Sabinne 158, 185, **199**
Beyond a Reasonable Doubt 110–111, 138
Les Biches 278
The Big Heat 58, 68, 103–108, **104**, **105**, **106**, **109**, 123, 126, 194, 233, 270–271, 288–289
The Black Countess 242
Blackman, Honor 154
Blade Runner 274
The Blue Panther 262, 276
Blumenschein, Tabea 248, 253, **255**
Boehm, Sydney 103
Bond, James 30, 89, 124–125, 156, 165, 178, 187, 193–194, 204–205, 207–210, 222, 224, 255, 271
Les Bonnes Femmes 273
Borsche, Dieter 138, **193**, 198
Le Boucher 273, 277
Brasseur, Pierre 241
Braun, Harald 198
Brauner, Artur 19, 110, 112–117, 123–125, 127, 129–143, **133**, **135**, 145–147, 154, 163, 173, 175, 177–179, 183, 187, 190, 194, 204, 212–214, 226, 230, 232, 235, 237, 239–240, 242–243, 252, 260, 276, 286, 288
Brauner, Wolf 133–134
Breathless 266

Brecht, Bertolt 20, 96, 98–99, 107, 288–289
Bresson, Robert 260
The Bride 272
Brides of Dracula 230
Broca, Philippe de 261
Broccoli, Albert 209
By Rocket to the Moon 31, 99, 109

Cabaret 153
The Cabinet of Dr. Caligari 24–25, 81, 85, 116, 283
Cabot, Bruce 95
Cahiers du Cinema 78, 93, 108, 124, 258–261, 277
Caminecci, Pierre 232
Capone, Al 58, 96
Casino Royale 157
Cave of the Living Dead 128
CCC Filmkunst 113, 116, 124, 131, 134–135, 137–142, 147, 150–151, 154, 162–163, 173, 177, 185, 187–188, 190, 197–198, 200, 202–203, 210, 212–213, 235, 239–240–241, 270
Celi, Adolfo 209
Chabrol, Claude 7, 11, 19, 84, 132, 210, 219, 222, 246, 252, 256–266, **259**, **261**, **264**, **265**, **269**, 270–273, 275–280
The Champagne Murders 210, 262, 277
Chaplin, Charlie 53, 125
Chemiker Null 11, 18
La Chienne 100
Chimes at Midnight 237
Churchill, Winston 286
Citizen Kane 237
Citopomar *see* Eitopomar
City in Darkness 154
Clash by Night 85, 106
Cloak and Dagger 100–101, 289
Clouzot, Henri George 125

301

Index

Club Extinction 7, 11, 108, 159–161, 219, 222, 267–280, 289
Cold War 3, 123, 132, 137, 145, 185, 190, 215
Confirm or Deny 97
Connery, Sean 209
Conqueror Worm 215–217
Conquest of the Planet of the Apes 285
Conspiracy Theory 282
Cooper, Gary 101
Cops 252
Coquillon, John 217, 224
Corman, Roger 233
The Corpse Packs His Bags 194, 235
The Corrupt Ones 154
Cotton, Jerry 147–148
Count Dracula 234–235, 242
The Crimes of Dr. Mabuse 75, **79**, 84, 90, 282, **284**
The Crimson Cult 216
Cry of the Banshee 224
The Cry of the Owl 276
Cushing, Peter 213, 216–218, 220–221, 224

The Daffodil Killer 200
Dagover, Lil 138
Dark Eyes of London 241
The Day the Earth Stood Still 210
Death Packs a Suitcase 194
The Death Ray of Dr. Mabuse 136, 151, 158–159, 178, 183, 200, 203–212, **206, 208**, 213, 271
Death Whistles a Blues 237
Decla-Bioscop 11, 23, 25–27, 40, 46, 55
Degen, Michael 267
Dern, Bruce 276
De Sade 153, 213–214
Desire 151
Destiny 20, 26–27, 110, 116
Destry Rides Again 103
The Device 188, 191–197, **192**, 200
Devil Came from Akasava 154, 235, 239
The Devils 222
Dialina, Rika 204
Dieterle, William 132
Dietrich, Erwin C. 235
Dietrich, Marlene 20, **97**, 101, 103, 154
The Disorientated Man **214**, 215, 218–219
Dr. Jekyll vs. The Wolfman 242
Dr. Mabuse auf dem Presseball 11, 16–17, 248
Dr. Mabuse der Spieler (book) 9, 14–18, **15**, 36, 41, 43, 45, 52, 58, 64, 80, 110, 112, 270–271, 282, 288
Dr. Mabuse the Gambler (film) 4, 7, 11, **12**, 16–17, 26–28, 30–32, 36–60, **37, 38, 42, 46, 50, 51**, **56, 58, 59**, 70, 87, 90, 93, 95, 102–103, 107–108, 118, 129, 131–132, 143, 156, 172, 213, 233, 248, 270–271, 276, 281, 289
Dr. Mabuse vs. Scotland Yard 31, 136, 159, 178, 188–202, **189, 193, 195, 196, 198, 199, 201**, 206, 213–214, 235, 270–271
Dr. Mabuses letztes Spiel see *Das Testament des Dr. Mabuse* (book)
Dr. No 209
Dr. Popaul 272
Dr. Terror's House of Horrors 215
La Dolce Vita 151, 210
Domergue, Faith 211–212
Don Quixote 237
Donde Mueren Las Palabras 211
Donovan's Brain 142
The Door with Seven Locks 200
Dor, Karin 148, 158, 163, **164**, 165, **171**, 185, 190, 210
Doyle, Arthur Conan 284
Dracula 6, 19, 45, 92, 234–235, 282, 284
Dracula vs. Frankenstein (Franco) 235
Dracula vs. Frankenstein (Fregonese) 210, 212
Drudge, Matt 252
Duryea, Dan 99–101

Einstein, Albert 16
Eisenstein, Sergei 60
Eitopomar 17, 172
Enemy of the State 7
L'Enfer 277
Eppler, Dieter 205
Erdmann, Otto 151–153
The Evil Eye 272–273
Expressionism 24–25, 45, 54, 176, 233
Eyck, Peter Van 118, **119**, 125, 135–138, 157, 198, 200, 203, 210, 222
Eyes Without a Face 230–231, 235, 240–241

Fahrenheit 451 273
Fanck, Arnold 145, 147
Fantômas 9, **10**, 11, 22, 39–40, 266, 276, 281, 284
Farrow, Mia 272
Fassbinder, Rainer Werner 142
The Fatal Passions of Dr. Mabuse 54
Fellowship of the Frog 147
Fethke, Jan 117
Feuillade, Louis 9, 11, 22, 39–40, 143, 276
Fiend Without a Face 127
The Fight for Rome 154, 243
First Man Into Space 127
Flashdance 272–274
Fleming, Ian 209–210
Flynn, Errol 154

Fodor, Ladislas 153–154, 157, 173, 180, 183, 185–188, 191, 194–195, 197–198, 200–201, 203, 212, 235, 241
Folies Bourgeosies 276
Fonda, Henry 20, 31, 95, 122, 154, 184
For Your Eyes Only 222
Ford, Glenn 103–104, 108, **109**
The Forger of London 147
The 400 Blows 261
The Four Just Men 188
Fowler, Gene, Jr. 96–97
Fraga, Manuel 229, 233
Frances, Stephen 215
Franco, Generalissimo 228–229, 233, 235
Franco, Jess 19, 26, 132, 126, 154, 194, 210, 214, 227–244, **230, 232, 236**, 246, 252, 255, 256, 258
Franju, Georges 124, 230–231, 235, 240–241
Frankenstein 6, 19, 225, 235, 272, 282–284
Fregonese, Diana 211–212
Fregonese, Hugo 19, 151, 203, 210–212, 252
Freud, Sigmund 283
Friedlob, Bert 110–111
Fröbe, Gert 11, 122, 124–125, 129, 138, 146, 148, **155**, 158, 162, 167, 180, **181, 182**, 187, 276, 289
Fuchsberger, Joachim 148
Furneau, Rudolph 163, 165, **170**
Furneaux, Yvonne 158, 185, 205, 210
Fury 59, 73, 94–95, 103, 105, 276, 289

The Game 282
The Games of Love 261
Garden, Eva 241
Gates, Bill 7, 282
Genn, Leo 207
Ghost Ships of the Blind Dead 242
Gilliam, Terry 224
Godard, Jean-Luc 228, 232, 258–259, 261, 263, 266, 273
Les Godelureaux 261
Godzilla 285
Goebbels, Joseph 5, 6, 18, 28, 34–35, 62, 68–70, 72–73, 76–78, 90, 98, 104, 110, 134, 146, 183, 190, 282–283, 285, 288
Goetz, William 102
Goetzke, Bernard 26, 36, 42, 46, **53**, 153
Golden Putrefaction 60
Golden Voyage of Sinbad 224
Goldfinger 124–125, 210
Goldmann 18–19
Gorbachev, Mikhail 275
Gordon, Richard 127–128
Göring, Hermann 146

Gossaerts, Jan 14
Gothard, Michael 222, **223**, 224
Grahame, Gloria 105, **106**, 108, **109**
Greene, Grahame 20, 99

Half-Breed 23
Hammer Films 178, 210, 215, 223, 230, 234, 242
Hand, Learned 80
Hand of the Gallows 147
Hangmen Also Die! 73, 98–99, 103, 107, 288–289
Harbou, Thea von 16–19, 25–32, **30**, 34–36, 39–41, 43, 45–46, 55, 60, 73–74, 78–81, 83, 96, 110, 112, 138, 146, 179, 218, 235, 285, 287, 289
Hardly a Criminal 211
Harryhausen, Ray 224
Hasse, O.E. 138, 204, **206**, 210
Hayworth, Rita 154
Heidi 145
Helm, Brigitte 28, 31, 151
Herzog, Werner 142, 199–200
Hessler, Gordon 19, 213–214, 217–218, 221, 223–224, 226, 252
Heydrich, Reinhard 73, 98, 183
Heyward, Louis M. 215–217, 220, 223–224
Hitchcock, Alfred 30, 58, 118, 165, 196–197, 200, 210, 218, 259, 263–266
Hitler, Adolf 5–6, 13, 21, 28, 34, 41, 54, 62, 64–67, 69–70, 72–74, 76, 78, 80, 83–84, 90–91, 97–98, 102, 104, 107–108, 113, 117, 134–135, 138, 145–146, 183, 190, 219, 281–290
Hogan's Heroes 180
Holmes, Sherlock 142, 215
Honecker, Erich 5, 275, 288
Hopkins, Miriam 101
Hotel Adlon 117
The House Un-American Activities Committee (HUAC) 34, 102–103, 125
Hoven, Adrian 234
Howe, James Wong 20
Human Desire 108
Hundhammer, Wolfgang 271
Hunte, Otto 51
Huth, Jochen 138

I Confess 210
The Image of Dorian Gray in the Yellow Press 7, 169, 245–256, **247**, **249**, **251**, **254**, 270–272
The Indian Tomb (original) 25–26, 46, 112, 138
The Indian Tomb (remake) 115–117, 129–130, 139, 141, 231
Ingenieur Mars 11, 17
Inkijinoff, Valerij 203

Invasion of the Body Snatchers 185
The Invisible Dr. Mabuse 31, 148, 151, 159, 163–173, **164**, **165**, **166**, **168**, **169**, **170**, **171**, 178, 207
The Invisible Man 163, 169

Jack the Ripper 235, 241
Jacques, Norbert 3, 5–7, 11–19, 27, 29, 34, 36–37, 39–40, 43, 45–46, 52, 55, 58, 61, 64, 76, 78–81, 83–86, 92, 103, 110, 112, 132, 140–141, 145, 157, 161, 173, 179–185, 189, 191, 201, 215, 218, 224–225, 238, 246, 248, 256, 270–271, 282–283, 285, 287–288
Jaffe, Sam 96, 98
Jagger, Mick 276
Janowitz, Hans 24–25
Johnson, Nunnally 99
Joloff, Friedrich 241
Jones, Marshall **219**, 220–221, 224, **225**
Joseph, Wilfred 224
Journey to the Lost City see *The Indian Tomb* (remake)
The Joyless Street 151
Juhnke, Harald 187, 200

Karloff, Boris 216
Katcher, Leo 75
Kennedy, John F. 285
Kettlehut, Erich 26, 129
The Killer Barbys 227
A King in New York 125
King Kong 189
Kinski, Klaus 190, **198**, 199–200, 214, 222, 234–235, 241
The Kiss Before the Mirror 154
Kiss Me Monster 234
The Kissing Bandit 211
Klein-Rogge, Rudolph 16, 25–28, 30, 36–38, **38**, 40, 41, **44**, 45 46, **50**, 78, 81, 86, 90, 124
Klingler, Werner 19, 180–181, 183
Kobe, Hans 46
Kohner, Paul 138
Kracauer, Sigfried 24, 49, 281
Krenz, Egon 275

Lang, Fritz 5–6, 11, 13–14, 16–35, 21, **30**, 33, 36, 39–47, 54–55, 58–60, 68–70, 72–74, 76, 78–81, 83–120, **94**, **97**, **100**, **111**, **119**, 122–130, 132, **133**, 135, 136–139, 143, 145–147, 149, 153, 156–157, 159, 161, 172, 173, 177, 179–185, 188, 197, 200, 218, 226–233, 236–239, 243, 246, 252, 256, 258–259, 263–265, 270–273, 275–278, 281–283, 285, 287–291
Langlois, Henri 257–258
Laocoon and Sons 253
The Last Will of Dr. Mabuse see

The Testament of Dr. Mabuse (original film)
Latte, Lily 92–93, 95, 98, 101
Lavi, Daliah 150, 157–158, 185, 212
Leavis, Q. D. 190
Die Lebenden Leichen des Dr. Mabuse 213, 224, 226
Lee, Belinda 127
Lee, Christopher 157, 213, 216–217, **219**, 220–224, 234
Lehndorff, Veruschka von **247**, 248, **249**, 251, 272
Leroux, Gaston 167
Liessen, Wera 88
Lilian the Perverted Virgin 235
Liliom 92–93
Lincoln, Abraham 285
The Line of Demarcation 262
Lipelt, Ernst 135
The Lodger 210
Loeb, Karl 129, 153
Lom, Herbert 234
The Longest Day 124
Lorre, Peter 20, 31–34, 108, 180, 227–228, 230
Lorys, Diana 231, 241
Losey, Joseph 110
Love and Death 125
Lucky the Inscrutable 235
Lugosi, Bela 241
Lupino, Ida 20
Lust for a Vampire 223
Lustig, Emile 127
Lynch, David 277

M 18–20, 29, 32–34, 73, 78–79, 81, 83, 86, 93, 99, 103, 105, 110, 112, 117, 129–130, 136, 149, 180, 227, 233
Mabuses Kolonie 11, 17, 61, 79–80, 84, 246, 282, 285
Madame Bovary 262
Madame X: An Absolute Ruler 253
Les Magiciens 276
Magritte, Rene 9, 11
Malraux, André 257
Man Hunt 73, 96–97, 100
Man in the Attic 210
The Man Who Knew Too Much 58, 227
Man Without a Country 96
The Manchurian Candidate 185
Mankiewicz, Jospeh L. 95
Mann, Thomas 11
Mannchen, Karl-Heinz 232, 235
Marks, Alfred 220
Marquis de Sade: Justine 214
Martin, Dean 157
Matejkos, Theo 11–12
Matthews, Christopher **220**, 222–223
Maurier, George du 283
Maurus, Gerda 31

Index

May, Joe 23, 25–26, 46. 112, 115, 139
May, Karl 147, 151, 154, 190, 212
May, Paul 19, 252
Mayer, Carl 24–25
Mayo, Archie 97–98
McCarthy, Andrew 38, 269, 274
McClory, Kevin 209–210
McGivern, William 103–106, 108
Meichsner, Eberhard 116
Mein Kampf 6, 66, 76, 125, 285
Metropolis 20, 22, 26, 28–31, **30**, 34, 46, 59, 68, 93, 99, 116, 131, 233, 283, 289
Ministry of Fear 20, 31, 99, 143
Miranda, Soledad 235
Miró, Pilar 235
Mr. Arkadin 237
Mitchell, Sollace 271, 276
Mock, Joachim 153
Molo, Conrad von 92–93
Monroe, Marilyn 20
The Monster of London City 153
Moonfleet 018
Moontide 97
Die Mörder sind unter uns 34, 136
Moriarty, Professor 11, 284
Morituri 135–138, 183, 286
The Mummy 210
Murnau, F. W. 132

Die Nachtwache 198
Naschy, Paul 210, 233
Navarre, René 39
Nazi Germany 3, 5–6, 13, 17–18, 21, 28, 33–35, 47, 54, 60, 62–70, 72–76, 78, 83, 88, 90, 92–93, 98, 101–102, 104, 107–108, 110, 113, 116, 124–125, 132–139, 145–147, 179, 183, 185, 190, 219, 231, 282–287, 289–290
Nebenzahl, Seymour 32, 73, 78–80, 92, 110
Nero Film 32–33, 80, 110
Never Say Never Again 209
New Wave 3, 11, 78, 139, 141, 228, 230, 240, 257–266, 273
Newman, Serge 230
The Nibelungen 26, 28, 34–35, 69, 103, 116–117, 131, 143
The Nibelungen (remake) 147, 154
Nichols, Dudley 96, 100–101
Nicholson, James 224
Niklas, Jan 267, 277
Nissen, Aud Egede 43, 46
Niven, David 154
No Time for Ecstasy 157
North to Alaska 154
Nouvelle Vague *see* New Wave

The Oblong Box 214, 216–218
Old Shatterhand 151, 154, 157, 190, 212
Olympia 146
An Orchid for the Tiger 262

Orwell, George 189–190
Ossorio, Armando de 233
Ott, Johannes 129
Ottinger, Ulrike 7, 19, 142, 169, 246, 248–249, 251–256, 270–271

Pabst, G. W. 132, 151
Paget, Debra **133**
Pal, George 154
Palance, Jack 210
Palmer, Lilli 101
Paranoiac 242
Paris Is Ours 261
Peck, Gregory 154
Peters, Werner 123, 125, 149, 154, 158, 168, 171, 190, 198, 200
Phantom of Soho 153–154
The Phantom of the Opera 163, 170
The Picture of Dorian Gray 246–248
Pinkerton, William 284
The Pit and the Pendulum 147
Pleasence, Donald 216
Pollock, Channing 29
Pommer, Erich 23–29, 47, 92, 137
Powell, Michael 232
Preiss, Wolfgang 117, 124, 128–129, 161, 163, 167, **181**, 183, 190, 201, 271–272
Pressburger, Arnold 98–99
Price, Vincent 20, 213, 215–217, **217**, **220**, 221–222, 224–226, 277
Propaganda 282, 287
Psycho 266
Psycho-Circus 200

Quiet Days in Clichy 274

Rabier, Jean 277
Radszun, Alexander 269
Rancho Notorious 103, 105–106, 110
Ray, Nicholas 276
Re, Gustavo 214
The Real World 252
Red Lips 229–230, 234
Redgrave, Michael 102
Reed, Carol 58
Reeves, Michael 213–214, 216–218, 221
Régent, Benoit 268
Regnier, Charles 179
Reimann, Hans 25
Reinhard, Max 210
Reinl, Harald 19, 117, 143–148, 151, 157, 159, 161–163, 165, 170–171, 173, 238, 252
Rennie, Michael 210
Renoir, Jean 100, 108, 260
Repulsion 210
The Return of Dr. Mabuse 31, 143–162, **144**, **148**, **152**, **155**, **160**, 173, 187, 194–195, 207, 212, 223, 238, 240, 286, 290–291

Return of Frank James 96, 103
Richards, Keith 276
Richards, Sylvia 101–102
Richter, Paul 43, **44**, 46
Riefenstahl, Leni 145–148
Rififi in the City 237
Rilla, Walter **181**, **182**, 183–184, 187, **195**, 197, 201
Riot in Cell Block 11 102
Rivette, Jacques 258–259, 261
The Road to Corinth 262
The Robe 125
Robinson, Edward G. 20, 99–101, 154
Rocha, Moises 241, 243
Rockwell, Alexandre 277
Roddam, Franc 272
Rogers, Ginger 154
Rohmer, Eric 258–259, 261, 263
Rojo, Gustavo 206
Rolling Stones 276
Romay, Lina 235
Room 13 147
Roosevelt, Franklin D. 286
Rosenberg, Max J. 215
Rosenthal, Lisa 26–27, 46

Sadisterotica 227, 234
Sag die Wahrheit 134–137
Saltzman, Harry 124, 209, 237
Sanders of the River 188
Sandloff, Peter 223
Saxon, Peter 215, 217–218
Sayers, Dorothy L. 189–190
Scarlet Street 20, 59, 85, 100–101, 106
Scars of Dracula 223
Schlettow, Adalbert 38
Schlöndorff, Volker 142, 255
Schmid, Helmut **184**, 185
Schüfftan, Eugen 20
Scream and Scream Again 159–161, 213–226, **216**, **217**, **218**, **219**, **220**, **223**, **225**, 238, 270–271, 288, 289
The Searchers 132
The Secret Beyond the Door 101–102
The Secret Ways 126, 231
Selznick, David O. 93, 99
Seyrig, Delphine 246, 248, **249**, 252
She Kills in Ectsasy 235, 239
Shub, Esther 60
Sidney, Sylvia 95–96, **100**
Siegel, Don 102
The Sign of Leo 261
The Silencers 157
Sinatra, Frank 211
Siodmak, Curt 150
Siodmak, Robert 132, 138, 154, 243, 276
Sommer, Elke 154
Soros, George 7, 282
Souvestre, Pierre 9

Index

Spartacus Uprising 6, 47, 63–64
Sperling, Milton 100–101
The Spiders 23–25
Spies 20, 29–31, 40, 58, 68, 96, 103, 108, 123, 143, 156, 197, 271, 289
The Spy Who Came in from the Cold 125, 200
The Squeaker 200
Stack, Robert 154
Stalin, Joseph 137
Stanwyck, Barbara 20, 85, 154
Starace, Gino 10–11
Staudte, Wolfgang 34, 136
Steele, Barbara 216
Steiner, Max 20
Stensgaard, Yutte 223, **225**
Sting 272
Strangler of Blackmoor Castle 147, 154
Strömberg, Eva 241, 242
Stürme über dem Mont Blank 145
Subotsky, Milton 213, 215–216, 218–219, 224
Succubus 233–235, 242
Surrealism 9
Swinn, Monica 242
Sydow, Max von 277

Tamiroff, Akim 276
Tani, Yoko 205
Taste the Blood of Dracula 234
Taylor, Jack 235, 241, **242**
Ten Days' Wonder 276–277
The Terror 147
Das Testament des Dr. Mabuse (book) 11, 18–19, 38, 80, 83–84, 86, 92, 179–185, 282
The Testament of Dr. Mabuse (original film) 5–7, 17–18, 32, 34–35, 46, 68–91, **69**, **71**, **72**, **74**, **77**, **79**, **82**, **85**, **87**, **88**, **89**, **90**, **93**, 98–99, 108, 117–118, 123, 127, 130, 133, 141, 149, 161, 173, 179–185, 218, 246, 251, 276, 282, 285–289, **290**
The Testament of Dr. Mabuse (remake) 161, **165**, 172–188, **174**, **176**, **178**, **181**, **182**, **184**, **186**, 197
The Third Man 58
This Island Earth 211
Those Magnificent Men in Their Flying Machines 124
The 1000 Eyes of Dr. Mabuse 7, 26, 30, 57–58, 81, 86, 108, 112–130, **113**, **114**, **115**, 119, 120, 121, **126**, **127**, **128**, **129**, 131, 136, 141, 143, 149, 153, 158, 163, 171, 200, 207, 221, 231, 241, 248, 270–271, 277, 289
Thunderball 207–210
Tiefland 146–147
The Tiger Likes Fresh Blood 262
Tigon 215
Todd, Richard 127
tom thumb 154
Topaz 165
Tourneur, Jacques 259
Towers, Harry Alan 234–235
Tozzi, Fausto 149, **155**
Tracy, Spencer 20, 95
Treasure Island 237
Treasure of Silver Lake 147
Treut, Monika 253
Triumph of the Will 146
The Trollenberg Terror 242
Truffaut, François 197, 228, 258–259, 261, 263, 266, 273
Turner, Lana 150
Der 20 Juli 138, 153, 288–290
The Two Faces of Dr. Jekyll 125

Ufa 23, 27, 29, 31–32, 129, 136–139, 214, 230
Ulbricht, Walter 176–177
Ullstein 16, 18
Ulmer, Edgar G. 20, 138, 259
The Usual Suspects 7, 282
Utopia 13, 17, 41

Valle, Ricardo 241
Valli, Alida 241
The Vampire Lovers 125
Les Vampires 39
Vampyros Lesbos 235, 239
The Vengeance of Dr. Mabuse 26, 159–161, 179, 194, 214, 226, 235, 238–244, **240**, **242**, **243**, **244**, 271, 289
Vengeance of the Mummy 242
Venus in Furs 233
Vernon, Howard 26, 38, 112, 125, **126**, 128, 231–233, 241–242
Vertigo 266
A Virgin Among the Living Dead 227

Wages of Fear 125, 200
Wagner, Fritz Arno 129, 138
Wald, Jerry 108
Wallace, Bryan Edgar 147, 188, 190–191, 194, 200–201, 219, 235
Wallace, Edgar 142, 147, 153, 154, 188–190, 200, 212, 235, 241
Walter, Wilfred 241
The Wandering Image 26
Wanger, Walter 95, 99–102
Warm, Hermann 25
Wayne, John 132, 154
We Are 18 229
Weigel, Helene 99
Weill, Kurt 89, 92, 96
Weimar Germany 6, 13, 14, 27–28, 34, 40–41, 47, 62–67, 107, 132, 287
Weismuller, Johnny 150
Welcker, Gertrude 42
Welles, Orson 124, 154, 236–237, 260, 276
Wells, H. G. 163, 169
Welsch, Howard 103
Wenders, Wim 142
Wernicke, Otto 32, 81, 83, **90**, 149
Western Union 96, 103
Whale, James 154, 163, 169
What? 157
While the City Sleeps 103, 110
Whitaker, David 223
White, Daniel 231
Wicking, Christopher 218–220, 224, 226
Wiene, Robert 24–25
Wilde, Oscar 246–249
Williams, Fred 241, **244**
Windeck, Agnes 200
Winnetou 147
Wives Under Suspicion 154
Wolff, Lothar 70, 74
The Woman in the Window 20, 99–100, 106
World War I 9, 13, 22–23, 40–41, 62, 67, 83–84, 98–99, 179, 283
World War II 41, 67, 83–84, 91, 98–99, 107, 113, 117, 146, 150, 190, 231, 286, 289–290
Worth, Adam 284
Wuttig, Heinz Oskar 117

X-312 Flight to Hell 235

You and Me 96, **100**
You Only Live Once 20, 73, 95, 99, 122
You Only Live Twice 165

Zanuck, Darryl 20, 97–98
Zischler, Hanns 267, 277

www.ingramcontent.com/pod-product-compliance
Ingram Content Group UK Ltd.
Pitfield, Milton Keynes, MK11 3LW, UK
UKHW050542150426
5217IPUK00026B/2033